WILD
AT
HEART

ALSO BY K.A. TUCKER

WILD
AT
HEART

a novel

K.A. TUCKER

ISBN 978-1-9990154-2-8
ISBN 978-1-9990154-1-1 (ebook)

Edited by Jennifer Sommersby

Cover design by Hang Le

Published by K.A.Tucker

Manufactured in the United States of America

To Lia and Sadie,
If you learn nothing else from me, I hope you learn the value of
determination.

To Stacey,
For laughing with me.

To Juanita,
Bless your heart.

CHAPTER ONE

November

"So ... I guess I'll see you when I see you."

I can't manage words around the flaring lump in my throat, and so I simply nod. The past four days with Jonah in Toronto have been a blur. A bliss-filled blur that I'm not ready to let go of yet. The Uber driver shuttling me home after this parting will have the privilege of a sobbing mess in their backseat.

An unreadable look flashes across Jonah's icy blue eyes. I still haven't grown accustomed to seeing him without a beard, though I'll admit I've enjoyed admiring that chiseled jawline and those dimples. He takes a deep breath and turns away, his carry-on slung over one broad shoulder, his boarding pass and passport dangling from between two pinched fingers.

I watch him hand his documents to the agent at the US-bound entry gate, who spends all of one second reviewing them before waving him toward the glass security doors. On the other side is his fourteen-hour flight home. In seconds, Jonah is going to be out of sight, gone.

Who knows when I'll see him again? He flew here to tell me in person that he's been miserable these past two months since I left Alaska, that he doesn't want to be a carbon copy of my father—spending his life pining over my mother—that he wants to find an "us" that will work. That he wants me beside him.

I haven't given him an answer yet, too afraid to leap.

Until now.

I feel the word rising inside me—an emotion about to erupt. "Yes!" My pulse pounds in my ears.

Jonah turns to regard me with a raised eyebrow.

Am I crazy? Maybe.

But I'm fully committing to it.

I take a step forward and swallow my nerves. "I'll come back to Alaska." Because being with Jonah again—laughing and reminiscing, having him in my space, waking in his arms—has only confirmed what I've suspected for months: I'm deeply in love with him, and living in Toronto when he's not here doesn't make sense to me anymore.

I'm done saying goodbye to this man.

Jonah leaves the line and retraces his steps to close the distance, dropping his bag by his feet. It's five A.M. and we're creating an obstacle, forcing travelers to weave around us on either side to get to their flights. Their grumbles touch my ears, but in this moment, I don't care.

The severe frown cutting across Jonah's handsome forehead as he stares down at me says he doesn't, either. "Are you serious?"

I nod. "Yeah. I mean, if you're serious about moving to Anchorage—"

"When?" he demands to know, his voice suddenly gruff.

"I don't know. As soon as I can?" How long does it take to pack up your life and move to a different country? Granted, a country I was born in and still have citizenship with but haven't lived in for more than two decades.

His eyes spark with determination. "Come for Christmas."

I laugh. "That's like *a month* away!"

"So? What else you got goin' on?" It's a challenge, delivered in Jonah's typical blunt style. "I'm not going to see my mom in Oslo anymore. And Aggie and Mabel would love having you there. Especially since it's the first one without Wren. You should come." His Adam's apple bobs with his hard swallow. "Come."

Somewhere in between his words and his tone and the way he's looking at me, I hear the silent plea. In truth, the idea of being near the people closest to my late father for the holidays sounds more appealing—and more feasible—by the second.

"Okay?" I say on an exhale, my voice shaky. "If I can figure it out, I will. I'll get there as soon as I can."

He pulls me into his firm body, leaning down to press his forehead against mine. "Damn, Calla, you know how to make a guy sweat."

I grin, reaching up to skate my fingertips over his stubbled jaw. I hid his razor two days ago to stop him from shaving. The act screamed of poetic justice to me, after he hid my cosmetics bags in his attic for all those weeks during the summer. Unfortunately, Jonah doesn't seem bothered. "Sorry. I only decided a few seconds ago." Though in truth, I think I've known all along.

"Are you sure, though? Because you can't tell me something like this and then chicken out. I'm gonna have to put the house up for sale *now* if we want any chance of being out of there by next summer—"

"I'm not going to *chicken out*," I promise. "I'm one hundred percent sure that I—" I bite my lip to stall the declaration that nearly slips out, my cheeks flushing.

Jonah's jaw tightens as he peers intensely at me. "You what?"

I love you. Those three words have been on the tip of my tongue since the second I heard his laughter from our porch, and yet I can't find the nerve to tell him. Crazy enough, I *have* found the nerve to move to Alaska for him. Probably because he asked me to. If Jonah told me he loved me, the same sentiment would fly from my lips in a heartbeat. But he hasn't said it yet, not in so many words.

"I'm sure," I say instead.

His gaze narrows in that assessing way of his, as if he's trying to read my mind. "Okay."

"Okay." I let out a nervous laugh. "Holy shit, we're doing this!"

"We are and it'll be great, you'll see." He kisses me again, slowly and deeply, his palm cradling the back of my head, his fingers weaving through my loose hair.

Someone grumbles, "Get the fuck out of the way," and Jonah breaks away to shoot a menacing glare. The small, pinched-faced man ducks his head and pretends it wasn't him.

"I should go." Jonah glances at his watch. "I'm already cuttin' it close. Plus, I think we've pissed off half the airport."

I stretch on my tiptoes to steal one more kiss. "Call me as soon as you land."

I get one of his crooked smirks in return, the kind I used to want to slap off his face but now clamber to catch a glimpse of. "Have fun tellin' Susan."

CHAPTER TWO

December

"I guess this is it!" my mother announces with a degree of finality, her hazel-green eyes glossy as they roll over the US-bound entry gate sign. Even at this ungodly hour, hordes of holiday passengers amble toward it.

"*Mom.*" I give her a look. "I'm not dying."

"Of course, I *know* that. It's just ..." She catches a tear with her freshly polished nail—cranberry, for the season. "I finally understand that look on my mother's face all those years ago, when I told her *I* was moving to Alaska. I should probably phone her and apologize."

My heart races with anticipation. It's been four weeks, five days, and twelve minutes since I said goodbye to Jonah in this very spot after his surprise visit to Toronto.

Since then it's been a flurry of preparation: copious forms, signatures, and exorbitant rush fees to renew my US passport; hours spent online learning about Anchorage; a myriad of "are you *really* sure you want to do this?" questions and cautionary "what if he's after your inheritance?" discussions with my mother that sparked more than one catastrophic fight; and carefully worded, psychoanalytical conversations with Simon over his secret stash of instant mashed potatoes—about how my feelings for Jonah *could* be a residual of our deep connection after facing my father's death together and, *if so*, not a strong foundation upon which to begin a life together.

And, of course, countless texts and phone calls to Jonah as I packed and planned and counted down the days.

And now here I am, standing in Pearson International at 5:17 A.M., gripping my phone that holds three boarding passes for three flights that will close the thirty-four-hundred-mile distance between me and Jonah's arms, because it's the only way I'll ever know where this can lead.

What would you think about this turn of events, Dad?

It's been over three months since Wren Fletcher passed away, and I still think of him daily. My chest still aches with each fond memory. My eyes still water when I flip through countless pictures from my time in Alaska this summer. My throat still clogs when I speak his name.

To think he was virtually a stranger in July—a man estranged from me since I was fourteen and nothing more than a distant voice over the telephone before that—and yet he has inadvertently shaped a future in Alaska for me.

Jonah was like a son to him. He'd be thrilled about this, I'm sure of it.

"Susan, we *really* ought to think about catching the train to our terminal," Simon warns in that gentle Hugh Grant-esque British accent of his, patting her shoulder while stealing a pointed glance my way. We all knew saying our goodbyes in the airport wasn't a smart idea. That didn't stop Mom from booking their flight to Turks and Caicos to leave twenty minutes after my flight, thus guaranteeing we'd be in this exact situation.

She adjusts the wide-brimmed sun hat perched atop her head as it was far too fragile to pack in her suitcase. My own hat much like it —the one I foolishly wore on my flight to Alaska the first time—is hanging on a hook in Jonah's house. I left it there, both to remind Jonah of me and because I was uninterested in the tedious effort of flying home with it.

I'm much more practically dressed this time, in leggings and a loose, cozy sweater, and suede hiking boots that will be a pain through security but are otherwise perfect for a day of travel.

"I wish you guys would reconsider spending the holidays with us," Mom mutters.

"It's a bit too late for that." On December 23, I doubt there are any seats to Turks available anymore. Certainly not ones that don't cost five thousand dollars per ticket.

But I know my mother isn't holding out hope for a last-minute switch. Jonah's not going to change his mind about needing to be with Agnes and Mabel this year.

And I'm not going to change my mind about needing to be with *him*.

"I'll text you when I get to Jonah's tonight," I promise. The guy *finally* invested in internet at his house.

"And call me as soon as you wake up."

"Yes, yes ..." I wrap my arms around my mom's shoulders, pulling her into me. "Have a merry Christmas, beachside."

Her returning embrace is fierce for such a slight woman. As she squeezes me tight against her, I inhale her floral perfume. So apropos for a florist. "I'll pray that the snow holds off until you get there," she whispers, and the hoarseness in her voice makes the knot in my throat flare. "Say hello to Jonah for me."

"Will do." I peel away from her, shifting my attention to Simon, who's been relegated to suitcase lackey and is busy tugging on the collar of his winter coat, his face flush from heat. Ever since I came back from Alaska in September, I've noticed his age that much more —the lines marring his forehead and mouth, his wrinkled hands, his sparse, graying hair. He was the only father figure I could turn to for twelve years of my life. Now that I've lived through the pain of losing my real father—a man I learned to love again—I'm acutely aware that I'll have to live through losing Simon one day, too.

I'm banking on that happening *many* years from now, though.

"Work on that tan, will ya?" I tease. Simon will no doubt spend his days hiding beneath the largest umbrella he can find, slathered in SPF 100, with a stripe of zinc down the bridge of his nose for added protection.

"You, too." I laugh as he pulls me into a tight hug. "She'll be fine. I won't let her mope," he says, too low for anyone but me to hear. "You do this Alaska thing with Jonah for as long as it makes sense to you, but you've always got a place here, if you find you need it, with no questions asked. Well ... maybe a few." He winks.

"I know. Thanks." My stomach stirs with butterflies as I hike my backpack over my shoulders, relieved that the three suitcases containing everything I need to survive are already funneling through security for the plane to Chicago. "Okay, so ... talk to you guys soon?" What else do you say to your parents on the day you move to the other side of the continent?

Mom's head bobs up and down, her throat shifting with a hard swallow, her hand blindly pawing for Simon's.

"I'm just a phone call or text or Facetime away," I assure her, the soles of my boots sliding across the polished tile as I edge away. "Safe flight."

"You, too." Simon offers an encouraging smile.

Fishing my newly issued US passport out of my purse, I trudge forward to hand it to the stone-faced man in uniform. It's the first time I've flown as a US citizen in over twenty-four years. He barely eyeballs it before thrusting it back, admitting me with a head nod.

I turn back one last time to see Simon's lanky arm encircling my mother's shoulders, pulling her tight to his side. She wasn't anywhere near this emotional the last time I left for Alaska. Then again, that was temporary. That was for my father. And for me.

This time ...

I'm moving to Alaska for Jonah.

The blunt, abrasive yeti who made my life hell, who I *hated* only months ago, who I've been through so much with since.

Now, I'm leaving everything I know behind to be with him.

With a deep breath, I step through the sliding glass door.

———

"They've *already* canceled it." I glare at the red word flashing on the screen next to my flight from Anchorage to Bangor, set to leave in four hours.

"Yeah, I saw. It's been snowing like crazy since last night. Way worse than they were forecasting. Everything's grounded on this side of the state," comes Jonah's gruff response in my ear.

I peer out the expanse of windows that overlook the runways. Nothing but blue skies and a crisp, white snowy vista, and a frosty coating around the windowsills to emphasize the cold temps. "There's *nothing* here."

"Well, there's four hundred miles and a mountain range between you and this apocalypse."

Jonah had mentioned the possibility of "some snow" in the forecast. At no point did he ever use the term *apocalypse*. "Do you think there's any chance it'll ease up?" We had decided it would be easier and cheaper if I grabbed a commercial flight rather than make him come all the way here to pick me up. But given the situation, maybe he could jump in a plane and—

"Not with the way it's lookin'. Supposed to keep going well into tomorrow."

"*Tomorrow?*" I feel my shoulders sag. And here I was, thinking how smooth today's travel was going so far. "This sucks!"

"Relax. It's the way it is around here. You'll get used to it."

"I don't want to get used to it," I say, pouting. Three airports, two planes, and eleven hours later, my frustration is swelling. More than anything else, I'm desperate to see Jonah.

He chuckles. "Yeah, well ... Let's hope your plane takes off tomorrow."

My jaw drops. Tomorrow is the twenty-fourth. If it doesn't take off tomorrow... "Oh my God. I'm going to be *alone* in an airport on Christmas Day, aren't I!"

"Don't get ahead of yourself. Things can change on a dime around here. Listen, I went ahead and grabbed you a room at the lodge down the road. It's nothin' fancy but most places are booked up, with it being the holidays. I know the owners, Chris and Andrea. They're good people. There's a shuttle that'll take you there."

"Thanks," I offer with resignation.

"You're welcome, Barbie."

I grin despite my sour mood. I used to hate it when he called me that. "Have you grown your beard back yet?" I keep asking and he keeps evading. I hope he has—a wish I never thought I'd be making.

"Guess you'll have to wait and see. Go. Grab your twenty-five overweight suitcases and head on over. Call me later."

"'Kay." I bite my lip against the urge to utter those three little words that I held back at the airport gate a month ago, that I hold back with every phone call, having convinced myself I can't say them for the first time from thousands of miles away.

But, deep down, I'm fearful Jonah doesn't feel the same way. Not yet, anyway. I'm confident his feelings for me are strong—we wouldn't be doing this otherwise. But, if Jonah is anything, it's blunt and undaunted, and he has yet to tell me that he loves me, which makes me think maybe he's not sure yet.

So I *can't* be the first one to say it.

"I'll talk to you soon?"

Jonah chuckles softly. "Yeah, for sure. See you soon, Calla."

I try not to drag my feet as I head for the luggage carousel. Thankfully, the belt is churning out suitcases from the Chicago flight. I don't see mine on the conveyor belt yet, so I stand and wait, my disappointment with being stuck in Anchorage for a night—sans Jonah—weighing heavily on my spirits.

Thirty minutes later, long after the suitcases have stopped sliding down the shoot for my flight and the last of the passengers have wheeled their belongings away, I add "missing luggage" to my list of "things that went horribly wrong when I moved to Alaska."

I'll be able to laugh about this … one day.

CHAPTER THREE

"What does Alaska have against me having clothes?" I accept my glass of red wine from the server—a man with unkempt brown hair and a black button-down shirt—with a nod of thanks, my phone pressed to my ear.

"You do look pretty good without them," Jonah says wryly.

My cheeks flush. The last time I was without my luggage was thanks to him and that tiny tin-can plane he came to get me in, back when he thought I was nothing more than a spoiled brat in need of a hard lesson. "Did you have something to do with this?"

He chuckles. "I wish. Have they located them yet?"

"*Apparently.* They got shuffled in Chicago because of some glitch with the overweight baggage. They said they'd have them on a late flight tonight and they'd get them to the hotel by tomorrow morning, first thing." I don't know if I believe them. The airline attendant apologized and offered to refund my exorbitant fees before offering me an emergency care pack of a cheap, disposable toothbrush and pint-sized tube of toothpaste. Fortunately, I packed my toiletries and cosmetics in my carry-on. Between that and the night shirt I grabbed at the Walmart down the road, I'll be fine for the night.

What I'm concerned about, though, are the Christmas presents I packed. "What if they don't arrive in time? My flight leaves at three." I spent two hours on the phone with the airline from my hotel room to secure that seat.

"Don't worry. You're not gonna need any clothes for a few days, at least."

My blood surges with Jonah's unspoken promise of what's coming, delivered in a huskier tone.

This last month may have seemed frantic at times with all the preparation for my move, but it also dragged. We went from essentially living together during those last weeks before my dad died to parting ways on a chilly day in Anchorage with no plans to continue our relationship, to reuniting two months later over a four-day-weekend visit.

In my third-story bedroom, directly above my mom and Simon.

Not exactly conducive to the kind of intimacy we were both craving, though we made the best of it. But this month-long wait has only left me with an unending ache of frustration. Hearing Jonah say things like that doesn't help.

I can*not* wait to be alone with him.

I swallow a gulp of wine. "Is it still snowing there?"

"*Still* snowing. How's the hotel?"

I drop my voice to a whispered hiss. "Aside from all the *dead* animals?" The lobby is full of bear skins and deer heads and stuffed fish. Pelts of every color and size adorn the walls of the hallways. A chandelier made from mismatched antlers—foraged in the woods or the prize of several kills?—dangles from the foyer, the dim light it casts adding to the eeriness of the place. "There's a freaking *water buffalo* beside the front desk."

"That's a musk ox."

"*Whatever*. This place is a wild animal tomb."

"Yeah, it's kind of their theme. Andrea's a taxidermist."

I feel my eyebrows pop. "*She* stuffed all these things?"

"*And* hunted most of them. You should see their house. They've got a full-grown male grizzly bear standing in the corner."

"That sounds delightful." I cringe, trying to picture the kind of woman who'd find pleasure in gutting animals and measuring their eye sockets for the perfect glass balls. Something tells me we won't be swapping favorite nail polish colors.

"You're in Alaska. People shoot and stuff things around here, and not only the men. It's the way things are. Get used to it."

I groan. "Get used to it" seems to be Jonah's new favorite slogan. "As long as *you* never bring home a carcass and ask me to clean and cook it." I know Jonah hunts. I've seen the collection of rifles and shotguns in his safe. I'm just not sure how I feel about it yet.

"Wouldn't dream of it." I hear the smile in his voice. "The restaurant's cozy, though, huh?"

"Yeah," I admit. It's plainly decorated in dark wood paneling and warmed by a rustic stone fireplace that blazes in a nearby corner. Picture windows overlook a frozen, snow-covered Lake Hood, cast in shadows of an afternoon sunset, all white save for the colorful small-engine planes, wearing skis in place of wheels. On the other side of the lake are humble brown-brick apartment buildings. Beyond them, in the far distance, majestic white-capped mountains loom.

I survey the tables with a curious glance. A third of them are occupied. How many of these people are also stranded, waiting to get somewhere?

"So, what're you gonna order?"

"I don't know." I flip through the pages. It's mainly pub fare, with a prime rib special. "A lot of wine, to drown my sorrows?"

"Go sit at the bar, then. Chris should be there."

My gaze wanders to the long, stately dark walnut counter—the fanciest thing in this place—and to the tall man with wiry gray hair. "Big, bushy mustache?"

"Yeah, that's him. He'll talk your ear off all night. Ask him about his huskies. He's got a dogsled team that their son races in the Iditarod every year. And get the burger. Andrea makes the patties herself."

"With *real* beef?" I ask pointedly. I've learned my lesson.

Jonah chuckles. And doesn't answer, I note. "Also, the butternut squash soup is good."

I grimace. "I hate squash."

"*What*? No, you don't."

"Yeah, I do. It makes me gag."

"No, it doesn't."

"Why are you arguing with me about this? Yes, it does! Same with beets. They taste like dirt."

Jonah groans. "Jesus. You're as bad as Wren was."

I feel a prick in my chest at the mention of my dad, who, in many ways, Jonah knew better than I ever will. "That's not true. He wouldn't eat a single vegetable. I only won't eat squash and beets." I add after a lengthy pause, "Or cabbage, or mushrooms. And I hate strawberries."

"*Strawberries?* Man, what have I signed up for?" There's a teasing note in his tone. "Okay, Barbie, give me the rundown. What else are you gonna be difficult about? Wait, wait ... lemme get a notepad. I have a feeling this is gonna be a *long* list."

I'm picturing him stretching out on his sectional in a pair of baggy jeans, a sinewy arm tucked under his head, a simple cotton shirt stretched across his broad chest, unintentionally showing off the many hard ridges that sculpt his muscular body.

I should have been lying on top of that body tonight, I think bitterly.

"Let me see ..." I settle into my own seat, propping my hiking boots up on the chair opposite me, and grin. "For starters, hairy, obnoxious men and cheap beer."

"*Nooo!*" I moan into my pillow as the news headline flashes across the bottom of the TV screen, claiming the worst snowfall in south-western Alaska in nearly fifty years. The accompanying videos and pictures from yesterday—snow blowing sideways, four-foot drifts over roads, cars buried—do well to emphasize that statement.

Worse, the weatherman, dressed in a red, fur-lined parka, his face hidden within the cove of his hood, is promising that Anchorage is going to catch a ribbon of that inclement weather beginning this morning. I checked in on my flight and it's already marked as delayed by an hour.

Dragging myself out of bed, I head for the window, the cool air chilling my bare legs, an odd comfort for the dull ache in my head. I took Jonah's advice last night and shifted my pity party of one to the bar to strike up a conversation with Chris, who turned out to be as nice as Jonah promised, albeit a bit awkward, telling stale jokes about Canadian accents and our horse-riding Mounties. Andrea made an appearance around nine and proved to be nothing like I imagined the killing, trophy-stuffing woman to be, her pixie-like face framed by a pale blonde bob, her wide smile offering nothing but warmth and friendliness.

They fed me red wine—a few glasses on the house—and entertained me for hours with stories of her hunting exploits and the lodge's crazy customers, until my body buzzed and my stomach hurt from laughing and I had earned myself an invitation to Christmas dinner, should I find myself stuck in Anchorage.

It was after eleven by the time I staggered to my room, but I forced myself to stay up, watching movies and plugging away at my computer until almost two A.M., trying to reset my internal clock against the four-hour time change.

I still woke up at six this morning.

I peel back the curtain and greet a sea of black nothing, the sun far from rising. The few dim streetlights that shine down over the parking lot show nothing of any falling snow. If clouds are rolling in above us, I won't see them for a few more hours.

But, with the way my luck is going so far, I fear I'll be spending Christmas dinner with strangers.

I stumble back to bed, dismayed, to check for a response to my "are you awake yet? How bad is it?" text that I sent to Jonah the moment my eyelids cracked open.

Jonah: *It's not looking good for today. Heading to Wild to help sort out the mess.*

I sigh heavily. He refuses to call my dad's charter company anything but, though the planes and small terminal have been sporting the shiny new crimson-and-blue "Aro" logo for weeks. That's the only thing that's visibly changed so far, from what he's told me. The new owner has been focused on getting the business's technology up to speed, with plans to freshen up the office and waiting area in the summer.

We will have left Bangor by then, if we can find the right place near Anchorage.

And if it *ever* stops snowing.

With my spirits low enough to threaten tears, I wash down a few Advil with a mouthful of water and burrow under the comforter.

The shrill sound of the hotel phone pierces the silence, stirring me from a restless sleep before noon. It's the front desk, telling me that my luggage has arrived. Relief amid frustration. It doesn't last long, though, as I check my flight on my phone to see that it's been delayed *another* hour. On the bright side, it hasn't been outright canceled. Yet.

There are no more texts from Jonah, though I'm not surprised. I don't normally hear from him when he's at work. Still, it doesn't help my mood. Neither does my growling stomach.

There is, however, a text from my mom, with a selfie of her and Simon on the beach, toasting to the camera, pasty-white-skinned and smiling.

Maybe I should have listened to her and gone to Turks. I wouldn't be spending Christmas with a stuffed grizzly bear watching over me while I eat.

I push that sour thought aside and get ready—yanking on my same traveling clothes from yesterday, brushing my teeth, pulling my hair into a quick topknot, and swiping my mascara wand across my lashes.

How funny it is that I wouldn't be caught dead barefaced six months ago, before Jonah intruded on my life. My appearance seemed vastly more important to me in the grand scheme of things then than it does now.

I throw open the door, intent on grabbing breakfast along with my things.

And gasp at the scruffy-faced male figure leaning against the wall, his tall, muscular body draped in a heavy plaid winter coat overtop layers of fleece, his ash-blond hair capped with a black beanie. His piercing icy blue eyes are locked on me.

"What are you doing here!" I exclaim, as waves of relief course through my limbs.

"Take a wild guess." Jonah's gruff voice rattles in my chest. God, I've missed hearing it in person.

"But I thought … the storm—"

"There was a decent break, so I took it, flew low, and prayed it would hold." His gaze skates over my hair, my nose, my mouth, stalling there.

"Was it bad?"

"Would you get over here already?" He heaves himself off the wall, taking a step toward me.

I dive into his chest, savoring the feel of his hard body against mine and the smell of him—spearmint gum and woodsy soap—as our lips find each other in a welcoming kiss. "My flight's delayed."

He curls his arms around me and pulls me tight to him, his bristly hair scratching against my skin as he bends to dip his face into the crook of my neck. He inhales deeply and then lets out a contented sigh. "I know. The airport's a mess. Tons of people trying to get places for Christmas."

I close my eyes. "I can't believe you're here." Suddenly, spending our first Christmas together at the dead-animal hotel doesn't seem so appalling.

"Of course, I'm here. As if I was gonna let you get stuck, alone, on Christmas."

"So, I'll fly back with you, then?"

"We're not going back that way today." There's an edge to his voice, one that makes me think the trip here over the mountains was far worse than he's letting on. And Jonah is fearless when it comes to flying.

A part of me wants to reprimand him—what if he had crashed?—but a bigger part is overwhelmed with emotion that he made the risky trip for me.

"I love you," I blurt before I can give it too much thought.

Several beats pass before Jonah pulls away, far enough to meet my gaze, a curious look in his.

I hold my breath, suddenly afraid that I'm going to have to add this moment to the top of my growing list of things that have gone terribly wrong so far with this move.

"I was wonderin' how long it'd take you to get up the nerve to say it. Especially after you chickened out at the airport." He brushes an errant strand of hair off my face. "Thought I might have to wait forever."

My mouth hangs open for a moment. "You knew?"

"You Fletchers never have been good at speakin' your mind." A soft, crooked smile curls his lips. "Of course, I knew."

I roll my eyes even as my cheeks flush. In the dingy Anchorage lodge hallway, being chastised by Jonah for how much like my father I am is *not* how I was envisioning this moment going. "Well ... great." What else am I supposed to say, especially since he hasn't echoed the sentiment?

His mouth splits into a perfect, white-toothed grin. "You're cute when you're vulnerable."

My indignation flares. "You know what? I take it back."

"Nah. You don't."

"Yeah, I do. In fact, I think I *hate* you right now." I make to pull free from his arms, but they coil tighter, keeping me in place.

"Look at me," he demands softly.

After a moment of reluctance, I do. His blue eyes are severe as they pin me down. "I can't remember what it feels like *not* being in love with you, Calla."

My pulse pounds in my veins.

He leans in, presses his forehead against mine. "I can't remember what it's like to wake up and not have you be the first thing I think about. Every morning, I roll over in bed to check for a message from you. Every night, I go to bed annoyed because you're not beside me. Because you're so far away. I need you in my life like I need to fly. Like I need this Alaskan air. *More* than I need this air."

"Wow. That's ..." I swallow the lump in my throat, about to float away on a euphoric high from his tender admission. *That's way better than just blurting out "I love you."*

He cups my chin with his palms. "You were made for me. I am madly in love with you, Calla Fletcher." His mouth catches mine in a deceptively soft kiss that threatens to buckle my knees. It draws a moan from deep within me, the agonizing month-long wait to feel Jonah's lips against mine finally over.

I grab hold of his forearms for support, my hands tightening over them, reveling in their strength. I ache to feel his corded muscle and smooth skin and soft hair beneath my fingertips again, to feel the weight of his body sinking me into a mattress.

Between us, the hard ridge of his erection presses against my stomach, taunting me.

A throat clears, pulling us apart. A housekeeper smiles sheepishly as she edges past to get to her cart on the other side.

I nod to my open hotel room door behind us. "Maybe we should take this inside?" Because I'm about five seconds away from unfastening his belt buckle, audience be damned.

Jonah takes a step forward, but then stops, shaking his head firmly. "If we want to make it out of here today, we need to go *now*. That system is movin' in slow, but it's comin'."

I frown. "I thought you said you weren't flying back today."

"We're not, but we're not staying here."

"Where are we going, then?"

"To see Santa."

"*What?*"

"Do you trust me?"

"Yeah, of course, but—"

"'Kay, then stop talkin', get ready, and meet me in the lobby. I'll check you out of your room." He plants a last, chaste kiss on my lips and strolls away, whistling "Rudolph the Red-Nosed Reindeer."

"But my suitcases—"

"They're at the front desk," he hollers over his shoulder, adding in a booming voice, "but I told you already, Barbie, you're not gonna be wearin' any clothes for a few days."

My cheeks burn as I seek out the housekeeper, hovering by her cart with her head down, pretending she didn't hear that.

And then I rush inside to pack my things.

CHAPTER FOUR

"I don't see Santa *or* his elves." I eye the A-frame cabin nestled at the edge of the tree line as Jonah circles our plane over the frozen lake. A narrow trail cuts through the forest leading up to it, the far end connected to another trail that snakes through the sea of tall, thin evergreens. A road, though I don't know how often it's been used.

"You just missed him." Jonah smirks and jabs a thumb toward the last town we passed.

It finally clicks. "The North Pole! Oh my God!" A wave of nostalgia washes over me. I can't believe I hadn't clued in already. "My dad always used to tell me he was flying there. I thought it was the coolest thing." Back when I only knew his face thanks to a picture, when I'd prattle nonstop over the phone and he'd listen patiently.

Jonah's deep chuckle carries through the headset. "Yeah. Well, it's not *the* North Pole, but it's North Pole, Alaska. Christmas all year round. They've got giant candy canes along the main street. We can take the snow machine in tomorrow for somethin' to do, if you want. It's not that far." He points to the expanse of buildings in the distance as a crop of lights ignite in the dusk, ahead of the coming nightfall. "That's Fairbanks up ahead. It's the second-largest city in Alaska."

Jonah wouldn't divulge any more hints about where we were heading as we loaded my luggage into the passenger seats. I snooped though the cargo area, packed with his black duffel bag, a cooler, a box of dry food, and several jugs of water. I badgered him as we fled the incoming weather system, heading northeast past the frozen plains, over the snowy, sawtooth ridges of the imposing mountain range, far enough that the looming clouds broke apart to allow slivers of sunshine through. Still, he told me nothing, enjoying my frustration while the radio frequency buzzed with chatter from other pilots, citing their coordinates, weather patterns, the odd joke.

Now, as the sun prepares to slip past the horizon at two thirty in the afternoon, I accept that Jonah has flown me farther north than I've ever been.

This is now my life.

Will the shock ever wear off?

I huddle in my heavy parka and thick winter boots, my body tense as Veronica—the four-seater Cessna that I spent so much time in when Jonah shuttled my father and me around Alaska on daily excursions—jerks and shakes violently on our descent. While I'm nowhere near as anxious as I was flying in a small plane that first day back in July, the few months away have robbed me of some of my unearthed bravery. "Whose place is this?"

"George and Bobbie's. They were gonna come for Christmas, but George got one of his funny feelings." Jonah gives me a flat, knowing look. The burly pilot from the Midwest is well known for bowing out of flights due to his superstitious tendencies. "So, they decided to wait out the snow. Offered their place to us for the next three days. It's fully stocked already."

"That was generous of them." A giddiness sparks inside me at the thought of three days alone with Jonah. The most time we've ever spent *entirely* alone was that trip into the mountains to pick up two hikers this past summer. We ended up grounded for the night because of heavy fog and wind and sought refuge in a rustic safety cabin. There was no running water or electricity, and nothing but a sleeping bag and muskrat jerky. And an insurmountable tension between us that rose to a boiling point, impossible to ignore. It was the night everything changed.

It was also the last night I was under the illusion that my father would survive his cancer.

Jonah releases the yoke long enough to give my knee a squeeze. "They're happy you came to your senses."

"That remains to be seen," I tease before my smile fades. "But what about Agnes and Mabel? I know you wanted to be there for them. Are they going to be upset?" My father spent every Christmas morning sitting on Agnes's couch with a mug of coffee in hand and a checkerboard in play.

"Aggie's the one who was watchin' the weather radar at four this morning, hopin' for enough of a break to let me fly. She didn't want you stuck in Anchorage alone. Besides, they're headin' to George and Bobbie's for dinner. A bunch of the Wild folks are gonna be there."

"That sounds … nice." For too many years, I blamed my dad's charter plane company for our estrangement. I hated everything about it. It took me coming to Alaska to see that it wasn't just some business, some job to make money. My father and Alaska Wild were improving lives. In some cases, saving them. And the employees were family to him. It still feels wrong that I'm about to inherit all that money from the sale of a place I used to despise.

I hesitate. "So, is my dad's house up for sale yet?" He owned all three modular homes on that stretch of road—his, Agnes's, and Jonah's. Properties passed down to him from my grandparents. My father was not known for acting swiftly or decisively, but in the last weeks before his death, he was busy adding names to deeds to allow immediate transfer when the time came. "To avoid all that messy probate stuff," he had said. It made it easy for Jonah to claim the house he was renting, and for Agnes and Mabel to take ownership of the other two houses to do with what they want.

"Not yet. She figures spring. She wants to give us a chance to sell first, and that's gonna take a while. We've only had one person come through so far."

I note how he says us and we, as if that house is somehow partly mine, and my heart warms. "I can help her take down the wallpaper in the kitchen, if she wants me to," I say, even as I grimace at the thought of scraping off all those mallards. I remember Simon's house being plastered with wallpaper when we moved in. It had been his English parents' house before he bought it. Primrose in the bathroom, apple blossoms in the kitchen, lilacs in the dining room.

I don't think my mother's suitcases were even unpacked before she attacked the powder room with a metal spatula. They ended up hiring someone to tackle the rest because it was too much for any one person, and I doubt Simon appreciated the disparaging remarks my mother muttered under her breath about his parents' decorating taste as she toiled away in anger.

But, *of course* I'll help Agnes. I'd do anything for that tiny, soft-spoken woman, the catalyst for me reuniting with my father, and the reason I'm here with Jonah. Besides, what else do I have to do while Jonah finishes up his last month at Aro?

How strange will it be for me to be in that house again, dismantling everything that made it my father's? A shiver of unease slides down my back with the thought.

"I'll help too," Jonah murmurs absently, his keen focus on the snowy stretch of lake ahead of us.

"It's frozen, right?" I ask.

"Should be."

"*Should* be?"

"I hope so."

I give him a high-browed stare. "This is you being funny?"

"No." He smirks. "But that's why we're gonna do a touch-and-go first, mainly to check the snow, but also for overflow."

I have no clue what overflow is, but Jonah's tight brow of concentration convinces me I don't want to be asking him questions right now. I stay quiet as he brings us down. I sense the plane's skis slide across the lake's surface for a moment, without slowing, before we're lifting off again. We circle around and, with Jonah eying the tracks and grunting "we're good," we descend once again.

Within minutes, Veronica's skis are gliding over the snow-covered lake. We ease to a stop some thirty feet from the cabin. With anyone else, I might have worried about crashing into it. According to my dad, Jonah is one of the best bush pilots out there and, if there's anyone who would know, it would have been Wren Fletcher.

Jonah leans forward to peer out at the place through the windshield. "Nice, right?"

"It's like a holiday postcard." A steep roof caps the two stories of the stained-ash cabin, with a deep overhang to shelter the wooden door from the elements. A tall chimney juts out from the left side. The space beneath the platform deck is jam-packed with chopped wood for a fire that I can't wait to curl up beside tonight.

It's certainly giving off cozy Christmas vibes, with traditional evergreen-and-red-ribbon wreaths marking each of the five windows and the door. On the deck sit two poinsettia-red Adirondack chairs, peeking out from beneath a layer of undisturbed snow and angled to overlook the lake. Above them dangle strings of patio lights, stretching the width of the cabin.

I'm about to say it's perfect until I spy a small wooden shed tucked into the thicket of trees behind, the telltale moon carving in the door. I groan at the unpleasant surprise.

"Come on ... You're tougher than that," Jonah goads, which only irritates me more. He knows how much I despise outhouses.

"No, I'm not. *Get used to it.*" I throw his favorite line back at him. "It's *freezing* out here! And dark for, what, fifteen hours?"

"More like nineteen to twenty right now."

"Oh! Even better."

He chuckles. "It's no big deal."

"Says the guy who gets to open the door and *whip it out*. Meanwhile I have to walk through ten feet of snow *in the dark*—probably with wolves and shit around—and freeze my bare ass *every time* I need to pee!"

"There's a heat lamp in there."

I shoot him a flat look, earning his laughter.

"What if I help thaw your ass after?"

"Yeah, you will," I mutter.

"God, I missed your bad attitude." His fingers curl around the back of my neck to give me a soft, playful squeeze. "Come on ... Let's get this place up and running."

———

"You can lose the coat and boots. I think it's finally warm enough." Jonah shoves another log into the woodstove. The orange glow from within flares.

I test his claim by blowing into the air. When we first stepped inside this quaint cabin of knotty pine, our hot breath billowed in the cold. Now, though, with a roaring fire and a heater pumping out warmth, only a mild chill lingers.

I kick off my boots and shrug out of my parka, swapping it for my red-and-black-checkered flannel jacket and wool socks that I dug out of my suitcase. With the glass of red wine I poured after unloading our food—mostly snacks and premade meals from Agnes's freezer, but also a turkey breast ready to go into the small propane stove—I settle onto the futon, careful not to knock the oil lamp that casts a dim but warm light. "How often do Bobbie and George come here?"

"A week or two in the summer, and a lot of weekends once the busy season dies down. They're usually here from Christmas till after New Year's." He prods the burning logs with a poker one last time before shutting and latching the little door. "They're gonna retire here. Get the place set up to live in comfortably year-round."

"Year-round? I think I'd get bored." My curious gaze drifts around the interior, with Bobbie's cute little touches—an embroidered cushion, a pastel watercolor of a bush plane floating on a lake, a kitschy sign about hearth and home—that feel very much like the bubbly grocery store cashier with a faded Alabama accent.

Above us is a tiny loft, with just enough room for a double bed and two narrow side tables. I'm struggling to picture George, a sizeable man with a handlebar mustache, ambling up that ladder at night. "How'd they get all that furniture up there?"

"Painfully, on ropes. I was here for that." Jonah sinks into the futon next to me with a groan. He hasn't stopped since his boots hit the snowy ground hours ago: emptying and securing the plane, bringing in firewood, loading and mounting his gun on the wall, setting up the various propane, oil, battery, and solar-panel power sources that keep this cabin operational. He's already talking about chopping more logs and taking the ATV to get water from the town well tomorrow.

I lean in to rest my jet-lagged head against his shoulder, inhaling the scent of burning wood as I absorb the silence, save for the sound of the crackling fire. I can't recall the last time I was so content. "It'd be nice to have a place like this to escape to."

His eyebrow arches. "Even with the outhouse?"

"I'd only come in summer." I discovered the three-piece bathroom in the back of the cabin, operational in warmer months when the water can't freeze in the pipes.

"There's my little princess," he teases, his hand sliding over my thigh affectionately. But then his voice turns softer, more serious. "We can have this, too, once we figure things out. Give us a few years to get settled somewhere and then we can look at buying a patch of land somewhere up here and building our own place."

"Like this?"

"Maybe a bit bigger." He pauses a beat. "Big enough for us and twelve kids."

"*Only* twelve?" I mock as flutters stir in my stomach. "How about we try for one and see how it goes?" Of all the things I appreciate about Jonah, his directness is near the top of the list. It forces conversations to happen that otherwise might not, if I'm left to my own devices. He first brought up the topic of kids back in Toronto. Almost as a checkpoint, I suspect, because his relief when I confirmed that, yes, I do want kids *eventually*, was palpable.

"Sounds good to me." Jonah seizes my waist and hoists me onto his lap to face him, guiding my thighs around his. A deep sound rumbles in his chest as his hands grip and outline my curves, working from my hips to my waist, to the swell of my breasts in one smooth motion.

I toy with strands of his ash-blond hair as my body responds with raw need. Meanwhile, my chest surges with a new level of appreciation for this man. I have no intention of becoming a mother anytime soon, but that Jonah is so resolute, so confident, so unafraid of the idea is unexpectedly sexy. And here, I didn't think he could become more so.

With dexterous fingers, he slides my flannel coat down my arms, letting it fall to the floor behind me. My sweater goes next, leaving me in a thin cotton shirt. I shudder, though I'm no longer feeling the cold.

"What did you think about that place?" I ask, smoothing my hands over his broad shoulders, across his hard chest, over the ridges of his defined stomach. Jonah credits his Norwegian genes for his physique. I haven't seen him venture out to a gym since I met him, so maybe it's true.

"Which place?" His calloused fingers slip beneath my shirt, skimming over my back to find the clasp of my bra. With a flick, the tension in the material gives way. An eager shiver runs through my body as he pushes the lace aside and cups my breasts within his palms, his touch far gentler than I ever expected from him.

"The one I sent you on Saturday?"

"You sent me a listing for a 3000-square-foot house in Anchorage, near a Walmart." He guides my arms up and then hikes my shirt over my head. He discards my bra as if it's a scrap, exposing my upper body to the cool night air. He leans back for a long moment, as if to admire my naked flesh and decide what he wants to do with it first. It's such a simple move, and yet my breasts grow heavy and my nipples harden and blood rushes to my core.

"It was a big lot. And the rent isn't too bad."

His gaze flickers to mine. "I'm gonna be thirty-two in April, Calla. I don't wanna rent anymore if I don't have to. Let's look for somethin' to buy. Somethin' that's a hundred percent *ours*. A smaller house with more land. No Walmart in our backyard." His hands splay across my back, pulling my body closer. He leans in to lick one peaked nipple before taking it into his mouth and sucking hard.

I revel in the conflicting feel of his bristly facial hair—it'll be another month before I can call that a beard again—and his wet tongue, but my mind is spinning with thoughts. Jonah has mentioned buying instead of renting once before. My mother has been pushing hard for the latter. It's far less permanent, she insisted. Less complicated to sort out should things not work between us. Easier for me to pick up and come home.

Like she did.

She insists she's only doing her job as a mother, warning me of pitfalls before I tumble into them.

But I am not her, and Jonah is certainly nothing like my father. He wants to settle down and have kids, *with me*. There are no accidental pregnancies guiding our decisions.

That he's so confident in us and our longevity gives me courage. "Okay. I can start looking at places for sale too—"

"Calla?" Jonah whispers against my skin, his hot breath sparking goose bumps. I love the sound of my name on his low, raspy voice.

"Yeah?"

He peers up at me, his gaze hooded in the low cast of lamplight. I remember the first time I saw those icy blue eyes—a gorgeous feature that he had kept hidden behind sunglasses and an acerbic personality. "We've got all the time in the world to talk about that. But, right *now*?" He grips my hips with his rough, strong hands and pulls my body flush against his pelvis. The rock-hard ridge of his erection is impossible to miss. "If I'm not inside you in the next three minutes, I'm gonna *die*."

I giggle, even as my body flushes with heat. "And you call *me* dramatic."

"I'm serious. I'll die right here, in George's cabin. The superstitious bastard'll never step foot in here again."

"We wouldn't want that," I say with mock seriousness, collecting his angular jaw between my palms. His face is impressively handsome, his features strong and masculine, and yet with those high cheekbones, pouty, full lips, and long lashes make him almost *pretty*.

Jonah's grin flashes with wicked intent. "No. Not when they've been so generous, lending us this place."

"Right. The *least* we can do is make sure he can come back." With a playful smile, I grind my hips against him, earning a whispered curse. I lean in and grant him a soft, teasing kiss, the tip of my tongue tracing his bottom lip before sliding in to stroke his mouth.

Jonah's fingers dig into my hips. "I wasn't kidding about the three minutes." I squeal as he shifts me off his lap and onto my back, sprawled on the futon. His hasty fingers hook around the elastic band of my leggings and panties and he tugs them down, his heated gaze rapt on every inch of me that he exposes in the process. In seconds, the last of my clothes has been stripped off me, socks and all.

I watch with greedy anticipation as he stands and shucks his clothes in record time. His body is perfect—powerful and well proportioned, his skin a golden olive, even in the dead of winter. I still haven't decided what my favorite part of Jonah's body is: his broad, cut shoulders, his columnar neck, the way his collarbones jut out around the pads of chest muscle, or the impressive cut of his pelvis, leading down to the part that's thick and velvety-skinned, and currently rigid, waiting for attention.

He dives in to cover my slight body with his massive one, settling his weight between my thighs. "I've thought about this moment every minute of every day for the last month." His fingers curl within mine as he stretches my arms above my head, pinning them to the mattress.

Our mouths find each other with hunger, our teeth clinking and nipping, our tongues stroking, our lips bruising as we taste and kiss with reckless abandon.

"It's been three minutes," I whisper, my inner muscles flexing with expectation. I rock my hips against him, seeking out his hard tip, lining it up with my body's entrance, aching to feel him inside me again.

He sinks deep with a single thrust and a moan.

And the eerie silence in the cabin fills with the heady sounds of our long-awaited reunion.

————

"Calla ..."

"Calla, wake up."

I groan as a hand jostles my shoulder.

"Seriously, Calla, you've gotta see this."

"What time is it?" I murmur, unwilling to open my eyes.

"Almost one A.M."

I let out a second groan, this one louder and laced with heavy annoyance, as I pull the blanket over my head. It was after eleven when we drifted off on the futon, our naked bodies boneless and coiled together, wanting to stay near the fire rather than climb the ladder to the loft. "That's five in Toronto. If I get up, I'm screwed for the night."

"You're screwed either way. Get up."

The hint of excitement in Jonah's voice is what has me unfurling myself and peering into the darkness. Jonah must have stoked the fire because the vibrant glow from the woodstove provides enough light to see.

He looms over me in nothing but a pair of sweatpants that hang low on his hips, showing off that intoxicating *V* of his pelvis. My hormones spike instinctively and I reach for him, my fingertips grazing his belly button, the dark trail of hair, lower … until I'm palming his flaccid but still impressive length. "Come back to bed."

He chuckles but takes a quick step out of my reach. He tosses my leggings, shirt, and plaid jacket at me, then reaches for his own shirt. "After. We're goin' outside."

"You're kidding me, right?" I tug on my clothes and trail him to the door, stopping long enough to shove my feet into my boots and pull on my parka and gloves. I make a point of shivering loudly as I follow him into the frigid cold, the shock of its icy fingers like a slap to my cheek.

All my complaints vanish the second I take in the shimmering green and blue lights that sway and surge and dance in the clear night sky, illuminating the expanse of stars above us and the frozen, snow-covered lake below.

"The northern lights!" I exclaim, mesmerized. It's as if the heavens have come to life.

Jonah shifts to stand behind me, draping his arms around my body, cocooning me in his warmth. "This is one of the best places in the world to see them." He presses his lips against my cheek. "That's why I wanted to bring you up here."

I gape at the spectacular light show, stunned. "Is it like this *all the time?*" I can't even see the *stars* back home, the city lights too bright.

"On a clear, dark night? Yeah, there's a good chance you'll catch them, especially in the winter. But you have to be watching for them."

"God, this is … incredible! I need to get my camera—"

"No." His grip of me tightens, keeping me in place. "I'll bring you up another time and you can sit out here all night, freezing your ass off and taking a million pictures. I promise. But tonight, this is for you and me. It's our moment." He rests his chin on my head. "The first night of the rest of our lives."

I relax into him. "Does everyone know you're such a romantic?"

"Shut up." His deep chuckle tickles my ear. "I figured you'd like seeing this."

"I *love* seeing this." I curl my gloved hand around his. "Thank you." Is this what a life with Jonah means? Will he whisk me away to remote places and show me awe-inspiring wonders? Things I had no idea about and things I may have heard about but never realized how much I would appreciate?

Because if that's the case, I'll never get enough of this new life with him.

His arms squeeze me tight. "Merry Christmas, Barbie."

I tip my head back to catch his lips with mine. "Merry Christmas, you big, angry yeti."

CHAPTER FIVE

January

"Simon burned the tops of his feet so bad, his skin blistered. He had to wear the hotel slippers from the resort *all the way* home." I hold my gloved hand in the air before me, studying the complex crystal pattern of a snowflake before it melts against my body heat. If that's even possible, given it's cold enough to make my nose hairs stick together. *At least it'll be sunny*, Jonah promised me over our morning coffee. "Mom made him use a wheelchair in the airport. He argued with her at first and caused this huge scene. Well, as much of a scene as Simon can cause. But then he remembered, through his 'acute, unyielding pain, to whom he is married and surrendered posthaste.'" A laugh escapes my lips as I mimic Simon's uppity British accent.

I don't expect a response, and yet the silence that answers is deafening.

"You would have liked Simon," I manage to choke out around the exploding ball in my throat, fighting the threatened rush of emotion. It's been a while since I've felt the loss of my father with such intensity, where a thought or a memory—a joke, a moment, a smile—would spark a burst of uncontrollable tears. But sitting here now, back in Bangor, next to his grave, so close to all that's physically left of him in this world, it all seems so fresh.

I hug my buckled legs against my chest as I study the solemn wooden cross, the name "Wren Fletcher" painted across it in tidy black lettering. The old cemetery is filled with these simple white crosses, scattered about in no particular pattern, some standing tall, freshly painted, the names unblemished, others leaning to one side, paint peeling, their owners unidentifiable. Worn, faded silk flowers loop around the wood and peek out from the heavy blanket of snow, where they'll sit until spring cleanup, to be replaced by fresh ones.

There are no grand monuments here, no expensive crypts to boast wealth, to stand out among the crowd. In the newer cemetery across town are plenty of headstones of varying sizes and styles and value, but in this one—the original cemetery that houses the earliest settlers of Bangor, where my grandparents were buried, and my father sleeps eternally—the graves are marked by simple white wooden crosses, regardless of whether the occupant of that plot could have afforded more. It's an oddly comforting notion—a show of solidarity for those embracing the simplicity of life in Alaska. And yet every time I see the sea of forlorn markers, a shiver runs along my spine.

Taking slow, calming breaths, I close my eyes and pretend I'm curled in my mother's shabby old wicker chair on the porch of my father's modular home, and he is sitting in the rickety lawn chair beside me, listening quietly.

"Jonah gave me a camo jacket for Christmas. Can you believe that? I mean, not like a cute, stylish army print that I might choose for myself. It's this big, bulky, green-and-brown thing with antlers all over it, for hunters." I wince. "And the inside is a fluorescent orange that I can reverse. You know, so no one mistakes me for an animal and *shoots me* while I'm out running." I shake my head. "And I can't tell if this is another one of his jokes, or if he *seriously* thought it was something I'd like."

We flew back on the twenty-eighth, to blue skies and a blustering, cold wind. We enjoyed a belated Christmas dinner with Agnes and Mabel, complete with Mabel's latest freshly caught chicken from Whittamore's and a four-foot, potted spruce tree purchased at the Saturday market. Agnes said she plans to plant it in her backyard come spring. Jonah's stony face betrayed nothing as I opened the bulky box, realized what it was, and did my best to appear gracious as I pulled it on. I don't know if he bought my act, but he hasn't mentioned it since, and it's been four days.

"Don't get me wrong, I *appreciate* the thought, especially coming from a guy who buys his clothes at the local grocery store." Which is why my gifts to him included designer dark-wash, straight-leg jeans that don't sag on his ass and a few ultrasoft crewneck shirts without a hint of plaid. I spent *days* looking for the perfect gifts for him, recruiting Mabel to seek out his neck and waist size. They're the nicest items in his closet, by far. "It's practical, I guess, seeing as I'm living in Alaska. And it looks well made, for a *hunting* jacket." I chuckle. "He also got me a children's book on wildlife safety. And Mabel and Agnes bought me a mosquito jacket and bear spray and bells, for when I go jogging."

After spending the day on Kodiak Island with Jonah and my father, seeing grizzlies roaming the river freely, I don't plan on running anywhere that puts me at risk of coming across one of those.

"I printed a twelve-month yeti calendar, for Agnes to hang in Wild's lobby. It features that picture of him cutting wood at the safety cabin. I even had someone design a logo that says 'The Yeti.' It was meant as a joke, but it looks good. We're trying to convince him to use it for the charter company but he's being stubborn. It's good, though, right? *The Yeti.* Like, 'Have you booked the Yeti yet?' *I* think it's catchy. Agnes agrees. Anyway, I told her to put the calendar up after we move, so he can't rip it down and hide it."

I smile, remembering the look on Jonah's face when Agnes opened it—like he wasn't sure whether he wanted to kiss or choke me. "You should have seen him, Dad. You would have laughed *so* hard." That soft, melodic chuckle that brings me back to the long-distance phone conversations of my childhood.

Another sharp flare of emotion triggers inside me, and I swallow repeatedly, trying to stave off the tears.

I huddle deeper into my parka—a Christmas gift from Simon—as a familiar black Ford pickup creeps along the desolate road, stopping at the cemetery's gate. The driver hops out, their knee-high boots landing solidly on the ground, their hood sheathing a face from view. I don't need to see a face to recognize the small figure approaching at a leisurely pace.

I watch as Agnes veers off to the far left corner, to where her late husband—Mabel's father, who died in a plane crash before Mabel was born—is buried.

What must it be like for her, to have not one but two men she loved to visit on this New Year's Day, and at only forty-three years old?

"Did you know Agnes sold her truck to that old accountant guy of yours? She's been driving your truck around ever since. Jonah gave her an earful. He can't understand why she did it. Apparently, it's in way worse shape than hers." I smile sadly. "I know why, though. It's because it smells like you." Like old, faded fabric permeated by years of tobacco smoke.

I found myself sitting in it for a short stretch yesterday, caught in a nostalgic moment about my first morning in Alaska, stranded and forced to trudge across the boggy grass in my suede wedge heels to beg Jonah for a ride to town.

"I'm getting my driver's license. I just need to sort out a bit more paperwork, but as soon as I have that, I'm going in to do the written test, and then Jonah will help get me ready for the road test. I should have it in time for our move to Anchorage, or shortly after, and then I'm going to buy myself a car." The lawyers anticipate that my father's estate will be wrapped up in a few more months and I'll have plenty of money to buy whatever I want with the proceeds from the sale of Alaska Wild. "Jonah's pushing hard for a truck. We got into a fight about it, after I told him I'm looking at a Mini Cooper. He's been sending me these *horrible* pictures of car crashes involving moose." I shake my head. "Don't worry, though. No matter what I get, I'm sure he'll make sure I learn how not to ditch it."

The snow crunches under Agnes's boots on her approach. In her gloved fist, she carries a cluster of pale pink silk calla lilies, to replenish the ones buried. My father's favorite flower, he admitted one quiet night in those last weeks, while he attempted to teach me how to play checkers.

"Happy New Year!" Her greeting is delivered in that accent I now recognize as common to a born-and-bred Alaskan, especially from this side of the state. My father spoke in that same slow, relaxed, folksy way. "Nice day for a visit with Wren."

"I think my butt's frozen," I joke, though the sleek black ski pants I'm wearing coupled with thermal pants offer decent protection.

"How about your feet?"

I tap the toes of my new white winter boots—bunny boots, they're called—another gift from Agnes and apparently, a must-have for any Alaskan, good for up to minus sixty degrees Fahrenheit. "Sweaty." It's not cold enough to be busting out the military-grade gear, but I wanted to test them.

"Good." She crouches in front of my father's grave, her wise, near-black eyes resting on the cross for a long, silent moment. She nods toward the small plane that I placed next to the cross when I arrived. "That's cute."

"It reminded me of Veronica. I thought he might like it." I found it online and painted my father's name and dates of life on its belly.

"Yes. I think he would." She tucks the silk flowers on the other side, fussing with them until they stay upright. "Is that Jonah's snow machine I saw parked out there?"

My gaze darts to the yellow-and-black Ski-Doo I left sitting in the field, outside the back fence. "Yeah. He taught me how to drive it, so I can get around town on my own."

"Look at you." She grins, flashing those slightly crooked teeth, the color of bone china. "You'll be fitting in here in no time."

If you'd asked me a year ago—hell, even six months ago—what I'd be doing on New Year's Day, racing around snowy plains of Western Alaska by myself would never have been invited as an option. "It's a lot more fun than I expected," I admit. "And fast." I had to slow down, the cold wind against my exposed cheeks biting.

"They can be. You best stay off the river," she warns.

"I already got the stern lecture from Jonah." We spent yesterday afternoon out along the Kuskokwim, where he showed me the trail markers to follow, and where the body of a man who went "water skipping" last November—an entirely idiotic concept I don't under-stand—was fished out with ropes and hooks by Search and Rescue.

"Jonah worries a lot about everyone but himself." She braces her hands on her knees and eases to her feet slowly. "Where is he today, anyway?"

"Good question. He took off before lunch, saying he had to drop off some supplies at a village."

A frown furrows her round face.

"Is that normal, to be doing supply deliveries on a holiday?"

She squints as she searches the bright blue sky. The sun will set at a quarter to five tonight, which is on par with Toronto, but it didn't rise until almost eleven. These long, dark mornings are a reality that will take some getting used to. I foresee myself sleeping in through the winter months.

"Who can say what's normal with that one? But I'm sure whatever it is, he had good reason." She offers me a reassuring smile. "What do you have planned for dinner tonight?"

"I think there's leftover soup?" I say half-heartedly, knowing Jonah will argue that soup is *not* dinner, and that Agnes is about to extend an invitation to her house, as she has every night since I arrived. We've fallen back into the same rhythm that steered us in those last weeks with my father—where we'd gather at one house or another, as any conventional family might.

"I have a moose roast in the oven, if you two feel like moseying on over later. You'll like it. Tastes like beef," she promises. "It's Jonah's favorite."

"What are we going to do when we're not living across the road from you anymore, Agnes? How are we going to survive? Does this mean I'll have to learn to cook?"

It's a joke, but I don't miss the fleeting sorrow that flashes through Agnes's eyes before it's gone, replaced by something else, something indecipherable. She brushes at the dusting of snow that has settled atop my father's cross. "You two will do fine, as long as you remember you're in this together."

"I think we've done pretty well at that so far. And we've been through a lot." Since the day I found out that my father would be refusing treatment for his terminal cancer, Jonah and I have stayed side by side to face the pain, the heartache, the tough decisions, each trusting the other for support. He has been my rock—steadfast and unfailing.

"Yes ..." Agnes hesitates, her gaze wandering to the distance.

I sense a "but." Agnes has never been one to deliver the "but," always the unobtrusive listener, the kind, supportive voice who keeps her opinions to herself. That one seems to be dangling off the tip of her tongue sets off alarm bells.

"You two are a good match for each other. Wren saw it right away."

"*Really?*" I grin, despite her ominous tone. My dad had hinted at the idea of Jonah and me getting together. He did it in his subtle way, never pushing. At the time, Jonah and I were at each other's throats.

"Sure, he did. We both did, or at least hoped. And right now, this must all feel like a whirlwind. Jonah, surprising you in Toronto; you, racing back here to be with him. So exciting and fresh and new. All these possibilities and big plans." Her easy smile holds for another second before it fades as quickly as it came. "But eventually, the days will start to feel longer, quieter. You may find yourself not so eager about what's ahead for you."

"So, basically like my life before coming here?" I let out a weak chuckle. My months in Toronto after losing my father to death and Jonah to distance weren't robust or inspiring. I spent much of it trying to heal—falling back into a mindless but well-worn routine of gym sessions and shopping, of bar nights with friends that suddenly felt hollow. I floundered over job listings and career discussions with headhunters, none of them appealing to me, the idea of going back to a nine-to-five job, crammed into subway cars like cattle, staring at spreadsheets all day with Micromanaging Marks and Type-A Taras hovering around me a soul-crushing prospect.

My mom and Simon assured me that the substantial inheritance I have coming my way was the cause of my lack of direction or motivation. I believe it, too. In part. But I also sensed the tectonic shift somewhere deep inside—my time in Alaska had changed me in ways I couldn't pinpoint but also couldn't ignore. Who I was and who I am now seem like two different people.

And then I found Jonah on my front porch, asking me to move to

Alaska, and I felt those plates shift yet again. This time, life seems to be clicking into place.

Agnes presses her lips together, as if to muzzle her words.

"Just say what you want to say. Please."

She sighs. "Following Jonah around Alaska while he flies planes won't be enough. Not for a girl like you, Calla. *Loving* him won't be enough. Not forever." Agnes smiles, as if to soften the blow of her warning.

My stomach tightens. I expected this from my mother and, to a lesser degree, Simon. Never from Agnes. Maybe that's why I'm not as quick to dismiss her words as scripture out of the *Standard Parenting 101* handbook. "What *will* be enough, then?" Because I can't imagine my life without Jonah in it anymore.

Several beats pass as she considers her answer, the corners of her eyes crinkling with thought. "Find *your* place here. Something that's going to give you—Calla Fletcher—purpose. Something that feels like *you*." She nods slowly, as if agreeing with her own answer. "Find that, and then give it your all."

I hear what she doesn't have to say out loud. My parents were madly in love—the kind of love that sunk its teeth in and held on despite decades apart—and they couldn't make it work. If I follow my mother's footsteps from twenty-seven years ago, newly pregnant and disillusioned about what life with a bush pilot in the wilds of Alaska would be like, focused on all that it's not, I won't last here, no matter how much Jonah and I love each other.

But Jonah and I are *not* my parents. We've already proven that. Jonah has already proven that.

I know Agnes is looking out for me, and so I smile when I say, "I'm really looking forward to starting this charter company with him." My website design skills may be self-taught, but my marketing prowess is intuitive, and I'm eager to learn everything else required. "Plus, he agreed to move if Alaska doesn't work for me." Jonah said he didn't care where he was, as long as he has me by his side. That he doesn't want to be in Alaska if I'm not here. I've "ruined Alaska" for him. And that right there is the main difference between Jonah and my father.

"That's … his intentions are good." Agnes's gaze darts to the distance, as if wanting to hide the thoughts—or doubts—it may reveal. "Well, I best get back to that roast or Mabel's likely to over-cook it."

I sense she has more thoughts on the matter, but as is usual with Agnes, she never pushes, never badgers you until she feels she's been heard. Maybe that's what makes her opinion so much more invaluable.

Maybe that's why I'd rather *not* hear what else she has to say on the matter.

"See you around five?" I offer.

"You can mash the potatoes. I've never liked doing those." She winks. "Don't sit out here too long. It's cold." With a wordless tap against my father's cross that lasts one ... two ... three seconds, Agnes turns and trudges back toward the truck.

Leaving me alone in the cemetery once again.

"You know you left a huge hole in our lives, right?" Would that bring people comfort in the afterlife, knowing they are so missed? "It's not a bad thing, but it's there, in all of us. Especially for Mabel." The bubbly, energetic twelve-year-old who used to storm into the kitchen and talk in rushed spurts and run-on sentences has been replaced by a more reserved, at times sullen creature. Agnes blames Mabel's behavior on burgeoning hormones but I don't think any of us believe that's all it is.

I linger for another half hour or so, until my hands are numb and my cheeks hurt, and Agnes's warning has taken root in the back of my mind. I ramble about nothing and everything, closing my eyes to recall the sound of Wren Fletcher's quiet chuckle.

Terrified of the day it fades from memory.

Whorls of smoke billow from the chimney into the frigid cold air as I coast past Jonah's forest-green Ford Escape. I park his Ski-Doo—ours now?—inside the ramshackle metal shed and hurry along the path that Jonah shoveled this morning toward the modular home, taking the time to kick the snow off my boots before stepping inside.

The linoleum floor wears a melted, brown-tinged mess from

Jonah's earlier entrance. "We need a mudroom!" I struggle to yank off my boots, using the wall and counter as leverage to keep my balance. "And a chair to sit on!"

"Where we gonna put that?" asks Jonah from the living room.

"I mean, in our new house." I take a stretching step over the puddles but land in one, anyway. I cringe as cold water seeps through my wool sock.

"You need slippers."

I look up to see Jonah leaning against the threshold wall into the kitchen, his arms folded over his chest. My stomach flips as it always does when he walks into a room. I toss my hat and gloves into the overhead basket and shrug off my bulky winter coat, hanging it on one of two hooks by the door. My new parka has done its job, leaving a thin layer of sweat trapped between my long johns and my skin, despite my chilled extremities. "When'd you get back?" I ask, opening and closing my fists to thaw my reddened fingers.

"Twenty minutes ago. You go to the cemetery?"

"Yeah." I shimmy out of my snow pants. "Agnes came by."

"When's dinner?"

I smile. "She said to be there for five. She's making a moose roast."

"Finally!" He groans. "George gave that to her *weeks* ago. I was wondering when she'd pull it out of her freezer."

I shake my head but laugh. "You're as bad as my father was, waiting for someone else to feed you."

"I'm *smart* like Wren was," Jonah corrects. His lips twist in thought. "You know, you should get some pointers from Aggie on cooking those. And venison, too. I hear that one's tricky."

"Get *your own* pointers. I told you, I'm not cleaning or cooking your kill." I peel off my wet sock and smooth the bottom of my damp foot on my other sock to dry it off.

"What about *your* kill?" he throws back without missing a beat, a playful lilt in his voice.

I saunter over to press my small stature against his firm chest, waiting for him to envelop me in his arms. "Last I checked, the meat at the grocery store is already dead. Even in Alaska."

He pauses for three beats, and then pulls me flush against his body, leaning down to kiss me, first on the lips, and then along my jawline. "You *are* going to learn how to shoot a gun, Calla."

"Why would I do that when I have *you*?" I argue, dragging my feet with mock reluctance as he steers us into the living room with backward steps, toward the couch.

"For safety."

"Me with a gun does not sound safe."

"For *me*, probably not." Flopping down, he pulls me onto his lap, guiding my thighs around the outsides of his. He sweeps my hair off my shoulders and grips it at my nape with one hand. "Close your eyes."

"Why?" I ask, narrowing my gaze to try to read him. As Agnes once said, Jonah likes to play little games. I'll never forget the time he made me believe he might cut off my hair in retaliation for the night I groomed his bushy face. So I can't help but wonder what game Jonah has in mind.

"Christ. Would you humor me? For once. *Please*."

The exasperation in his tone convinces me to follow directions. I bite my bottom lip as I wait impatiently for whatever he has planned, willing myself to keep from stealing a peek at the sound of crisp tissue paper unraveling.

Calloused fingers slide over the back of my neck where they fumble. I sense a cool chain trail against my skin, and something weighted settles against my chest. His fleeting touch straightens it. "There. You can look now."

"What is it?" I ask, reaching for the object, my fingers grasping cool metal as I lift it into view. A dainty plane dangles from a chain, its white gold glimmering from polish.

"That's your *real* Christmas present. The guy making it took longer than expected."

"Oh my God ... it's ..." It's so delicate and detailed, right down to the windows and doors, the propeller blades, the wheels. Tiny diamonds cover the wings, winking at me as their facets catch the late-afternoon sunlight that invades the living room through the bay window.

But the detail on the tail, the minuscule replica of the Alaska Wild logo, is where my attention locks and my emotions swirl. "It's *beautiful.*"

"Something you'll actually wear?"

"Yes! Absolutely." I'll wear it with nothing but pride.

"Is it better than the hunting jacket you hated?" The corners of his mouth betray him.

"That was a joke?"

"Of course, it was a joke." He grins. "And *so* worth it. Man, you are a shitty actor."

"God, you are *such* a jerk sometimes!" I let go of the pendant to smack my palms hard against Jonah's chest. Beneath my fingertips, I feel the vibrations of his low chuckle, as his hands settle on my hips, warming my body even through two layers of clothes.

"Thank you for this," I offer, more contritely. "It's beautiful, Jonah. Seriously. It's the nicest piece of jewelry I own." I shouldn't be surprised. Jonah has good taste, something I discovered when I first walked into his house, expecting a dingy bachelor pad complete with pork-chop bones and empty beer cans.

He inhales deeply, his smile fading. "I can't take all the credit." He holds the small gold plane between his thumb and index finger. "This necklace, it's not only from me." His pale blue eyes dart upward to meet mine. He swallows hard. "About a week before he died, Wren asked me to get in touch with this friend of his, up in Nome."

The lump in my throat inflates.

"He wanted you to have something to remember him by. Something you could open on Christmas morning." Jonah clears his throat. "For a while there, he was hoping he'd last this long."

I clasp my hand over my mouth to muffle my sob. Tears blur my vision, slipping down my cheek in a steady, hot stream. It's been months since my father's death and just like that, again, it feels like he died yesterday.

Jonah's jaw tenses. "He was hell-bent on getting you something you'd wanna wear. I never saw him like that before, so determined. But he knew how you are, with your clothes and stuff. Anyway, the plane was his idea." Jonah finally meets my eyes again and I note their glossy sheen, the gruffness in his voice. "I added the diamonds 'cause I know you like sparkly things."

It takes me a moment to find my words and when I do, they're barely a whisper. "It's the most perfect thing anyone has ever given me. I'll never take it off. *Never.*"

Jonah simply nods and then pulls me into him, his hairy face tickling the crook of my neck as I cry.

CHAPTER SIX

The hollow thump of heavy boots against the porch steps announces Jonah's return a moment before the kitchen door creaks open. I steal a glance at the clock as my heart skips a beat. It's almost nine P.M. Jonah was supposed to be home hours ago.

"Calla?" comes his deep, raspy voice, carrying through the unnervingly silent house. That's one of the most jarring differences between here and back home. In Toronto, I'd be lying in bed, listening to the blare of horns and the scrape of metal against pavement as the snowplows cleared the streets. Here, in this little house surrounded by a vast expanse of land and little else, nothing but the fridge's odd and intermittent rattle-and-hum makes a sound. During the day, I've taken to leaving the television on to drown out the silence.

"In the bedroom," I holler back, hitting the Save button on my laptop.

The floorboards groan beneath Jonah's heavy footfalls. He rounds the corner, filling the doorway with his broad shoulders, his ash-blond hair standing on end, mussed from a day under a knit hat. I'd laugh if he didn't look so tired.

"Sorry. Stayed to help them cover the planes." Even his voice sounds exhausted. He shrugs off his jacket and tosses it onto the dresser. Beneath it is one of the sweaters I brought him—an azure knit that makes his blue eyes bright and hugs his chest and collarbone nicely. "Fucking guys up in St. Mary's did a shitty job patching that hangar back in the summer. The whole damn thing is ready to cave in. I had to meet with the insurance adjusters and sort all that out, then explain it all to Howard."

"The hangar with the roof leak that my dad was complaining about, back in the summer?"

"Yup." He flops backward into bed with a heavy sigh and rubs his eyes, then his beard. It's grown since I arrived three weeks ago—long enough for clippers and a bit more style. "Can't wait to be done with all this Aro bullshit."

Neither can I.

The blustery air clings to him, and I burrow deeper within my cozy cocoon. "You know you could be done tomorrow if you want, right?" It's not like he signed a contract.

He gives a firm head shake. "I said I'd stay until the end of January, so that's what I'm gonna give 'em."

Of course, he is. Jonah is nothing if not loyal. To the detriment of himself, my father once hinted. "Okay. So, two more weeks. That's nothing."

"And then I'm officially unemployed."

"Join the club. On Wednesdays, we wear pink." I can't ignore the thrill of knowing that Jonah will be with me and one hundred percent focused on building this charter company soon.

"Pink?" He frowns at me, confused.

"You know, from *Mean Girls*? It's a movie. Never mind." Jonah didn't have a television in his house until I moved here. "And you won't be *un*employed. You'll be *self*-employed. That's different."

"Yeah, I guess ..." He smirks. "I can't remember the last time I didn't have a boss telling me what to do."

I burst out laughing. "When have you *ever* done as you're told by *anyone*?" According to my father, Jonah was a young, "full of piss and vinegar" punk when he showed up at Alaska Wild ten years ago, and stubborn as they come. But he quickly became an indispensable part of the team, and my dad's right-hand man. From what I saw in the summer, it seemed like he was running the company. Wren Fletcher was more the quiet, passive type.

"I do, sometimes. When I feel like it." Jonah reaches out to seize my chin beneath his thumb and forefinger, pulling my face down to steal a slow, lingering kiss. A small groan slips from within his chest. "And I've been feeling like doing *that* all damn day."

I can't keep the beaming smile from my mouth, an instant reaction to whenever Jonah says anything even semi-romantic, which is more often than I would ever have expected, though usually woven in among playful jibes.

"There's a plate of spaghetti in the fridge for you. Homemade." My best friend, Diana, in her desperate attempts to keep my presence in our *Calla & Dee* lifestyle blog alive, has a new brainchild for a segment: "Calla Learns to Cook." It's not the worst idea given these winter days are long, there is no premade meal service in Bangor, and we can't rely on Agnes to feed us forever.

Jonah's eyebrows arch with doubt.

"Homemade sauce from a can," I amend sheepishly. "But I went *all the way* into town to get that overpriced can." Which is about as exciting as my cooking content gets, but Di is convinced that pictures of me going grocery shopping on a Ski-Doo are hilarious.

"Thanks. I'll eat in a bit." He nods toward my computer, sitting open on my lap. "What'd you do today?"

"Lots of *very important* things," I say with mock seriousness. We are two weeks into the new year and have fallen into somewhat of a routine, where Jonah goes off to Aro well before sunrise and I take breaks from toiling away on my computer to stoke the woodstove with logs that Jonah cut. Last week I focused on website design for the charter plane company, which is now ready for final touches and then launching, once he stops arguing with me about the fact that *The Yeti* is the perfect name for it.

This week, it's real estate and a crash course in business operations from Agnes, who has basically been running the administrative side of Wild for years. I've taken copious notes about nautical miles, basic pilot jargon, radio frequencies, topography maps, and flight itineraries. Just a scratch in the surface of this exciting world, Agnes promised.

I flip to one of many website tabs I have open to show Jonah the house listings. There aren't many this time of year. "What do you think about Eagle River?"

"Eagle River," Jonah echoes.

"Fifteen miles northeast of Anchorage. A nineteen-minute drive. They have an airport and all the basic amenities. They even have a Walmart. And, look, they've got some nice houses." Modern, new builds that surprised me, with high ceilings and tile floors and Corian countertops—all things I'd never given a moment's thought to before I suddenly found myself entering the house-hunting market. "Look at this one. It's got an extra-wide, two-car garage, and the view outside the kitchen window with the mountains is to die for. Or this one ..." I flip through to another house, a few streets over, and show him the pictures.

"How much land?"

I scroll the cursor downward to reveal the details. "Almost an acre?"

Jonah laughs. "That's nothing, babe."

I frown. "But look at the yard. It goes way back."

"What about the planes?"

"The airport's like five minutes away. See?" I zoom out on the map. "It's the same distance as Wild is to you here."

He rolls onto his back, his gaze settling on the ceiling tiles above us. "I'd love to have my own airstrip."

"What do you mean? Like, a private *airport*?"

"Nah. Just a simple airstrip. A gravel stretch on my own property with a hangar to keep the planes, so I can come and go as I please, not have to deal with all the bullshit of using public airports. No one tellin' me what to do."

"Do places like that even exist?"

"In Alaska? Sure. All you need is enough land."

I know without checking that none of the listings I've looked at have enough property to land a plane. "What would something like that cost?"

"Around Anchorage?" He sighs. "Too much."

"Well ... we can always rent a place and invest in some land for later?"

"I told you, Calla, I don't wanna pay anyone's mortgage for them, not when we can afford to buy. Do you?"

"No, but ..." Simon has now jumped onto the "rent first, buy when you're sure about Alaska and Jonah" train, whether upon my mother's insistence or because he felt obliged. Regardless, it's more difficult to dismiss his advice than it is my mother's.

But I'm turning twenty-seven this year. When will I stop letting them influence me so much?

Especially when Jonah doesn't seem to have any doubts about us.

Neither should I, I realize, because how can this work if I keep making contingency plans for it *not* working? "No, I think I'd rather buy, too." I consider alternatives. "So maybe in a few years, after The Yeti is established, we can look at moving to a house on more land?"

He shoots a severe glare my way. "We're not goin' with that name."

"We'll see ..." I mock in a singsong tone, closing out the tab, ready for Jonah to begin disturbing my clothes. That's become his pattern, within five minutes of his body hitting the mattress, no matter how long his day has been—me, naked.

My blood races with anticipation.

But he doesn't make a move yet. "Aggie had an interesting conversation with Barry earlier today."

It takes a moment to connect. "The farmer down the road?"

"Yeah. He's interested in buying our houses. This one and Wren's."

"Really?" They've already got a nice two-story home.

"Business is booming and he wants to expand his crops."

"Well ... that's good, right? We were afraid it'd take forever to sell."

"He wants the *land*, Calla. He might demo the houses."

It takes a second to process. "What, you mean, like, *tear them down?*"

"Yeah." I feel Jonah's gaze on me. "What do you think about that?"

Houses where my father and grandparents lived for decades, where my mother and father lived and loved, where *I* lived, a place that still wears my mother's hand-painted flowers from almost twenty-seven years ago. These two simple modular houses on this cold expanse of tundra—one a mossy green, the other a buttery yellow—that meant nothing to me when I first saw them, now feel like a lost childhood somehow rediscovered.

And Barry Whittamore wants to make them disappear?

But do I even have a right to be upset? Jonah and I are leaving Bangor, starting our lives elsewhere.

"Honestly, I don't know what I should think. What do *you* think?"

He bites his bottom lip in thought. It's a moment before he answers. "I've got no use for this place if we're moving. Still ... I guess I always saw another family living here."

"Right. Same. And Agnes? What does she think?"

He snorts. "Well, of course *she* doesn't like it. The damn woman is driving around in Wren's shitty-ass, beaten-up truck with bald tires because she's so nostalgic. But she doesn't need two houses to look after. She told Barry he should rent the houses out and farm around them. He sounded open to it. And selling to Barry would be the smart move. Otherwise who knows how long we'll be sittin' on these listings. And who's to say that whoever buys them doesn't tear them down, anyway."

"Right." I wait for him to continue, sensing a "but."

Jonah shrugs. "It seems wrong, you know? Wren's gone, Alaska Wild is gone. And now even his house might disappear. It's like he's being erased."

I feel what he's saying. My dad said there'd always be a home for me in Alaska, and yet it won't technically be true.

Silence lingers, and I study the struggle in Jonah's features—his jaw tensing, his eyes tracing the lines of the ceiling tiles as if my dad set them there with his own bare hands. What is he really asking me?

Perhaps he's looking for *my* permission to let someone possibly level my family's history.

"What would my dad say if he were here?" I hate that I can't confidently guess, that I didn't know him that well.

But Jonah did. My father was more a father to him than he ever was to me.

Jonah thinks on it a moment and then a slow smile curls his lips. "He'd ask if this is some karmic twist for refusing to eat his broccoli and carrots. Somethin' like that."

I laugh, because I can almost picture my father standing at the living room threshold, scratching his chin, his weathered brow furrowed with consideration, saying those exact words.

Jonah's smile turns wistful. "But then he'd tell us to sell. That it's just a house. To not make the same mistakes he did by tying ourselves down at the expense of people we love."

My head bobs in agreement. Jonah's right. My father sold Alaska Wild—our family's fifty-four-year-old legacy—because it was time for everyone to move on. That house next to us is just a bunch of walls and a roof and two hundred forty-four mallards with hand-drawn nipples. The Fletcher family is gone. "Then there's your answer. You guys should sell to Barry."

He nods slowly. "I guess it's time to do some serious house-hunting, then. What else you got here?" He flips through tabs on my laptop, pausing to frown. "You wanna live on a farm?"

"No. That's an Instagrammer I've started following," I admit, scrolling through the pretty array of pictures. Since deciding to move here, I've been branching out with different lifestyle bloggers for inspiration, specifically ones who live in rural settings. "She's an interior designer, and she's been renovating this old place in Nebraska with her husband, and chronicling it. I love her style. And the house has so much character. That's what I want—a house with character."

"It's all *white*," he scoffs.

"No, it's not."

"The walls are white, the floors are white, the curtains are off-white ..." He smirks. "Even the couch is white! Where the hell do they sit?"

"It's slipcovered."

He shakes his head, chuckling. "For the love of God, please don't make me live in an all-white house."

"Her story is interesting! She's all about upcycling and sustainable living. They've got animals and she grows all her own vegetables."

Jonah's eyebrow arches. "So you *do* wanna live on a farm."

"No! I didn't say that—"

"I can see it now." He stretches out on his back, tucking his arms under his head in a mock-relaxed pose, the hem of his shirt creeping up, exposing his taut stomach muscles. "Calla Fletcher, farmer. I'll get you some big, ugly rubber boots and a straw hat for your birthday. And a basket, for all the eggs. We have to have chickens."

I scrunch my nose. "Chickens smell. And don't they attract bears?"

"And a cute little goat or two," he goes on, ignoring me.

"I *hate* goats."

"What?"

"*No* goats."

Jonah turns to stare at me, his brows raised in shock. "You're being serious."

"Yes!"

"*Goats*. Those cute little farm animals."

"With the creepy horizontal pupils. Yes."

"How can you hate goats?" He sounds legitimately baffled.

"I have my reasons. So, what do you think about solar panels? Do they work in Alaska with the short—"

"Uh-uh." Jonah shakes his head, his blue eyes twinkling with mischief. "No way, Barbie. Spill it or I'm gonna come home with ten cute little pygmy goats for your farm."

Knowing Jonah, he will. I mean, we have an unofficial "pet" raccoon living under the porch.

I groan, already knowing how this will play out. "Fine! When I was six, I got mauled by a bunch of them on a school trip and ever since then ..." My words are drowned out by Jonah's burst of laughter.

"*Mauled* by *goats*?"

I elbow him. "It's not funny!" Even though I'm struggling to suppress my smile.

"Okay, okay. You're right. It's not." He holds his hands in the air in surrender. "Show me your scars."

"Well, I don't actually have any *physical* scars."

"Because they're all on the inside?" he asks with fake seriousness.

"Shut up! When you're six and you're surrounded by a herd of animals nipping at your clothes and fingers, and you get knocked into a fresh pile of shit, you never forget!" I shudder for emphasis.

He shakes his head, his laughter dying down to a soft chuckle. "Come here, my little goat hater." He slaps my laptop shut and pushes it off to the side. In one smooth roll, his heavy body is pinning me down and his mouth is on mine.

CHAPTER SEVEN

February

"This is George's friend?" I ask, huddled in the depths of my parka as Jonah steers Veronica toward a long, flat stretch of land, lined on either side by tapered evergreens. Two forest-green, metal-roofed buildings sit off to one side—both simple rectangles; one large structure, the second a small replica of the first. Next to the frozen lake is a log cabin. A plume of dark smoke curls from its chimney, dissipating into the murky sky. Elsewhere, tucked in among the trees, are several lean-tos and sheds. A staple for any home in Alaska, I'm learning, to shelter everything from chopped wood and propane and water jugs to ATVs and snow machines.

"Who, Phil? Yeah. They knew each other in the air force. I've met him a few times over the years. Good guy. He lost his wife to a stroke, back in the fall. Around the same time Wren passed."

"Is he all alone out here?" There aren't any other cabins on the lake, from what I can see.

"Yup. His son lives somewhere south. Oregon or Idaho, something like that." Jonah nods toward the back, to the cooler of moose meat that George asked us to drop off on our way to Anchorage's suburbs to check out open houses. "He'll appreciate that."

Our plane catches a wind current and jolts, and my hand shoots out to clutch Jonah's forearm on instinct. He chuckles, offering me an easy, confident wink of reassurance that everything is fine, that we're fine.

That's how things have been between us since he rescued me from a Christmas alone over a month ago—easy. We've fallen seamlessly into our old rhythm, except without that once-persistent cloud of dread that lingered in the background as we watched my father deteriorate, day by day, and wished for more time.

Now our conversations are dominated by excitement about our future—of must-haves for the house we're going to buy, of what we need to do ahead of launching the charter company, of which sunny, warm destination we'll vacation at when we need a break from the long, dark winter. Our nights are filled with laughter as we lay tangled in sheets, talking and planning and teasing each other, our contentment palpable.

And now that Jonah is officially done at Aro—they had a farewell party for him yesterday—and the lawyers are working on paperwork for the sale of the houses to Barry, our life together is moving ahead, faster than I anticipated.

It's everything I imagined being in love could feel like, back when I was trying to figure out what love is, when I couldn't form a definition in my mind for it.

It's this.

It's us.

It's the swell of emotion every time Jonah first walks into the room, it's the impatience I feel whenever he's not around, it's the way my heart skips every time I make him laugh.

On impulse, I lean over and press a quick kiss against Jonah's cheek, above his freshly trimmed beard.

He regards me, a curious glint in his eye. "What's that for?"

"For being you." I shift my focus back to the approaching ground below. Even painted the same stark white of winter, this area of Alaska is a vastly different landscape from the frozen tundra we left at first light. On this side, the houses are dispersed but more numerous, the lakes and rivers clearly marked by the cut of dense forest around their shorelines.

Jonah follows my gaze. "This is a really nice part of Alaska."

I'm momentarily enthralled with the jagged white peaks of the mountain in the distance, even more distinct against the crisp blue backdrop of the sky. Will all these mountain ranges ever become commonplace to me? "Which one is that?"

"Denali. Highest mountain peak in North America."

I sigh. It *does* seem nice here. "Too bad it's so remote."

"It's not *that* remote. It's considered part of the Anchorage metropolitan area."

"And how far is the actual city from here?"

"Only about an hour and a half."

"An *hour* and a *half*." I emphasize. "That's a *three-hour* commute. In good weather."

Jonah shrugs. "Not like Bangor, though."

"No, I guess not," I admit.

Jonah brings Veronica down on the snowy airstrip, her skiis sliding effortlessly over a lane that's been plowed recently, likely by the tractor parked off to the side. "Beautiful sight line ... nicely graded ..." His voice is full of admiration.

"I'll bet you say that to *all* the runways."

He yanks off his headset and flicks a multitude of switches by rote, bringing the plane's engine to a halt. Leaning in to plant a fast but hard kiss on my lips and to whisper "smart-ass," he pops open his door and hops out of the plane.

My boots hit the ground with a crunch, the stark contrast between the heated plane cabin and the frigid temperature outside making me shrink into my coat.

A man emerges from the tall metal building—a hangar, I realize, spotting a red plane wing inside, through the gaping door. He approaches, his steps hobbled and chosen prudently as he moves along the narrow, shoveled path. He must be in his seventies, his face weathered with age, the wisps of hair peeking from the base of his black toque white to match the snow.

Jonah closes the distance to meet him halfway, the cooler of meat dangling from one hand. He offers him a hearty handshake with the other. "Phil. Good to see you again."

"It sure has been awhile." Phil grins, highlighting a missing front molar. Gray-blue eyes shift to me, and I note how the left one is cloudy. "This the missus?"

"Not officially yet but, yeah."

My heart sings at Jonah's response, at all the promises and intentions buried within—though we haven't discussed marriage seriously yet—and delivered without hesitation or fear, in typical blunt Jonah style. It's a quality I despised when I first met him, how he so brazenly told me what he thought of me in less-than-glowing terms, and now I'm not sure I could survive here without it. It's easy to trust a person unequivocally when you don't have to worry about what they're *not* telling you.

Jonah stretches an arm back to beckon me forward. "This is Calla. Wren Fletcher's daughter."

"Sorry to hear about your father. What a shame. Gone way too soon."

"Thanks." I rush to add, "And Jonah told me about your wife. I'm sorry, too."

His lips press together and he offers me a curt nod of acknowledgment, as if he can't manage more than that.

I know the feeling all too well.

Phil spies the cooler in Jonah's grasp. "George mentioned he was sendin' something from his hunt with you."

Jonah pats the hard case. "It's a good cut, too."

"Yeah, he was braggin'." Phil chuckles, and it reminds me of an old car engine, struggling to turn. "Well, come on, then. Why don't I give you a tour around, if you want, and then we can drop that off at the house?"

"We'd love that. Right, babe?" Jonah's eyes shine with curiosity as they dart about the property before landing on me, an odd, buoyant smile touching his lips.

I can't help but return it and lean in to whisper, "You have such a hard-on for this guy's place right now, don't you?"

He loops an arm around my waist, pulling me in tightly. "I'm about to come in my pants."

———

"Colette and I bought this place back in the '80s. Spring of '85, I think it was." Phil pauses in front of the kitchen sink, scratching his chin in thought. "That's right, it was my fortieth birthday. We came out this way to fish on the river. If you like fishin', we have one of the best spots for it. There's a whole network of rivers, west of us. People come in droves through the summer. Anyway, we fell in love with the area. I remember thinkin' I was at least halfway to dead and needin' to make a big move. So we did it. Almost a hundred acres, plenty to live on. Goes way back that way." He waves a dismissive hand toward the back of the house. "Need snowshoes to get around there this time of year."

"That's something I haven't tried yet," I admit. I can't fathom what a hundred acres looks like, but I suspect it would take hours to cross on foot. After the tour of the hangar and workshop, we climbed into a rusty red GMC pickup truck and *drove* here, the distance to the house too far for Phil to walk.

Phil studies me curiously. "Now that ya mention it, you don't look like you're from here."

"I was born in Alaska, but I've lived in Toronto most of my life."

"Huh. A city girl." He holds up the bottle of whiskey that was sitting on the counter toward Jonah. "You thirsty?"

Jonah shakes his head. "Better not. I've gotta fly."

Phil waves the bottle my way in a taunting manner. "*You're* not flyin' the plane."

I school my expression. It's barely noon and Phil is into the hard liquor. There's a tumbler sitting next to the bottle and I can't be sure whether it's yesterday's glass or if he's already imbibed. What must his life be like, all alone out here? Maybe I'd be downing shots of whiskey, too. "Thanks, but we have a long day ahead of us. A glass of water would be great, though."

"Sure, I think we've got a bottle somewhere in here, from when my son was here." He shuffles over to the fridge to pull out a plastic bottle, his movements every bit that of an elderly man. I haven't missed his use of "we" and "our" and "us" throughout our tour of his property, as if his late wife is still present. It must take awhile to adjust to the status of widow after being married to a woman for fifty years. That or Phil has no intention of ever adjusting to the idea of her being gone.

I smile in thanks as I accept the water from him.

"Got a nice, big vegetable garden back there. About a quarter acre in size. Big enough to grow a winter's worth of preserves and all fenced off and electrified to keep the critters away during the growin' season. You a gardener?" He's looking directly at me.

"No, that's more my mother's forte." Though she herself admits she finds more enjoyment from her rose bushes and lilacs than carrots and corn.

"Well, anyone's thumb can turn green if they stick it in the dirt long enough," he dismisses with a wave. "There're also the pens where we kept the livestock."

"Your farm, Barbie," Jonah murmurs, earning my subtle eye roll.

"'Course, got nothin' left but a few hens that give me my morning eggs, and Zeke." Phil slaps that heavy tumbler down on the counter and fills it halfway with whiskey. "That ol' goat's nothin' but a pain in my ass. Doesn't like men. Has no use for me, now that Colette's gone. Used to follow her around everywhere."

Jonah's face splits with a grin. "What do ya know? Calla *loves* goats."

"So, how old is this place?" I ask, spearing Jonah with a warning glare. My gaze drifts over the log cabin's wooden interior, intentionally skirting the enormous moose head that watches us from its mounted perch between two large windows. A pair of deer heads flank the fireplace. A black fur pelt trimmed with red felt hangs opposite it—I can only assume that's a bear, because there's no head to go with it.

I'll never understand why people feel the need to surround themselves with the things they've killed.

"Let's see ... The old owners started buildin' about ten years before us. Fell on hard times, which is why they had to sell before it was even finished. So, I guess that makes it"—he squints in thought —"close to forty-five years old, now? We've updated some. And we did a lot of work to the basement. All that stone was us. Colette thought'd it'd look nice. Break up the wood."

"She was right. It does." The log cabin is built into a small incline, allowing for a walk-out basement level with several sizeable windows. The exterior is clad in fieldstone that matches the fireplace.

"'Course there're small things that need doin'. Trim and closets. The bathrooms could use new faucets and paint." He takes a swig of his drink, wincing at the first bite. "You know, things you say you're gonna tackle when you have a free weekend and then before you know it, thirty-five years have passed, your kid is gone, your wife is dead, and you're still staring at primed drywall." A forlorn tone lingers in his voice.

I hope I manage to hide the pity from my expression as I say, "You have a lovely home." In a rustic, cluttered way, where the décor is dated and cobbled together, and yet cozy. Despite all the dead animals watching me.

Phil may be the only one living here—evident by the dirty dishes and empty frozen-dinner packages littering the counter, the clothes strewn over almost every piece of furniture, the visible cobwebs dangling like tinsel from the chandelier—but there's still evidence of his late wife. The fridge's surface is plastered with floral magnets that secure pictures of grandchildren splashing in the lake. A calendar pinned to the wall sits on September, a tidy woman's handwriting marking appointments, a birthday, an anniversary. A hand-painted "Bless this Alaskan home" wooden sign, adorned with purple wild-flowers, hangs at the threshold of the side entrance—a long, narrow corridor lined with a dozen hooks housing everything from light sweaters to hip waders. My guess is the medley of pale blue and mauve articles hanging there were Colette's.

"It's all hand-hewn logs, you know," Phil says, his eyebrows arching as if sharing a shocking secret. "Colette insisted that if I was gettin' a hangar for my toys, she was gettin' her log house by the lake, with a big fireplace where she could spend the cold winter days. Couldn't argue with that." His cloudy gaze reaches the peaked ceiling of the two-story living room where the grand, rustic fieldstone hearth reaches. Cheap, worn, moss-green carpet veils the long, plank-wood floor. "A lot of good memories in that there spot. Anyway, the hangar and the workshop didn't come for another fifteen years."

"They look well built," Jonah says with that same appraising tone that's lingered in his voice since we landed.

"Oh, they are. The hangar needs a few repairs. Regular maintenance that no one can avoid. But you won't find a place like this anywhere around here. Those builders, I tell ya." Phil shakes his head. "I was on those guys every day like a fly on moose shit, and it shows."

I hide my cringing smile behind a sip from my water. "Jonah's been admiring it ever since we landed." I shoot him a wry glance. More like Jonah has been strolling around in sub-zero temperatures with a full-blown erection for a giant metal shed.

"Hoped you would. George swore up and down you'd appreciate this place." Phil swallows another hearty sip of his whiskey. "That's why I'd rather sell to you than that couple from Homer. So, when do you reckon you'll have the money to buy me out?"

CHAPTER EIGHT

"I'll have the bison burger and the pale ale on tap." Jonah folds the lodge's menu and hands it back to Chris. "And Calla will have a steak knife to drag across my jugular."

Chris's bushy eyebrows arch as he regards me, his eyes shining with a mixture of delight and curiosity. "I'm guessing he deserves it?"

"Does the leek soup have dairy in it? I have an allergy." I force a polite smile. I'm angry, but I'm also starving.

"Let me double-check. Back in a minute. I'll bring some coasters to fix the wobble in this table." Chris collects my menu. "And a knife to fix Jonah." He ambles away, his cheeks lifting with his grin. He's amused. That's nice.

I pin my steely glare back on the man sitting across from me.

Jonah leans back, his chair creaking with the weight of his considerable frame. He regards me with a calculating stare—the kind that says he's gauging how he's going to persuade me to go for this harebrained idea of his, living in the woods in the middle of nowhere. "You've gotta admit, it's perfect for us."

"For *us*? No. Not for *us*. For *you*."

"You wanted a place with character. What's got more character than a log cabin with a prime view of Denali out your front door?"

"In the middle of *nowhere*," I remind him.

"Trapper's Crossing is *not* the middle of nowhere. Wasilla's only twenty-five minutes away. It's got ten thousand people and every-thing you need. They've even got a Walmart."

"A *Walmart*. You think that's what I need?"

He throws his hands in the air. "Hell, I don't know! You're the one who keeps bringin' up Walmart!" His gaze furtively searches the wall behind me as if there's a convincing argument buried somewhere within the wood paneling. "Marie lives near Wasilla."

"Your super-close female friend who is secretly in love with you. Even better," I mutter, though there's no animosity to go along with that. When I met the pretty girl-next-door veterinarian, it was just after Jonah and I had kissed for the first time, and I was burning with jealousy. It was clear to anyone paying attention that she was hoping their friendship was a stepping stone to something more. Jonah himself admitted that they'd kissed once. He also said that he couldn't give her what she wanted.

I've seen Marie twice since then—once at my father's funeral—and she seems to have retreated a step, as if trying to respect an invisible boundary that's been put in place, now that I'm in the picture. In any case, I have no issues with Marie, but it's not exactly a selling feature for buying Phil's place.

Jonah rolls his eyes. "She's *not* in love with me."

"We agreed on Anchorage," I remind him.

"No. We agreed on *closer* to Anchorage. This is a hell of a lot closer to Anchorage than Bangor." He folds his hands on the table in front of him. "Come on, Calla ... You *seriously* don't want to move to the suburbs, do you? A plain, subdivision house with a tiny yard and people on either side, lookin' into your windows at night? A house with *no* character?"

I sigh with exasperation. He's using my words against me. And, I hate to admit, effectively.

"How would I fly my planes? Where would I keep them?"

"*At an airport* like a normal human being. Like my father did."

He bites his bottom lip. If I weren't so annoyed with him, the subtle move would likely stir my blood. "This isn't a shock, Calla. I've mentioned having my own landing strip. More than once." He adds more softly, "Remember, the other night when I was landing that little toy plane on your—"

"One day!" I cut him off, flushing, my eyes darting to the nearby table to ensure the family seated there isn't listening. "I thought that was 'one day,' like, five or ten years from now." Not *today*.

"That's what I thought, too. But why wait five or ten years when the perfect place is right there for the taking, *now*?"

"You don't even get why I'm angry, do you?"

"Because you really want to live in a subdivision?" he says.

I give him a flat look. "How long have you known that Phil was selling his place?"

Jonah's bearded jaw tightens. "George may have mentioned something to me about it last week," he admits.

"So then, why didn't you tell me last week? And don't say you haven't had a chance. We've been talking about moving *every day* for the past month."

He sighs heavily. "Because I knew you'd pull out your damn map and decide that it's too far without even hearing me out."

"So, instead, you tricked me into going there. You *lied* to me. Moose meat, my ass!"

"That was *not* a lie." It's Jonah's turn to steal a glance at the nearby family, but they seem engrossed in their own conversation. Still, he drops his voice. "George asked me to drop that off for him if we were goin' to see the place."

"And, what? Did you think that when I walked into a log cabin in the middle of the woods with animal heads all over the wall, I'd jump at the chance to live there?"

"Honestly? Yeah, I thought you might."

A burst of incredulous laughter escapes me.

"What? You said so yourself, it's beautiful there, with the mountains and the lake."

"Yeah. To visit!"

"It's not *that* remote, Calla. The place is fully functioning. A well for water, plumbing, heating, everything. Anchorage is within easy driving distance. There's a lot of cabins in Trapper's Crossing. It's a big tourist area." Frustration furrows across his forehead, the small white scar from last summer's plane crash falling naturally into a crevice.

"I don't like these kinds of surprises." The life-altering ones.

"Can you blame me for tryin'?"

Maybe not. But that's not the point. "We're supposed to be in this together, Jonah." I realize as I say them that I'm echoing Agnes's words. "Don't manipulate me to get what you want."

"I wasn't trying to manipulate you," he says slowly, as if his conscience is reevaluating that declaration as he makes it.

"Maybe not intentionally, but that's what you were doing. And that's not you. You've always been open and honest. You speak your mind. That's what I love about you." Hadn't I just finished thinking about *how much* I love that quality about him? "This deceptiveness? It isn't you." It's why I never caught on to his plan, which, in hindsight, I'm an idiot to have missed.

Jonah's lip press together. "I'm sorry. I guess I just got caught up with how perfect this place is. I was banking all my hopes on you falling in love with it when you saw it. Phil was supposed to keep quiet until I tested the idea out on you." He picks up a salt packet, only to cast it aside. "I was hoping you'd see the potential. Or you'd at least hear me out *before* you shot it down."

An unpleasant silence falls over us, Jonah's frustration palpable.

The urge to break through it—to solve for it—overwhelms me. I wonder if I'm going to regret this. "Fine."

Jonah's gaze flashes to mine.

"I'll *hear you out* before I shoot down the idea." And then I'll shoot it down.

He takes a deep breath, his demeanor visibly shifting from stark disappointment to brimming excitement as he decides where to begin. "It'd be turnkey for the charter business. I mean, we'd still have to apply for an operations license if we're letting customers onto our property but we wouldn't have to deal with landing strip usage fees or rent, or any of that bullshit for me to fly. I wouldn't have to get guys in to build a proper airstrip and hangar, and all the headaches that come with that, because it's already done. That walk-out basement is the perfect space for an office, so I'd be around when I'm not flying. We wouldn't be in some shitty little trailer at an airport all day."

From sunup until sundown, as my mother often complained my father was. *He was never there.*

"And it's a nice house. Well built, tons of character."

"Dated. And unfinished. And wood-y," I counter. With three pint-sized bedrooms and only one bathroom on the second floor.

"Nothing that can't be finished and updated."

"Or gutted."

"Maybe." He shrugs. "If anyone can make something look pretty, it's you. Remember?" He gestures at his beard and I struggle to keep my smile at bay. I'm annoyed with him.

Jonah leans in a touch, almost conspiratorially. "And the place would come fully loaded. Phil said he's got no use for any of it anymore. He's moving down to live with his son. Everything comes with the sale. *Everything*, Calla. The old GMC pickup truck, the tractor, his-and-her snow machines and ATVs. He's even selling his plane, if I want it. Needs some work but, with his eyesight going, he can't fly anymore." Jonah grimaces momentarily at the idea of that—before his expression smooths over.

"And, yeah, it's *a bit* quieter around there than what you might have had in your head, but everything outside of a major city is gonna feel remote. It's not like Bangor, though. There's a great highway all the way to Anchorage and plenty of paved roads. As soon as you have your license, it'll be nothing for you to drive there to get whatever you need that you can't get nearby. But Wasilla has everything."

I sit back and listen to Jonah ramble on about all the benefits of this location—the hunters who've already booked him for their fly-in this coming fall will be happier flying into Anchorage than Bangor; the tourists who come to the area in droves who'll be looking for daily trips over the Denali mountain range—and I can't help but find myself nodding along with him. He's making many good points.

And having a place where he can readily access and fly his planes *is* ideal. I'd much rather roll out of bed and walk two floors down to our "office" than venture out into the cold every morning.

I don't think I've ever seen Jonah so excited before. I certainly haven't seen an ounce of this enthusiasm over any of the other prospective house listings I've showed him.

Maybe he's right. Maybe this *is* perfect for *us*.

I feel my resolve begin to wear away. "You should have told me before we got there, Jonah."

"You're right. I'm sorry." His light blue eyes brim with sincerity. He reaches across the table to collect my hands. The rough calluses he's earned chopping wood and shoveling snow scrape against my palms. "It's a good setup for us though, Calla. I wouldn't be pushing for it if I didn't think so. It's the best of both worlds. It's got somethin' for both of us."

And we are in this together, which is going to mean compromise, I remind myself. Truthfully, I've been trying to picture Jonah—a guy who lands planes on glaciers and mountains—feeling at home on an urban street lined with houses and minivans, and I've been struggling. Worrying that we'll choose the wrong house, in the wrong area, that he'll regret leaving Bangor for me. I am not the only person giving up what I know and love. I need to consider Jonah's needs, too, and he's been hinting subtly—that is so unlike Jonah, I missed the cues—what would make him happy.

An hour-and-a-half drive to Anchorage.

Twenty-five minutes to ten thousand people. And a Walmart. I spent that much time commuting into work every day for four years, I remind myself.

"Aggie thinks it's a good idea."

"You've already talked to Agnes about this." I'm not irritated though. If there's anyone who knows how to listen and not judge or cajole, it's her.

"I wanted to make sure I wasn't insane. And, for the record, she told me I shouldn't spring this on you." He offers me an apologetic smile.

"How much does Phil want for it?" All that land, a hangar, and a log house that does have its own charm. "It can't be cheap."

Jonah shakes his head. "Double what we were planning on spending. And Phil is lookin' to move sooner than later. Before the winter's over."

I let out a slow whistle. "If Phil can't wait, we'd have to try to get a mortgage." Something Jonah was vehemently opposed to, and frankly something that may not be an option at all, given our current employment status.

His head shake only confirms it. "We don't have time for that. He'll sell to the other couple. But I've gone through the numbers and we can do this. Between the money I got when I sold Jughead to Aro, the sale of the house, and my savings over the last ten years, it'll more than cover the cost."

"I won't be able to give you my half until March or April. Maybe later." There's still some estate red tape to process before the funds are released to me.

"About that." Jonah's brow furrows. "Look, the land and hangar must be worth at least half the cost, so I'm willing to cover all that plus half the house—"

"What?" I glare at him. "No."

"Come on, Calla. Wren left you that money so you can set yourself up for life. So you can invest in something."

"I *am* investing in something." I frown. "Us."

He shakes his head. "I know what Wren sold Wild to Aro for, and I don't ever want you or anyone else thinkin' that I'm takin' advantage of you."

"Since when do you care what anyone else thinks?" My tone is escalating again, along with my irritation.

"I care what Susan and Simon think," he says.

Did my mother say something to him? I make a mental note to confront her. "The only thing they care about is that I don't go and blow it all and have nothing to show for it."

Jonah's jaw sets in that stubborn way of his. He's being a prideful ass.

For once, though, I have the upper hand. "We are in this together. This is going to be *our* home together, and *our* life together, which includes the charter company. There's no reason why I shouldn't be paying for half of it." I make sure to enunciate the next words slowly and clearly. "The *only* way I'll agree to this is if we're in it together, *all* the way. Fifty-fifty."

He opens his mouth to speak but then closes it, as if thinking better of whatever he was going to say. "So … does that mean you're saying yes?"

I let out an exaggerated sigh. "I am saying I will *consider* it." Maybe

I should also consider therapy, because I *can't believe* I'm humoring Jonah with this.

"Hey, Jonah!" Chris hollers from the bar, the phone receiver pressed to his ear. "You still planning on taking Andrea's truck up to Trapper's Crossing today?"

"Uh ..." Jonah watches me hopefully.

I feel my face twist with bewilderment. "Unbelievable! So, they were in on this, *too*? It's a conspiracy!"

He shrugs sheepishly. "We needed to borrow their truck, anyway, for the open houses. I figured we could drive up and check out the area while we're here. See what you think."

I fall back into my seat, letting out a groan.

The slow-blooming sly grin on Jonah's face tells me he thinks he's already won.

I shake my head at his arrogance. "I have conditions."

His eyes narrow warily. "Like what?"

"I'll let you know when I come up with them. And they're nonnegotiable, by the way." A thought strikes me. "But for now ... two words"—I hold up my fingers for emphasis, leaning across the table toward him, to mouth in a mock seductive way—"The Yeti."

Jonah grimaces and I catch the whisper of "Ah, fuck" under his breath.

My lips curl into a vindictive smile.

Jonah's hands grip the steering wheel of Andrea's pickup truck as we ease to a sliding stop on the slick road. Nothing of Phil's property is visible here, the driveway a long lane curving around the trees— spruces with their limbs sagging beneath the weight of snow and naked deciduous trees serving as a natural wall.

But ahead of us is where my attention settles, on the vast white wilderness, on the jagged peaks that reach far into the dusky sky, the mauve hue of the last moments of sun caressing the looming mountain before nightfall.

Never in my wildest dreams did I expect a view like this where I live.

And we can have this every day.

"You haven't said much." I feel Jonah studying my profile, hear the worry in his tone. "Tell me what you're thinking."

I'm thinking ... Trapper's Crossing is sleepy, but it's not dead. I watched as we drove along the main road—Main Street would be a misleading name for the paved, two-lane highway banked by a handful of shops and services—and I saw signs of life. A man huddled in winter gear, briskly walking his golden retriever among the trees that dapple the properties; three young kids laughing as they dart out of the colorful bus that has been artfully converted into a burger shack; dozens of cars angled around gritty, plow-made snowbanks in the small grocery store parking lot. A lumber mill, a hardware store. It reminds me of the Northern Ontario towns I've driven through on my way to cottages—quiet, functional communities who thrive on tourism, collections of people, some born and raised there and others having escaped from elsewhere. A place where you find yourself wondering what people do with themselves all day long, what their Friday nights look like.

It didn't take long to see the bulk of what Trapper's Crossing has to offer. Jonah navigated around the town, pointing out the community center and library, the one-floor health center for minor ailments only. There is nothing resembling an urban subdivision here. It's all roads cutting through a seemingly endless forest, with houses interspersed.

But then he settled his palm onto my thigh, squeezing gently as we passed the small, boxy elementary school. A memory of him holding a chubby toddler at Sharon and Max's farewell party flooded my mind, and my thoughts suddenly shifted from all the things Trapper's Crossing isn't to all the things it could become, if I embrace it.

If I give this dream of Jonah's an honest chance.

A life for Jonah and me. A log cabin in the woods with a million-dollar view has a lot of charm, I must admit, especially when I'm sharing it with this man. Thoughts of George and Bobbie's cabin come to mind—with the Christmas bows and strings of light. Christmas will be nice here.

I meet Jonah's blue eyes, see the unease in them. The hope. I think he's holding his breath. "We'll need a sign to advertise. Over there." I point at a crop of naked birch trees. "And it's not going to be one of those ugly billboard-looking signs, like the ones I keep seeing all over the place." Corrugated plastic with faded print lettering advertising business hours and peddling wares.

Jonah releases the air from his lungs in a heavy sigh. "You can put up whatever the hell you want. You're better at that stuff than I am, anyway."

"Wait, is there cell reception out here? Because I can't survive without basic—"

"There's a tower nearby. We get four bars here."

It's my turn to sigh with relief, though I'm far from finished. "And you are not going to take off all day, every day, and leave me here, all alone, to fend for myself."

"I make my own schedule. And you can fly with me. It'll be like old times."

"And no overnight trips. I'm not spending my nights all alone."

"Believe me, I don't wanna be anywhere but lying in bed next to you every night."

"And you need to take me driving more, so I can get my license as soon as possible."

"Good, 'cause I'm tired of cartin' your ass around."

"And I'm in charge of decorating. This will not be one of those dingy log cabins with dead animals and guns all over the walls."

He puts his hands in the air in a sign of surrender. "You can paint the whole goddamn place white if you want, Calla."

I frown. "Seriously?"

"I mean, it'd be a fucking horrible idea and Phil will probably come back here and shoot us both if he finds out, but I don't give a shit." He smirks. "Just don't get pissy with me when I get it dirty."

"Maybe just one white room," I mock.

He collects my hand and brings it to his mouth to press a kiss against my knuckles. "Whatever makes you happy."

I've only ever seen that look on his face once before—standing in front of the US entry gate at the airport, when I told him I'd move to Alaska for him.

"Making *you* happy makes me happy," I answer truthfully.

"Well then … you've just made me the happiest guy on earth. God, I love you so much." Cupping my face between his two large hands, he gently pulls me to him and captures my lips in a deep kiss. The kind of kiss that stirs instant need in my body. The kind that has me unfastening my seat belt and sliding over to get closer to him, ready to fog these windows and defile Chris and Andrea's truck on the side of this desolate road.

Jonah breaks free as my palm finds an appealing spot pressed against his fly, his breath ragged. "You know what this means, right?" His forehead rests against mine. "This is a big commitment."

"I moved to Alaska for you, didn't I?" Haven't I already committed to him?

"Holy shit." Jonah exhales. "So? Should we go tell Phil that we'll take it?"

I steal a moment for my own calming breath as I eye the long driveway ahead. "Do you think he's even sober enough to have this conversation?" It's been a few hours since we first visited. That's a long time for an old man and his bottle of whiskey, alone in the woods.

"Let's find out." Throwing the old truck into Drive, Jonah eases up the driveway. *Our* new driveway, soon. A nervous flutter churns in my stomach.

My hand is firmly clasped within Jonah's the entire way.

CHAPTER NINE

March

"I swear, I *really* do want to come, but I don't think we can afford it this year, with all these bills! Plus, there's his sister's wedding. We have to fly to *freaking* Costa Rica. Who makes their *entire family* pay *thousands* of dollars to see them get married?"

I smile, thinking about that time Diana mentioned how nice a destination wedding would be. Now's not the time to remind her of that, though. "What if I pay for your tickets?" Since Diana moved into an exorbitantly priced one-bedroom condo in Liberty Village with her boyfriend this past January and decided she's going to law school, she's been nonstop complaining about money. Or maybe I've noticed it more because money isn't going to be an issue for me soon.

"That's generous of you, Calla, but you know Aaron … He'd never accept that." And God forbid Diana spent a few days away from him to come here on her own. "We'll figure it out. When are your parents coming up?"

"I don't know. My mom mentioned end of June for my birthday, but the shop is so busy with weddings that it's probably going to be impossible."

"I'm sure she'll make it work. And I will, too, I promise! If not this year, then *definitely* next year." Diana's remorseful voice rings in my ear.

"I can't wait." It's been two and a half months since I hugged my best friend goodbye, an emotional farewell the night before I flew here. While we still text like we're in the same city, the weight of missing weekly meet-ups and laughs lingers in the background, suitably masked by the flurry of activity tied to my move, flaring on the rare occasion that I hear her voice.

"I know! Oh my God, Aaron hasn't shut up about Alaska since I brought it up. I regret ever mentioning it."

"No, you don't."

"No, I don't," Diana agrees, and I can hear her smile. "Our own personal pilot and our own airstrip! Jonah will fly me wherever I want to go, right?"

I laugh, picturing the flat look on Jonah's face when he finds out he gets to play chauffeur to my high-spirited friend. If he thought *I* didn't fit into Alaska, just wait.

"Calla! You ready?" Jonah's deep voice booms from my father's kitchen.

"Almost!" I holler back, tracing the faint pink edge of my mother's hand-painted calla lilies with a fingertip. Agnes will be effectively erasing them with a coat of warm white next week, in preparation for the renter. She sold the house to Barry on condition that he rent the house for the next few years. While I don't know if that stipulation would ever hold up in court, a handshake and neighborly goodwill seems to be enough for Agnes.

There's more than enough land around it to cultivate. She even found Barry his renter—a new pilot working for Aro—and agreed to do the painting and cleaning up. Jonah and I offered to help, but she smiled and shook her head, and said we have enough on our plates, that this is something she needs to do on her own.

We've spent the last month sorting, cleaning, and packing up Jonah's house. Most of the furniture is staying behind. It's not worth the cost of flying to Trapper's Crossing. All that's left to take are clothes and personal effects, and a few sentimental things—namely my father's impressive collection of Julia Roberts movies. Some of it will remain here, boxed up, to come when George flies Archie, Jonah's second plane, to Trapper's Crossing in a few weeks.

"Listen, Di, I've gotta go, but I'll text you when we're all settled.

It'll be a few days before we have internet and cable and all that set up."

"Okay, but don't wait too long to post something."

"I'm on hiatus, remember?"

"I know! But everyone wants to know when your hot Alaskan pilot proposes."

I roll my eyes. Diana has created an entire section on our website dedicated to my new life in Alaska, lovingly coined "The Beauty and the Yeti." It has become fodder for the romantics among our followers. While neither of us are as active as we once were with *Calla & Dee*—absorbed by moves and our future careers—we made a tearful pact the night before I left that we'd make the effort to keep our site going in one form or another.

For me, that has become chronicling my new life in Alaska.

"Don't roll your eyes at me!" she exclaims, as if she can see through the phone. "I'll bet he proposes by the end of the year."

"Oh my God. Don't start with that." I laugh, even as a rash of nervous butterflies erupts in my stomach. It's not that the thought hasn't crossed my mind. It has, more than once. But I've promptly pushed it out, telling myself that it's far too soon. "We have enough on our plate with this house and the company."

"Calla!" Jonah hollers.

"I've gotta go. The yeti is getting impatient."

"'Kay. Enjoy your first day in your log cabin in the wilderness. You're crazy! Love you! Bye!"

She hangs up before I get a chance to respond.

Yes, maybe I *am* crazy for agreeing to this.

But I'm also crazy in love with Jonah.

I slide open the empty dresser drawers in one last perfunctory check to make sure we haven't missed something important of my father's, and then I make my way down the hall, stealing a glance at the vacant living room, my focus instinctively darting to the corner where my father's hospital bed once sat. The old, shabby furniture is gone and the scent of fresh paint permeates the air.

It's no longer Wren Fletcher's home, I remind myself.

I walk into the kitchen to the sound of tearing. Jonah is ever so slowly peeling a strip of the atrocious mallard paper off the wall. "Figured I'd help Aggie out."

"Did that feel good?"

He studies the letter-sized piece he managed to pry off. "Yeah, actually. Fuck, yeah."

He holds it up for me, the nipples that he and Max, another Wild pilot, drew on each duck as a joke visible. "What do you think about framing this and puttin' it up on the wall at our place?"

"It's a great idea." I grin as warmth blooms in my chest. "And I think you need to stop giving Agnes grief about driving my dad's truck and come out of the closet, you big nostalgic baby."

He smirks, tucking the scrap between the pages of a hardcover book to protect it.

A rattling metal pulls my attention to the far corner of the kitchen where Bandit sits in a small pet carrier, his plump body twisting against the gated door, his dexterous paws stretching and fumbling with the latch in a frantic attempt to break free.

"He doesn't look thrilled," I note.

"He will be when he sees his new digs." Phil arranged for a neighbor to take the last of his livestock—including the goat, thank God—which frees up the pen for our *raccoon*. And of course, we have no choice but to take him, according to Jonah. If we leave him here, he'll get into Barry's crops and Barry will shoot him.

I shake my head. "Remember when you said he wasn't a pet?"

Jonah closes the distance. "Remember when you said I was an asshole?"

"Jury's still out on that one," I tease.

He leans over and captures my lips with a soft kiss. "Almost forgot this." He pats the coffeemaker on the counter. "You want to carry that or him?"

"I'll take the one that won't claw my leg, thanks." My hand smooths over the plastic, reminiscing. It's a cheap appliance that was an integral part of my father's simple daily routine. I made the worst pot of coffee known to mankind one morning, using this machine. Dad drank the entire cup without complaint.

"All right, all right ... relax." Jonah retrieves a chattering Bandit.

Both of our gazes roll over my father's kitchen one last time, each caught in a moment's reflection of our own memories here.

Jonah looks to me. "Ready?"

To leave what I know of Alaska, for something entirely unfamiliar and new?

I take a deep breath. "Yes."

With a silent, firm-lipped smile, Jonah leads me out.

―――――

"I thought he was supposed to be gone," I whisper. My eyes don't know where to land first.

The front door was unlocked when we arrived. The long, narrow hallway is still lined with coats and shoes and scarves. The worn couch and side tables still fill the living room. Plates and glasses still sit in the dish drainer. The forlorn moose and pair of deer still stare morosely at me from their predicaments on the wall.

Jonah's boots leave snowy tracks on the plank floor as he strolls over to the kitchen counter, to where the pile of keys sits, next to a piece of paper. His brow furrows as he scans the handwritten note. "Phil's gone. Left on a flight this morning," he confirms, dropping the page on the counter with a heavy hand. A grim smile touches his lips. "He wasn't kidding when he said he'd leave *everything*."

"No shit," I mutter. I wander over to the fridge where glossy pictures of little boys—strangers—stare back at me. I guess I'm supposed to throw these out? "This is weird."

"Yup," Jonah agrees. "But I guess it'd be a lot for him to clear all this out by himself. Probably hard, too, with all those memories of his wife here."

I open the fridge. "Yeah, I'm sure this half-eaten sandwich was *way* too sentimental to throw out." My voice is thick with a mixture of bitterness and frustration. There are bite marks in it. Next to it is a jug of milk, a few loose processed cheese slices, and several jars of preserves—pickles, beets, jam ... eggs? Smears of grease and food drippings coat the bottom shelf. Nothing has been wiped down.

Jonah opens a cupboard to reveal an array of spices and canned goods. The cupboard beside it is equally full, this one with mismatched mugs and glassware. He slowly spins in a circle. "At least he cleaned up the kitchen a bit."

I cringe at the dried soap suds and crusted food particles at the bottom of the sink. "Jonah, this place is filthy!" And something tells me cleaning products to tackle the mess are the only thing Phil *didn't* leave for us. The dull ache in my head that appeared halfway through the bumpy flight here blossoms with my dread for the work ahead of us. I pinch the bridge of my nose to quell the pain. "How are you not *snapping?*" Because I'm ready to scream, or cry, or both.

As wary as I was about buying Phil's place in the beginning, I've been imagining this day with excitement since we signed the papers a month ago. I pictured us strolling into our new house, the rooms barren, the walls bare, our gazes greedily taking in all the empty corners, spotting little secrets and imperfections previously hidden. We'd start making a mental list about what we'd tackle first as we toasted to this exciting new beginning. I even packed champagne flutes in my purse.

This is not at all what I pictured.

Jonah comes up behind me, roping his arms around my waist. "It'll take no time for the two of us to get through this. And I'll bet there's a lot we can use. That cold cellar was full of preserves the last time we checked."

"And what about all the stuff we *can't* use?" Decades of it, I'd imagine. They were married for fifty years! They've lived in this house since 1985!

"We'll donate or dump it. Or burn it. We can have a big-ass bonfire. Looks like there's a nice pit down by the lake."

He's far too even tempered right now.

I rest my head against his chest, trying my best to focus on the positives—I'm in Alaska with Jonah, and we've bought our first home together. A place that's going to see so many important milestones for us. It's a bit of clutter, some dirt. Nothing we can't easily deal with. Nothing compared to what we've already faced together.

"I am *so* damn annoyed," I growl.

Jonah chuckles. "I know you are. But you'll laugh about it one day."

"Will I?"

Jonah dips his head to graze the side of my neck with his lips, tickling me with his beard. "I promise." His breath skates over my skin.

"You're right. Maybe in an hour, after I've finished guzzling that bottle of champagne George and Bobbie sent with us, this'll be really funny."

"Drunk, angry Barbie. Can't wait," Jonah says wryly, drawing out my chuckle. "Before you pop that cork, though ... we have a problem we have to deal with out back." He sighs heavily. "And you're gonna be *really* pissed about this."

———

"You have *got* to be kidding me."

Jonah scratches his beard. "Nope."

"What happened to his neighbor taking it?" I was sitting right across from Phil at his kitchen counter when he confirmed—several whiskeys in—that the guy on the other side of the lake was taking his livestock.

"The note says they had a fight and the guy changed his mind. He took the chickens, though." Jonah stands in front of the sizeable animal pen, enclosed with wire fencing, his hands on his hips, in a staring match with Phil's black-and-white goat.

Our black-and-white goat now, apparently.

I wrinkle my nose against the faint, acrid scent of bird poop that permeates the cold. The empty chicken coop is a ramshackle box of plywood and haphazardly nailed shingles that sits three feet off the ground to our left. Next to it is a much larger but equally dilapidated structure. I assume, nighttime shelter for Zeke. "A fight about what? What kind of argument ends in 'I'll take your chickens but keep your goat'?"

"No idea. That's all the note said—that him and this guy, Roy, had a falling-out, and there should be enough hay and grain to last Zeke until spring." Jonah presses his lips together in thought.

I don't like that look on his face. I've seen it before. He's problem-solving, weighing options.

There are *no* options here.

"So, we're going to convince Roy to change his mind, right?"

"I guess." Jonah cocks his head. "You're *seriously* scared of this little guy?"

Zeke lets out a loud bleat and turns those disturbing horizontal pupils my way. A shiver runs down my spine. "We don't need a goat."

"Bandit might like a friend."

"Raccoons don't have friends."

Jonah sets his jaw. "Who says he can't be friends with a goat? And goats don't like to be alone."

I see where this is going, and my frustration flares. "I agreed to move to a log cabin in the woods for you. I didn't complain about the raccoon in the cage. I'm about to sort through *fifty years' worth* of someone else's shit and there is piss all over the bathroom floor because Phil was too drunk to hit the toilet bowl. I draw the line at owning a *goat!*" My voice carries through the dense, quiet forest that surrounds us.

Jonah's lips twitch.

"This is *not* funny!"

He rubs his forehead. "Fine. You're right. I'm sorry."

"Okay." I take a calming breath. "So, let's go meet Roy."

Jonah's eyebrows spike. "What, like, right *now*? We just got here. I thought you wanted to go pick up the mattress today."

Zeke bleats loudly, his hoof kicking at the steely wire fence of the enclosure.

"Yes. Like, *right* now."

CHAPTER TEN

"This has to be it." Jonah slows at the end of the road where a rustic wooden sign with R. Donovan carved into it is nailed to a tree. It's a good thing he suggested we take one of Phil's old snow machines because the path ahead looks more like a hiking trail than a drive-way, unfit for any full-sized vehicle. A trail that's not in use. It hasn't snowed in almost a week, according to the local weather reports, and yet there isn't a hint of tracks in or out of the property from this direction.

My arms are roped tightly around Jonah's waist as we coast down the lane, deeper and deeper into the woods, passing two neon yellow No Trespassing signs. A little farther ahead is yet another sign, this one wooden with carved letters painted black, that reads, "I support the right to stand my ground."

"What does that mean?" I holler over the low, rugged hum of the engine.

"Different things to different people," Jonah answers cryptically, rounding a bend of trees, only to discover that the trail continues.

"I don't think this is the right way!"

Jonah points at a spot above the trees, and I see the haze of smoke that sails upward, countering my worries. The snow machine's engine whirs as he speeds up.

The forest finally thins, revealing a tiny weathered one-story cabin with a screened-in porch off the front, missing a porch door.

Beyond it is a barn at least three times the size of the home and several smaller shacks and lean-tos. In between is a whole lot of *everything*. Barrels, pails, used tires, gas cans and propane tanks, wood in various states—from fallen trees to neatly chopped kindling. Three old trucks sit off to one side, two of them rusted and missing parts.

It looks like a junkyard.

Jonah cuts the engine as two enormous dogs round the corner of the barn, charging toward us, their growl-barks unsettling. The closer they get, the less they look like dogs and the more they look like wolves.

"Jonah?" I call out, lifting my left leg, readying to kick in defense as the black one moves in, teeth bared.

The front door of the cabin opens with a loud creak, and a man emerges. "Oscar! Gus! Heel!" His harsh tone cuts through the chaos.

The wolf dogs quiet instantly and settle back on their haunches, licking their maws. The mottled-gray one—the seemingly calmer of the two—locks its sharp yellow gaze on me. As if waiting for a twitch, a cough—some reason to lunge.

Chickens cluck frantically from the coop nearby, stirred by all the commotion.

"You Roy?" Jonah calls out.

The man, who has moved to the opening at the top of the porch steps where a door belongs, stares hard at Jonah for a minute, as if considering his answer. He's in his fifties, at least—maybe older—and weathered looking, either by age or hardship or both, his salt-and-pepper hair combed back neatly off his face much darker than the scruffy solid-gray beard that covers his jaw. Sawdust clings to his blue jeans and heavy flannel jacket. "Who's askin'?" he demands, in an accent that belongs somewhere in the Deep South.

With a wary glance at the wolf dogs and a comforting squeeze of my thigh, Jonah climbs off the snow machine and strolls over to the front porch. He slides off his right glove as he eases up the three steps. "I'm Jonah Riggs."

Roy studies Jonah's proffered hand for a long moment before accepting it in a single up-and-down handshake.

"We moved in next door. Bought Phil's place."

Next door is a stretch. We're *miles* away from this guy. At least, it feels like it, with the two lengthy driveways.

"Right." Roy sniffs. "The pilot who wants to fly his goddamn planes over my head all the livelong day." There's no small amount of bitterness in his tone, nor in the steely glare he settles on Jonah. A challenge, perhaps. To what, I don't know. Jonah is a physically intimidating man—well over six feet tall and broad shouldered. It's hard to compare Roy, standing several steps above, his shoulders hunched, but I'd bet money Jonah has as many pounds on Roy as Roy has years on Jonah. And yet, if Roy is the least bit intimidated by his visitor, he doesn't show it.

Jonah eases back down the porch steps, glancing over his shoulder, to give me a look—part amused, part "can you believe this guy?"—before facing our friendly neighbor again. "Phil said you were plannin' on takin' his goat. We thought we'd check to see if you're still interested."

Roy's attention swings to the barn where five goats of varying size mill along the fence line, curious of the newcomers. A large clearing stretches out beyond the barn. "Got enough goats."

"I see that." Jonah nods slowly. "So, what's one more, then? Looks like you've got a big barn there. And you obviously know what you're doin'. I'll even throw in some hay and grain. Enough to get you through till spring."

"Why don't *you* want him?"

"We're not in a place to take on livestock right now. We're just startin' out."

"Huh. Just starting out." Roy smirks. "All you outsiders, coming here to 'just start out.'" Again, that bitter tone laces his words.

I may be an outsider, but Jonah certainly is not. I feel the urge to point out that Jonah grew up in the Anchorage area, that's he's as Alaskan as they come, but Jonah speaks before I get a chance to decide if I should.

"It'd be a big favor to us if you took him off our hands, added him to your herd." I hear the strain in Jonah's voice. He doesn't have patience in the face of attitude.

Roy shifts on his boots, moving out from behind the porch post and into full view. It's only then that I see the gun propped against the floor in his left hand.

Tension skitters down my spine.

"Nah. He ain't good for nothin'."

"He's a *male* goat. I can think of *one* thing he's good for." Jonah looks pointedly at the animal pen. "You've gotta have some females in there?"

"They're *all* females." Roy chuckles darkly. "And he ain't even good for *that*."

"Shit," Jonah mutters.

"Maybe you can find some fool who don't know nothing about goats to take him off your hands. Or someone who likes the taste of old meat. I don't."

"Thanks for your time," Jonah says, not hiding the annoyance from his tone. He marches toward me.

"Tell you what … bring him on over."

Jonah stalls. "Really? I appreciate it—"

"The hounds have gotten fat and lazy over the winter. Figure a good chase an' kill ahead of the summer might do 'em some good. Though I doubt he'll give them much of a chase."

I grimace. I may not like goats but the picture Roy just painted is far more disturbing than creepy pupils and unpleasant childhood memories.

Jonah's jaw hangs in a rare moment of speechlessness before he regains his composure. "Good to meet ya, Roy." His brow is furrowed as he trudges back to take his seat and start the engine.

The black wolf dog slinks away as if nervous by the hum, but the gray one hasn't so much as twitched. It's unnerving how it watches us. Me.

Curling my arms around Jonah's torso, I steal a glance Roy's way in time to catch the knowing smirk on his tight, thin lips before Jonah squeezes the throttle.

"You're gonna have to get over your goat PTSD because there is no way in hell we're givin' Zeke to that asshole!" he hollers over his shoulder as we race back down the long trail toward the road, much faster than we came, Jonah's body tense beneath my grip.

———

"Who greets people with a gun?" I take a healthy sip of chardonnay from an ornate etched-crystal glass I found in the cupboard and then drop to my knees to finish scrubbing the fridge. After our meet and greet with the neighborhood lunatic, we took our new old truck—that smells of motor oil and is plastered with silver duct tape to keep the worn leather on the seats in place—to Wasilla for a few groceries and a mattress.

"He's just an old man trying to intimidate us." Jonah gives the logs in the fieldstone fireplace a stab with the cast-iron poker. Of the two of us, he's certainly handling today's unpleasant surprises with more grace than I am.

"Well, it worked because we're never stepping foot on his property again. Especially not with those wolves. You can't keep *wolves* for pets. We should report him."

"They're not wolves. Hybrids, maybe, though I haven't heard of any trained to listen like that. But sendin' the cops to our neighbor on our first day probably isn't the best way to start out here." Jonah eases away from the fireplace. "Whatever. That's another plus to living where we are. If you hate your neighbors, you don't have to see 'em."

Finally satisfied with the interior of the fridge after having worked on it for the past hour, I peel the rubber gloves off with a sigh. "That's one thing done." Only a million more to go.

I catch the telltale whir of speeding snow machine engines. Jonah wanders over to the big bay window to peer out on the frozen clearing as several race past, their headlights dull beams in the evening's dusk.

"Isn't this our private lake?"

"Yup." He sucks back a sip from his bottle of beer. "Phil probably didn't care, though."

"Phil was probably already unconscious from whiskey by now." My focus trails the departing taillights. "Wonder if they trespass on Roy's property, too."

"I hope so. Screw Roy." He frowns as he inspects the sliver in his index finger, earned while fussing with the gate into the animal pen earlier.

"How's Bandit doing out there with his new *friend*?"

Jonah chuckles. "He's confused. I cleaned out the chicken coop and locked him in there for the night so they can see each other but they're separated." He drags his index finger along a row of book spines on the bookshelf tucked beneath the stairs. It's stuffed with dust-covered books, magazines, and board games.

Much like *every* other corner of this house, stuffed with one thing or another. I opened a closet earlier and was assaulted by an avalanche of mismatched Tupperware containers.

"I don't know where to start," I admit, fumbling with the stack of black garbage bags, my gaze drifting to the garish five-light chandelier hanging above. It's too small for the double-story room, and three of its bulbs have burned out. "Did you see a ladder anywhere?" Phil has left *everything* else. He must have left a ladder, too.

"Think I saw one in the workshop. We'll get to that tomorrow." Jonah stretches his arms above his head as he saunters over to me. "Start with this." He tops up my wine to brimming. "And this." He flips open the lid on a pizza box—the one without cheese, for me—that we grabbed at the only pizza shop in Trapper's Crossing on our way home. "I'll haul the mattress upstairs and we can make our bed. And then we'll crack that bottle of champagne and relax. Tomorrow, we'll start dealing with everything else."

"You make it sound so easy." My arm feels heavy as I reach for my drink. My mental exhaustion has drained me.

He gently clinks the neck of his bottle against my glass. "It is."

"I'm glad you think so." I plaster on an innocent smile and pat the extra-large yellow rubber gloves on the counter. "Because these are for you, to scrub the drunk-man pee off that bathroom floor up there."

He slips my glass from my hand and scoops me into his arms. "Told you, Calla, I don't care. I have you and my planes, we have this place ..." His eyes are bright and wistful as they roam the beams in the pitched ceiling. "We have it all."

CHAPTER ELEVEN

"What did the contract say?"

"I'd have to go back and check."

"Well, you must be able to do *something*." My mother's astonished tone carries well over the phone's speaker, even from thousands of miles away. "Bill him for a cleaning company or for your time. At the *very* least, you need to complain to the agent. Didn't they inspect it before you arrived?"

I stifle my groan, knowing I'm about to get an earful as I admit, "There was no agent. It was a private sale." A lawyer in Wasilla managed all the paperwork—the contract, the title and lien search, and a bunch of other things I don't care to know about.

"No agent!" She makes a sound. "Well, no wonder!" To say my mother is unimpressed that we haven't heeded her warnings and rented rather than bought is a glaring understatement.

"I'm sure it saved them some money on commission fees, Susan." Simon's typically calm voice is a challenge. I can picture them squaring off in the living room—my mom with her face painted and her hair coiffed, spearing Simon with an exasperated look; Simon, with his afternoon cup of tea in hand and a BBC special on mute in the background, his eyebrows arched in a "she's a grown woman, living with a grown man, making her own decisions and mistakes" way.

"We did save money. Phil knocked the price down by six percent,"

I confirm, reaching deep into the cabinet with a gloved hand to fish out something metal from the corner. I frown at the manual hand beater that appears. Likely forgotten about decades ago. One for the donation box. "Whatever. It's not the end of the world. The upstairs is completely cleared out and we're making good headway down here." Four days in and we've turned over decades' worth of household goods and sentimental junk from almost every cupboard. Our main floor looks like a hoarder's paradise but there's a system to the chaos—boxes line the narrow hallway, waiting for Jonah to haul burnables to the fire; items worth keeping are piled on the kitchen counters and the small dining table, for washing and organizing later; donations for the local Salvation Army fill the living room floor. Everything else goes straight into a black plastic bag. There are seventeen bags of trash and counting.

"And the old owner doesn't want *any* of it?" My mother can't seem to get past her abhorrence.

"Nope." I climb to my feet and head for the living room, where we've pushed aside the floppy couch and scuffed side tables to make room. "Jonah called him yesterday. He said to throw out whatever we don't want."

"That's bizarre." My mom's sigh carries over the speaker. "Where's Jonah, anyway?"

"At the fire pit." He's been out there since the sky began to lighten this morning. The plume of smoke that rises is dark and thick and full of ash, and every time he comes in to swap an empty box for a full one, he carries with him the scent of charred paper and burnt wood.

Not that I can complain. I've been cleaning in the same clothes for the past four days—a baggy sweatshirt and a pair of sweatpants that I found in a dresser full of women's clothes in the bedroom. They're now coated in grime, dust, and cleaner.

"Have you had a chance to photograph anything good yet?" Simon asks, with a glimmer of excitement. He once admitted that, at one point in his life, he dreamed of being a nature photographer. My own skills with the camera—his Canon that I have claimed as my own—are in part thanks to his amateur teachings.

I smile, silently thanking him for shifting off the topic of this house. "No. Jonah said he saw a fox running along the tree line, down by the hangar, but I've been too busy inside cleaning to do much of anything else." I haven't even pulled my camera out. Diana has been harassing me to share something online, but I haven't wrapped my head around this disaster to decide how I want to frame it for spectators.

"Don't get too close for the sake of a picture," Mom warns. "Even a moose can turn on you."

"I don't think that's something we need to worry about with Calla," Simon says dryly.

We chatter for another five minutes before Mom signals an end to the conversation. "Well, I guess we should let you get back to it."

"Yeah, I'm gonna tackle these valances next." I stretch my arms over my head, wincing with the ache in my lower back and shoulders. I long for a long, hot soak in the bathtub.

"Ugh. Valances. I've never understood the point."

"Right?"

"Say hi to Jonah for us."

"I will. And figure out when you're coming!"

We end the call as Jonah's voice carries in.

"... refuses to go back there if he's there. Bandit seems okay with him so far, at least." The front door creaks open.

"I'll ask around and see if anyone is interested," comes a familiar female voice.

"Somethin' tells me there aren't many people looking for a useless old goat who hates men. Hey, Calla, Marie's here!" Jonah calls out, as the tall, willowy woman steps into our house.

I peel off my rubber gloves and toss them aside before turning to meet Marie's teal-blue eyes. It's been two months since we last saw her, when she flew to Bangor to provide veterinarian services to the villagers.

And now she's here, living only fifteen minutes away.

"Hi, Calla," she offers, her hands fidgeting around a house plant and a gift bag in the shape of a liquor bottle. "I thought I'd stop by to see how you guys were doing."

I drag my fingers back through my hair, smoothing my wayward topknot. "It's good to see you." And it genuinely *is* good to see a familiar face while we're in the depths of house-purging hell, even if Marie and I have exchanged little more than polite conversation and I'm one hundred percent positive she's in love with my boyfriend.

Marie tucks the gift bag under one arm, freeing a hand to brush a strand of long, golden-blonde hair off her face. She tucks it behind her ear. "So ..." She edges around the mountain of trash bags. "How's it going?"

"Well ... I'm wearing a dead woman's clothes while I go through her belongings. I just found a hemorrhoid cushion in the back of the hallway closet. I've broken every fingernail, and I'm seriously considering opening a bottle of wine at"—I glance at my watch—"noon."

Marie presses her lips together to hide her smile, her gaze pausing on the bleach stains that I earned yesterday while on my hand and knees scrubbing the main-floor bath. "You look great. But you *always* do."

"Thanks, but I look like a vagabond," I counter, borrowing a favorite word of Simon's.

Marie's appearance is more polished than her usually casual, fresh-faced style. She's still in jeans, but the sweater showing through her opened winter coat is pink and hugs her slender body. A light dusting of shadow coats her eyelids, a stroke of brown mascara makes her already thick fringe of lashes longer, and the beachy waves in her hair were likely created by an iron.

I wonder if this is how she looks when she's not the crusader, flying around Western Alaska, or if she put extra effort in, coming here today?

Marie laughs and her focus drifts over the space. "There's a lot of stuff here."

"They were married for fifty years. Do you have any idea what this is?" I ask, tapping a round plastic appliance I found in the pantry closet.

Her nose crinkles in thought. "I think that's a dehydrator. You know, to dehydrate fruits and vegetables and ..." Her words drift as she takes in my grimace. "Some people like it."

I swiftly carry it over to the donate pile.

"Anything else to burn today?" Jonah asks, shifting the empty cardboard box on the floor with his boot.

"That stuff." I cast a wayward hand at the pile in the corner.

"You want me to burn our living room furniture?" Jonah looks at me, amusement in his tone.

"It's not *ours*. It's Phil's. We're getting all new stuff. And why not? It's mostly wood."

"How about we wait until we have something to replace it with, so we're not sittin' on the floor. And then I'll take it all to the dump. Someone else can use it."

"Someone's going to pull that couch out of the *dump* and bring it *home*?"

"One man's trash ... Anything else for the fire before I put it out?"

"Those?" I nod toward the wall of animal trophies.

Jonah glares at me the same way he did when I tossed an old, tattered book into the burn box. "We're *not* burning those."

"Fine. Then, just *me*," I grumble, reaching back to rub the painful knots in my neck, wincing with the ache. "End my suffering." I'm desperate to have an empty, clean house to start with.

Jonah saunters over and drops his rough hands on my shoulders to knead them with skilled fingers.

I let out a deep groan of appreciation.

"I take it that helps?" He dips his head to press a kiss against my jawline.

Marie averts her gaze, staring intently at a cheap, framed poster print of Denali National Park that I haven't yet taken down. Is it to give us privacy? Or is it to avoid the inevitable sting that comes with watching someone you care about being intimate with someone else? Jonah may be oblivious, but I'm not. I'm also not naive. You can't just turn off feelings for someone because they love someone else, as much as most people would like to.

What if our roles were reversed? What if Jonah and I were "just friends" and I had to stand idly by and watch him fall in love with another woman?

A sharp prick of sympathy stabs my chest at that thought.

"To be continued later," I whisper, giving him a knowing look as I slip my hands over his, squeezing them until they stall.

Jonah steals one last kiss from my neck before stepping away. "You got big plans for today, Marie?"

She refocuses her attention on him. "I didn't, but I just got called for an emergency as I was pulling in here. I have to head back to take care of a sick cat. Otherwise I would have offered to help you guys."

"Run. Save yourself while you can!" I moan.

Jonah playfully swats my backside. "Got time for a quick tour?"

"A *really* quick one?"

"That works. I need to get this hellion out of here before she burns the entire place down." He cups the back of my neck, giving it another rub. "What do you think? Drive into Wasilla to check out some new furniture?"

"A couch?" I ask, excitement stirring in my sore limbs.

He smirks. "Sure."

My hopes for finding something suitable are not high but the idea of going somewhere—*anywhere*—has me saying goodbye to Marie and rushing upstairs to shower in our dingy, dark bathroom with newfound energy.

"Calla, wake up." A gentle hand jostles my shoulder.

I whimper. Every muscle in my body aches.

"Come on. You gotta see this."

"Is it the northern lights again?"

He chuckles. "It's almost nine. The sun's already coming up. Come on."

I crack my eyelids to find Jonah already dressed and holding the red terry-cloth robe I bought at the Wasilla Target the other day.

"This better be worth it." With a shiver, I pull myself out of bed and trail Jonah downstairs. The gentle gurgle of my father's coffeemaker brewing a fresh pot carries through our empty main floor. Seven days in and everything of Phil's that we've decided not to keep is gone, to the dump or the thrift shop, or charred to ash. Even the animal heads have found a temporary home in the work-shop because I couldn't handle them watching me anymore. And after three days of spelling out all the disgusting things that have likely spilled into the moss-green sisal rug, Jonah finally agreed to roll it up and drag it outside. He's left it next to the old couch that I also made him remove, in preparation of our new one arriving Friday from a warehouse in Anchorage.

I wasn't expecting to find anything in the furniture shop in Wasilla when we went that day but, lo and behold, they had the perfect midcentury modern sectional in a dark briar-gray tweed material. Of course, Jonah balked at the price tag. It took two days of whittling him down until I threw it on my credit card and told him he needs to get on board. I am far more excited than I ever thought I could be about a couch.

All that's left in the house are piles of things I need to clean and organize, furniture that we'll use until we can replace with new purchases, and a thousand repairs and improvements to make— wood floors to refinish, bathrooms to remodel, nail holes to fill, cracked outlet covers to swap out, door handles to tighten, hinges to oil, appliances to replace. The list goes on and it's daunting at times, but we have time. Most importantly, though, this log cabin is finally starting to feel like *ours* and not Phil's.

I turn toward the kitchen and coffeemaker, but Jonah loops an arm around my waist and pulls me in the opposite direction, past the crackling fire in the stone hearth, and toward the living room bay window.

"Oh, *wow* ..." Two moose stand at the edge of the frozen lake no more than thirty feet away, grazing on dead foliage. The entire vista before me is awe-inspiring—the vast expanse of freshly fallen, crisp snow, the sun that has been hiding behind cloud cover for days on end visible and climbing, its yellow glow bouncing off the stark, white landscape blinding in its intensity. Not until we moved in did I truly appreciate our house's location—on a peninsula of sorts, where we get the morning sunrise from the east and the evening sunset from the west.

"They're probably gonna disappear the second I start the tractor to clear the snow," he murmurs low in my ear, as if they can hear us. And maybe they can.

"That one on the left is *huge*." I've only ever seen moose from the air, flying above.

"Yeah. She's probably nine hundred ... maybe a thousand pounds. The males can weigh up to eighteen hundred."

"How do you know it's a *she*? I mean ..." I tip my head to the side, but I can't see anything from this angle.

Jonah chuckles. "Definitely that, or the fact that she has no antlers. The males lose their antlers every winter, but they start growing new ones right away."

"Well, aren't you a wealth of knowledge."

"You know, this is all in that wildlife book I gave you for Christmas. That you told me you've already read."

"I was just testing you," I lie, the humor in my voice betraying me.

"Uh-huh." He smirks. "The smaller one beside her is a bull calf. She probably had him last summer."

The two enormous animals continue to graze, undisturbed and seemingly unaware of our presence, though the mother's ears twitch a few times. "I need to get a picture of this before they leave." I make to move but Jonah's hands on my hips hold me in place.

"Don't worry, they tend to stay within a five-mile radius so you'll be seeing them around. Just don't get too close." He steals a kiss from my neck.

I lean back against Jonah's chest, content as we watch the mother and her baby. "I'm shocked Phil didn't add them to the wall."

"Nah. He would have liked having the wildlife around here."

And so do I, I realize, as I take in the picturesque scene. "Okay. Fine. You're allowed to wake me up for stuff like this."

His deep chuckles carry through the quiet morning, earning another twitch of the moose's ears.

CHAPTER TWELVE

"Do you think we can fit a bigger tub in here?"

"Not a chance."

I hit the bathroom light switch on my way out, fresh from a long bath to help ease my aching muscles after ten days of kneeling, lifting, and scrubbing. "Fine. Then we're turning the little bedroom into another bathroom and taking some space to make this one an en-suite."

"That'd leave us with only two bedrooms." Jonah's back is against the bed frame, his attention glued to my laptop screen. The sleeves of his navy-blue T-shirt stretch over his muscular biceps, distracting me momentarily.

"So? Seriously, Jonah, how many guests are we ever going to have at one time?"

"I was thinking more about kids."

"*Oh*. Right." I consider the bedroom that spans the back of the house as I settle onto my side of the bed. There's a chill to the air, despite the forced heat pumping through the vents and the logs that Jonah shoved into the fireplace before coming up to bed. Replacing the windows might help, at least in part. "They can have bunk beds."

"That'd work for two of them. What about the other six?" he says with a solemn tone, his brow furrowed intently on the picture of him and my father on the About page I built for The Yeti website.

"I don't know. You'll have to ask the animal you're breeding with. Maybe she has a den somewhere that can fit them all in."

His deep chuckle fills our bedroom.

"Any bookings yet?" I ask, teasing. The Yeti's site has only been live for three days.

"How would I know? You haven't shown me how to see them."

I ease in closer to him, resting my chin on his shoulder. "That's right, I haven't. I have to make myself indispensable to you somehow."

Jonah's blue eyes crawl over my face. "You *are* indispensable to me. Seriously, I couldn't have pulled together anything half as good."

"Wait till you see the *itinerary template* I finished," I say, dragging out the two words seductively. Agnes walked me through several examples of forms and gave her official seal of approval—an emailed response with a smiley face on it.

The bed shakes with his laughter. He leans in to skate his lips along my jawline. "Thank you. For everything."

I inhale the scent of body wash on his skin from his shower. "This is only the beginning. By the time I'm done with my marketing plan, every Alaskan man, woman, and child will have heard of *The Yeti*," I promise, repeating the seductive tone.

"Would you stop saying it like that?"

"Like what? *The Yeti*—ow!" I squeal, feeling his teeth playfully nip at my throat.

With a soothing kiss over the spot and a smirk of satisfaction, Jonah shifts back to his previous position, his attention on my laptop screen again.

"I called Chris today. He agreed to promote us at their front desk, front and center. I've already ordered the pamphlets." I spent the weeks leading up to our move designing promotional material and now that we have an official address, there's nothing stopping me from printing.

"Please tell me there aren't any half-naked pictures of me in them?"

"No! Of course not. That would be totally unprofessional." I pause. "Those are only for the calendar. I've sent one to Andrea. She said she has the perfect place to hang her copy at their front desk."

Jonah grits his teeth "You better be kidding."

"Guess you'll have to find out." I waggle my eyebrows at him. "Hey, when do you think Phil's plane will be up and running? I want to take some pictures of it and add it to the fleet page."

He shakes his head. "Who knows? I couldn't even get the engine to turn when I tried earlier. I'm not thinking about that right now, though, not when I've got two reliable planes to choose from. Well, semi-reliable. Veronica's gas gauge is acting up." When he sees the concerned look on my face, he quickly adds, "It's no big deal. I have to pay closer attention. I'll get it fixed as soon as I find a mechanic around here I trust to look at it."

I force away the fear of Jonah's engine stalling midair because he's run out of gas. "Speaking of mechanics, the blue snowmobile sounds like it wants to die."

Jonah sighs. "We'll have to get that fixed, too."

I curl up against his side, craving his body heat. "I want to go into Wasilla tomorrow to do some shopping, so maybe we can ask around?"

"*More* shopping? For what?"

"Stuff."

His eyebrow arches. "Stuff?"

"*House* stuff." I shrug. "Maybe something to go with the couch? I'll let you know when I find it."

He shakes his head. "I'll be gone most of the day tomorrow. I'm gonna do a run to Unalakleet."

I frown. That's far in the west, if I remember correctly. "For what?"

"A possible TB outbreak."

"*TB?*" My voice fills with alarm. "Isn't that, like, *highly* contagious?" And, I thought, eradicated?

"It can be. The doc doing rounds there called while you were in the bath to see if I can pick up an X-ray machine from Anchorage. Aro is backlogged and Nome doesn't have one to spare. They're telling him they can't make the run for at least another week. He's got two sick kids he's worried about and a half dozen more people who aren't doing too good." Jonah doesn't sound nearly rattled enough by this.

"Can't you call Howard and yell at him to make this a priority?" That's what Jonah's good at, according to my dad—shaking trees until the fruit falls.

"I could, but the doc and I go way back, and it's business for me. It's supposed to be clear for another day before the snow starts again. Good time to go."

Not that that can't change in an instant, from everything I've learned about Alaska. I push that worry aside. "I thought you were going to focus on this side of the state."

"Eventually. Right now, I need to take whatever I can get. Plus, these villagers know and trust me to help them out. I will, whenever I can."

"Why don't I come with you, then?"

He shakes his head. "I might have to fly those kids to the hospital."

"Right. Well ... I guess I'll wait to go shopping, then." It'll be the first day since we moved here that Jonah's flying anywhere. An unexpected pang of longing for tomorrow night hits. I wish I could hit a button and fast-forward until then.

I *really* need to book my road test soon.

Jonah pushes the laptop closed and sets it on the nightstand. We're using Phil and Colette's old mismatched bedroom furniture, save for the mattress, until I can find a set I like to replace it.

I let out a heavy, dramatic sigh. "I guess I'll just hang out here ... all *alone*."

Jonah reaches back and pulls his T-shirt up over his head, revealing the web of muscle that fans his back, his broad, hard chest, and the ridges in his taut abs. He tosses the shirt haphazardly toward the corner, missing the hamper entirely. I know that before bed tonight, he'll get out of bed to move it back. He's a closeted neat freak. "You're not alone. You've got Bandit and Zeke."

I pause in my admiring gawk of his upper body to shoot him a look. Jonah has been single-handedly dealing with our livestock problem. I have yet to even venture to the pen, let alone bond with my childhood nemesis.

He pulls the tie on my robe and, with a casual flick of his wrist, throws both sides wide open. I feel his heated gaze drag over my naked flesh as if he were touching me with his fingertips. "There's plenty to keep yourself busy with around here all day while I'm gone."

"Like what?" I shiver from the cold against my bare skin, even while my body begins to fire with the promise of what's coming.

He works our comforter out from beneath my body and back up, covering my lower half. "Oh, you know ..." He slides over to press his body against mine, the feel of his hot skin against me pulling a soft moan from my lips. He's wearing boxer briefs, a problem I hope to fix momentarily. "Make sure the house is clean and warm for me when I come home ..." He brushes his lips along my jawline. "Wash and fold my laundry ..." His lips find my neck. "Cook me dinner ..."

I school my expression—Jonah knows the mere suggestion of catering to him like a 1950s housewife will get a reaction from me—and respond with, "Maybe I'll order those tables. You know, the ones I showed you yesterday?"

"Nope. Don't remember," he murmurs, but the flash of recognition on his face before his head dips down and his mouth closes over a peaked nipple says otherwise.

I inhale sharply, his teasing tongue sparking heat between my legs. "From that store in Seattle. The live-edge ones that cost a grand each, and you said a person would have to be a moron or certifiable to consider paying that much for a hunk of wood?" I smile as I quote him, weaving my fingers through his ash-blond hair as he shifts his attention to my other breast. Even from this angle, I can see the grimace he's trying to hide as I push his buttons. "I maxed my card out with that couch, so should I use your Mastercard or your Visa? Which one has more room—ah!"

I squeal with laughter as Jonah moves fast, maneuvering his big body to fit between my thighs.

"It's a fucking piece of wood that someone slapped lacquer on and screwed four legs to." He props himself up on his elbows, his brawny arms framing my face. "I'll make you one for free."

I have no idea if he could or not, but seeing Jonah riled up is too much fun. "But we get a shipping discount if we order both end tables and the coffee table together. I think it was two hundred to ship all three? Of course, I'd choose express, so it'll be more."

"Don't you *dare*, Calla. Those are a huge rip-off," he warns, his eyes flashing with grim amusement as he peers down at me.

Part of me wants to stretch the verbal foreplay a little longer. There's nothing but his cotton boxer briefs separating us, and I can feel how much he wants me pressed against the apex of my thighs. Also, these kinds of games always lead to fervent sex, which is exactly what I'm in the mood for.

My hips shift of their own volition, enticing him to make the next move.

With a knowing smirk, he obliges, shoving his underwear down with one hand and entering me without preamble, his lips crashing into mine.

I cry out with abandon into the cold, dark night, again and again, my jagged nails dragging across his back with each powerful thrust, my fists tightening through his hair, my legs curling around his hips.

Taking full advantage of the fact that there's no one to hear us for miles.

CHAPTER THIRTEEN

The snow machine's engine churns loud and ragged as I race along the driveway toward the plane, holding out hope that it doesn't die on the way, and that Jonah spots me coming before he takes off.

When the door pops open and Jonah hops out, I sigh with relief.

I come to a stop on the edge of the strip and wait for him to reach me, his strides long and purposeful, his brow furrowed.

"What's wrong?"

I cut my engine. "You didn't say goodbye." He was gone before I stirred this morning, leaving nothing but the smell of brewed coffee in his wake and the faint memory of a kiss against my temple.

"Yeah, I did. You were half-asleep."

"Then it doesn't count."

He reaches out with both hands to tug the sides of my winter hat down over my ears. The temperature is above average by a few degrees for this time of year, according to the local radio station, but there's still a wintry chill in the air. "I found your itinerary form. It's filled out and sitting on the desk."

"Great. Thank you." Agnes said to make sure Jonah never leaves without completing an itinerary. It has his destination and his flight plan. It's the only way I know where to direct help, should he not arrive. "What time will you be home?"

"Around five. It's far, and it took me a while to get that stupid thing goin' before I could clear the snow." He juts a chin toward the tractor, the cherry-red plow attached to the front wearing several dents. Another engine in need of a mechanic. "I'll call you on the satphone when I get to Unalakleet."

"*Right* when you get there?" I give him a threatening stare. Agnes warned me that one of Jonah's few faults around piloting is his inability to promptly and reliably check in. It's an odd and uncharacteristic difficulty for a guy like him, who prides himself on his communication skills.

"Yeah, yeah." He smirks, leaning in to steal a quick kiss, obviously in a rush to get off the ground.

I grab hold of his neck before he has a chance to pull away and hold him there, prolonging the feel of his lips against mine.

He's frowning curiously when I release him. "Am I gonna get this kind of goodbye every time I fly off somewhere?"

"Yes," I say with more seriousness than I intended. "Don't ever leave without saying goodbye to me. Please."

He studies my face a long moment. "I'm not gonna crash, Calla. I promise." His voice is soft, lulling.

"You can't promise that." Though I desperately want to believe him.

He leans in to kiss me again, this time more deeply. "Fine. But I *will* always find my way back to you," he whispers against my lips. "Love you. See you in a few hours."

"I love you, too." My heart sings as I watch him head toward the plane, a buoyancy to his step that I've come to recognize as Jonah when he's about to get in the sky—cheerful, energized, but also at ease, as if slipping into something comfortable. Today, he seems more charged than usual. Probably because he hasn't flown since the day we arrived almost two weeks ago. The longest he's ever gone without being in the air since he moved to Alaska, he noted last night, as we lay naked and out of breath, in postcoital bliss.

Suddenly, he spins to face me, walking backward. "By the way, what is that stuff in the fridge? In the jars?"

"Chia pudding. I made it for breakfast. Like it?"

"No." He screws up his face. "Not even a little bit."

I shrug. "It's healthy for you."

He waves off my words, turning his back to me. "You should go for a run!" he hollers over his shoulder. "You must have cabin fever by now!"

"Yeah! *Log* cabin fever, thanks to you!" A run isn't a bad idea, though.

He climbs back into the plane. Moments later, the engine purrs loud and then Veronica is taking off.

I huddle in my parka with my Canon pointed, capturing stills of Jonah's first official flight from our airstrip. Veronica's wings tip and wobble left and right as she climbs into the sky, until the plane is nothing more than a speck and I'm all alone, surrounded by snow and trees and an eerily calm silence.

The snow machine's engine chugs and coughs a few times in protest before finally coming to life. I coast back to our empty home, the panoramic view of the mountain range against the crisp, blue sky following me the entire way.

————

I slow my pace to a walk, my hot breath producing a billow of misty cloud as it merges with the icy air. My body is suitably warm from the three layers I dressed in, but my lungs burn from the cold.

Six kilometers.

That's the distance I had to run—past chained driveways and smokeless cabins—to spot signs of another living being.

I pause to suck back a small gulp of my water from my insulated bottle while reading the tacky array of corrugated signs ahead. They're nailed to a half-dead spruce tree on the right of the driveway leading into Trapper's Crossing Resort, and they promise everything: fully equipped two- and four-person cabins and spacious camping spots for rent, excellent fishing and dogsled rides, free Wi-Fi, a hot breakfast, and small-engine repair.

Phil boasted about the fishing in the network of rivers nearby. I imagine that's a seasonal thing. Right now, the rustic little cabins with red-tin roofs sit idly among the thinned-out trees, their curtains drawn, the snow-covered ground around them free of tracks.

Utterly lifeless.

The main building stretches off to the left—a simple, long and narrow log cabin capped with a red-tin roof to match the rest of the property's structures. A string of old, multicolored Christmas lights like the ones I dug up in my father's shed dangles across the front, from one end to the other. Above a solid forest-green door is a colorful decal of a fish and a sign that reads Ale House. In the window is a blinking neon Open sign. One lonely pickup truck sits in the lot, its burgundy color coated with dirt.

The sign for small-engine repair, which points with an arrow to a metal garage off to the other side of the main building, is what sparks my interest and spurs me toward the Ale House's green door. This might be a good place to service our snow machines, before we find ourselves stranded.

I stomp my shoes—specialty winter runners my mom gave me for Christmas—on the thinned doormat that reads Dogs Welcome, Humans Tolerated, and push inside.

Warmth and the smell of freshly brewed coffee envelop me as I allow my eyes to adjust to the darkness. The only light in the room is a pot light shining over the bar where a burly man in a camo baseball cap and a heavy gray sweater is hunched over a spread newspaper, staring at me.

"Hi," I say through a slightly ragged voice, still catching my breath. I'm out of shape, having only run a dozen times since leaving Toronto last December.

The man's appraising gaze skitters over me, all the way down to my shoes, as an AM radio broadcaster's voice chatters in the background, filling the otherwise empty, quiet room with news of this weekend's weather forecast. "You need somethin'?" Unlike Roy, this guy sounds like he might be from here, his voice carrying that folksy lilt. Like Roy, though, he isn't showing any hint of friendliness.

My stomach quivers with unease at the possibility that Jonah and I have found ourselves surrounded by assholes. "Yeah. I was out for a run and I saw the sign for small-engine repair?" I throw a thumb in the air, pointing out to the road. "Anyway, I was wondering if you fix snowmobiles. Sorry, snow *machines*. Still getting used to saying that," I mutter, more to myself. "We just moved in down the road and the ones that came with the place sound like they're about to die." When he frowns, I clarify, "Did you know Phil Gorman?"

"Oh, right. I heard he sold." His thumb drags over his short, brown beard. I'd put him in his midthirties. "That explains it."

"Explains what?" I dare ask, unsure whether I want to hear his answer.

Suddenly, his face splits into a wide grin, one that softens his hard features and makes him look five years younger. "The *four* bear bells. You're not from around here, are you?"

I can't help but laugh, even as my chilled cheeks heat from embarrassment and my hand instinctively reaches to cover the bell secured to the opposite hand's wrist. I also have one on each shoe and one attached to the bear spray chest holster. "I'm actually from Toronto. But I will have you know that a born-and-bred Alaska Native gave me these for Christmas and made me promise I'd never go running without them."

"And you should definitely use *at least one* of them. Especially when the bears come out of hibernation next month." He pulls himself off the counter—he's barrel-chested and only a few inches taller than I am—and comes around the bar to offer a hand that's rough, the nail cuticles stained dark. The hands of a mechanic. He's clearly the one doing the engine repair promised on that sign out front. "I'm Toby McGivney." His entire demeanor has shifted, much to my relief.

"Calla." My focus drifts over the interior again, from the wood-stove in the corner to the small tables, all covered in mismatched vinyl table cloths, to the kitschy signs and stuffed fish and countless photos of people and their fish secured to the walls with thumbtacks. If I had to guess, everything in here was salvaged from a basement or a garage sale or a thrift shop. Maybe even the dump.

There's a bulletin board on the wall near the door. It's littered with flyers and scraps of paper in every color, with phone numbers scrawled on the bottom, ready to be torn off and called. A good place to advertise a new charter plane company in town, perhaps. Tucked between a container of napkins and a bottle of ketchup is a small stack of laminated menus. I guess they serve food here, too. "So, do you own this place?"

He lifts his baseball cap to reveal unkempt sable-brown hair before resettling it on his head. "Yeah. Well, my family does. We live on the other side of this." He points to the wall and, I assume, the other half of the log building. "How do you like it in Trapper's Crossing so far?"

"It's really ..." I stall on my choice of words to describe the town. "So, what do you do around here for fun?"

"Leave?" he offers with a grin. "Nah, I'm kidding. There's a ton to do around here for the right kind of person. Mainly outdoors stuff. A lot of fishing, hiking ... The hunting's not great, though."

"That's too bad." I struggle to keep the sarcasm from my voice, and can't help but note his choice of words—*the right kind of person.* Has Toby already figured out that I'm all wrong for Trapper's Crossing?

He chuckles, an easy, warm sound. "Summer is busy as hell." Reaching for a full pot of coffee, he asks, "Want one? On the house."

"I'm good. Thanks, though." Above the coffee machine is a gilt-framed picture of Toby and another guy in camo hunting jackets, standing side by side over a moose carcass. Identical smiles plaster their faces. Cousins or brothers is my guess.

"Something stronger?" Toby offers mildly as he tops up his own mug, jutting his chin toward the five beer taps jutting out of the counter.

I laugh. "No, and do me a favor, if I ever jog here so I can drink, it means Alaska has finally gotten to me. Please put me out of my misery. Rope a steak to my neck and tie me to a tree for the bears."

His eyes widen with momentary surprise. "Uh ... So, what brought *you* here?"

"An airstrip." His heavy brow furrows and I laugh. "My boyfriend's a pilot and he wanted his own airstrip. And I needed to be within easy-ish driving distance to Anchorage." I shrug. "He fell in love with Phil's place and suckered me into it. It's been an adventure ever since."

"Right." Toby nods, adding quietly, "of course."

"Sara called!" comes a loud male voice from somewhere unseen. "Did you hear Jax got trampled by a moose?" A moment later, a round man with a long, bushy white beard and wearing mustard-colored overalls pushes through a two-way swinging, saloon-style door. He stops abruptly when he sees me—and the horrified look that must be splayed across my face. "Sorry, didn't mean to scare ya, dear. Jax is a sled dog.

"Oh." I'm not sure if that makes me feel any better.

"Yeah. He crossed paths with a mama and her baby during the Iditarod. Turned nasty fast."

"Dad, this is Calla. She moved into Phil's place. Calla, this is my dad, Teddy."

"Toby and Teddy. I think I can remember that."

"He plays Santa at the town's Christmas dinner every year. You'll never guess why."

Teddy gives Toby a playful slap upside the head before coming around to offer his hand. "Phil told me he was sellin' to a nice young couple. You're from Canada, right?"

I smile. "I am."

"From what I've heard, your husband's one heck of a pilot."

I don't correct him on the husband label as my chest surges with pride. I already knew Jonah was one of the best around—my father said as much. But to hear complete strangers say it feels somehow more authentic. "He is. He flew for Alaska Wild for ten years and now we're starting a charter business here." It still sounds surreal. Me, part owner of a charter plane company?

"Alaska Wild." Teddy strokes his beard in thought. Beneath the mass of wiry white hair, his cheeks are a rosy red, with tiny capillary lines marring his skin. "That went under, didn't it?"

"No." I say more abruptly than I intend, but Wild—and Wren Fletcher—did not fail. "My father had terminal cancer. He decided to sell."

Sympathy passes through Teddy's blue eyes. "Well, we get all kinds of people coming through here. We'll be sure to pass along your hubby's name if they mention lookin' for a ride somewhere."

"That would be amazing."

"Sure, sure. And Toby here also works on planes so if you're ever in need of a mechanic, you've got one right down the road."

"Really?" Running six kilometers has paid off. "Because we have Phil's Beaver and it needs some work if we want to get it in the air again." I suppress my goofy grin as I realize I've begun talking about planes by their model, as if it comes naturally to me. I remember a time when everyone around me did it, and it sounded weird.

"Well, good, then. Glad we can help each other out. That's how it works around here."

This is going so well, I decide to forge on. "Actually, if you don't mind, I'd love to leave some pamphlets here when I get them. Or even just put one up on that bulletin board."

"Sure, sure. You go on right ahead, dear. That's what it's there for." Teddy waves a hand toward it, then turns his attention to Toby, patting the counter. "Hunter called. He's bringin' his machine in. His engine died on him, out on the middle of the lake. They had to drag him all the way home."

"I guess I'll go stoke the fire in the garage. Get it warmed up." Toby studies his cracked hands. "You sure you don't want a coffee, Calla?"

"No. I should get back." Jonah will be calling soon.

"'Kay. Come by tomorrow and I'll look at that engine for you. Probably just needs some regular maintenance. Phil was never good at keeping up with that."

Teddy's cheeks lift with his jovial smile. "You swing by whenever you want, dear. I know Muriel would love to meet you. She and Colette used to spend a lot of time together, mucking around in the garden. And bring that pilot of yours here on Friday night! It'd be good to meet him." Teddy waggles his eyebrows. "It's *ladies'* night."

"Ladies' night," I echo, eying the giant stuffed fish on the wall next to a sign that reads "I love a big rack," before meeting Toby's gaze.

"There'll be exactly four old drunk men here on Friday," he confirms soberly. "No ladies."

"*One* lady," Teddy corrects him with an arched brow. "Your mother is always here."

"Except she ain't no lady," Toby counters. "She'll tell you that herself."

"Yeah, fine. No ladies," Teddy agrees with a chuckle. "Until May, that is, when this place wakes up. Anyway, you're welcome any time. And here ..." He grabs a scrap of paper and a pen and slaps it down in front of his son, stabbing the counter with his stubby index finger.

"You should have our number, in case of anything. This is a tight-knit community. We rely on each other whenever there's a need. Make sure you go out and meet your neighbors."

"We've already met Roy." I school my expression as best I can.

"Oh boy." Teddy gives me a knowing look. "Dealing with that guy is like flipping a coin and getting the wrong side nine out of ten times. Just remember, his bark is worse than his bite."

"His bark's pretty bad," Toby says, scribbling his number down.

"Yeah, Muriel and him have gone at it a few times. They haven't shot each other yet, but there's still time for that. He's not too keen on the tourism industry and ..." Teddy waves aimlessly around him. "Here we are, survivin' on it."

No wonder we've already started off on Roy's bad side. A good chunk of The Yeti's business will come from catering to tourists. Phil must have mentioned our plans to Roy during their livestock trade discussions.

I accept the slip of paper that Toby passes over with a smile. "Thanks."

"Uh-huh. Any issues, anything you guys need, you give us a call, dear." Teddy sees my bear spray and my bells and nods to himself. "Can never be too prepared."

"*Right?*" I'm beaming from this pleasant and advantageous introduction as I take one last long look around the Ale House, in all its mismatched glory. The place feels far less empty and uncomfortable now than it did when I walked in. These neighbors, though six kilometers away, more than make up for one curmudgeon.

"I'll be by tomorrow morning with one of the snow machines," I promise, heading for the door, my eyes grazing the antlers mounted to a plaque on the far wall. A thought strikes me. "Hey, you know what you guys could use in here?"

Teddy and Toby both frown and, while they look nothing alike, there is a definite family resemblance in that expression.

I grin. "Some animal heads for your walls."

CHAPTER FOURTEEN

I freeze, my heart hammering in my chest as I survey the trees, searching for whatever just moved within them. It's the second time in as many minutes that I caught motion from the corner of my eye. The first time, I dismissed it as my unease playing with my imagination. But when it happened again ...

There's something out there, in broad daylight, shifting among the shadows, and every hair along the back of my neck is standing on end.

Fumbling with the can of bear spray attached to the holster, I pull it out with shaky hands and grip it tightly. I march along the driveway toward home, the bells jingling with each step, blood pulsing in my ears, my head on a swivel as my eyes dart this way and that. I struggle not to run, in case whatever it is would prefer to give chase.

I'm so tense that when the satellite phone rings in my coat pocket, I yelp with surprise. "Jonah!" I yell into the phone.

"Hey. Landed in Unalakleet. What are you up to?" His voice is a bit distant and distorted. And I don't know if I've ever been so happy to hear it.

"I think I'm being followed," I say loudly, hoping the sound of my voice scares whatever it is away.

"*What?*" I can picture him, his brow furrowed, his hand on his hip.

"There's something in the trees. I went for a run and ..." I give him the thirty-second explanation, my words rushed as I keep walking toward the house.

"Okay. Relax, Calla."

"I'm trying to!" But I'm out here in the middle of nowhere, alone, with any number of wild animals surrounding me.

"Where are you now?"

"Halfway between the hangar and the house." I can make out the green of our roof up ahead. Jonah drove the truck down to the planes this morning. I wish I'd jumped in and driven it back.

"Okay, you're not that far. Keep walking. I'll stay on with you until you get home."

"Thank you." While he can't reach through the phone to protect me, talking to him has a calming effect.

"It's gotta be that fox. It must have a den around us."

"No. The fur wasn't orange. It was brown or gray, something like that." A fleeting blur of dull color. "And big."

"Probably the moose, then."

"Oh, yeah. Great. Did you know mama moose like to trample things?"

"Tell me about your run. Where'd you go?" he asks, steering me clear of that thought. It's a distraction tactic but I gladly accept it.

Jonah listens as I walk and talk, filling him in on the resort down the road, Toby and his father Teddy, my voice shaky as I keep a steady pace. By the time I reach the door to our basement walk-out, my fear has abated some. "Okay, I'm home."

"You good?"

"Yeah." And feeling slightly embarrassed, to be so frightened by something I didn't actually see. "I know there was something out there, Jonah."

"Maybe it was a yeti."

"Not funny."

"Whatever it was, it's probably already a mile away."

"I hope so."

His heavy sigh carries through the phone. "But you've gotta get used to this, Calla. You're living in rural Alaska. You're gonna see animals, especially if you're out running. But as long as you don't bother them, they won't bother you."

"I know. I just ... I know." Living at my father's wasn't anything like this. The threat of dangerous animals roaming around his house was low. You had to go up the river to find black bear and moose.

"'Kay. Gotta go. See ya in a few hours."

I slide the satellite phone into my coat pocket, looking forward to getting inside. I've pushed the key in the lock when I catch the sound of crunching snow behind me. The hairs stand on the back of my neck as I whip around, a scream curdling in my throat.

Zeke is standing ten feet away.

"Oh my God!" I exclaim, sinking against the door as relief bowls me over. "How did you get out?" I demand to know, my voice thick with accusation.

He answers with a loud bleat, marching toward me, his hooves leaving little round tracks in the snow.

"No. What are you ... Shoo!"

He ignores my wild waving hand, moving in to nip at the bell on my right wrist. I wrench it away and step back. He follows, making another attempt, flashing his gnarly brown teeth, the smell of his fur making my nose curl.

As much as I'd love to go inside and leave him out here until Jonah comes home to deal with him, there's a chance he'll wander off and get himself eaten. A vision of Jonah flying home to find a goat carcass lying on the runway hits me, and I know what I must do. "Ugh ... come on." I follow Jonah's boot prints from earlier around to the back of the house, checking over my shoulder several times to confirm that Zeke is following. The snow is deep, and by the time I reach the unlatched door to the pen—set some distance from our house—my ankles are chilled with snow and the hairs on the back of my neck have risen again with that eerie sense I'm being watched. I give a furtive scan around the trees but see no movement.

"Relax, Calla," I say out loud as I pull open the gate—the only part of the enclosure that isn't electrified—hoping my voice carries. Little good it does for my nerves.

Raccoon chatter answers a moment before Bandit's tiny black-and-gray triangular face pokes out from the door leading into the chicken coop. He's taken to his new home and companion more readily than we expected, though it'll be interesting to see if he's as willing to be penned up come the warmer weather.

"You let him out, didn't you?" I accuse Bandit, luring Zeke back in, avoiding the piles of goat poop littering the trodden snow. I push the gate shut behind him, taking a few minutes to figure out how to fasten the latch. If I didn't know better, I wouldn't believe that Bandit could have managed it.

With the goat safe within his cage, I pause, taking a moment to study the two faces staring back at me. I shake my head. "Is this my life now? Spending my days talking to a raccoon and a goat?"

Zeke bleats and kicks at the fence, rattling the entire structure.

I hurry inside, my gaze on the surrounding forest the entire way.

———

Jonah plows through the door, bringing a wave of blustering cold with him. Temperatures have dropped with the impending storm. "Hey, babe."

My eyes dart to the clock, though I already know the exact time, down to the minute. 7:04 P.M. Two hours from when he was supposed to arrive. Just one hour before sunset.

"Hi," I push through gritted teeth. When I heard the plane coming in thirty minutes ago, relief coursed through every fiber of my body. Now, I've also had a half hour to stew in my anger.

He tosses his coat onto the hook and kicks off his boots. "Somethin' smells good."

"Soup."

"Is that the mix you bought the other day?"

I hesitate, weighing civility over my irritation. I've learned that Jonah despises canned soup, so when I saw the packaged mix—spices and dry ingredients, with instructions to add meat and vegetables, as if from scratch—I threw three into the cart. "Yes," I answer crisply.

"Nice. I was thinkin' about that. Sounds like we're gonna get snowed in starting late tonight. I've gotta bring in a bunch of wood for us." He empties his pockets onto the desk—a wad of cash that I assume is from the run today, a fuel receipt, the satellite phone, and his iPhone. He leans in to kiss me.

I give him my cheek.

It might be the first time I've ever done that.

Finally, he seems to get the message. "Is something wrong?"

"Seriously?" I meet his blue eyes, his furrowed brow. Is he that oblivious? "You were supposed to be home at *five*."

"I got hung up talkin' to Bo Sterling and ended up givin' him a ride to Talkeetna. It was on the way."

"And you didn't think to call me?"

"I *did* call you. When I landed in Unalakleet. Remember? I stayed on the line with you for almost ten minutes while you walked home?"

"Jonah! I was two seconds away from calling the state troopers and reporting you missing!" My voice cracks.

"Oh, come on." He groans, pinches the bridge of his nose. "You're overreacting—"

"I am *not* overreacting, and you know it! The first day you're out there with me in the office and you were *an hour and a half* late!" Angry tears escape, hot as they roll along my skin. "You have an itinerary to follow and a satellite phone to call me with if you change plans. It's that simple! And it's the only way I know something hasn't happened to you." I brush my palm against my cheek, annoyed with myself that I couldn't keep my emotions in check. "I don't have a network of people to reach out to and track you down. I had to call Agnes!"

She's the first person I called, when the minutes kept passing with no sign or word from him and I wasn't sure if I should be worried. She told me to sit tight while she made a few calls and was able to confirm that Jonah had left the airstrip in Unalakleet an hour later than he was supposed to, with this guy Bo. That led her to calling a pilot at the Talkeetna airport—because she knows Bo and knows that's where he's from—and confirming that Jonah landed there.

But I don't know Bo. I don't know anyone who works at the Unalakleet airport or any pilots who might have been in Talkeetna at the same time as Jonah. All I know is that Jonah was supposed to be here by five o'clock and he wasn't, and he didn't call to tell me otherwise.

"You might have gotten away with doing this kind of stuff back when you were flying for my dad, but it's just you and me out here, and just me when you're gone, and I don't know who to call or how to check up on you, and I can't be calling Agnes to track you down every time you don't show up when you're supposed to. I can't be sitting here wondering if I should be worried, if I should be phoning someone, or doing something. Wondering if you're sitting in a pile of metal somewhere in the snow!" The berating words tumble out of me. "You know better than to change plans without calling it in!" He said as much, that day we left the safety cabin and went on a run to find the missing hikers. He knew my father and Agnes would be unhappy with him, but he did it anyway.

Now, as the person sitting by the phone, waiting for news from him—as the only person keeping track of his comings and goings—I appreciate what an asshole he is when he does it.

Jonah grits his jaw, and I hold my breath, expecting him to double down on why he's right and I'm wrong. "I'm sorry. I lost track of time."

His words instantly deflate some of my anger. An unexpected wave of relief washes over me as he drops into the other desk chair, wheeling closer to me. "Look at me, Calla."

I meet his sincere light blue eyes.

"I'm fine—"

"That's not the point."

"I know it's not." He collects my hands in his. "Bo and I got to talking. He runs a hiking expedition company. He wanted to know if I'd be interested in doing some runs for him this summer, getting people in and out of Ruth Glacier. His usual pilot is out with health problems and he heard I was doin' my own thing. We go way back."

"You go 'way back' with half of Alaska," I mutter.

"What can I say? I got excited. Bo's a great guy and he's nearby. It's income for the summer." He sighs. "I've been stressing about having enough business to bring in decent money."

"Really?" He hasn't mentioned it once, hasn't even hinted. "But, Jonah, you're going to do fine. Everyone loves you."

"They can love me all they want. Until we see steady work coming in, it doesn't mean anything. Keepin' these planes in the air is expensive, and I feel like I've been burning through savings faster than I expected to."

"Well, yeah. We just bought this house."

"I know. And I know there are a lot of expenses that come with that—new windows, a better bathroom, furniture. It's all money. And now there's a ton of things I have to worry about with the company that I didn't have to while I was working for Wren. I mean, I worried, but none of it was ever coming out of my pocket. It's just ... a lot for me to get used to, and sometimes I wonder if I dragged you all the way out here to watch me fail."

I notice how his shoulders sag with those frank words—either from the relief of finally admitting his worries to me, or from the weight of them. Either way, it's the first time he's openly wavered about The Yeti or about buying Phil's place. It's the first time he's shown anything other than steadfast confidence in his plan.

He bows his head. "Anyway, I got so wrapped up in Bo and the opportunity, I lost track of time. That was shitty of me and I'm sorry. It's not fair to you, and I'll try my best not to do it again."

Silence lingers in our tiny office with a prime view of the frozen lake and the mountain range beyond as I decide what to say, how to appease his worries. Anxious Jonah leaves me disconcerted. He's the steady, level-headed one in this relationship.

"First of all, you didn't drag me out here. I came because I wanted to. And if The Yeti fails, then *we* fail, because we're in this together. You and me. But we're not going to fail." I give his hands a squeeze. "Remember, I owe you half of what this place costs. You'll see that money soon. And when my inheritance comes in, I can cover us for—"

"No." He shakes his head firmly. "I told you already, that's your money. Wren didn't leave it for you to support my ass. Besides, he's already left me more than enough."

I give him a flat look. "You're being pigheaded."

"Maybe, but I don't care. *I* need to know that I can support us. That's important to me. If I can't make this work with what Wren gave me, then maybe I shouldn't be doin' it." He picks up a pen and then tosses it.

"You *should* be doing it." I believe that to my core. I've seen Jonah at Wild, and out flying around Alaska, helping people. If Jonah belongs anywhere, it's in the air.

But I also know that part of this is about ingrained male pride that makes Jonah who he is. Pointing out that I could probably support us for decades on what my father left me won't aid my cause here.

I reach for a pad and pen. "What's Bo's company's name?"

"Alaska Expeditions." He pauses. "Why?"

I jot it down. "I'm going to have to call him and get all his information, so we can properly invoice him. And I also need information about this doctor from Unalakleet so I can add it to the books. You can't just come in and drop wads of cash on my desk at the end of the day. That's not how you run a legitimate business."

Jonah lays his hand over mine, stalling my scribbles. "I'm sorry."

I swallow the last of my anger. "You're going to do fine, Jonah. You're not going to fail. I don't think you're capable of that."

He brushes strands of hair off my forehead. "And you can't live every day thinking I'm going to crash, Calla. It'll drive you crazy."

"I know." It's what drove my mother crazy, and a big part of what made her run in the end. "I guess it'll take time, to get used to this."

"I didn't help today, did I?"

I shoot him a glare, but there's no heat behind it.

He chuckles as he presses a kiss against my lips. "Any more animals hunt you down after we talked?"

"Still not funny," I warn. "By the way, Zeke got out. Bandit must have figured out how to unfasten the latch."

He shakes his head. "The little shit. I'll have to add something to stop him."

"Yeah, good luck with that." Tim and Sid, my mom and Simon's resident raccoons, have gotten into the secured compost bins too many times for me to believe there's anything that can keep a determined raccoon out. Or, in this case, in.

"So …" Jonah's hands smooth over my thighs with affection.

"How did you escape today's goat attack? It must have been a harrowing ordeal?"

I'm smiling now. "Shut up."

He pulls me onto his lap. "You know, I'm not used to being lectured by anyone, especially not a Fletcher." His lips are cool as they graze my collarbone, sending shivers through my body. "Coming from you, it's kind of hot."

I revel in the feel of Jonah's arms around me, my anger with him having vanished in mere minutes, as if it never existed. How ironic it is that there used to be a time when *not* wanting to throttle Jonah felt foreign. Now, holding even a shred of animosity toward him throws my entire world off-kilter.

"Find another way to get turned on," I say.

"I know of a good one. It works every time." His icy hand slips beneath my sweater, making me shriek.

"Oh my God, stop! You're freezing!" I cackle as I fight to wriggle free. But Jonah holds tight, grinning as his fingers coast over the small of my back and slide up my spine to unfasten my bra.

His phone rings then, and Agnes's name flashes across the screen.

"You need to answer that."

He groans. "No, I don't. She's gonna yell at me."

"Agnes, *yell*?" The woman is the most docile person I've ever met. I don't think she's capable of showing anger. I've certainly never seen it.

"In her own way." His palm weasels beneath my bra to cup my breast, his hand still a cold shock but less so than it was a moment ago.

"Too bad. Time to pay the piper." I grab his phone before he can stop me and, hitting Accept, hold it to his ear.

He glares at me. "Hey, Aggie ... yup ... uh-huh ... I know ..." His hand falls from beneath my shirt—the moment temporarily doused —and, collecting the phone from me, urges me off his lap. With a playful swat against my ass, he heads up the stairs.

And I breathe a sigh of relief that everything between Jonah and me is back to normal.

I take a few minutes to finish the post I was working on for *Calla*

& Dee—about Zeke and my disturbing, possibly imaginary, animal experience from earlier—and then save and close.

On a hunch, I open The Yeti's in-box, to see an unread email sitting at the top. When I see the subject line, I click through, scanning the details.

And let out a little shriek at the details of our first official website booking.

CHAPTER FIFTEEN

April

"All right, Miss Fletcher, turn right up here." The brunette woman shrewdly watches from over the frame of her bifocals, clipboard in hand, pen poised to strike her checklist, as I flick the signal switch and navigate our battered old truck down a side street in Wasilla.

When I woke up this morning—the day of my road test—and saw the plump snowflakes falling and the fresh layer of snow that had landed overnight, I panicked. But the plows have already been out to clear and sand the streets. Fifteen minutes into the test and, so far, I haven't slid through any stop signs or otherwise screwed up.

"See that Ford ahead?" She points at the green pickup truck parked on the side of the street, at the end of a driveway. "I'd like you to parallel park behind it."

"Okay." I say a silent prayer of thanks. She's kind—she's chosen a quiet street and a car with nothing behind it. I sidle up beside the truck, checking my rearview mirror. It's early in the day; no one is behind me.

I give the steering wheel of this big old beast a tight squeeze to calm my nerves. Why couldn't Phil have left us a small sedan? Taking a deep breath, I check my mirrors again and, shifting the truck into reverse, I begin backing up.

A flash of movement in my side-view mirror catches my eye before the truck suddenly jolts.

———

"How was that *my* fault?" I stare at the failed test form in my hand, close to tears.

"You can't hit anything during a road test. It's an automatic fail." Jonah lifts his baseball cap off his head, only to smooth his hair out and put it back on. "How did you *not* see a *moose?*"

"It came out of nowhere!" I burst.

His hands go up in a sign of surrender. "Whoa ... Okay. I'm just tryin' to understand how it happened," he says.

"I don't know how it happened! She told me to parallel park behind that truck. There was a driveway and this big hedge, and a tree ...," I sputter, trying to rationalize how a full-grown bull moose managed to make its way down the driveway and into the path of my reversing truck, without me spotting it first. "I was nervous, and I was looking for cars on the road, not moose?"

"Fair enough," Jonah says, but I sense he doesn't buy that.

"The tester didn't see it, either." A thought strikes me. "Unless maybe she did? Is *this* how they test drivers in Alaska? Do they put moose around town and get them to ambush you as part of the road test?"

Jonah chuckles and collects my hand in his. He gives it a squeeze. "No, babe. It was just a crazy fluke."

"Why did it have to happen to *me?*" I was ready. Jonah and I have been out every day practicing since I got my test date. Now I'm a twenty-six-year-old who failed her driver's test because she backed into a damn *moose*! I'll bet this has never happened in the history of road tests! I'll bet the people working at the licensing office are having a field day with this. Beyond my anger and disappointment, I'm embarrassed.

He starts the engine. "At least you were goin' slow. No one got hurt." The right taillight on Phil's truck is cracked, but the moose walked away. Literally. "It's no big deal. People fail their road tests all the time. You can rebook in a week and try it again."

And what if I fail again?

How much longer am I going to be stranded at our house, relying on snowy ditches to get around town in a snow machine while Jonah's working?

Jonah pulls out of the parking lot.

"Don't tell *anyone*. Please."

"Won't say a word."

"And don't you dare *ever* tease me about this," I warn in a severe tone.

The corners of his mouth twitch. "I would *never*."

Right.

He reaches over to rest his palm on my thigh. "Don't worry, you'll laugh about it one day."

"I have *a lot* of laughing to do later on in life," I mutter.

CHAPTER SIXTEEN

"Mark Sheppard said he's been keeping Jonah busy."

"Mark Sheppard, John McGee, Nathan Mineault ... Jonah's been flying somewhere almost every day that the weather cooperates." I rotate a cream crockery pot to check the price. And while he's been flying, I've been slowly building a list of contacts all over Alaska, for business but also in case he forgets to call me and goes off course again. So far, he has kept his word.

"I figured he would be. He knows a lot of people. I get someone coming into Aro every single day, asking about him."

I can hear the smile in Agnes's voice. She sounds like a proud mother. "I can't believe he was so worried. We've had a few bookings through the website already, too. He's taking a travel journalist around to a bunch of places next week. And a film-scout crew wants to book him for a solid week in early May." It's a good thing the days are getting long—the sun crept over the horizon at six today and it won't dip past it until ten tonight—because he'll need all the daylight he can get. It also means less time with him for me, when I can't tag along.

I try to keep myself busy on those days.

"So, what are you up to today?" she asks.

"I'm going to bake Jonah a chocolate cake for his birthday, even though he's refusing to take the day off."

"I've *never* been able to get him to celebrate his birthday," she confirms.

"So I'm learning. I have two days to convince him." I put the crockery pot back on the shelf—it has a noticeable chip in the lip. "And I'm doing a little shopping. Figured I'd check out this thrift shop in town." A double-wide trailer dropped in a barren parking lot about ten minutes from our house. With Jonah gone, I'm limited with how far I can venture unless I want to spend an exorbitant amount on an Uber to Wasilla.

I can't wait to get my license. I've rebooked the test for three weeks from now.

"*You're* in a thrift shop?" Agnes does a terrible job hiding the shock from her voice.

I laugh. "I'm trying to embrace this whole upcycling and recycling thing for decorating our place." Ever since Jonah divulged his worries about finances, I've been reining in all spending to avoid stressing him out. "It's a challenge. Gives me something to do." And it gives the gray-haired woman behind the counter who has been watching me intently (as if I'm going to steal something *from a thrift shop*) something to do. Maybe if I had come with Jonah the day he donated a truck's worth of trinkets and trash from our house, she'd seem friendlier. "How are things at Aro?"

"Oh … it's fine. Not the same, but nothing stays the same forever." Agnes sighs. "So, what about Diana? When is she coming up?"

"She's trying for August, but Aaron said he can't make it work and she won't come on her own." I try to not let my annoyance show in my voice. I shouldn't be surprised. We've never been able to manage so much as a girls' night without an appearance or at the very least, a phone call, from him.

"August will be nice. Fewer bugs," Agnes rationalizes. "And your mom?"

"They're saying Christmas." Another prick of disappointment that I'm trying to ignore, though I understand my mother's rationale —two Christmases in a row apart is not an option. "But Jonah's mom wants us to go to Oslo for Christmas."

"Maybe you should invite Jonah's family to Alaska, then."

I wince at the idea. "Yeah … I don't know." We have three

bedrooms, so we could *physically* handle both sets of parents under the same roof. Mentally and emotionally is another story. "Have you ever met Astrid?"

"No, I don't think she's been back to Alaska since they left all those years ago."

I wander down the cluttered aisle, pausing long enough to lift the metal handheld beater that I found buried in the depths of our corner cabinet. "I've said hello to her on the phone when they talk, but that's about it." Which is about once a month, the ten-hour time difference difficult to navigate. She *seems* nice—a soft-spoken woman with a heavy Norwegian accent who often cuts over to her native tongue, frustrating Jonah to no end, because he's lost the language over the years.

But what if she hates me? What if she doesn't think I'm good enough for her son? Would that bother him? I know it would bother me. Jonah and I will have been living together for a year by that point. Will we have broached the topic of marriage?

Will we be engaged?

An unexpected, fluttery wave stirs in my chest at that prospect.

"Well, a big family holiday in a log cabin sounds lovely to me." There isn't a hint of sarcasm in Agnes's tone. "Have you found anything good in there?"

"I have! An old ladder that I'm going to use for blankets and this big, ornate picture frame that I think I'll paint and turn into a tray." I'll need to come back when Jonah's home to load it into the truck.

"I can't wait to see the place."

I smile and nod, though she can't see it. "How's Mabel?"

"Oh …" There's a long pause. "She's okay."

An alarm bell goes off in my head. "What's going on?"

"Nothing for you to worry about. Just teenager stuff."

"Like?" I push.

Agnes hesitates. "She quit her job at Whittamore's last week, with no warning. And she's been hanging around with a couple kids that I'd rather she didn't."

"Sounds like teenager stuff," I say in agreement. Unfortunately, I'm not sure that Agnes has the demeanor to parent a kid through the rebellious stage, especially alone. "When are you guys coming to visit?" It's been more than a month since we moved here.

"Maybe in a few weeks? George said he was flying that way. We'll see. But I should let you go. Howard is wavin' me down. Have fun upcycling."

"Talk soon." I end the call and head toward the cash register, intent on paying for my finds and negotiating with the lady to keep them here until I can pick them up.

A low table in a corner catches my attention, stopping me dead in my tracks. I bend over to trace my finger along the edge of raw wood to confirm it's what I think it is, before moving the box of porcelain trinkets and lanterns cluttering its surface. Beneath is a beautiful, lacquered slab of wood, the rich markings in the grain mesmerizing. There are a few scratches on the surface, but I would think nothing that can't be buffed or sanded out. It's as fine a piece of furniture as the ones I was eying online, and it's being used as nothing more than a place to hold a dusty collection of trash.

"Is this for sale?" I call out, a thrill coursing through me.

The woman working at the counter ambles around, a hobble in her step as if her hip is giving problems—to ease up beside me. "Which one?" She reaches for a rusted lantern.

"No, not those. The coffee table."

"The table?" She peers over her reading glasses at it. "I mean, I guess I could sell it. Fit these things on a shelf somewhere else ..." Her voice trails as she looks around. The little thrift shop is crammed.

I'm wishing I hadn't insisted that Jonah take Phil's side tables to the dump. I could have offered them to her. But now's not the time for regret. My stomach stirs with excitement at the prospect of getting my hands on this piece. "How much do you want for it?"

"I dunno." She frowns, waffling with indecision—on price or parting with it, I can't tell. "How much you willin' to pay?"

Probably a hell of a lot more than she suspects. "Forty bucks?" I throw out and hold my breath.

Her lips twist in thought. "How 'bout fifty?"

"Done!" I blurt. Too fast, because the woman is peering at the table again, her eyes narrowed in thought. Probably wondering if she has something more valuable than she realizes.

"Well, I don't know. It *is* pretty handy to have around here for—"

"My mother had one just like it," I lie, schooling my expression as I think fast. "She's going to be *so happy* when I give this to her. For her birthday."

The woman studies me shrewdly. "What happened to hers?"

"House fire?" I nod somberly, even as my answer sounds doubtful. I can't believe I've resorted to making up a horrific tragedy. I'm going to hell, all in the name of a coffee table.

After another long pause of consideration, the woman turns and wobbles back to the counter. "You'll need to carry it out. I can't manage it with my hip actin' up and Kent is out."

"No problem." I press my lips together to contain my delight—I would have forked over ten times that amount—and dig the cash out of my wallet. Lifting the heavy, awkward table, I scurry out the door like a lucky thief.

Until I get outside.

"Shit," I curse under my breath, as I eye the old snow machine sitting in the parking lot.

I was so overjoyed, I momentarily forgot how I got here.

I spend five minutes cursing Jonah for being at work and the moose for stepping into the path of my truck during my road test while trying to maneuver the table onto my lap in a way that will allow me to steer. I finally accept that I have no way of getting this thing home without risking either getting pulled over by the cops or crashing.

I consider taking it back inside and asking the old woman to hold it for me but quickly dismiss that idea, afraid she'll wise up and change her mind. I would deserve it, given I lied to her.

Jonah won't be home for hours.

I call the only other person I know in Trapper's Crossing.

———

Toby's burgundy pickup pulls into the thrift shop parking lot fifteen minutes after I texted him. I haven't seen him in two weeks, since I brought the second Ski-Doo in for maintenance.

He eases in next to where I'm sitting on the seat of my snow machine, hugging my precious find. He cuts the loud, rumbling diesel engine and hops out, his boots landing heavy on the ground.

"Hey. Thank you *so much* for coming. And so quickly."

"Yeah. No problem. That engine can wait." He scratches the scruff on his chin—it's grown even longer in the weeks since I first met him—as he surveys the coffee table on my lap curiously. "You said you needed my help with something important?"

I pat the surface and drop my voice to a conspiratorial whisper. "This table is worth a shit ton of money and I scored it for fifty bucks, which is insane, but I can't get it back on my own and I don't trust that lady in there not to change her mind about selling it to me."

"Moving a coffee table. That's what you needed help with," he says slowly.

"Yeah." I wince sheepishly and wait for annoyance to appear on his face.

But he only shakes his head. "Why didn't you bring your truck?"

I groan. "Because I backed into a moose while parallel parking and failed my road test and, *I swear to God*, if you tell anyone, we are no longer friends!" Which would be more a punishment to me than him, I suspect, given he's my only friend in Trapper's Crossing and he's barely more than an acquaintance.

"You backed into a moose." His voice drifts as his features transform with a grin. "Hey, have you ever watched *Schitt's Creek*?"

"No? Is that a TV show?" The name does sound vaguely familiar. "Does someone hit a moose during their road test on it? Please tell me someone does."

"No. Nothing like that. This entire moment reminds me of that show for some strange reason." He shifts his attention back to the table. "Can I throw that thing in the truck bed, or do you need it Bubble-Wrapped and swaddled in blankets?"

"Do you *have* Bubble Wrap and blankets?" I'm only half joking.

He chuckles. "No. But maybe Candace does? She's the lady who runs the store."

"Why don't we try sliding it into the backseat?" Because my guilt over my lie is beginning to fester, especially now that I know her name.

He pops open the door and heaves the table off my lap. "Did you carry this out?" When I nod, he frowns curiously. "You're a lot stronger than you look."

"More like highly motivated. There's a table like this for a grand online that I've been dying to buy, but Jonah was giving me grief."

He lets out a long, slow whistle. "Don't blame him. Especially since someone probably donated it to her. That, or she found it in the trash."

I gasp, which earns his laugh.

Toby eases the table in carefully, whether to protect the table or his truck, I can't be sure. The table just fits. "Candace gave me my first pair of skates when I was nine. Found them out in a dump, good as new. Then every year after that, she'd show up at my door in October with a pair one size bigger. She did that right up till I was like seventeen. She's always been good to me."

"Well, I feel like a real asshole," I mutter.

Toby slams the door shut. "Why?"

I pull on my helmet. "Never mind."

He reaches for the driver's-side door handle. "Meet you back at your place?"

"Go slow!"

———

Toby is sitting on our front steps when I speed up the driveway a few minutes after him, the table already unloaded and waiting by the front door.

Zeke stands about twenty feet away, eying Toby, shifting on his hooves as if ready to bolt at any sudden movement.

I groan as I cut the engine. Jonah must have forgotten to coil the wire around the latch this morning when he went to feed them. It's the only thing Bandit can't figure out.

The second I slide my helmet off, the old goat trots toward me, bleating noisily.

"I tried catching him but he wouldn't come!" Toby hollers.

"Yeah, he hates men." I climb off the snow machine.

"You probably shouldn't let a goat wander around loose like that. He's easy pickin' for wolves and bears."

"We don't let him. Our raccoon keeps letting him out." I scowl as I sidestep to avoid Zeke nipping at my coat. At least I don't have the same visceral reaction when I see him anymore. It's worn off, replaced by general annoyance.

Toby's eyebrows arch. "Your raccoon?"

"Unfortunately. Be back in a minute."

"If you unlock the door, I can put this thing inside for you," Toby offers.

I toss him my keys and then head around back, scolding Zeke as he trots after me, a spring to his step. When the goat is safely back in his pen—for the moment—I make my way inside, happy for the warmth.

Toby is standing in our living room, his hands on his hips, taking in the relatively barren space.

I feel the stupid grin stretch over my face as I eye the coffee table he's already set in front of the couch. It looks even better than I'd imagined. The area rug I have sitting in an online shopping cart, waiting to be ordered, will finish off the room. "Thank you *so much* for helping me."

"Yeah. No problem." He waves it off. "Man, this place looks so different."

"That's the goal." In the weeks since we moved in, we've managed to refinish the floors on the main floor—a messy, six-day process that involved renting a sander, knee pads that didn't completely eliminate the ache, and gallons of stain and polyurethane that, despite wearing gloves, I'm still scrubbing off my skin. But the result is worth the effort. Our dark-walnut floors bring a fresh, new feel to the space.

"I should consider shopping at the thrift store more often. Or the dump, maybe." I toss my purse onto the kitchen counter. "Words I never thought I'd say."

Toby laughs and two dimples appear high on his cheeks, beneath his eyes.

"Do you think I could find matching end tables there?"

He shrugs. "Never know. Ask Candace to keep an eye out." He pauses. "Or you could see if Roy would make them for you."

"Roy?" I frown. "As in my crotchety old neighbor with the gun and the wolf dogs *Roy*?"

"Yeah. He's a carpenter by trade. Makes furniture in that big barn on his property. Probably wouldn't be too hard for him to make something like this. It's not complicated."

"That's why he was covered in sawdust," I murmur, more to myself.

"I've heard he's real good, too, but he doesn't take custom orders. He builds what he feels like and then sells them on consignment, here and there."

"That doesn't surprise me." I can't see him working well with people. "What's his deal, anyway?" Besides hating Jonah and me.

Toby shakes his head. "That's a nut no one's been able to crack yet. He's been here for years. Keeps to himself, building furniture, raising goats and chickens. Cheap as they come, too. Counts his pennies and doesn't give out of neighborly kindness. He's come out a few times to the town council meeting, if there's a big vote on the agenda. Usually ends with a shouting match between him and my mother out in the parking lot. A few years back, during one of those fights, he dropped from a heart attack. We had to rush him to the hospital. He was lucky he wasn't alone at home when that happened." Toby smirks. "Then again, I don't think he gets that worked up unless my mother is there to push his buttons."

The more I hear about Toby's mother, the more I'm curious to meet her.

"He's always been alone out there?"

"As far as I know. My mom said he was married before he came here, but his wife took off on him. Don't ask me why or how she found that out."

I sigh. "Probably because he's an asshole."

Toby grunts with agreement. "By the way, how're your snow machines working? My dad was asking about you the other day. We haven't seen you since you came in for the engines."

"Yeah, I know. I've been too freaked out to go running, even with the bear spray," I admit sheepishly. "I keep getting this feeling when I'm outside, like something's watching me." I didn't feel that eerie sense today, thankfully, but I've felt it more than once. "I know it sounds crazy."

"It takes some getting used to, I guess?"

"You mean, not worrying about being chased by a bear or stalked by a wolf or trampled by a mama moose every time I go for a jog? Yeah."

Toby chuckles.

"Anyway, I'm looking forward to getting my license so I can get to the gym again. I just wish it wasn't a half hour away."

His gaze roams the stone fireplace. He doesn't seem in any hurry to get back home to his engine.

"Did you come here a lot before?"

"A few times. Mainly to fix problems on Phil's plane." He wanders over to the bookshelf where I've lined up framed family pictures—the ones from Jonah's place and a few of my own. "My mom and Colette were pretty close. She'd call me over to help, especially in the last few years, with Phil not able to handle so much."

"So, why are you working on small engines when you know how to fix planes?" I ask curiously. Jonah and Toby *really* need to meet, and soon.

He shrugs. "Not a good setup for workin' on planes at the resort. I've helped out a bit at Sid Kesslar's, over at Mile 68 off the highway, but between you and me, he rips off his customers. I can't stand the guy. Anyway, it wasn't really part of the plan, me bein' back here."

"Why'd you come back, then?"

"Shit happened." He picks up the picture of Diana and me. "Your sister?"

I'm momentarily distracted. "Best friend. I'm an only child." Though there was about five minutes last summer when I had convinced myself that my father had a secret daughter—Mabel. "What about you? Any sisters or brothers?"

"One brother. Deacon."

I recall that framed hunting photo on the wall in the Ale House. "Older? Younger?"

"Younger. By two years."

"Does he help run the resort, too?" If he does, I haven't seen him around.

"He used to," Toby says, setting the picture back. "Before he disappeared."

I frown, replaying that in my head in case I heard it incorrectly. "*Disappeared*, like, he moved to Miami and you guys don't talk anymore?"

Toby's gray eyes flash to me, a hint of grim amusement in them. "Like he went out hunting one day five years ago and never came back."

A chilling feeling washes over me. "Oh my God. Is he ... I mean ... do you think he might still be out there, somewhere?"

"Nah. Not alive, anyway. We spent months looking for him. State troopers, local Search and Rescue, volunteers."

My stomach has sunk to my feet. I feel like I'm prying—I don't really know Toby—but I can't help myself. "What happened?"

"Well ..." He perches against the arm of the couch, folding his arms over his chest, as if settling in for a story. "Him and two of his buddies drove up to a spot outside Fairbanks for the hunt. I tore up my MCL earlier that year and was recovering from surgery, or I would have gone with him. Anyway, the weather was shit and they weren't having any luck. The other guys wanted to head back to camp early but Deacon, that stubborn ass, stayed out, alone. Said he'd be back to camp within a few hours and call them over the walkie-talkie if he bagged anything, so they could come out and help him dress it."

I assume "bagged" and "dress" are hunting terminology for killing and cleaning, but I don't interrupt to ask questions, too engrossed in the tale.

"When he didn't come back after dark and he wasn't answering his radio, they went out to look for him. Found his ATV right where he'd left it. They tried hiking in, but it was a good mile and a half off the trail, and dark. That's when they reported him missing. They went out again at daybreak, but they couldn't find him."

"They found *nothing at all*?"

"No, they found his radio, lying on the ground. And footprints."

His brow furrows as he studies me. He hesitates. "His and a brown bear's."

A sinking feeling stirs in the pit of my stomach.

"There were some empty casings lying around. It looked like he fired a few rounds before he took off. They followed both sets of prints all the way to the river where they stopped."

"And then?" I dread the answer.

Toby shakes his head. "They combed the area but never found Deacon or the bear. The way the ground looked, they figure he stumbled down the embankment and fell into the river, got carried away. That, or the bear caught up to him while he was trying to cross. There's usually a body when that happens, though."

"*When* that happens?" I echo, my voice a touch shrill.

"*If* it happens," he amends, smiling as if to ease my panic. It doesn't reach his eyes.

"I'm ..." I shake my head, unsure what to say. "I'm so sorry."

He nods slowly. "It's not the craziest thing in the world, for people to go missing up here. It happens more than you think. Especially when people aren't smart. Deacon, he wasn't smart. You don't go out there alone."

Silence lingers as I search for the right words. I've caught myself imagining what Agnes went through, when Mabel's father didn't arrive at his destination. That fleeting worry, as I kiss Jonah goodbye before he climbs into his plane, that it'll be the last time I kiss him, is always present. But I've never imagined Jonah going out one day and disappearing without a trace. My stomach roils at the thought. "That must be hard, to not have any answers after so long." No sense of closure. No peace.

"Yeah." Toby scratches at his bristly beard. "My mom still drives up there and goes out looking for him every summer. I think she's accepted reality, but she's too stubborn to give up completely."

"He's her child."

"And Deacon knew what he was doin'. There're people who have no clue how to survive heading out into the middle of nowhere. Thinkin' Alaska's like any other trail hike."

"I don't know how anyone would go out there thinking that." I don't know what else to say except, "I'm sorry about your brother."

"Yeah ... So that's why I ended up coming back to Trapper's Crossing. Deacon was the one who wanted to take over the family business. I was workin' at a shop in Anchorage with plans to go out on my own one day." He shrugs. "Now I'm back here."

Much like my father came back to Alaska Wild. Though, it was always the plan he'd run the company eventually. But tragedy struck, forcing him home sooner than he'd expected.

Clearly, Toby feels the same sense of obligation to his family's legacy. But is he doing so willingly, or because it is expected of him?

Sometimes I wonder what *I* would have done, had my father—in those final weeks, once our relationship had been mended—asked that I carry on the Fletcher family business. Barring the fact that I'd have no idea how—Agnes and Jonah would surely have helped—how would I have felt, pressured into following my family's footsteps rather than having a choice in my own path?

Toby heaves himself off his perch on the couch. "I didn't want to tell you about it, given how nervous you already seem to be around here, but I figured you would have found out, anyway."

And there I was, on the first day we met, making jokes about tying meat to my neck and leaving me out for the bears. No wonder he had that weird look on his face. I unwittingly stuck both feet in my mouth.

"Do me a favor?" Toby wanders over to the bookshelf and holds up the wildlife book Jonah gave me for Christmas. When he speaks again, his tone is lighter. "Promise you won't go off in the bush alone because you've read this cover to cover."

"I can't even walk to the pen to lock the goat up without thinking something's waiting in the trees to run out and kill me."

He chuckles, sliding the book back in its spot. "You have a bit of a wild imagination, don't you?"

And stories like the one about Toby's brother certainly don't help, but I keep that to myself.

I'm about to offer Toby a drink when a hard knuckle raps against the glass window panel of our front door, startling me.

"*See?* Don't worry. I won't be heading into the forest alone!"

Toby's laughter trails me as I head to answer the door. A courier waits outside, bundled in a heavy coat. He grips a thick, legal-size envelope from my father's estate lawyer and a signature machine in his hands, the tips of the gloves cut off, his naked fingers poking out.

A strange sensation overwhelms me as I scrawl my name in the box and collect the envelope, mumbling my thanks.

I know what this is.

In the months that followed my father's death, I've faced a wide range of feelings when talking about my inheritance—shock, guilt, sadness, discomfort, regret—but at no point would I say I was "excited" for it. It felt wrong to look forward to the day the money hit my bank account, given the cost—my father's life, my family's legacy.

But now I'm back in Alaska, living a life that I believe would make my father happy and proud, and it's in part because of the money he left both of us.

I feel a thrill coursing through my veins over all the new possibilities.

CHAPTER SEVENTEEN

"They found the bear sitting on top of the hiker, *eating* him!" My eyes are wide with horror as I read the rest of the report out loud. "And then it attacked and mauled *three* of the searchers!"

Jonah's electric toothbrush buzzes through the cracked bathroom door, but I know he can hear me.

I continue scanning the list of fatal bear attacks, unable to shake the heavy feeling that's been clinging to me since Toby left this afternoon, after telling me about his missing brother. "This other bear? It dragged the guy out of his tent at night. And then it mauled two other people before someone shot it!" I scan further. "Oh my God. This one? It broke into their cabin and—"

"Okay, you're done here." Jonah suddenly appears to shut my laptop and strip me of it in one smooth movement. He sets it on the dresser, well out of my reach.

"Don't *ever* try to get me to sleep out there in a tent with you, Jonah. I don't care if you have three loaded guns under your pillow, I'm not doing it."

He sighs heavily, his broad, shirtless back hitting the mattress as he falls into bed. "You're not gonna get eaten by a bear."

"I'll bet they thought the same thing." I point accusingly at my laptop.

"How many people did that list name? Like, twenty? Thirty? Over the last ten years? In *all* of North America?"

"That they know of! And that's Wikipedia. It's not gospel."

He turns onto his side to face me. "Do you know how many people die in car accidents in the US every year? Try thirty *thousand*. At least."

"Yeah, I'll take death by car crash over bear mauling for a thousand, Alex."

He rolls his eyes. "You're being dramatic."

"Am I? Toby's brother went out and never came back. How does that happen?"

"Did Toby say his brother died from a bear attack?"

"He didn't *not* say it. There was definitely a bear involved."

Jonah shifts onto his back again, his gaze on the ceiling. "There's a hundred different ways Alaska can kill you."

"Yeah. Not comforting."

"A lot of people go missing every year."

"Two thousand people. I looked it up. Twice your country's national average. *Again*, not comforting."

"Also *your* country, now."

"And Toby's brother had a gun!"

"Remind me to thank Toby for telling you this story," Jonah mutters.

"He didn't want to, but I would have heard about it eventually."

"And now you're gonna be freaked out every time you step outside, thanks to him."

"I already was!"

He groans. "Calla, you've never actually seen whatever has you spooked. You haven't even seen the fox and that thing is around *all the time*."

"Exactly my point. Who knows what else could be out there? I was doing some reading this afternoon, and I want to get cameras."

He gives me a flat look. "*Cameras?*"

"Yeah. Motion-sensor cameras. Tons of people use them to see what's coming onto their property. Even in Alaska." And now that my bank account has more zeros than I know what to do with—my jaw dropped when I checked to confirm the deposit, because even though I knew it was coming, actually seeing it was a shock—I feel no need to worry about stressing Jonah out over finances anymore.

He pinches the bridge of his nose as if pained. Or possibly annoyed. "Did you burn something in the kitchen today? Smells like something burnt down there."

"Uh ... yeah. I was trying to bake something, but I went wrong somewhere." I smile sheepishly. What went into the oven was a promising birthday cake for Jonah. What came out of the oven was a flat, goopy mess that had dripped over the sides to burn on the oven floor.

He chuckles. "I don't have to fly until tomorrow afternoon. I was thinking we could drive up to Talkeetna."

"Do they sell cameras in Talkeetna?"

He seizes my waist and pulls my body onto his with little effort. My elbows find a natural spot on either side of his head. "I have no idea. If it makes you feel safer, get cameras. You can watch moose trip the motion sensors all day long, for all I care. You'll probably go years without seeing a bear around here."

"And what if you're wrong? What if one comes and you're not around?"

"That's why I keep tellin' you that you need to learn how to shoot a gun." He kisses my jawline. Such a contradictory move for his words.

"And I keep telling you that I hate guns."

"Fine." He smirks. "Then I guess Zeke'll protect you."

"That stupid goat's going to get eaten one of these days."

"Better him than you." He smooths his hand down along my spine to settle on my backside, where he fills his palm with a squeeze, and pulls my body tighter against him. Beneath me, I feel him hardening.

"We're hiring Toby to be our mechanic," I say, before I lose my chance to bring it up tonight. "He came back to help run their resort because his brother died ... disappeared ... whatever. Anyway, his passion is plane engines, but he let that go to come back and help his family here, and, I don't know, I feel like it'd be good to use him for the planes."

"He's gotta be a good mechanic. I'm not messin' around with any clowns that might put me into the ground."

"The snow machines are working great."

"Those aren't planes." Jonah sighs. "I guess I should probably go and meet this guy soon, then."

"Yeah. Definitely. You'll like him."

"Really? 'Cause you're about to turn our peaceful log cabin into a fucking military base with all your surveillance, thanks to him, so I don't think I like him too much right now." He hooks his thumbs on the waistband of my pajama bottoms and begins drawing them down, ending our conversation.

CHAPTER EIGHTEEN

May

"The guy's coming out on Monday to quote us."

Jonah tosses the heavy brochure on the kitchen counter. "I told you already—I can screen in the porch. It's just two-by-twos and a couple rolls of screening."

"And you can make it look like *this*?" I tap the picture of the log cabin—much like ours, only far nicer—with the enclosed porch off the front.

"Who cares what it looks like? It'll keep the bugs out. That's what you want, isn't it? And at a tenth of the price that guy's gonna charge."

I glare at him. "Hi, have we met? *I* care what it looks like. And when were you going to do all this, anyway? You've been gone all day, every day, for the past week!" I shouldn't complain because it's great for the company and has been keeping me busy with paperwork and collecting referrals, but I feel like I only see him when he's sliding into bed at night.

"I don't know! The next time the weather's too shitty to fly. It's supposed to be overcast on Monday."

"This is more than a day's work. Are you going to be able to finish it before the hot tub goes in?" I ask doubtfully. "Because those guys are coming in two weeks."

"Are you kidding me?" Jonah groans. "You did *not* order that already."

"I told you I was going to!" I had added it to my list of conditions for agreeing to the move—an ever-growing catalogue compiled mostly after mining "log cabin" hashtags on Instagram, searching for decorative inspiration.

"That thing was *nine grand!*" His booming voice carries through the house, his expression offering not a hint of humor.

"So what? We can afford it!" Which is the same thing I said to him when I climbed into the empty shell in the showroom and imagined us relaxing in it on our porch while we gazed out over the lake and the mountain range. "What we can't afford is for me to go insane cooped up in this house once mosquito Armageddon arrives." From what the lady in the grocery store said, it's coming soon. Agnes has already warned me that, as bad as I thought the bugs were in Bangor, they're a hundred times worse here, near the lake and among the trees.

Jonah shakes his head. "Wren didn't leave you all that money so you could piss it away on custom screens and hot tubs and a *fucking* three-thousand-dollar fake antler chandelier!" He throws an accusatory hand toward the large box that arrived last week sitting by the fireplace. The local electrician is coming to hang it tomorrow. "You said you didn't want it lookin' like a hunt camp in here!"

"Hunt camps don't have three-thousand-dollar chandeliers!" I yell as my indignation flares. "I am *not* pissing my money away. And he left it to *me*, Jonah. I don't need your approval on how to spend it!"

"I'm not saying you need my approval," Jonah begins through gritted teeth, as if struggling to control his temper.

A heavy knock sounds on the side door, interrupting our shouting match.

Jonah glares at it. "Is that another delivery guy? Jesus Christ, woman, what *else* have you bought?"

"I don't know! Let's find out!" I have no idea who that could be at eight A.M. and why they'd come to the side door—the barista machine I ordered couldn't be here this quickly. Maybe it's the new bedding. But Jonah's attitude is making my insides burn. I storm down the hallway with him in hot pursuit and throw the door open, ignoring the fact that I'm in my pajamas.

A short, heavyset woman with a helmet of tight gray curls and a hard, weathered face waits outside.

By the way her shrewd gaze flits back and forth between us, I'll bet she heard the shouting match.

"Hello. Can I help you?" I ask in a forced polite tone.

"You must be Calla." Her voice is huskier than I expected. "You're even prettier than the guys said you were." The moment she smiles— a wide, feature-transforming grin that reaches her gray eyes—I know exactly who she is.

"You're Toby's mom," I say before she can introduce herself. The resemblance is uncanny. And I'm even more embarrassed that she's a witness to our fighting.

She thrusts out a rough-skinned hand wrapped in bandages. A hand that sees daily manual labor. "Muriel." She turns to Jonah, sizing him up with a single astute look. "And you're the pilot."

"I am. Come on in." Jonah settles a hand on the small of my back —as if we weren't just screaming at each other—and holds the door open for her to shimmy through. She heads down the long, narrow hall without pausing to remove her boots, leaving a trail of mud on our freshly finished wood that I'll have to mop up the second she leaves.

"So, he's been tellin' his mom how pretty you are," Jonah whispers.

I ignore him and move ahead, my anger set to a low boil for the moment.

"You two have been busy." Muriel surveys our house as she ambles into the kitchen, her jeans rolled at the cuffs to fit her short legs. She seems comfortable in our home, which would make sense seeing as Toby said she was close with Colette. It must be odd, though, to have two strangers invade your friend's space, especially when that friend died so suddenly. "I'm guessing Phil left you with quite the mess."

"He didn't take much with him, that's for sure," Jonah confirms.

He didn't take *anything* with him, I silently correct.

She shakes her head. "I offered him help but he refused, obstinate old ass. He was never the sentimental one, though. It was all her." She pauses another moment, lost in thought, and then pulls a page out of her pocket. "Toby said you're afraid of goin' out running on your own, so I've got here the name of two gals who run on Saturday mornings. Jodi and Emily. They know the area well. Meet 'em outside the Burger Shack at eight A.M. tomorrow. They're expectin' you." She caps that off with a smile that's so contradictory to her harsh tone.

"Thanks. That's … nice of you," I stammer. And presumptuous that I don't have plans, that I would want to join a running group.

"You can't live in Alaska and hide inside like a mole. You'll go mad," she says matter-of-factly. "How's your garden lookin'?"

"I … uh … don't have one yet?"

"Sure you do. That big space with the eight-foot fences out back! It can't go to waste. You've gotta get the soil ready for planting. The days are long but the summers are short." Her eyebrows arch, as if waiting for an answer.

I can't help but hear the hidden meaning in her words and that look. *If you can't get over your fear of wildlife and take up gardening, then you may as well reconsider living out here.*

"Yeah, we've been so busy with the house and the charter business, we haven't been back there lately." But do I dare admit to this woman that I have no plans to become a gardener?

"Okay, come on. Let's go and see what state it's in." She marches for the side door, her heavy boots clomping on the floor, leaving more muddy prints.

"Right *now*?" I peer down at my pajamas. "But I'm not dressed."

"Who you got to impress? The goat?" She snorts.

"Uh … I …" I'm momentarily stunned, unsure how to respond. But she's Toby's mother and one of only a few neighbors, I remind myself. Someone I might need help from in the future. And a woman whose son disappeared five years ago, never to be seen again.

My annoyance softens with that reminder.

I just need to nod and go along with this charade until she's gone.

She gives Jonah a broad smile. "It was nice to meet you. Make sure you get Toby in here if you have any issues with your planes. He's the best mechanic around, and I'm not sayin' that because I gave birth to him."

"I'm planning on giving him a call in the next few days," Jonah promises.

"Good. Come on, let's go, Calla. I haven't got all day!" She caps off her request with a wave of her hand, one that tells me I'm coming with her whether I like it or not.

I shoot a glare at Jonah—he's still grinning, amused by Muriel's stern demeanor or by my visible discomfort over my predicament, or maybe both—and head for my rubber boots.

———

"There's a good boy." Muriel pulls chunks of banana peel from her pocket and tosses it over the fence to Zeke. "You're looking a little thin. Aren't your new owners takin' good care of you?"

Zeke bleats and rushes to gobble it up, as if he hasn't eaten in weeks.

"Jonah comes out every morning and night to feed and check on him," I say, a touch of defensiveness in my tone.

"Well, no wonder he's not eatin'. You know, Zeke doesn't like men." Again with that matter-of-fact voice.

"He doesn't mind being fed by one." Something tells me my childhood horror stories wouldn't earn any sympathy here.

She harrumphs, and it could be in agreement or disappointment with me—I can't read this woman—but then says, "Probably the stress of change. First Colette gone, then Phil, though Zeke never liked ..." Her words drift as her eyes go wide, locked on the triangular face watching us from the tiny opening. "Is that a *raccoon* in your chicken coop?"

My stomach tightens instinctively. There's no mistaking the displeasure in her tone. "Yes?" He's taken to his new home. Though he has free range of the entire pen, he usually lingers inside the coop.

"You can't have a *raccoon* living in your chicken coop. How are you gonna have any chickens?"

We're not, I want to say, but admitting that would somehow feel like another strike against me. So, I say the next best thing I can think of because I'm tired of bearing the brunt of Muriel's disapproval and I'm still angry with Jonah. "Bandit is Jonah's pet."

Maybe she'll scold him, too.

The jerk would probably enjoy it, though.

Another harrumph, and then she continues traipsing through the boggy, brown grass as if this property is her own, leading the way to the spacious clearing and the enormous rectangular enclosure that Phil put at about a quarter acre in size. "That's your greenhouse." She points out the small, dilapidated structure on the far end of the pen —the wooden frame missing pieces, the plastic sheeting tattered and dangling. "Bad storm came through and twisted it all up last summer. Never got around to fixin' it in the fall." She flips open the lid on a panel next to the gate and flicks a power switch. "This is a voltmeter," she announces, pulling a black rectangular box from her plaid coat pocket.

"I think I found one of those." I put it in the hallway closet with everything else that Jonah said we couldn't throw out, but I have no idea what to do with.

"Course you would have. You'll want to make yourself a little garden kit, so you have it at the ready when you head out here every morning."

I struggle to school my expression. *When I head out here every morning?*

"And check your fences often." She taps it against the electric wire and watches the screen. Nothing appears. "See? Not workin'. They've been having issues with this one and the animal pen for years. I remember foxes got into their chicken coop one winter years ago and slaughtered the lot of them. Another year it was a wolf. Jonah'll need to fix this soon, or you'll have critters in here mowin' down everything, and you don't want to lose an entire summer's worth of work overnight."

Does Jonah even know how to fix an electric fence? Should I be embarrassed that I moved across the continent for a guy and I can't answer that?

She tucks her tool back into her pocket. "I harvested and cleaned the beds up as best I could last September. Buried the leftovers for some good compost. Colette was always good at keepin' on top of the weeds so there wasn't too much of that, at least. And I didn't get a chance to amend the soil, but we can do that once the ground warms up a bit more. Spring's takin' its sweet time comin' this year."

My attention wanders beyond the garden to where patches of snow persist within the thicket, despite the warmer temperatures. The last claims of winter, holding on tight. "When do you think that'll be?"

"Another week or so, if we don't get too much rain." Reaching the gate, she pauses to inspect a cinch in the wire. "Before you have that hot tub in and screened porch of yours finished."

Muriel must have been standing by the door for a moment, listening, before she knocked.

I pretend to survey the patch of dirt within the fencing but really to hide the heat in my cheeks. "I don't know the first thing about gardening," I admit, wishing my mother were here to navigate this conversation so I wouldn't feel so inept.

"You'll know more than the first thing by the end of summer," Muriel assures me, emphasizing her determination with a firm nod, as if she's made it her personal mission. "You'll need to pick up all your seeds at the local Feed & Mill. We'll get your little greenhouse set up for next year's seedlings but for this year, I should have some extra lettuce, peppers, onions, and tomatoes you can use. Oh, and cabbage, for your sauerkraut. You've been saving all the jars from the cellar, right?"

"We have," I confirm. Mainly because I'm not sure what to do with them, so I just put them back on the cellar shelves after Jonah's done polishing off their contents. But right now, under the perpetually disapproving eye of Muriel, I'm relieved I've done something right.

"Smart girl. Good. Makes it easier when you go to do all your preserving."

Right. My preserving. I recall the day I walked into Agnes's house last summer while she was pickling vegetables from Whittamore's —payment to Mabel for her labor. Her kitchen was a war zone of jars and dirty pots, her skin and shirt stained purple from beets, despite having worn gloves. My nose curled from the vinegar and cloves in the air. I remember asking myself why anyone would go to all that trouble when they can go to the store if they want a jar of beets.

"Colette's strawberries are over there, under the straw. That's the trick with them. You need three to five inches of mulch to over-winter the plants."

I follow her stubby finger to the far corner. "That looks like a lot of strawberry plants." The patch takes up at least a quarter of this entire garden.

"Colette loved her strawberries. Sold almost forty quarts at the farmers' market last year!" Muriel says proudly.

I have no idea how much forty quarts is, but I can guarantee it's far more than a person like me—who doesn't eat strawberries—could ever want. "So, there *is* a local farmers' market where I can *buy* fresh produce?" As in, I can avoid all this work?

"Yup. Every Friday afternoon from end of June till September in the community center. They sell all kinds of stuff. Produce, local honey, jam. Colette made wonderful jam. We served it at the Ale House for breakfast. People can't get enough of it. If this year's growin' season's as good, I reckon you'll be elbow-deep in mashed berries for a good three weeks." Muriel's head bobs up and down. "Don't worry, though. I'll help you with your first batch, so you get the hang of it."

"Thanks," I murmur, though I feel anything but thankful. Yet again, Muriel assumes I intend to spend my entire summer gardening and preserving.

She doesn't clue in to my reluctance. Or maybe she does, but she refuses to acknowledge it. "We need to make sure things keep growin' in here." Her brow is furrowed as she studies the barren dirt again. Her best friend's garden, that she laid to rest after she laid her best friend to rest.

Maybe that's what is at the root of Muriel's dogged determination to mold me into the consummate gardener—loyalty.

"I best be gettin' going. I promised Teddy I'd make him an omelette." She makes to step away but then stalls, her lips twisting, the wrinkles around her mouth more pronounced. "This ain't none of my business—"

I struggle to school my expression. Sentences that start with those words are never welcome.

"But I'm guessin' Jonah likes to have control."

Hearing her use the word "control" to describe Jonah makes my irritation flare. A controlling man is *not* appealing. "He likes to have his say. It's not about control," I correct. Jonah is assertive and he knows what he wants. Those are appealing qualities.

Her head tilts in a "you silly, naive girl" way. "Men like him don't do well havin' no say over things like finances."

She's Toby's mother, I remind myself, biting my tongue and forcing a smile.

"You know that resort? All those acres we own?" She juts her thumb in the direction of the Trapper's Crossing resort. "That's *my* family's property. Teddy married into it. But the day I told him that we were gettin' married or to quit wastin' my time, I knew it would become as much his as mine. I still had a hard time lettin' go, seein' him as having an equal say. Took a few years to get used to the idea of that, especially for a stubborn broad like me. And I'll tell ya, those were some hard years." She shakes her head. "But there is no labeling 'mine' and 'yours' once you're married."

"We're not married."

"And you won't ever be if you two let a big pile of money get in the way of it happening." She points at the house. "It seems you've already made some big commitments to each other, buying this place, all the way out here. Rings and a ceremony … that's all for show. It's the day-to-day stuff that makes a real marriage, and out here where the winters are long and cold, you don't wanna be at odds with your other half, believe me. You'll need him." She smiles knowingly. "I get what I want when it comes to the resort. Teddy thinks he's runnin' things around there, and I let the fool think it. Everybody wins." Her pat against my shoulder is firm, and yet somehow comforting. "Do me a favor and listen to a willful old goat who had to learn the hard way."

I find myself nodding dumbly.

———

"You two need to come down to the Ale House at the end of the month!" Muriel hollers, throwing a leg over the seat of her ATV. Behind it is a metal rack and on that rack sits a long, slender gun. The sight of it is unnerving. "It's our annual chili cook-off. A good way to meet locals. The seasonal folk start lurking then, too. Comin' up to open their cabins."

"I like chili," Jonah announces from his spot on the covered porch, leaning against the post, his shapely arms even more pronounced folded over his chest.

"I'll have Toby send a list of everything we need to prep the soil. You go on and get that stuff for Calla. She's got *a lot* of work ahead of her this summer."

Jonah grins, enjoying this far too much. "I'll be happy to help Calla with her garden in any way I can."

She waggles her finger at me. "And don't forget, tomorrow, eight A.M. at the Burger Shack. They'll ..." The low rumble of the ATV drowns out the rest of her words, and then she's off, speeding down our driveway.

"Bet she could shoot a sprinting deer from a thousand yards with gale force winds," Jonah says, equal amounts amusement and admiration in his voice.

"If she doesn't just order it to drop dead." I sigh with defeat, my gaze drifting over the expanse of water. The snow melted weeks ago, leaving behind a frozen blue surface that gleamed in the sunlight but that locals no longer dared test with their recreational toys. It seemed like the spring thaw happened overnight. It began with patches of dull black ice and slush appearing, and then the jarring sound much like a cracking whip as fissures formed and ice chunks broke off, to nudge each other like slow-moving bumper cars as they floated to the shoreline. There, they dissolved into the cold blue lake that stretches before me. Early in the day, the surface is glass, a perfect reflection of the sky and clouds above. But now a slight breeze in the air creates a ripple across its surface.

Lately I've found myself inclined to sit on the porch with my morning coffee and admire the yawning expanse of water, land, and mountain. I never thought of myself as a person who gravitated to water, but in this vast wilderness and solitude, there is an unparalleled calm that comes with starting my day here.

This morning, though, there will be no finding calm, my peace suitably disturbed. I don't have the energy to deal with Jonah, not after dealing with Muriel.

I climb the porch steps and push through the front door, kicking off my rubber boots along the way to the kitchen, aiming for the laundry room where our mop bucket is stashed.

"Hey." Jonah catches up to me, reaching out to rope an arm around my waist.

"I'm not in the mood—"

"I know it's your money. I'm just trying to ..." He spins me around to face him. "Fuck, I don't know what I'm tryin' to do. Anytime I come into some extra money, it goes straight into the bank."

"It's not like I don't have most of it invested already." Simon's financial adviser—I guess I should start thinking of him as mine, too —has tied up most of it in a dozen different ways, ranging from short- to long-term, low risk to high yield.

"I know you do." He brings his forehead to mine for a few beats before pulling back to show me earnest eyes. "I'm sorry for being an asshole earlier."

"A *big* asshole," I correct, feeling my lingering anger—and hurt, now that I consider it—disintegrate.

"Fine. I deserve that. I guess my priorities are different. I have no idea how we'll be doing in five years, and I like safety nets. I wasn't raised to drop cash like this."

I curl my arms around his waist. "Unfortunately for you, I was."

He shakes his head, but he's smiling. "Simon doesn't seem like an extravagant guy."

"His car is older than I am." In mint condition because he coddles it and keeps his mileage low, but *still*. The only time he gets new clothes is when my mother buys them for him, because she's tired of seeing him in the same five outfits every week. She's been trying to convince him to redecorate his office for the past ten years and he's fought her on it. I think it might be the only argument against her that he's ever won. "Simon's very ... *fiscally responsible* with his money." Much like Jonah, I'm beginning to see.

"So how does he deal with Susan, then?"

"They agreed on a monthly budget for her 'frivolous spending.'" I let go of Jonah long enough to air quote that word. "She stays within her budget, and he's not allowed to so much as blink at her purchases, no matter what. Not a word."

Jonah bites his bottom lip, hesitating. "Is that something we should maybe consider doing here? Or at least talk about purchases over a certain amount before they're made, to make sure we're both thinking clearly?"

I shoot him a flat look. "By *both*, you mean me, though."

Jonah's lips curl into a small, playful smile.

Muriel's advice—though unwanted—loiters in my mind. "I'd be willing to discuss anything over a thousand."

"Five hundred," he counters.

"So, *two* thousand?"

His brow furrows.

"I'm trapped in a log cabin in the woods, with a goat and a raccoon and no driver's license. A crazy woman with a gun just told me I'm making strawberry jam and growing cabbage this year. Frivolous spending is all the joy I have!"

His burst of laughter carries through the stillness. "Fine. A thousand, but only if you plant brussels sprouts back there."

"Ew. Really?" I grimace. "Fine. And you can't argue with me just because it's not important to you."

He glares at me. "A five-thousand-dollar dining room table is fucking ridiculous, Calla. We'd use it once a year, if that!"

"Fine," I agree begrudgingly.

He pulls me in tight. "We're gonna have to come to a more reasonable common ground eventually, though."

"Eventually," I agree with mock innocence, smoothing my fingertips over his coarse beard. It's finally back to the length it was when I left Alaska the first time.

"I hate fighting with you." He leans in to capture my lips with his.

"Stop being insufferable, then." I trace the seam of his mouth with my tongue.

"You want insufferable?" The wicked grin that flashes across his face sets my pulse pounding. With a swift tug, he yanks my pajama pants down, letting them fall to my ankles. My panties follow in a split second, and before I can balk, he has a grip of the backs of my thighs and he's hoisting me onto the kitchen counter.

CHAPTER NINETEEN

"We need a new truck," I lament, gripping the steering wheel with both hands, my biceps tensing as I turn into the parking lot of Burger Shack. It's empty of cars and riddled with potholes.

"Nah. Just need to fix the power steering," Jonah says from the passenger seat, his focus on the local newspaper in his grip. "We'll have 'em look at it when they fix the taillight."

"It's *ancient*."

"It's got power windows." Unlike the SUV Jonah drove in Bangor. But he had an excuse for driving it there. In a place where vehicles are brought in by boat, you hold on to whatever you can find until the engine takes its final breath. Anchorage has every dealership imaginable, albeit pricier.

Still, there is no excuse for keeping this leaking, creaking, duct-tape-covered beast.

I come to a stop in what might be a parking spot, if there were actual lines painted on the gravel. There's no sign of these local runners Muriel set me up with, but we're ten minutes early, to give myself a chance to warm up. "I was thinking something bigger, manlier."

Jonah pauses his reading to frown at me. "You've gone from wanting a Mini Cooper to something manlier?"

I roll my eyes. "Not for me. For *you*."

He moves back to his paper. "I told you, this is good for me."

"Of course, it is." I let my focus wander. A thin, older man jogs past, a black Labrador on a leash keeping pace next to him. Maybe that's what I need—a dog to keep me company when I'm outside. "Fine. But *I* want something nicer to drive."

"Like what?" He drops the newspaper again. "And don't say a fucking Mini Cooper or I swear to God, Calla, I'll find more crash pics to send." There's no hint of amusement in his voice.

"I was thinking a Jeep. A Wrangler. They're supposed to be good in snow."

Jonah makes a grunting sound that could be approval, but also might not be. "Hardtop, right?"

"I think soft, actually. They say it's easier to take off—"

"Bears can tear right through canvas."

"Hardtop, it is."

He smiles. "How much are they?"

I press my lips together, deciding how I want to answer, given the fight we just had yesterday over my spending. "More than the hot tub." Especially with the leather interior and all the bells and whistles the website let me choose.

He studies me a long moment, and I hold my breath, waiting for him to start giving me a hard time. "Get your license first, and then maybe we can go check out the dealership. You should test drive one before you make any decisions."

"Yeah. That's smart." I leave the keys in the ignition and hop out of the driver's seat, inhaling deeply. It's overcast, but not raining. The morning air, though crisp, is clean. It's a nice day to run.

The passenger door slams shut behind me and Jonah's boots drag across the gravel, sending stones skittering.

"What are you going to do while I'm out running?" I ask, stretching my legs.

"A few errands."

I glance over my shoulder to find him leaning against the hood of the truck, his thumbs hooked in his pockets, his steady gaze on my ass. I spin around to face him, ending his show. "Pervert."

"You don't know the half of it …" He flashes a wicked smirk that makes my heart race and my cheeks flush and a thrill course through my core. We've been living together for almost five months, and he can still cause an instant reaction in my body with a single look. Enough that I'd be willing to skip this run with strangers and find a private spot to christen this old truck.

I clear my throat. "Errands?"

He grins, as if he can read my thoughts. "I figured I'd go and see about Muriel's list of demands."

I groan. "How did I get myself into this?" Toby sent a text last night with an itemized list—manure, triple mix, and seeds for everything from carrots to squash to pumpkins—that Muriel wants me to have at the house by Monday. He also apologized if his mother seems a bit controlling. That choice of words made me laugh.

"You did mention trying out gardening, didn't you?" Jonah reminds me.

I pivot into a leg lunge. "I was thinking more along the lines of a pot of basil on our windowsill."

"Well, you can have a jungle of it." Jonah chuckles. "Look, she's willin' to help so let her help."

"She's a dictator, and she made me feel dumb and clueless."

"Then prove her wrong," he challenges.

"But I *am* dumb and clueless when it comes to gardening."

He shakes his head firmly. "You'll figure it out. And I don't think she means anything bad by it. She set this run up for you. Maybe you'll make some new friends around here."

"Yeah, I guess. I could definitely use one of those right now."

Jonah lifts off the truck, closing the distance to seize my shoulders and pull me against him. "I'm sorry about Diana," he offers, his voice conciliatory.

"I'm so disappointed." I press my cheek against his chest, the feel of his soft cotton shirt and the smell of his woodsy body wash a comfort. "I was really hoping she'd come this year." Diana called me last night to break the news that, with Aaron's sister's wedding and needing to take time off around exams, she won't have enough vacation days left to visit me. I can't begrudge her situation—I'm competing against a wedding and law school. Still, I'm disheartened.

"So, she'll make it here next year."

"Yeah. We'll see." It's been five months since I saw my family and my best friend. It'll be a year by the time Mom and Simon come for

Christmas. A year and a half, at least, for Diana. While I *could* fly to Toronto to see them at any time, the selfish part of me wishes they'd have made coming here to see *me* in my new world a priority.

"My mom said that was one of the hardest things about living in Alaska—how little she saw of her friends and family. They all say they're gonna come but they don't. 'Course, most of them were in Oslo, which is *way* farther than Toronto." Jonah smooths a comforting hand over my back. "Don't worry, though. They'll make it here."

A hollow ache stirs in my chest. "Muriel said eight, right?" I check my watch. It's five after eight. "What if they don't come?" I can't even remember their names.

"They'll come."

"How do you know?"

"For the same reason that I'm driving halfway to Wasilla for manure and why you're planting a garden."

I peer up at Jonah's handsome face. "Because we're all terrified of Muriel?"

He chuckles. "I'd call it more of a healthy respect. Look, that's got to be them there." He juts his chin toward the road behind me.

I peer over my shoulder to see two female runners jogging side by side at a slow pace turn into the parking lot. They're wearing matching head-to-toe neon running gear—one yellow, one magenta—and I have to wonder if any part of that is for fashion or if it's all for visibility.

"You good? Or do you want me to stick around until you're sure you're doin' this?" Jonah asks.

"I'm fine. It's just a run." And it's much needed. I've been feeling sluggish lately. "This is only going to take a half hour, tops."

He leans down to kiss me, lingering a long moment, his beard tickling my face. "I'll meet you at the grocery store after."

"Fine. Don't take too long, Jeeves. Ow!" I let out a yelp—of surprise, not pain—at Jonah's swift parting slap across my backside before he climbs into the truck.

"Calla?" the older, wiry woman in yellow—in her late forties or maybe even early fifties—calls out.

I smile, even as my cheeks flush. There's no way they missed that. "Yeah. Hi."

She slows to a walk to close the last ten feet. "I'm Jodi." She gestures to the softer-bodied, raven-haired woman next to her who is closer to my age. "This is my daughter, Emily."

My glance flips back and forth between the two, looking for the resemblance, finding it in the slender bridge of their noses and their closely set eyes.

Emily offers a lukewarm smile in return.

So far, this feels as awkward as walking into a stranger's house for lunch uninvited.

"You all warmed up?" Jodi's gaze flickers over the can of bear spray in my holster and the bell on my wrist. I limited myself to one today.

"I am."

"Great. The bike path is over there." She points to a narrow opening in the trees, beyond the lot, and begins leading us in that direction. "Have you been on it yet?"

I shake my head in answer.

"It goes all the way down to Wasilla. We obviously won't be going that far."

I fall into step beside them as uncomfortable silence lingers. I wonder if they find this as awkward as I do.

"Thanks, for letting me come with you."

"Safety in numbers, right?" Emily offers, her voice wispy and timid.

I match their pace as we close the distance to the trail ahead. "So, have you lived here long?"

They both nod but offer no opportunity for more conversation, and so I give up, keeping my attention ahead to where the cautionary yellow signs appear, warning of bicycles and runners.

And moose.

And bears.

My anxiety spikes.

"We've been running this trail for years and we've never run into a bear on it," Jodi says, seeing where my eyes have landed. Muriel must have told them about my paranoia. I can only imagine her version: that girl from Canada who's afraid of her own shadow.

"How far are we going?"

"We do ten miles on Saturdays. Muriel said you'd be up for that?" They both watch me expectantly.

Did she, now ... That's sixteen *kilometers*. I could barely handle *six* kilometers back in March and I haven't run since.

I do a quick glance to confirm that Jonah is already gone. Too late to turn back.

I'm the stranger here, crashing mother-and-daughter time, I remind myself. I force a smile. "Sure, should be fine."

CHAPTER TWENTY

I hear the distant buzz of Muriel's ATV long before I spot her through the window, coasting up the driveway.

Toby texted me twenty minutes ago, warning me his mother has decided today's the perfect day for us to prep the garden, with the soil warm and dry enough.

With a groan, I hit Save on a draft of my latest *Calla & Dee* blog post, entitled "The Reluctant Gardener." The original title, "The Hostile Gardener," sounded too ... hostile.

I wince as I stand, my thighs still sore from Saturday's run. Grabbing my gardening cheat sheet—a compilation of basic tips from my mother and notes I gathered from an *Alaska Gardening 101* blog—I step into my rubber boots and drag myself outside to face my determined neighbor.

———

"You almost done there?" Muriel bellows from the far end of the garden, wiping the back of her gloved hand across her brow.

"I think so!" My back and shoulders throb as I drag the rake one last time. We've been working tirelessly for hours, churning the old dirt with the mounds of fresh, black soil and manure that Jonah dumped in here the other day, until the mixture is loose and level.

My stomach is growling, my body is coated with sweat, and I can feel the dirty streaks that paint my cheeks.

Muriel treks between the long, tidy rows of soil she built using a hoe, her boot prints remaining behind. "You need some water. Here." She reaches down into her cooler and pulls out a bottle. "Drink up. Come on now."

I accept the bottle, downing nearly half of it in under twenty seconds, no longer fazed by the way she herds and cajoles and demands.

"Better?"

"Uh-huh," I manage through a pant.

"You're all out of breath." She snorts. "I thought you were a runner!"

"This is different ... from running." Though I sounded about the same by the time I reached the end of my ten-mile run with Jodi and Emily—two quiet-mannered women who I learned speak little and smile even less. I've already politely declined their invitation to join them next weekend.

Preparing this soil is backbreaking work. And this woman, who has three or four decades on me, is out here by choice, her breathing even. The only sign she's exerted herself is the damp gray curls stuck to her forehead.

She leans against the garden gate, settling a bicep over the top that would give most guys I've dated a run for their money in an arm-wrestling match. Beyond, Zeke grazes on a patch of newly sprouted weeds. Muriel insisted that he should be allowed to wander while we're working out here. Meanwhile, Bandit took off into the woods, to climb a tree. "You've got yourself a good first garden, Calla," she says with a satisfied nod. "We can start planting tomorrow."

"The porch guy's coming to install the screens tomorrow." Thank God. The bugs haven't risen from their winter nests, but I know they're coming, each day growing a bit longer and warmer.

"And are you helpin' him build?" Her wrinkled lips twist with a doubtful smirk.

"Well, no, but—"

"So, I'll bring the seedlings in the morning. We should be able to get everything in by noon."

There's no point trying to explain that I don't want to be all the way back here when a stranger is working on my house. What if he has questions? What if he needs my opinion? I'm sure she'd have an answer for that, too. Right now, though, I want her to leave so I can shower, eat, and rest my throbbing body until Jonah comes home.

"Have you seen the rest of your property yet?" Muriel asks suddenly.

"Uh, no. There's, like, almost a hundred acres." I haven't ventured beyond the driveway and the pen. My guess is I'll never see all of it.

She lifts her chin in that way she has sometimes when she talks. Like she's about to tell me a secret, something she knows I don't know—which is undoubtedly a lot. "I'll bet Phil didn't tell ya about the old cabin."

I pick through my memory and come up blank. "What cabin?"

The broad smile that fills her face makes me instantly regret asking. "Come on. You and me are goin' for a little ride."

The back of Muriel's jeans and coat are splattered with mud by the time she hops out of her seat in the middle of the thicket.

I check my own pant legs to confirm that my clothes are equally dirty. The narrow, wet path she led me on to get here was sinking and churning beneath the weight of our ATVs.

We're surrounded by tall, leggy spruce and birch trees that are still mostly naked, though I see tiny buds on the ends of skinny branches. Fallen trunks lay in every direction, many rotted and coated with patches of bright green moss. A blanket of crumpled brown leaves from last fall's shedding layers the forest floor in clumps, like soggy newsprint, waiting to decompose fully.

"Is this my property?" I feel like an idiot asking that, but it seemed like I trailed Muriel forever.

"Sure is." She unfastens her helmet and hooks it on her handlebar, then reaches for the brown rifle strapped on her ATV's rack. "I imagine we made enough noise comin' in that there won't be a sane critter within a mile of us, but I like to be prepared, just in case."

What about *insane* critters? I want to ask. The predatory grizzly that dragged a man out of his tent in the middle of the night? The protective moose that trampled a dog because it got between her and her baby?

I haven't seen our moose in weeks. Jonah thinks the noise from the plane taking off every day may have caused them to venture elsewhere.

Muriel checks something on the gun before throwing the strap over her shoulder. "Jonah's taught you how to use one of these, right?"

Here we go ... "I don't like guns."

"It has nothin' to do with likin' them. Though, plenty of people love their guns." She picks through the loose branches, her boots kicking away clumps of wet leaves. "It's about feeling safe."

"That's just it. I don't feel safe around them." Even seeing this one in her grip unsettles me. "I didn't grow up around guns."

"What? Your dad never took you out huntin' in the tundra when you came to visit?"

Toby and Teddy know I'm from Toronto and that my father owned Alaska Wild, so I have to assume they are Muriel's source of information. "I never came to visit. My father and I ... we weren't on speaking terms until last summer. I hadn't seen him in twenty-four years."

She steals a gray-eyed glance back my way, quiet for a moment, and I brace myself for the invasive prodding, the wise-woman lecture, the uninvited opinion.

"Well, you know what's more dangerous than a gun? Being in Alaska and not having one when you need it," she says instead.

Your son, Deacon, had a gun and look where that got him.

I trail her as she pushes through the brush, her rubber boots heavy as they fall. I wonder, deep down beneath the rough exterior of this woman—never a lady, according to her loved ones—how often she thinks about the son who disappeared one day five years ago. Is that startling truth still the first thought she wakes up to every morning, in that precise moment when the fog of sleep dissipates?

"There's a ton of history about the Mat-Su Valley that I'm guessin' you have no idea about."

"You're right. I don't," I admit.

"When you have kids, they'll learn about it all in school. Of course, most of the focus is on the colonists. They get all the fanfare. Parades and special days and all that hoopla for them. But they didn't start comin' up here until the Great Depression. There were plenty of people here before them who helped settle the area. Farmers, miners, people wanting to be free and live off the land. They began headin' up this way as soon as homesteading was allowed, back before the turn of the century, when we were a district of the United States. That's how my family ended up here. They were originally from Montana." She pushes a low tree branch back, holding it for me to pass. We round the thick crop of trees to find a small, dilapidated cabin ahead.

"What is this place?" I take in the sunken, moss-covered roof and the rough wood logs that make up the four walls. Boards have been nailed across what I guess are windows, sealing them. It reminds me of the safety cabin Jonah and I sought refuge in while waiting for the murky weather to pass.

"The original homestead on this property." Muriel steps over a rotten log in her path, then kicks another one. "You've heard about that, right? Homesteadin'?"

"When the government gave away land for free? Yeah, I watched a documentary about it." I watched everything I could find about Alaska after returning to Toronto, grieving for the loss of both my father and Jonah, and desperate to hold on to it for a little while longer. My mother lovingly accused me of masochism.

Muriel's eyes widen with surprise. "That's right. They'd give a parcel to you, and you had five years to build a dwelling and cultivate a certain portion before the land was yours, free and clear. A man came up here sometime in the '60s, in the spring to settle with his wife and two young boys. He was from Montana, too. He staked his claim, paid his entry fees, and away he went, thinkin' he'd made off like a bank robber, ready to show everyone how it's done.

"He built houses down there, so he assumed he'd be fine. I remember my parents talkin' about what an obnoxious fool he was.

Didn't have the first clue about survivin' up here, though, of what it's like to be part of a community. Well"—she peers over her shoulder as she walks to give me a knowing look—"one boy was gone before Christmas. Caught somethin' that he couldn't shake, livin' in this drafty, cold place, half-starved. The wife went out in a blizzard a month later and didn't make it home. Took days to find her body. The man up and left with his remainin' son before the snow melted. Didn't last a year."

My jaw hangs open as I regard the tiny cabin before me, equal parts amazed and horrified by its dark history. What is it with the McGivney family telling me these terrible stories?

"Might have gone a completely different way, had they been willin' to help, and be helped. They didn't even know how to keep a proper root cellar so their vegetables wouldn't rot!" She shakes her head. "Eventually, the Beakers showed up with money to spend. It was the '70s and this area was startin' to grow, with the Parks Highway finished and talk of movin' the state capital to the area from Juneau. The government was sellin' land, so the Beakers bought up a bunch and made somethin' of it by settling over on the other side of this lake, building the log house where you live. They put in a good decade here before deciding they were ready for something a little easier, so they sold to Phil and Colette, who *really* made somethin' of it."

She caps off her story with a prideful smile, that grin that transforms her face and softens her harsh tone. "Now it's your turn to leave your mark."

Things have changed, I want to tell her. Even in Alaska. We're not trying to settle the land. I certainly have no intention of living off it. But this little trip has helped me begin to understand Muriel. Her family not only survived but thrived in what that documentary I watched described as the harshest of conditions—poor soil and short summers that challenged crops, wild animals that threatened livestock, the blistering cold, long winters, the endless assault of mosquitos deep in the thicket, the grueling daily labor required. It's in her DNA. She's proud of her heritage, of what her family has accomplished.

She sees only one right way to live in Alaska.

Leading me around the corner to where the roof hangs over a single wooden door, Muriel points to the glimpse of water beyond the trees. "That's your lake. You're over on the other side."

"Seriously?" I've spent countless hours looking across to the far shoreline. Never did I catch even a hint of a cabin hidden within. We can't even see it from above, everything so overgrown.

"Okay, let's see if this will budge." She gives the doorknob a yank and the old door opens with a hair-raising creak of the hinges. Muriel looks impressed as she pushes it all the way back. "Move that rock over here, will ya?" She nods toward a small boulder on the ground a few feet away.

My back and arms scream in protest from the earlier soil tilling as I struggle to roll it over. I prop it against the bottom corner of the door to hold it open.

"Haven't been in here in years," she admits, leading me into the small room that smells of damp wood. It's dark, the only light streaming in from the door and the few cracks within the boarded-up windows. It's empty of everything but dust, debris, and a few chunks of broken glass.

I do a slow spin, trying to imagine where four people slept and ate, where the kitchen was situated. A black pipe in one corner hints at the location of the woodstove, but nothing of it remains.

"Locals cleaned the place out as soon as they caught wind of the family takin' off," Muriel explains, as if reading my mind.

"How old is this place again?"

"Well, it was built in the '60s, so well over fifty years old now." She paces in a slow circle. "That man might have been a shmuck when it came to survivin', but he built a sturdy enough cabin. Phil's done some repairs and upkeep over the years and made sure it stayed boarded up, or else he was bound to find a sleeping bear in here, come winter. Thomas used to come out here with his friends and get up to no good. That's their son, by the way. My boys would come out with him from time to time, too."

It's the first time she's even alluded to having more than one son.

"And of course, Thomas would sneak out with his girlfriend, too. What teenager could resist a place to shack up." She raises her eyebrow with meaning. "Anyway, thought you should see some good Alaskan history on your land."

I may have been reluctant at the start, but now I find myself appreciative. "I had no idea. There wasn't any mention of the cabin in any of the paperwork."

"They probably lost track of it." She shoos me out the door with a wave of her hand, then gives the boulder a swift kick with her boot, sending it rolling enough to loosen its grip of the door. With the cabin secured, she leads the way back through the bramble. "That spot where you have your garden, it wasn't too much better than this when Colette and Phil took over. Of course, the Beakers had a little garden. Colette wanted bigger, so Phil gave her bigger. Lord, did that man ever love her, bless his heart.

"Anyway, it took them a good five years to get it to size. Every year they'd clear and churn more. So much hard work put into it. That's why it needs to continue being used." Muriel straps her gun onto the rack and climbs back on her ATV. "Okay. You'll want me to lead again so I'm gonna go around you and cut back onto the path—"

A loud metal snapping sound followed by a howl of pain cuts through the silent forest, the echo sending countless birds from their perches, flapping into the air.

"What was that?" I ask in a rushed voice.

"Shhh!" Muriel holds a hand up to silence me, her head cocked in the general direction of where the noise came from.

A second howl, less piercing but full of agony, carries moments later. It's to our right, and it's close. Too close.

"Somethin' got caught in a trap. Probably a wolf."

My stomach drops at the idea that there was a wolf lurking that close to us and we had no idea.

"Okay, come on," she says with a heavy sigh. "Let's go and deal with it." She cranks her engine and takes off in the direction of the wounded animal, forcing me to hurry to follow.

———

Muriel's already off her ATV and heading toward a pile of fallen trees when I pull up and cut my engine.

"A leg-hold trap! Big enough for a bear!" she announces, nodding to herself, as if she's delighted for having guessed correctly. "Got 'im good, too."

I spot the mound of mottled, tawny-gray fur. With trepidation, I close the distance. "Oh my God." I wince at the jagged metal teeth that dig into the wolf's hind leg.

"I heard you've already had the pleasure of meetin' your next-door neighbor?" she says, her tone grim.

"Who, Roy? Yeah. Why ..." My question fades as I take in the poor creature's face, sharp, fear- and pain-laden eyes intent on our every move as it whimpers. "That's Roy's dog." The one that seemed to be sizing up my jugular that day.

She snorts. "Dog, my ass. He'll swear up and down that he's got malamutes, but he ain't foolin' nobody, includin' himself. Lucky for him neither of 'em have caused any trouble that needed reportin'." She shakes her head with dismay. "Roy ain't gonna be too happy about this. Those hounds are like his kin." She glances around. "Wonder where the other one went to. They're usually a combo deal." Branches crack beneath her footfalls as she heads toward her ATV, leaving me with the wounded animal.

As little as I cared for Roy's threatening beasts, the sound of it in agony stirs a natural response to end its misery somehow. "Is there a way we can pry this thing off?"

"Not without you needin' a few dozen stitches in that pretty skin of yours. That there ain't no friendly mutt. Besides, even if we could get the trap off, that leg is so mangled, I doubt he could keep it."

I study the trap again, meant for an animal *at least* twice the size—its giant metal teeth gripping flesh without mercy, cutting through tendon and muscle, anchoring into bone. I cringe with the thought of it clamped over my own leg. "What the hell is a bear trap doing out here, anyway? A *person* could have stepped in this!"

"Who knows how long it's been there. I remember Phil havin' a bear issue a few years back, so maybe this was him. I don't see any fresh bait anywhere."

I crouch, and with a tentative hand, reach for the nearby chain. The dog bares its teeth and emits a grating growl, warning me back. Muriel's right—I'll only end up getting hurt trying to help it.

I stand, sighing with frustration. "So, what do we do?"

A click sounds that raises the hairs on the back of my neck. It's a sound I've heard only a handful of times, when Jonah loads his rifle.

"What are you doing?" I ask warily, cold dread seeping into my stomach as I watch Muriel approaching with her gun. I know exactly what she's about to do.

She gives me a blank look. "I'm puttin' the thing out of its misery."

"You can't just shoot it!"

She shakes her head at me in disbelief. I'm sure my face is painted with horror. "We can't leave it here. It'll gnaw its damn leg off to get out of that thing and then bleed out in the bush! This is the humane thing to do, Calla!"

"Well ..." I stall, looking for an answer that doesn't involve a bullet in this poor dog's head in the next five seconds. "Shouldn't we go and tell Roy? It's his dog."

"And what do you think Roy's gonna do for the wretched creature? Sing it lullabies?" She snorts. "This is a kindness. Now go on and get out of the way." The gun is gripped within her rough, calloused hands, ready to point, aim, and fire.

"No." The word comes out before I can even think about it. My feet are rooted in place.

Her eyebrows arch. "What do ya mean, no?"

"I'm not letting you shoot the poor dog without first giving it a chance!"

She sighs heavily. "Look, Calla, I know this might seem cruel to a girl *like you*, but what else are we gonna do? How are we gonna help it, all the way out here?" She waves a hand around us, emphasizing the fact that we're deep in the bush. "Can't even get it out of that trap without tranquilizing it first. I don't have a tranquilizer. Do *you*?" She snorts derisively.

A tranquilizer.

Of course. I dig out my phone. I have one bar of reception. It might just be enough. "Yes. Actually. I do."

CHAPTER TWENTY-ONE

Jonah slows the ATV to a stop. Ahead of us, the ruts stretch beyond the bend in the trees. Someone's been driving along Roy's laneway with big tires, tearing up the soggy ground, churning the mud into a mess.

"Tell me again why we're goin' to all this trouble for this asshole?" Jonah yells over the hum of the idling engine.

I huddle within my jacket, chilled within the shade of the forest. "It's not for *him*."

Jonah peers over his shoulder at me, takes in my grim, weary face, and his blue eyes soften. He gives one of my hands clasped around his waist a squeeze and then hollers, "Hold on!"

I cling to Jonah's body as we bump and jostle and dip through the trenches, my teeth rattling, tiny specks of mud splattering the back of my clothes like raindrops. A feel some land on my neck.

And I remind myself that this is the right thing to do, even as my anxiety over telling this foul old man that his beloved dog is probably going to die twists my stomach into knots.

Marie answered her phone on the third ring and, when I rushed to explain the situation, said she was hopping in her truck straight away. Muriel, who couldn't stop shaking her head at me every time our gazes met, got hold of Toby, gave him an explicit "two hundred yards southwest of the old homesteader cabin" location, and told him to be waiting for Marie at our place with a trailer.

It took almost half an hour before we heard the familiar hum of an approaching ATV engine in the woods. It was the longest half hour of my life, with the poor dog taking turns whimpering in pain and baring its fangs every time Muriel tried to get anywhere near the trap. Marie got to work immediately, sinking a dart between the dog's shoulders and, as soon as his lids shuttered, releasing the metal teeth with deft skill. Toby and I helped lift the unconscious dog—who Toby put at a hundred twenty pounds—onto an old bedsheet that Marie brought, and then she wrapped his mangled leg, wearing a furrowed brow the entire time.

Our convoy of ATVs emerged from the woods as Jonah was landing, Marie sitting cross-legged in the trailer, cradling the animal's head in her arms as best she could, a grim mask of determination on her pretty face.

She never complained once through all of it. Not as the wagon hit bone-jarring bump after bump, not as the dog's blood seeped through the gauze and blanket, staining her jeans, not even as Muriel attempted to instruct her about where she should put the tranquilizer, on how best to release the trap, and how tight to bandage the wounds.

The woman who still secretly pines over Jonah was, for lack of a better word, *inspiring*. Also, incredibly intimidating for her even temper and skill.

The least *I* can do is deal with this asshole while Marie tries to save a life.

Roy is outside when we approach the cabin, removing slabs of wood from the back of his pickup truck. The barn's door is propped open, giving me a glimpse of the many tools and work benches inside.

His truck is caked with dried mud, its sides wearing countless scratches in the paint. From the tree branches along his narrow driveway, I surmise. The oversized tires are likely what tore up the ground.

The enormous black wolf dog is nearby, growl-barking.

"Settle down!" Roy yells. The wolf dog instantly quiets and sits on his haunches. I wonder if it's the words or his tone that get such an immediate response. Is the dog as daunted by Roy as I am?

I steel my spine as Jonah cuts the engine. "Hey, Roy. How's it goin'?" He doesn't bother climbing off to shake the man's hand this time.

Roy makes a grunting sound that *might* be a greeting. His old worn blue jeans and checkered jacket—possibly the same outfit he was wearing last time we came here—are covered in sawdust again. The rifle is nowhere in sight, thankfully.

"Listen, we found your dog caught in a bear trap, out in the woods. We called a good friend who's a veterinarian to help. She took it to her clinic to see if anything can be done," Jonah says, cutting all pretenses of small talk.

"Damn animal ... He's been wandering off for weeks." Roy's tense jaw the only sign that the grim news has any impact on him. "He gonna lose his leg? 'Cause I got no use for a lame dog."

Jonah sighs heavily. "I don't know, Roy." He slips Marie's business card out of his shirt pocket. "Here's my friend's number. She'll give you an update, and you can decide what to do."

Wait a minute. "What does that mean? Decide what to do?" I whisper.

Jonah shoots a pointed look over his shoulder at me that tells me it's exactly what I think it means.

My anger flares, at Roy for his callous attitude and at Jonah for his indifference. "I just spent the last hour fending off Muriel and her trigger finger. Marie's trying to save him. He can't turn around and tell her to put it down," I hiss, my words meant for Jonah but too loud, apparently.

Roy's eyes narrow. "I can do whatever the hell I want." He casts a hand toward the black beast that's watching us intently. "I could shoot him if I wanted and you couldn't do a goddamn thing about it."

My jaw drops as I grapple with a suitable response, but I can't think of one. Didn't Muriel claim these animals were like family to him?

"Muriel." In that single name, it's obvious her displeasure with Roy is mutual. His lips twist in thought. A long, silent moment drags as he regards his other dog. "You probably shoulda let her shoot him. 'Course, a young, city slicker like you wouldn't have the guts for that."

I glare at him. It's like he's *trying* to antagonize me. "Well, I didn't let her, so now you get to be a decent human being and take care of your *wolf*. Of course, a miserable, curmudgeon like you probably doesn't have the guts for *that*."

Roy cocks his head, seemingly astonished by my retort.

So is Jonah, by the arched eyebrow he flashes me. "On that note ..." He's still holding the business card up between two fingers. "Do you want Marie's information or not? I've got shit to do."

I hold my breath. What if Roy says "not"? What happens to the animal?

Roy saunters over and accepts the card, examining it as he steps backward. "She gonna give me issues?"

"Nah. Not unless he bites someone." Jonah starts the engine.

"You're welcome!" I yell, unable to contain my annoyance with this man, especially after the day I've had because of his wandering animal.

The corners of Roy's mouth twitches, almost as if he's about to smile, but then the fleeting moment is gone and he's left glaring at me as Jonah pulls away, back down the muddy path.

"I hope that dog bites *him*," I say to myself, assuming Jonah can't hear me over the engine.

His body shakes with laughter.

——————

"Come on!" I whine as Jonah steers us left toward the hangar instead of continuing home. I'm desperate for a shower and food. I haven't eaten since this morning.

He pulls up next to Archie, the Piper my dad left him, wrapped in canvas and sitting outside the door until Jonah can swap out Phil's old plane, the hangar only able to accommodate two. "Gimme two minutes. I didn't get to finish up properly."

Two minutes is *never* just two minutes when Jonah's with his planes.

With reluctance, I release my grip of his torso. He swings a leg over, hopping off. It always amazes me, how he moves so gracefully for such a tall, broad man.

"It's fine. I'll be over here, gnawing my arm off," I call out, my tone dry.

"Just like Roy's dog would have had you not been out there to find him."

I cringe. "Jonah!"

"Too soon?"

"*Not* funny!"

"Who knew you had a soft spot for wild animals." His chuckle carries as he disappears through the small door into the hangar, leaving me alone to pick at my thoughts about the turn my day took.

After five minutes and no sign of Jonah, I waver between leaving him here to walk home and going inside to rush him. In the end, I cut the engine and head for the door, annoyed. He's exactly where I expect him to be, circling Veronica with his clipboard, going through all his postflight notes and safety checks with a mask of deep concentration.

"I think he's been coming around here."

"Huh?" Jonah murmurs absently.

"Something Roy said, about the dog taking off a lot lately. I think maybe he's been lurking around here. And I think he followed us out to the cabin today." Why else would he be out there?

Jonah finally looks up from his clipboard. "What do you mean, lurking?"

"Like, I think he's been out there in the trees, watching me." A shiver runs down my spine at the thought. "I told you how sometimes I sense something out there. And that day I thought I saw movement in the trees? I'll bet that was him." He's the right size and color.

Jonah shakes his head. "Doubt it, Calla."

"I'm serious!"

"So am I. Zeke keeps gettin' out. Don't you think that dog would have slaughtered him the second he had a chance?"

Jonah does have a point.

He goes back to his clipboard and I let my gaze roam the hangar. Why Phil needed a place big enough to house two planes when he's only ever owned one, I have to wonder. "I still think I'm right."

Jonah doesn't answer, too focused on his clipboard. Or ignoring me.

I wander over to Phil's blue-and-white Beaver that sits on a trailer off on the far side, the panel for the engine pulled off. He told us he hasn't had it in the air for three years because his eyesight issues. What does lack of use do to a plane after that long? "What year is this, again—'69?"

"Fifty-nine."

"Even better." I use the narrow ladder propped against the pilot's side to open the door and climb in. I let my feet dangle out the side while I take in the silver strips of tape holding together the red fabric on the seats. Phil and his duct tape.

The control panel of dials and switches is a replica of Veronica in my opinion, but I'm sure Jonah could point out a thousand differences between the two with a glance. "What do you think is wrong with it?"

"For starters, it needs a new propeller. Phil said I could probably get another three hundred hours on the engine, but I'll leave that to Toby to figure out." They finally met today, under less than ideal circumstances, and shared a few quick words before we parted ways. At least Jonah seems lukewarm to giving him a shot, happy with how well the snow machine and ATV engines have been running since Toby worked on them.

"You two should go out for a beer sometime." It'd be nice for Jonah to make a local male friend, and soon. It seemed everyone in Bangor knew—and liked—him, but my father and Max were the only guys Jonah hung out with, outside of work. Now my father is gone and Max is back in Portland, suitably occupied with baby Thor.

Jonah merely grunts in response.

I drag my fingertip over one of the plane's gauges, and it comes back with a thick layer of dust. She'll need a good clean once she's ready to go.

That's when it hits me. "We need to name her!" I holler. It was my grandfather's tradition, then my father's. Now, it needs to be ours. I can't believe I hadn't thought of this before.

Jonah has finished his checks and is dangling half out of Veronica as he stretches to reach for something inside. His boots make a heavy thump against the ground as he hops out of the plane. In one hand, he clutches a crinkled brown paper bag and another package wrapped in newspaper. "I already did."

"Seriously?" An unexpected prick of disappointment stirs inside me. "How could you name her without—"

"Wren. I named it Wren." Jonah reaches up to smooth a hand over the fuselage. "It's a *he*."

"Oh." I bite my lip as a smile emerges in tandem with a bubble of emotion. "That's a good name."

"Yeah. I thought so, too." Jonah's blue eyes are sad. It reminds me, yet again, that I am not the only one who lost—and still feels the loss —of my father.

"Help me down?" It's far too high to jump with the plane on floats and a trailer.

Jonah obliges, stretching out his arms and opening up his broad chest.

I lean down and, wrapping my arms around his neck, let myself drop, knowing he can bear my weight.

He grunts but barely shifts, easing me to the ground with an arm roped around my back.

I steal a kiss from his lips on my way down.

"Here." He hands me the awkwardly shaped package that's wrapped in newsprint, secured with twine. There's weight to it. "It's a housewarming gift from Ethel."

"Ethel? When did you see her?"

"Today."

I frown. "What was she doing up in Crooked Creek?"

"I stopped at her village on my way home. Wanted to see how they survived the winter."

"What the hell, Jonah!" Ethel and her family live a subsistence lifestyle in a village up the Kuskokwim River. I'm not sure how far they are up the river from Bangor, but I know it's not anywhere near Crooked Creek. "Remember the *itinerary*?" He arrived home a half hour later than expected but I was so distracted by the ordeal with the dog, I didn't think much of it.

"I'm here and I'm fine, okay? Come on, relax."

My hackles rise instantly. "Don't tell me to relax!" I *hate* being told to relax.

He gives me a look and then juts his chin forward. "Come on, open it."

I sigh. "This conversation is not over." But I'm too tired and hungry to argue with him. I pick at the twine that holds the wrapping together. "How is she? Still threatening to chop off her son's limbs?"

Jonah smirks. "He still has both hands. For now."

"And her grandson?"

Mention of the boy who's alive today because of Jonah's bravery —or insanity, depending on who you speak to—brings a wide smile that instantly melts my irritation. "Huge and running around."

"Must be all that muskrat his grandma feeds him. What *is* this?" I break through one layer of newsprint, only to find another beneath. It's something hard, that much I can tell. Hopefully not something morbid. That woman has an odd sense of humor.

Jonah pulls out a long, brown strip of jerky from the brown bag and offers it to me.

I shake my head. I already learned the hard way that it is most certainly *not* beef.

"Can't be that hungry, then," he teases, ripping off a chunk between his teeth.

"You're not kissing me again until you brush your teeth." I unravel the last of the paper to find a sculpture inside. It takes me two hands and a moment of rolling it this way and that, taking in all the angles, to identify the two coiled birds. "Wow. Is this handmade?" I ask, sliding my thumb over the surface. It's smooth.

"Yeah. Ethel carved it over the winter," he says between chewing. "It's ivory."

"*Ivory?*" I feel the apprehension fill my face.

"*Walrus* ivory," Jonah corrects. "Alaska Natives are allowed to hunt them. And don't worry, every last part of that animal would have been used to help Ethel's family survive the winter."

"I don't doubt that." I study the two birds. They've been shaped to perfection. "The raven and his goose wife." I smile softly as I hold it up for us to admire.

Jonah shakes his head. "That woman loves her stories."

"She got this one wrong." I am *not* Jonah's goose wife. Or perhaps I am, but I'm a goose wife who survived to see the spring thaw, and who is determined to thrive alongside her raven. "It's beautiful." I already know where I'm putting it—on the top shelf of the rustic curio cabinet that I ordered last week. That Jonah doesn't know about yet.

Jonah's gaze isn't on the sculpture, though. It's on me, and his face is a grim mask.

My stomach sinks. "What's wrong?" With that look, something is definitely wrong.

"I don't know how to tell you this, Calla, but ..." He hesitates for a few beats, long enough that my anxiety spikes. "You *really* need to take a shower. I've never seen you so *filthy*." A grin splits his face.

"Shut up!" I smack his chest, equal parts relief and outrage slamming into me. "Believe me, I'm trying to, but *no one* will let me go home! First Muriel, now you!"

"You have dirt *all over* your face." He rubs the pad of his thumb across my jaw and pulls back to show me the smear of brown sludge. "It looks like you were trying to avoid enemy fire out there."

Great. I went to Roy's looking like I was playing war games? "Do you have *any idea* what my day has been like?"

"Did it involve rolling around in a pile of mud?" he asks with mock innocence, reaching up to pick a twig from my topknot. "What were you trying to do? Blend into the forest?"

"Okay, you know what, smart-ass? I'm leaving." I stroll past him, housewarming gift in hand. "If you want a ride on the ATV, you better get moving."

"I'd rather walk, thanks."

I can't help but laugh, even as I throw my middle finger in the air.

"Seriously, though, if you wait by the side of the house, I'll be there in ten minutes to hose you off. You shouldn't step inside our house like that."

"You know what? Screw you and your brussels sprouts!" I holler as I push through the door.

———

I'm working my shampoo into a rich lather—the muscle ache from today's labor already settling into my shoulders and arms—when the bathroom door creaks open. A moment later, Jonah is pushing the shower curtain open and stepping into the tub behind me.

"Need some help?" He doesn't wait for my answer, gripping my hips to spin me around.

I revel in the feel of his touch as he massages my scalp with strong, skilled fingers.

"Marie called."

My heart skips a beat, nervousness splicing through the moment of peace. "And?"

"He's gonna survive."

"Oh, thank God!" I fall against Jonah's broad, bare chest, the soft blond hair tickling my cheek. I'm surprised with myself for feeling this much relief over an animal that isn't mine, that I'm quite certain has been scaring me to death, lurking around for the past two months. "What about his leg?"

Jonah's hands keep working, sliding all the way down to the ends of my strands. "Still attached. She doesn't know how much use he'll have of it, though. He'll definitely have a limp forever."

"She really is amazing," I murmur, even as a troubling thought stirs. "Roy said he didn't want a lame dog."

Jonah snorts. "Roy's full of shit. He called her office, like, thirty seconds after we left his place and demanded she do whatever is necessary to save him. No cost was too high. And when Marie called him back with the news, he thanked her."

I feel my eyebrows pop as I try to consolidate that with the miserable old man we dealt with not that long ago. "He actually used the words?" He knows the words *thank you*?

"A few times. And then he asked when he'd be able to come get him."

I shake my head. "What is that guy's problem?" Teddy did warn me that, more times than not, we'd face the wrong side of Roy Donovan. But, to be that confrontational just because we want to run a charter plane business? It doesn't make sense.

"I don't know." Jonah's soapy hands smooth over my back. "But you did good today, Barbie."

"I *did* do good. Muriel was about to shoot him." The dog would be dead.

"She was doin' what she thought was right. And if Marie hadn't been there, it probably would have been the right thing to do." Jonah gives my shoulder a squeeze, earning my whimper. "From workin' outside?"

"Yeah. Muriel is not only an executioner, she's a tyrant. I'm amazed she didn't bring a whip with her."

"It looks great back there. You did an incredible job." Jonah gives my shoulders a soothing rub.

I wince, even though his hands feel like a masseuse's touch. "It's going to take *way* more ass-kissing to get me to plant your stupid brussels sprouts, Jonah."

His chuckle fills the tiny bathroom, carrying over the running water. "Believe me, we haven't even gotten to the ass-kissing part."

CHAPTER TWENTY-TWO

"Hey ... Calla." Jonah's voice stirs me from my slumber.

I crack a lid to find him standing over me. It takes a moment for me to register that he's already dressed for outside, the collar of the navy-blue wool jacket I bought him for his birthday flipped up. It's a sexy look, likely unintentional on his part. "You promised you wouldn't work today." Even groggy, my voice is heavy with disappointment. I was hoping for one full day with him this week.

"I'm not." His rough fingers caress my temple, pushing my wayward hair back off my forehead. "We're going out. Get dressed."

"Where to?"

"Out." An indecipherable look flashes across his face. "I've switched out the skis on Archie and wanna take him out for a spin so he's ready for the season. He's been sittin' too long."

"Okay," I say through a yawn. "Give me an hour?"

He smirks. "So you can log in more sleep?" He knows me too well, because that's exactly what I was envisioning. And to think there was a time when I'd use every one of those minutes to primp. "Be ready in twenty."

I check the clock. "It's only seven A.M.! What is wrong with you? Don't people sleep in on their days off in Alaska?" I've been getting up at six every morning lately to see Jonah off on a rash of supply runs from Anchorage to remote locations in the interior. I went with him for two of those days, mainly so I could meet people and get scenic shots for social media, both for The Yeti and for my own personal use. But the carpenter was here to install the screens for the porch, so I've had to be around. It's not a hardship, if I'm being honest. As much as I love spending time with Jonah, the supply trips are becoming repetitive and mundane. I feel more productive in the office with paperwork and marketing than I do rattling around in turbulence and delivering boxes of ground coffee to a remote resort for the tourist season.

It was different last summer, when all this was new and thrilling, when the clock was ticking on my time in Alaska and with Jonah. It's still exciting to be in the air with him, but now that I'm here for good, I don't feel the necessity to tag along on every flight.

Though, if we leave soon, I might get a day off from Muriel. True to her word, the day after the bear-trap disaster, I heard the buzz of her ATV coming up the driveway at seven A.M. She arrived with trays of tiny green plants strapped next to the gun on her rack and a hand-drawn map to mark where everything had to be planted. A replication of Colette's garden.

Every morning since, she's shown up at our side doorstep, rain or shine, dragging me out to check on the electric fence and the piles of dirt and tiny seedlings, confirming that nothing has changed save for the few weeds that pop up here and there. She even makes a point of releasing Zeke and Bandit from the pen along the way.

"Come on, sun's been up for hours. It's a nice day out." Jonah punctuates his words by strolling over to yank open the curtain.

I attempt to block the beam of light with a hand, squinting against the brightness. "Half an hour," I negotiate.

"There's coffee ready downstairs."

"A latte?" My barista machine—a duplicate to the one Simon bought—arrived yesterday.

"You know I have no damn clue how to use that thing." Jonah drags our comforter off the bed, leaving my bare skin exposed to the chilly morning air.

I groan loudly as I stretch my arms above my head. "Stop being such a morning person. It's annoying."

He opens his mouth to respond but stalls, his blue eyes surveying my naked body.

I could still win this. "So ... an hour?" I taunt, arching my back just enough to bring his heated gaze to my chest.

He curses under his breath and then spins around and marches out the door, hollering, "Twenty minutes!"

"You're in full-on yeti mode. Great." I stare up at our wood-planked ceiling. Jonah doesn't fall easily to distraction when he's like that. With my attempts at seduction thwarted, I haul my tired body to the bathroom.

———

Exhilaration courses through me as Jonah cuts the engine on Archie and I take in the familiar valley—the walls of sheer rock climbing into the sky on either side of us; the snaking river that stretches ahead, its water trickling over rock and pebble, circumventing fallen logs, the rivulets converging and diverging again.

The last time we were here, we were on a mission to pick up a couple who'd been hiking in the mountains for a week, and the inclement weather forced an overnight stay. Now, fluffy white clouds float above us, breaking up an otherwise crisp blue sky.

Jonah hangs up his headset. "Worth draggin' your ass out of bed for?"

"Absolutely." I clasp his cheeks with my hands and pull his face into mine, planting a hard kiss on his lips. "This is the best surprise, Jonah. Seriously."

The floats attached to the amphibious plane make it too high for me to hop down easily. I wait for Jonah to appear on my side and then reach for his shoulders and jump onto him.

He stalls my descent with a searing kiss, leaving my feet to dangle midair for several long moments before touching down on the dirt airstrip.

"You're acting weird," I note. I can't place a finger on what exactly it is that's odd, but whatever it is, he's been doing it since waking me.

His brow furrows. "Because I kissed you?"

"Yeah. Or, I don't know. You seem ... happier than normal? What gives?"

"Can't I be in a good mood?" He pulls out our small orange cooler from the seat.

I frown. "Are we staying over?"

"Nah. It's just a light lunch." He smirks. "Figured you wouldn't want jerky again."

My eyebrows arch. "*You* packed a lunch? Because I was fairly certain you didn't know how." I've taken to making sandwiches for him that he can grab on his way in and out for work. It's easier than dealing with his grumpy mood when he's hungry and standing in front of the fridge, glaring at my salads and overnight oatmeal, complaining that there's never anything to eat.

"All right, smart-ass." He slings his rifle over his shoulder—a reminder that, while we're entirely alone out here, we're never actually alone—and, taking my hand, he leads me toward the tree line.

Wistfulness flutters in my stomach as we trek through the forest, passing the familiar archway with the antlers fastened to them. Our surroundings aren't as lush as they were in the depths of summer. Everything is still waking from a wintry slumber—the deciduous tree branches bare, the ground cover only beginning to emerge. There isn't a sound save for the weight of our boots along the time-worn path.

"What if someone's using it?"

"Then I'll kick 'em out," he answers, his eyes dancing with mischief.

The safety cabin is exactly as we left it, a quiet, rustic shack nestled among the forest, the windows boarded up, a stack of wood piled next to the door, waiting for occupants to seek shelter.

"This is *so* weird." A wave of nostalgia overwhelms me as we step into the dim interior. The tiniest rays of sunlight creep through the cracks in the window boards, offering little light. But it's enough for me to make out important details—the spot on the floor where I made up a bed, unsure who would be occupying it; the rope line where Jonah hung my clothes, soaked from the downpour; the tiny kitchen with the dry sink and the dented pots, where he ordered me to strip; the black woodstove in the corner that warmed the air and our tangled bodies well into the night. It even smells the same—like musty wood and soot.

It was the night that the tension brewing between Jonah and I erupted.

Jonah's gaze drifts over the interior for a long moment. I wonder what he remembers of that night, and how vividly. Me? Now that I'm standing here, I remember every touch, every kiss, every shudder of my body. At least it seems that way.

He sets the cooler onto the table. "Gimme a minute to open it up a bit." He brings my hand to his mouth to kiss it and then takes a deep breath and exhales slowly, his eyes steady and thoughtful and hinting at something—worry or fear?—as they lock on mine.

"Jonah, seriously, you're beginning to freak me out. Are you about to tell me you're dying or something?"

"Jesus." He releases a breathy laugh and, shaking his head, heads out the door.

"Okay, I guess not," I murmur, adding louder, "Don't cut yourself again! I like this shirt too much for you to bleed on it!" I wander over to the rustic kitchen table to unzip the cooler bag, curious to see what he packed. Inside are multiple containers of grapes, cheese and crackers, a thermos of the barley soup I made yesterday. "Wow. You actually made sandwiches." I peek under the croissant to find a tidy pile of ham. There's a small, two-glass bottle of champagne tucked into the side. He even remembered to pack flutes.

"Didn't you eat breakfast?" Jonah asks from the doorway. With a window uncovered on either side, there's plenty of daylight streaming in.

"Just snooping." I hold up the bottle. "What are we celebrating?"

He shrugs. "How about being here again?"

"Fair enough." I smooth my hand over the rough surface of the rustic table, smiling slyly. "Remember this?"

He kicks the door closed with the heel of his boot and strolls toward me. "I remember *everything* about that night." He comes to a stop in front of me, his fingers coasting over my cheek, tucking my hair behind my ear.

I hop up onto the edge of the table, allowing my legs to dangle off the side. "Feel like reenacting it?" I waggle my eyebrows.

I expect him to laugh but instead, a contemplative look passes over his handsome face. "You ever wish you could hit rewind and relive that night?"

I take in the tiny space again as I consider his question—and remembering everything that came after. I shake my head. "It was an amazing night. But so much happened after it that I wouldn't ever want to face again." So much pain. I found my father, only to lose him again, this time forever. And for months, I thought I had lost Jonah forever, too. That was agony of a different kind.

I hook my heels around his thighs and pull him toward me, fitting his hips between my legs. Reaching up, I let my fingers drag through his beard. I smile as I recall the night I trimmed it the first time, exacting my revenge while he lay unconscious after the crash that totaled the plane. I can still hear my father's laughter the next morning when he realized what I'd done to his golden boy, and why.

So much has changed between us.

That night we found ourselves stranded here, Jonah was an enigma to me. That sexy but intimidating man who spoke his mind, even when it wasn't something I wanted to hear. My father's right-hand man, the bush pilot who would never leave.

He was temporary, as was my time in Alaska.

Now … He still steals my breath and my every thought, but he's all mine. He doesn't intimidate me anymore because I know him inside out. I know the origin of every scar on his intoxicating body. I know that he gets irritable when he's grounded for too long and giddy when the propeller begins to churn. I know he hates it when freshly dried clothes sit in the hamper for too long, and he can't stand skin on chicken. I know he's a light sleeper and a heavy snorer. I know he likes to be in charge of most any situation, but he'll give a stranger the shirt off his back if they need it. I know he feels guilty for not seeing his mother more often, but every time he calls her, the sound of his step-father's condescending voice in the background makes his fists ball up.

I know Jonah loves me. Maybe as much as I love him.

"Where we are now is perfect," I say. Almost too perfect.

"It is." Jonah's throat bobs with a hard swallow, his gaze searching my face, lingering on my mouth before shifting to the small gold-and-diamond plane that sits nestled against my collarbone. I wear it every single day. He collects it between his fingers, studying it a moment. "I remember thinking that night how I was gonna fall hard for you."

"Really? Because I remember you being ready to stop doing *this* so I'd stay." So we didn't *complicate* things.

"Nah, I was just tryin' to be a nice guy." His smirk is fleeting before it falls off. "One thing is for sure, Barbie. *This* was never gonna end. Not if I had anything to do with it," he whispers, his hands coming to rest on either side of my jaw, cupping my face. "And in the year that I've known you—"

"It hasn't even been a year. It's only been, like, nine months," I correct him. How has it *only* been nine months? It feels like I've been living with him for *years*.

"Almost ten, if you wanna be picky. May is more than half over. And stop interrupting me," he scolds through a kiss. He takes a deep breath. "In all that time, I've never doubted that you're the woman I want to spend the rest of my life with."

May is more than half over.

An alarm triggers in my mind—a gut feeling that I've missed something important—and I feel the blood drain from my face as I abruptly pull away from him. "Oh my God."

Jonah pauses. "What's wrong?"

"What's the date?" I mumble, scrambling to pull my phone from my pocket to check my calendar. I do the math. "No, no, no, no …" My stomach drops as realization takes over. "I'm late."

"For what?"

I shoot Jonah a flat look. "I'm *late*."

His frown instantly smooths as realization hits him. "*Oh.*"

It's a good thing I'm sitting down because I suddenly feel off-balance as panic settles in.

"How late?" he asks.

"Four days."

"That's not—"

"I'm *never* late, Jonah. Never. My cycle is like clockwork. Oh my God, how could this happen?" My hands fly to my forehead, as if that will somehow help soothe the shock of this situation. "I mean, I missed *one* pill this month but I took it the next day. That shouldn't have messed things up."

"Hey … Slow down, Calla." He collects my hands in his, giving them a gentle squeeze. "We will be *fine*. We can handle this. So, it's a bit sooner than we planned—"

"*A bit?* I'm not even twenty-seven yet! Try *years* sooner, Jonah. Like five, six years too soon." I don't even have a timeline in my head for having kids, that's how "too soon" this is. "This is … Oh God! I'm becoming my mother! I'm *literally* reliving my mother's life!" Sure, she was pregnant before she decided to move to Alaska, but she sure as hell didn't plan on getting pregnant when she did.

Jonah watches me quietly as I tumble into a full meltdown until his silence only exacerbates the situation.

"Please, say something."

"I'm not sure what to say, Calla," he begins, his voice even. "It's not crazy to have a kid at twenty-seven. And I'm thirty-two. Five or six years sounds like a long time to wait for me." He chews his lip. "We're living together, we have a house, and more than enough money to get by."

"Yeah, but a baby changes *everything*, Jonah. It's permanent. It's *for life*."

Jonah's jaw tenses. "As opposed to what *we* are?"

"No, I didn't mean it like that. I'm just …" I search for the right words. "We're barely settled here. I'm still trying to figure out what I want my life to look like. Is The Yeti going to turn into something big enough to keep me busy all day? Will I be happy doing that for the rest of my life? Am I going to go back to school? Are we going to stay in Alaska long-term? And what about traveling? I want to take a vacation with you at least once before I'm trapped at home with diapers and bottles and whatever the hell else comes with all that. I'm just … I'm *nowhere* near ready to start popping out babies!"

The questions and wishes and doubts fly out of my mouth in rapid fire, and Jonah's expression … well, it looks like he just had the wind knocked out of him. "I'm not saying *no* to kids, Jonah. I do want one or two eventually—"

"No, I get it." He releases my hands to hold his up in the air in a sign of surrender. "It's okay, Calla. Really. You're right. It *has* been only a few months." He voices these words, but his frown says something different.

"I'm sorry."

"Don't apologize." He shakes his head. "I'm always pushing you to be honest with me about what you want. Or don't want, in this case."

"So ... What are we going to do?" A fresh wave of panic hits me as reality sets in and I look down at my abdomen.

Is there a human growing inside me?

"I guess"—he pauses, searching for words—"we need to find out for sure first. There's no point worrying until we know for sure."

As usual, Jonah is right. "I'll do a test as soon as we get home."

Uncomfortable silence fills the cabin, the previous nostalgic mood obliterated, replaced by something sour. Jonah has stepped away from me—to give me space, perhaps?—his hands now occupied with his coat pockets.

I'm searching for the right words to get back to our previous conversation when Jonah sighs heavily. "Maybe we should head back. I don't think either of us will be able to think about much else."

That's probably for the best.

I barely nod before he's moving for the door.

———

I steal another glance behind us but all I see are jagged mountain peaks. The cabin and valley are long gone from view.

Jonah has been chattering back and forth with another pilot on our frequency. I can't tell if it's because he's enjoying the idle conversation with a stranger, or if he's avoiding conversation with me.

Right now, I'm fine with either.

A baby.

I take a deep breath, trying to reconcile myself with the concept of becoming a mother at twenty-seven years old. It certainly wasn't part of my plan. Then again, moving to Alaska wasn't, either.

If there is anyone's baby I'd want to have, it's Jonah's. I've felt the desire, in momentary flashes and twinges, whenever I've seen him watching a child at the grocery store with amusement. He'll make an excellent father—a quality I never even considered in any guy I dated until I met him. These facts tell me that I'll get there, eventually.

But we've only been living together for five months, in this house for not even three. It's far too soon. We're just finding our bearings as a couple. Things between us are perfect.

A baby would change that.

I think of Sharon, twenty-three and sitting in the receptionist desk at Wild, her belly bulging, her ankles swollen, rocking a passenger's mewling newborn. She confided in me that she'd been waiting to have a baby since she was seventeen, after her first date with Max. The fact that I'm feeling nothing more than shock and fear tells me that no matter how much I love Jonah, I'm not ready to go there yet.

A warm hand slips over my thigh. I turn to meet Jonah's furrowed brow. He offers me a thin-lipped smile but says nothing. He doesn't seem to hate me for my glaring lack of excitement about our predicament, but he can't hide the disappointment in those blue eyes.

Jonah is ready to go there now.

"When do you have to work again?" I ask, craving a safe topic of conversation.

"Day after tomorrow. I *was* thinking we could fly out to Bangor. Visit Wren's grave and see Aggie. Yell at Mabel, get her to smarten up."

"Yeah, because rebellious teenagers respond well to that," I say sarcastically, noting how he emphasized the "was," as if flying west is no longer an option.

"Maybe not, but I need to say something before she fucks up her life—" He stops talking abruptly and frowns at the gauges in front of him.

"What's wrong?"

He curses under his breath.

"Jonah?"

His attention darts between the sky ahead and his panel, up and down, up and down. Not answering.

My pulse begins to race. "Jonah, what's going on?"

"Just, uh … an issue with the oil pressure," he says in an oddly calm, detached tone that only makes his words sound more ominous.

"What does that mean?"

"It means we're gonna land."

"What. Like *now*?"

"Pretty much."

I scan our surroundings. Everywhere I look are jagged mountains and trees. "*Where?*"

He chews his bottom lip in thought as he studies the river below us. "I think I remember there being a lake up ahead. Around that bend."

"*You think?*" Everything looks the same around here. People have gotten lost following the wrong river; they've crashed into mountains, misidentifying peaks and making the wrong turn.

He pulls a map from a side pocket, instructing me to open it up as he angles the plane to fly lower. "Can you find Rainy Pass on there?"

"I … uh …" I fumble with the paper. "I don't know." In our office, with the map stretched out, I've gotten pretty good at reading these things. Cramped in a tiny plane as we descend toward the trees? Not so much.

"Here. Lemme see." He keeps a keen eye on our flight path as he traces a river down through the mountains. "Yeah, there. I think that's up ahead."

It's the second time he's said, "I think."

"Can't we turn around and fly back to the cabin?"

His gaze flickers to the gauge again. "No. You're buckled in, right?" He does a quick glance over.

My adrenaline surges as a mental flash of twisted metal and rivulets of blood running down Jonah's forehead hits me. A scary day that I never wanted to repeat, and yet here we are. This time, in the mountains, where there are far bigger things to hit than a crop of field stones. "Jonah, are we going to crash?" I hear the panic in my voice.

"No, Calla. We've gotta land." He begins calling out our location over the radio as we descend.

———————

"We're not dead." I release a long, shaky sigh as we float on the placid water in utter silence.

Jonah lets out a weak chuckle as he rubs his brow. "You don't have a lot of confidence in my flying ability, do you?"

"I do. But I also thought we were going to hit those trees back there." Jonah brought us down so close to the tree line, I couldn't keep the screams of panic from escaping. Even now, cold sweat coats the back of my neck, and there's a fifty-fifty chance I still might vomit.

"I wasn't sure how big the lake was, and I wasn't gonna risk having to do a second pass to get enough runway."

Especially not when he had already cut the engine before the floats touched down. I heard enough of his radio chatter to understand the gist of what was going on. Things like "in the red," "burning up," and "stall out."

It was far more serious than Jonah was letting on.

He nods to my chest. "You can let go."

I look down and see that my hands are curled so tight around my seat belt that my knuckles are white. I release my grip and peer out the window. "Where are we?" Besides in the middle of nowhere.

"Here." Jonah points out the lake on the map, surrounded by mountains and far from any town or landmark. We couldn't walk, even if we wanted to.

"Is that guy going to come?"

As if on cue, our headsets crackle with the man's voice, asking if we're okay.

Jonah responds, giving him our coordinates, and then yanks off his headset. "He should be here soon. I need you to listen and relay any messages from him."

"Where are you going?" We're in the middle of a lake!

"I need to see how bad this is." He reaches behind my seat for his tool bag. His mouth is mere inches from mine. Normally he'd have stolen a kiss by now. He *always* does when he's reaching for anything behind my seat.

But he hasn't this time.

I'd like to think it's because he's too focused on our current engine predicament, but I can't help but worry that it's about the other, more serious problem at hand.

On impulse, I lean in and capture his lips with mine. He responds with the briefest of kisses, his soft sigh skating across my cheek as he pulls away. "Listen for this Sam guy, okay?"

"Don't fall in." Who knows how deep that lake is, and the floats are likely slippery.

He pops open his door and eases out.

Leaving me alone with worry gnawing at my insides.

"What kind of plane is that?" I study the mustard-yellow one-seater that taxis along the lake toward us. It looks like a brightly painted fighter plane, with the little pilot hatch on the top.

"A Fire Boss." Jonah watches its approach while standing on a float. "They use them to fight forest fires. The pilots fly down low over a lake, slurp up a bunch of water into the floats, and then dump it on the fire from above. It's pretty cool." Jonah's words don't match his flat voice and grim face. Whatever he found under that engine panel had him cursing Bart, Alaska Wild's mechanic.

The silence drags as we wait.

"So, how bad is it?" I finally dare ask.

"Don't know yet. I need to get Toby here."

The yellow plane stops twenty feet away, and Jonah tightens his grip as the subtle waves rock us. The hatch pops open and a bald man waves. "Not havin' a great day, are ya!"

You have no idea.

"Thanks for comin', Sam," Jonah hollers.

"No problem. You need a ride outta here? I can come back with another plane, but it'll be a bit. Or I've got a friend not too far away I can call."

"Either would be much appreciated."

"Lemme get a hold of my friend. Probably faster."

Jonah gently thumps his fist against the fuselage. "I'll start tyin' him up."

"Did you do it right?"

I look up from my perch on the closed toilet to glare at Jonah. "How many ways are there to pee on a stick?"

"More than one, based on this." He scowls at the pregnancy test instructions. "It's less complicated to fly a damn plane."

I stare hard at the tiny window, turning it this way and that under the light of the naked bulb above, searching for the second pink line that's supposed to appear within two minutes. It's been five and there's not even a hint of one. Based on this test, I'm not pregnant.

Relief sweeps over me, though I know we're not in the clear yet.

Jonah crumples and tosses the pamphlet into the trash can. "So, what now?" His mood hasn't improved since Sam's friend brought us home. We left Archie at the edge of the lake, secured by ropes and anchors, and I know it's eating at him.

"I'll do another test in the morning, to make sure. Maybe my hormones are messed up this month." I can't hide the hopefulness in my voice.

Just as Jonah can't seem to hide the disappointment from his face. He nods slowly. "Did Toby respond yet?"

"Yeah. He said he's free to go today if you want," I say.

"Today would be ideal." He hesitates. "You good with staying home, or did you want to come with us?"

I can't help but sense that Jonah would prefer the former of those two options. After my epic meltdown at the cabin, I wouldn't blame him.

I smile, even though it stings to think he wants time away from me. "I think I've had enough flying excitement for one day." My nerves are frazzled by that emergency landing. "Go do what you have to do."

He peers at the second, unopened pregnancy test. He opens his mouth to say something but decides against it. Leaning down, he plants a quick kiss on my forehead and then turns for the door.

"Jonah?"

He pauses, his back to me. "Yup?"

"Are we okay?"

"Of course, we are." He turns back to flash a comforting smile that doesn't reach his eyes.

CHAPTER TWENTY-THREE

I'm practically skipping out of the bathroom and down the stairs the next morning, despite the heavy cramping in my abdomen, buoyant with the knowledge that the crisis has been averted. I am without a doubt *not* pregnant. I don't know what caused the delay in my cycle, but I will certainly never forget a single pill *ever* again.

It's only 6:30 A.M. and a quiet calm hangs in our house. I heard Jonah leave through the front door as I was waking, likely not expecting me up for another hour or two. My guess is he's in the hangar, itching to fetch Archie from his temporary parking spot in the remote wilderness.

Toby dropped everything yesterday to come help him. They took off in Veronica, first to the plane so he could assess the damage. He confirmed what Jonah suspected—that several seals and lines weren't tightened properly during maintenance, causing an oil leak. All fingers point to Bart, or whoever he had doing the work because Alaska Wild's mechanic was known for pawning off basic maintenance to grounds crew who swore they knew what they were doing. He would normally double-check their work, but maybe, with everything going on at Wild, he missed that step.

The guys flew to Anchorage to buy the necessary parts, then back up the mountain to try to fix Archie on-site—because what else do you do when your plane is stranded on a lake? There's certainly no tow truck you can call.

The sun was setting by the time Veronica's floats broke the calm of our lake once again, both men wearing tired faces but chuckling over the idle threats Jonah plans on making to Bart the next time he sees him. Toby seemed confident that there wasn't any permanent damage to the engine. Jonah, less so, and he's already hired Toby to do a full, top-to-bottom service of the plane next week to make sure nothing else arises.

Something so simple as sloppy maintenance could have killed us had we not had somewhere to land, had Jonah pushed our luck, had the engine stalled before we touched down.

But it didn't, and the plane is fixed, and I am not pregnant, and everything needs to go back to the way it was between us when Jonah yanked the covers off the bed yesterday morning.

My nerves stir as I text Jonah.

Calla: *You at the hangar?*

I make myself a latte while I wait for an answer.

Jonah: *Yup. Sam's giving me a ride up the mountain to get the plane. He'll be here at eight. I'll swing by the house before I leave.*

Jonah seems to have bonded with the wiry, bald firefighter in the yellow plane who rescued us from our predicament yesterday.

Calla: *So it's safe to fly?*

Jonah: *It better be or Toby's a shitty mechanic.*

I smile. At least he's starting to joke about it.

Calla: *BTW ... False alarm.*

I watch for the three bouncing dots that signal a response. It takes a full minute before they appear.

Jonah: *OK.*

"Okay?" I don't know what answer I expected from him.

You must be so relieved.

Let's make sure we're more careful.

Don't worry, I love you and next time, we'll both be ready for it.

"OK" seems so ... not okay.

That feeling begins to gnaw in my stomach again, that our relationship took a major hit yesterday with this pregnancy scare. But I could also chalk it up to Jonah not being keen on texting. And it's easy to misinterpret thoughts and feelings in texts. It's *too* easy for your own insecurities to breed falsities in a simple word.

What I do know is that I can't let him fly off like this, with my head and my heart spinning, not until I've talked to him, face-to-face.

I charge for the hallway, for my red plaid jacket—the one Jonah bought me last year after he bled all over my favorite cardigan—intent on getting out to the hangar and spending the next hour fixing this tension however I can before Sam gets here. In my haste, I knock Jonah's wool jacket off the hook.

A small box falls out of his pocket.

I frown at the small black jewelry box as I collect it from the floor. It takes a few beats to process what it could be.

No way ...

With my pulse pounding in my ears and a furtive glance out the door to confirm Jonah is not about to walk into the house and catch me snooping, I pop open the lid.

I gasp at the diamond ring that stares back at me, and the pieces fall into place.

Jonah was wearing this jacket yesterday. The surprise trip to the cabin ... the lunch ... the bottle of champagne ... him, acting so strange ...

He was going to propose.

Before his words triggered the pregnancy scare, he was talking about spending the rest of his life with me. I remember—vaguely—one hand leaving my face, reaching toward his pocket.

He was literally in the process of asking me to marry him when I panicked about being late.

"Seriously?" Wild flutters stir in my stomach. With no warning? No marriage conversations beforehand? I mean, we've only been living together for five months! We've known each other less than a year, and yet, here is this ring—this stunning diamond ring designed to look like a snowflake, with countless diamonds of various sizes—and he was going to propose to me yesterday.

And I would have said yes, I realize with absolute certainty.

I would have been shocked speechless when he asked, but I would have said yes, as I said yes to Alaska and yes to this house, because being with Jonah is not optional. Because, despite knowing him for less than a year, I can't imagine my life without him in it anymore. I never want to be without him again.

I would have said yes.

I would be wearing this ring. We would be engaged.

Instead, I freaked out about the possibility of being pregnant and probably not in a way that screamed, "We should get married!"

An ache stirs in my chest as I think back to that look on Jonah's face—of hurt and disappointment. He'd planned the entire day—the location, the lunch. He'd even brought champagne. And me, being entirely caught unaware, never put two and two together.

Oh my God.

What if he doesn't want to marry me anymore?

"Yeah, but a baby changes everything, Jonah. It's permanent. It's for life."

"As opposed to what we are?"

Did I unwittingly create a fissure between us with my rambling?

I shut the box and slide it back into its hiding spot in his pocket, fixing the jacket as best I can so I don't let on that I've discovered Jonah's secret.

And then I head for the door, hoping a walk to the hangar will give me enough time to figure out what the hell I'm going to say to him.

I frown at the silver truck parked next to ours outside the hangar. There's no doubt whose it is. A magnetic sign with her veterinarian clinic name clings to the door.

But what is Marie doing at our house at 6:45 A.M.? Does this have something to do with Oscar? As far as I know, the wolf dog is back home with Roy, slowly healing from his leg wound.

"... and then everything blew up from there." Jonah's voice carries from the gaping hangar door, stalling my feet.

"So, I guess you didn't get a chance to ask her, then." Marie's soft, sympathetic voice answers

"You kidding? There wasn't exactly a way to segue back to marriage after that."

It's clear they're talking about what happened yesterday. Jonah must have told Marie he was going to propose. I guess I shouldn't be surprised. She's his closest friend. And yet, an unpleasant feeling settles in the pit of my stomach, knowing that he has obviously divulged the pregnancy scare to her as well. It feels like a betrayal of confidence. It's something private between the two of us that we haven't fully discussed, and yet here he is, talking about it with *her*.

That's why Marie is here. Jonah must have called her. He needed to talk about it with someone who *isn't* me.

Hurt pricks my chest as I edge in closer and eavesdrop shamelessly.

Jonah sighs. "I've never seen her like that before. I mean, I've seen her snap plenty, believe me ... but this was somethin' else."

"She is only twenty-six, Jonah. And she's gone through a lot in the past year. Her whole life has been turned over, more than once. She's obviously not ready to have it flipped again yet. Cut her some slack."

Yes! Exactly!

"No shit." He snorts. "But five or six years? I'll be almost forty."

"You're not *that* old," Marie chides.

"I will be if it turns into eight or nine. And it might. You should have seen her, Marie. It was like the idea of being pregnant was a death sentence."

I feel my cheeks flame. I know having children is important to Jonah, but he told me it was okay that I wasn't ready, that I shouldn't apologize for not being ready.

Was he lying to me when he said that?

"Or it could turn into two or three years, once she settles and her priorities change," Marie counters. "Don't forget, when you met her, she was living at home with her *parents*. Her focus was on looking good and going out to clubs."

Is that what Marie thinks of me?

"But, Jonah, you haven't even started trying to have kids. What if she ends up not being able to at all? What are you going to do then —*divorce* her?" There's an accusatory tone in Marie's voice, almost a challenge to admit he'd be so callous, and my heart softens for her again.

"Fuck, of course not! I just ..." His voice trails for a long stretch. "Maybe I *am* moving too fast."

No! No, you aren't! I want to cry out. I mean, it *is* fast, but I'm ready for this, for us. I never realized how ready I was until that ring fell out of his pocket.

"Yeah, you're not known for your patience," Marie says, and I hear the smile. "But you can't help it. You're so passionate when it comes to someone or something that's important to you." There's a pause, and when she speaks again, there's a hint of yearning in her soft voice. "It's one of the things I've always loved about you, Jonah."

Despite Marie's earlier words of seeming support for me, a wave of jealousy burns my insides, hearing her remind him in a not-so-subtle way that, yes, they may be just friends but she's still waiting on the sidelines for a chance at more. I'm sure Marie would be more than happy to deliver Jonah's baby on the ground of the hangar right here, right now, given the opportunity. That I'm not ready feels like a strike against me, a competitive edge that she has over me, even though the diamond ring in Jonah's pocket is meant for *my* finger.

"Marie, you know how I feel about Calla—"

"Of course. I wasn't trying to …" Her words drift. "I care about you, and I only ever want to see you happy."

"I know, and I *am* happy."

"Are you, though? Completely? Are you happy turning down jobs because you're afraid to leave your girlfriend alone?"

Jonah's been turning down jobs because of me? What jobs?

"It's not like that. I promised Calla I wouldn't drag her all the way out here and then take off for days at a time."

"And how long is she going to hold you to that?"

"I don't know! Until she feels comfortable, I guess."

"I hate to break it to you, but I'd be more worried about how long *that*'s going to take than I would be about when she'll be ready to have kids. I mean, she's terrified of stepping outside!"

"Don't worry about Calla. She's figuring things out and doin' fine, running the office stuff and getting the house settled. She's got that big garden out back—"

"I'm not worried about her, Jonah. I'm worried about *you*."

Just like that, any goodwill I felt toward Marie withers.

"You wanted to be free to fly wherever, whenever. It's why you didn't take over Wild from Wren when he tried to give it to you, remember?"

"It wasn't mine to take."

"You were like a son to him, Jonah. No one would have thought anything of you for accepting his offer. You could have had the entire thing."

I frown. What does she mean by that? My father did ask Jonah if he'd be willing to buy Wild at one point, but Jonah didn't have the money.

"And here you are, turning down jobs that you *really* want so you can do supply runs all day long while she blows that money, *decorating*." There's no missing the critical edge in her tone.

"That's outta line, Marie," he warns, his tone sharp.

"I'm sorry." She sighs. "I do like her. Please don't think that I don't. I just hate seeing you giving up what you love."

My heart pounds as I waver between storming inside to scream at Marie and demanding that Jonah tell me what the hell she means about giving things up. In the end, I keep my feet grounded where they are, wanting to see what more I'll glean from this conversation.

The silence stretches.

"I should probably go. I told Roy I'd be by at seven to give Oscar his shots ..." Marie's voice grows louder as she approaches the hangar door. I shift backward, not wanting to get caught eavesdropping. But there's nowhere to go, the driveway between the house and here stretching too far to hide.

The workshop.

I dart for the smaller building adjacent the hangar, thankful that the door is propped open. I make it inside just as Marie appears, her long, golden-blonde locks loose down her back, her hiking boots kicking gravel on the driveway.

I've only been in the workshop twice, the clutter Phil left behind too much for me to digest. There are countless old tools and jars of screws and everything under the sun that a person might need to survive, but also straight-up junk—old rusty license plates and dented hubcaps cover the back wall; an old fridge that's missing a door, rendering it useless, sits in the corner; old, used paint cans and supplies are stacked in a heap. It's another major clean-out task for us that we're both avoiding.

I find my way to the small, grime-covered window in time to see Jonah grab Marie's hand, stalling her from climbing into her truck. My anger flares over the fact that he seems to be consoling her after her harsh words—does she deserve comforting after what she said about me? And do I have a right to say anything, given I was listening in on a private conversation?

They exchange words I can't hear. With a quick parting hug, she ducks into her truck and peels away, leaving Jonah standing by himself, rubbing his forehead as if the day has already been too much for him.

Abruptly, he turns and walks along the driveway toward the house.

He's on his way home to see me.

Shit.

There's no real way around this, short of sprinting from tree to tree to try to get home in time, and lying that I was out here—a decidedly immature and high-risk charade I don't want to take part in.

Taking a deep breath, I step into the doorway and holler, "I'm in here."

Jonah's head whips around, his face momentarily marred with surprise.

Then with realization.

His brow is furrowed as he doubles back and approaches as he no doubt replays his conversation with Marie, wondering what I caught of the exchange.

"Sorry, I came down to see you and then you were talking to Marie and ..." And what? Do I tell him that I know about the ring?

He leans against the door frame, close enough that I can inhale the intoxicating scent of soap on his skin. "What exactly did you hear?" he asks.

I falter. "Enough to know that you've been turning down jobs. And what's this about my father giving you Alaska Wild?"

He curses under his breath.

"What jobs?"

"Doesn't matter."

I'm not sure what annoys me more—that I don't know about it or that Marie does. "What jobs have you been turning down?"

He bites his bottom lip. "A hunting outfit mentioned wanting me to work for them in September. It's not a big deal, and I don't even know if I'd want it."

"That's not how Marie made it sound."

He scowls. "She doesn't know what she's talkin' about."

That, or Jonah isn't willing to tell me.

I decide to leave that alone for the moment. "And what was that about my dad giving you Alaska Wild?"

"I don't know why we're doin' this—"

"Because I want to know. Marie shouldn't know things about your life that *I* don't!" *Especially as the woman you want to marry.* "The last I heard, my dad offered to sell you Wild, but you couldn't afford it."

He sighs heavily and shakes his head. "There was a brief point when Wren was thinkin' about how to keep Wild running after he was gone. He asked if I wanted to buy it off him for whatever I could pay him, which wasn't nearly what it was worth. He suggested it about a week before you showed up. That's when I knew something was goin' on with him. It didn't make sense for him to walk away from the kind of money he could get sellin' to Aro, who I knew was interested in buying him out."

"So, why didn't you take it?" My dad did say that Jonah was the one person who would do right by Alaska Wild.

He shrugs. "Didn't feel good, takin' advantage of the situation like that. He'd basically be giving it to me. Plus, I knew he had a daughter, even if you hadn't seen each other in forever. It'd be like robbing you of what was rightfully yours. Anyway, as soon as you showed up, Wren came to his senses and realized it was time to let Wild go completely. I even offered to run it, if he wanted to leave it all to you. And I would have, for however long you wanted me to."

"Why didn't you tell me this?"

"Because he wouldn't agree to it. He didn't want to put that kind of pressure on either of us. It'd mean tying you down to Alaska and something that kept you two apart for so many years. So, he took that option right off the table and sold it to Aro." Jonah watches me. "He said he could die peacefully, knowing you'd always be taken care of. Financially, at least."

What if my father had agreed to Jonah's proposal, that he leave the company to me and have Jonah run it? For starters, I'd be screwed if Jonah decided he didn't want to do it anymore. It's not like I was about to move to Western Alaska to try to run things. And for how long would I be expected to keep it alive? What if I wanted to sell it? I'd be selling my family's legacy—that my father loved and gave up everything for—to the highest bidder.

The guilt with that decision would have weighed me down. It'd be a thousand times worse than Agnes signing over the deed to his house for possible demolition. Would I find myself resenting my father for putting me in that position, for tying me down to his life?

Jonah would still be attached to Western Alaska—for life, or as long as I was relying on him. We wouldn't be living here.

We might not be living together.

Jonah probably wouldn't have a ring in his pocket.

In the end, my dad made the right call. He put me ahead of Alaska Wild. Something he never seemed to be able to do before.

"You should have told me."

"It doesn't matter."

Maybe not. Though, if I ever needed proof for my mother that Jonah isn't after me for my money, I have it.

Jonah places a hand against the small of my back and pulls me closer to him. "How are you feelin' today?"

I reach for him. My palms smooth over the hard curves of his chest, his collarbone and shoulders, settling on his biceps. "I'm fine. A bit achy." I always am on the first day of my period.

"How long were you listening for, exactly?"

"Long enough to know I'm not a big fan of Marie's right now."

He smirks. "She was challenging me. That's what a good friend does."

I level him with a look.

"Tell me Diana wouldn't have a few harsh words about me if she was worried about you."

I can't tell him that because Diana would shred Jonah's character if she thought I was sacrificing my happiness for him. "But Diana isn't *also* in love with me."

He sighs, but he doesn't deny it this time. "What else did you hear?" He's fishing for vital information. Mainly, do I know about the botched proposal?

I've never been able to lie successfully to Jonah. "What else *should* I have heard?" I ask instead.

His jaw tenses as his gaze roams my face, as if he's deciding whether to take the plunge and admit his true intentions in yesterday's trip. "How much I love you, and that we don't need to rush *anything*."

What does "*anything*" mean?

Babies, I assume.

But is he pulling back the reins on the idea of marriage, too?

I hesitate. "Please tell me we're okay, because I feel like we're not okay—"

"We're okay, Calla. I promise," he says, brushing a strand of hair from my forehead, his voice turning gruff. "We're more than okay. I'm sorry if I let you think we weren't."

"I was so scared," I admit in a whisper, my fingers clawing at his waist, gripping him tightly.

"I'm sorry." Clutching the back of my head, he leans in to kiss my lips, stroking his tongue against mine in a deep, tantalizing way he normally reserves for the bedroom, when our clothes are off and our bodies are tangled.

A soft moan escapes my throat, unbidden.

"Sam won't be here for a bit," he whispers between ragged breaths, one hand fisting my hair, the other moving down to grip my backside and pull me flush against his arousal. "You want to go back to the house and get in the shower?"

My cramps have temporarily vanished, the promise of feeling Jonah's body within mine an antidote for any discomfort. Yet the idea of trekking all the way home seems anticlimactic, and I feel the overwhelming desire to please him. I catch his bottom lip between my teeth in a teasing nip. "I can't wait that long." My hands slip under his sweater. His stomach muscles tense beneath my cool fingers as I unfasten his belt and zipper and slide my hand past the elastic band of his boxer briefs to grip him firmly.

"That's fine with me," he rasps. "You've just always wanted to do it in the—" His words die as I drop to my knees before him, tugging his jeans and boxers down his powerful thighs along the way.

"Fuck," he hisses, his blue eyes flaring with heat as he watches me take him in my mouth. Plaiting his fingers through my long hair, he settles back against the door frame with a guttural moan, his appreciative gaze wandering between me and the vast wild vista surrounding us.

CHAPTER TWENTY-FOUR

"Wow. She wasn't kidding," I say as we pull up to the Ale House. The parking lot is filled with vehicles—mud-splattered pickups, ATVs, the odd shiny sedan. More have found space on the grass behind.

Jonah groans as he slows to search for a vacant spot. "Do we have to do this?"

"You think dealing with Muriel isn't exhausting for me?" Though, she has only been by twice in the past week to make sure I haven't ditched my daily garden duties. Oddly enough, I've found myself out there every morning without her prodding, curious about what new growth I might find. It's early days, but tiny stems with two leaves are cropping up where I sowed beet seeds. Today I compared the tomato plants to pictures I took on the day we planted them, to see that they're noticeably taller, thanks to the long Alaskan days.

"She said this place'll be full of fishermen and hunters, and people who rent their cabins out to tourists who want to go sightseeing. We need to meet people if we want to drum up more local business, right?"

"Weren't you complaining I was gone too much?" He backs the truck into a spot on the grass in between two others.

"Actually, I was complaining that you spend too much time playing with your planes in the hangar." I do my best to not complain about the hours he puts in for work. "Since when did you become so antisocial?"

"Seriously, Calla?" His blue eyes sparkle with humor. "I've *always* been this antisocial." He nods toward the front door where two burly men in black jackets and camo hats step out, reaching for cigarette packs, one of them studying the unlit string of colorful lights as they chatter. The sun is high at seven P.M. It'll set after eleven tonight, leaving the sky dusky until it rises again at four thirty, a reality I'm no more accustomed to now than I was last summer, staying at my father's house. "This isn't my scene."

A middle-aged couple wearing matching plaid jackets hurry across the lot as if late for something. In the woman's grasp is a Crock-Pot. "Uh ... Just so we're clear, *this* is not *my* scene, either. But I need a night out to talk to someone besides you, a goat, and a raccoon, so suck it up. For me, please."

"Fine," Jonah grumbles, but he leans in to press his lips against mine. "You look good tonight, by the way."

I smile. It's the first time since moving to Trapper's Crossing that I've made "night-out" effort with my hair and makeup and clothing, choosing a pair of tight blue jeans, my black leather riding boots, and a flattering yellow-and-black checkered button-down over our new branded, form-fitting T-shirts—an outfit that in my opinion says "Alaskan chili cook-off," but with style.

"So do you." I drag my fingernails—that I spent an hour filing and painting after scraping out garden soil despite wearing gloves—through his freshly groomed beard.

It's been a week since our trip to the safety cabin and the pregnancy scare and, much to my relief, things between us feel right again. *More* than right, actually. We've been all over each other—the touches frequent, the kisses lingering, the showers long enough to empty the water heater. It's as if we're both wordlessly trying to reassure each other and ourselves that all is okay. Or maybe that sharp slap of reality—two, if I count the engine-failure scare—has brought us even closer.

Either way, we feel perfect again.

Though, there's been no hint of an impending proposal or mention of marriage. When I went to sneak another peek at the ring, it was no longer in his jacket. I've had to bite my tongue more than once before I let on that I've seen it.

I hadn't given serious thought to marriage before that day, and now I catch myself peering down at my naked left finger and wishing things had played out differently. But I keep telling myself that he'll ask when the time is right.

Jonah slides a warm hand over my thigh and leans in closer, his mouth finding the crook of my neck. "You wanna skip this and go test out that overpriced hot tub? It should be warm."

"Funny how you're suddenly so interested in it," I whisper, reaching over to cut the engine and snag the keys. The installers left around four, after maneuvering the deluxe unit onto the porch to set it up, fill it, and test it. "The sooner we go in, the sooner we can leave." I hop out of the truck, pausing to smooth a finger over the new Yeti vinyl decal I affixed to the door.

An annoying buzz catches my ear. "Hurry up! The bugs are out!" It's like the mosquitos and black flies all woke up one morning. I stepped outside and got swarmed. Since then, I've had to wear a bug-net jacket or bug spray if I want to venture beyond the screened-in porch, and even then, they hover.

Toby promised they'll ease off a bit later in the season. Until then, I'm trying to not let them get to me, but I've caught myself hiding indoors and praying for a scorching heat wave or some sort of blight to come and kill them all.

Jonah takes his time easing out of the truck, much to my annoyance. "Told you to wear bug spray."

"I don't want to smell like that on a night out!"

"What do you think everyone in there smells like?" He pulls me into his side as two men step out the front door. Loud, boisterous voices, a lull of old rock music, and the pungent scent of simmering meat and spices carries out in the space between them.

I scrunch my nose and quietly admit, "I don't actually like chili."

———

Within minutes of us settling onto the last two vacant stools at the bar, Muriel marches over, shimmying to fit her broad hips between the tables. "Well, don't you look cute tonight, Calla," she exclaims, in a tone that could be a compliment but also might not be. It's hard for me to read this woman. "Maybe we should stick you behind the bar, instead of that face." She juts her chin toward Toby who's busy pouring a pint from the tap.

"We'd definitely sell more." Toby casts a friendly wink my way. I can't get over how much younger—and more like Muriel—he looks without facial hair. I saw him this morning when he came to work on Archie in the hangar, and he still had his beard then. He shaves it off for this weekend every year, he explained, when I first saw him tonight and gawked at his baby face.

"Jonah, have you met Jack Thomas yet?" Muriel asks by way of greeting.

"Can't say I have," Jonah says slowly.

She points out a man with a mop of unkempt gray hair and a thick, untrimmed mustache sitting at a nearby table with two other men. "You should go and talk to him. I think you two will get along well."

"And why is that?" That faint amused look lingers on Jonah's face. He's probably wondering what I am—how would Muriel know who Jonah might get along with? She's had three brief conversations with him since they met. She doesn't know Jonah at all.

"'Cause he's lookin' for a pilot!" she says matter-of-factly, and perhaps a touch annoyed. "He owns Big Game Alaska. The one Toby was tellin' you about the other day."

"Right." Jonah's gaze flickers to me.

This must be that hunting outfit that wants him to fly for them in the fall.

"Well then, go on and say hello!" she urges, and I can't help but smirk, relieved that for once, I'm not the target of her doggedness.

As hardheaded as Jonah can be, I've noticed he always shows the utmost patience and respect to the Agneses, the Ethels, and apparently the Muriels of the world. So I'm not shocked when he murmurs, "Yes, ma'am," and hops off the stool. The hand he had settled on my thigh earlier slips around my waist, his thumb stroking my side. I've felt his constant touch since we strolled through the door and into a boisterous, crowded room of about fifty, and I'm beginning to think it has less to do with affection and more to do with the attention I seem to be corralling.

I've felt the looks—in this casual sea of flannel and jeans and angler- and hunter-branded baseball caps, I stick out. Some glances are merely curious. Others are leering.

And Jonah seems intent on marking his territory.

"You good here?" he leans in to kiss my lips.

"Of course she's fine!" Muriel answers for me, then shoos him away with a flick of her hand. "These men ... It's like he thinks you can't handle yourself!"

And, if I didn't know better, that would sound like a compliment coming from her.

"This one's on me." Toby sets a pint in front of Jonah.

With a murmured thanks, Jonah collects it and heads off.

Muriel's gaze trails after Jonah, as if needing to witness this introduction. The guy I assume is Jack Thomas stands and shakes Jonah's hand, then gestures toward the empty seat, which Jonah settles into in his signature legs-splayed way.

"Good. Yes, that'll work out just right." Muriel nods with satisfaction, as if making a check mark on her to-do list. With that, she turns her attention to me. "I'm the chair for the Winter Carnival planning committee, and I think you'd be a good addition to it. I've already mentioned it to the group. We meet the second Thursday of every month, at the community center."

"Oh ... I ... Okay," I stammer, unsure if that's a suggestion or demand. In the end, I likely have little choice, if Muriel deems it so. "What kinds of things would you need help with?" It better not be something insane, like dumping me into an outdoor dunk tank in the middle of an Alaskan winter.

"We'll think of something. Paige moved to Kansas with her new beau, so the outhouse race is up for grabs. You'd be perfect for that."

"I'm sorry, did you say the *outhouse* race? Why would I be perfect for that?"

"Because you like makin' things look pretty," she says, as if that's an obvious answer.

"Muriel!" Teddy hollers from the long buffet table stretched out at the far end of the room, where six slow-cookers simmer and a small horde eagerly awaits their next paper-cup sample. He waves a frantic "come here" hand at her.

"I swear, that man can't wipe his own ass without me standing around the corner to coach him through it. We'll talk more about the carnival later."

"Can't wait," I mutter as she bulldozes through the crowd, moving fast to get to his side. Suddenly a winter dunk tank sounds appealing.

Toby leans over the bar counter on his elbows, watching his parents. "If he doesn't call her over, she'll chew him out because she should be there. If he calls her over, he can't do anything without her."

"It's a no-win situation for him," I agree grimly.

Toby flashes that wide, dimpled smile, even more noticeable on a clean face. "What can I get ya?"

"Something strong, so I'm drunk when your mother comes back."

He chuckles. "All I've got are these on tap," he says, pointing to the branded handles, "and those in the bottle." A small chalkboard behind him lists five beers. I recognize Muriel's scrawl from the garden schematics she drew up. All capital letters. Even her handwriting demands you listen to her.

"Really? No vodka hidden anywhere?"

He drops two coasters in front of me, one advertising Bud, and the other the local Trapper's Crossing IPA.

"What kind of *ale house* is this?" I let out a dramatic sigh. "A bottle of Corona, I guess." It's the only name I recognize, besides Budweiser.

"Comin' right up."

I study the large, crowded room while he fetches my beer from the white kitchen fridge in the corner. The energy here tonight is casual but charged. It feels like a family reunion of sorts, where everyone is a familiar face.

And most of those faces are Caucasian, I note. Much like the population of this area. It's a vast difference from Bangor, where at least half the population is Alaska Native—a mixture of Yupik, Athabascan, and Aleut.

"A bit busier than that first time you came in here, huh?" Toby asks.

"A bit," I agree with a laugh. "Who are all these people?"

He pops the cap and slides the beer across the counter. No lime, I note. Based on the price of them at the grocery store, I can't say I blame them. "A lot are locals, but we've got more of the seasonal crowd coming around now, too."

"Yeah. I noticed them on our way in." Cabins showing signs of life —chains down, cars parked. One woman was nailing a new wooden Welcome sign to a tree at the end of her driveway.

"The rest are from the resort. Most of our cabins are rented out for the weekend. There's even a bunch of campers in."

I shudder at the thought. It was barely above freezing last night.

"We'll have them straight through until snow. Just wait until peak salmon season in July, when the resort is booked up and all the cabins are in use. It gets busy around here. They'll be fishing shoulder to shoulder. You fish, right? I can't remember ..."

I give Toby a cockeyed look that makes him laugh.

He drags a rag over the counter, though there doesn't appear to be anything spilled. "So, how's the garden coming?"

"You know what? Surprisingly ... okay."

"Mom said you're so bored, you've started decorating out there, too."

I can only imagine Muriel's tone when she said that. "I put in new plant markers." The recycled orange-juice-jug tags that Muriel made to identify the vegetables were small and unappealing. I replaced them with bigger, nicer ones I designed using old paint stir sticks I found in the workshop—an idea I came up with after seeing something similar on Pinterest.

I also painted Calla's Garden in white across a rusty shovel that I found in the dilapidated greenhouse and propped it at the gate, to give the old tool purpose and to give me cute Instagram content. It was so simple and yet followers loved it enough that Diana has been texting me once a day to start doing a weekly Alaskan garden post. Of course, Muriel noted, with a frown, the shovel is still functional, and the white markers will get dirty every time it rains.

Toby's gaze wanders over to where Muriel stands, having nudged Teddy away with an elbow to take over doling out samples. "I know she can be a bit opinionated. Pushy, too."

"No way," I say with mock surprise, but I add a smile to let him know I don't harbor any ill will toward her.

He laughs. "She likes you, though. Talks about you all the time."

"Really?" This time, my shock is genuine. "I'm convinced she thinks I'm an idiot."

"Yeah, I get that. Happens to me, too, and I'm her son. But do you think she'd bother with you if that were true?"

"Honestly? I don't think she can help herself, no matter what." Muriel's the type of person who likes to be the one holding all the answers.

A wiry man three seats down waves his empty bottle in the air, and Toby swiftly and wordlessly replaces it. "She likes to keep busy with tasks and projects, is all. She's always been like that. And then after Deacon died ..."

My attention veers toward the two faces surrounded by the gilded frame.

Toby shakes his head. "Let's just say she sometimes bites off more than she can chew, not that she'd *ever* admit to it."

"I guess I'm her latest project?"

"Guess so." He pauses a beat. "She's definitely bitten off too much there."

"Funny guy!" I grab a coaster and throw it at him.

He smoothly catches it. "Our family has been here for over a hundred years, and she thinks it's up to her to make it feel like a real community. It's why she's the chairman of the town council and has her hands in almost every committee there is to sign up for. It's why we have nights like these, to draw people out. It's hard, when the winters are long and half the population is seasonal, and the residents have to leave town to shop and work. Anyway, she doesn't think you're an idiot, Calla. She was impressed with how hard you worked out there. Said you never complained once."

"Not out loud." Again, I'm shocked by my own interpretation of Muriel's frowns and comments compared to what her son is telling me. "It's important to her to see that garden go on, isn't it?"

He nods. "She's loyal to a fault, and Colette was a good friend to her. One of the few people willing to call her on her bullshit." He watches his parents for a moment. "Plus, she's convinced you and Jonah are going to starve to death before the winter's through."

I laugh. "Because there aren't any grocery stores around here?"

"Exactly." He chuckles. "She's got her way of doing things, and she won't back down until she's convinced you that her way is right, but …" He shrugs. "Her heart's in the right place."

"I know it is." Which is probably why I'm tolerating her more than I thought I'd be capable. I observe Muriel for a moment, her broad smile infectious as she ladles from the pot marked #2 and hands a paper cup sample to a woman, before her gaze seeks the next recipient. I'll bet she knows every name and address in here and, if she doesn't, she'll make sure to by the end of the night. "You know she's going to be a nightmare for any girl you bring home, right?"

"Why do you think I'm single?" His cheeks flush as he collects an empty draft glass from a man who approached the bar and refills it from a tap. I guess fresh glasses for each drink are a luxury around here.

"You know who else is single?" I wait for his eyes to flicker to me. "Marie, the veterinarian."

Toby grins, his face turning a deeper red. "She seemed nice."

"And smart, and pretty …" And maybe if she starts dating someone else, she'll stop playing the dear, considerate friend to Jonah while waiting for our relationship to run its course. That's what I've convinced myself her angle is. I mean, that's what *I* would do, if I were in love with a good friend and didn't think the woman he was with was right for him.

As much as Jonah might value their relationship, after last week's ordeal, I'll never entirely trust her around him, whether her intentions toward me are insidious or not.

Thankfully, I trust him.

Jonah's boisterous laugh carries over the crowd. I know him well enough to know he can't fake that. Not that he can fake *any* laugh. The guy has the worst poker face when he doesn't like someone.

It means he's enjoying himself with his new acquaintances.

"So, do you think Jonah'll fly for Jack?" Toby asks, pouring a round of pints for a guy who could be Teddy's doppelganger— another rotund, Santa-bearded man.

"I'm not sure yet. What's this Big Game Alaska thing? Hunting, right?"

"Yeah. People pay serious cash to use Jack. I'm talking twenty, thirty grand for a fly-in, a full camp, and a guide."

A low whistle escapes my lips. "For how many people?"

He gives me a look. "That's per person."

"Holy shit." I automatically do the Canadian currency configuration in my head. I wonder how long it'll be before I stop doing that math.

"Yeah. And he just lost one of his pilots to an airline down south somewhere. Mom mentioned Jonah to him. The guy's got a good reputation because Jack already knew about him."

My pride swells, hearing that.

"So ..." Toby leans forward again to rest his elbows on the counter. "If Jonah can get in with Jack, that's some good, solid cash coming in every September, before the season starts to die down."

"I don't know if he wants to do it." Why wouldn't he, though? Having work that pays well every September is exactly what Jonah is interested in.

"No offense, but he'd be crazy not to for what Jack pays. But I get it ... Some people aren't keen on being up in McGrath for that long."

"McGrath?" I don't recall where that is on the map.

"Yeah. Of course, they'd put him up at the lodge there. It's not the greatest, but it works."

"A lodge. So, he'd be *away* for the month." As in, I'd be alone at home for *an entire month*. The conversation I overheard between Jonah and Marie is starting to make sense.

Jonah doesn't think he can take it because of the promise he made to me. But he told Marie about it, and if he's talking about it with her, then he must be interested, despite what he said to me.

Another loud burst of laughter comes from Jonah, along with the other men at the table. I don't think I've heard him laugh like that since ... Well, since he was joking around with my father.

Guilt pricks me as Marie's words come to mind. *Are you happy turning down jobs because you're afraid to leave your girlfriend alone?*

How long will she hold you to that?

I'm holding Jonah back from doing something he wants to do, and for what? Because I—an almost twenty-seven-year-old woman

—don't want to be home alone. And of course he'll keep his word, because that's who Jonah is. But are my reasons justified?

I've noticed that on the days Jonah's grounded because of the weather, he's irritable and restless, scowling at the clouds as if trying to scare them away. He hates being held back from doing things. Agnes says he's always been like that—like a high-strung toddler who needs his daily dose of outdoor exercise to regulate his mood. I laughed when she made that comparison, but I'm realizing she's not wrong.

How long before he begins resenting me?

"Ah, shit ..." Toby bows his head, his hand working a cloth over the counter.

"What's wrong?"

His gray eyes dart to the door and I see rare annoyance on his face. "Don't look now, but the woman who walked in—I said *don't* look!"

"Sorry! It's a natural reaction." I wince sheepishly. "The one in the leopard-print crop top?"

"Yeah. If you mean the short shirt." He leans closer. "That's Jessie Winslow. Her husband works on the north slope."

"What's that? Like a ski slope?"

"Nah. It's what we call the northern tip of Alaska. A lot of people from around here go up there to work on the oil rigs. Anyway, he's gone for, like, two weeks at a time, and every time he's on shift, she goes on a bender. Ends up coming in here and getting smashed, and then my father makes me drive her home. She gropes me *every* time!"

I peer over my shoulder again to catch a better look at the woman. I'd put her in her midforties—a good decade older than Toby. "She's pretty." She's certainly put a lot of effort into her appearance, though her jeans are suctioned to her body and the crop top isn't the most flattering for her figure, but if she's looking for attention, she'll certainly get it in this room.

"You know who's *not* pretty? Her six-four, two-hundred-seventy-pound husband."

I burst out laughing.

"It's not funny!" Toby declares, but he's struggling not to smile.

"You're right, it's not." But seeing him so flustered is.

"I'm not driving her home tonight. She can take a cab," he says with firm resolution, but something tells me he's made that declaration before, too.

I steal another look at the married vixen who has sidled up to a tall, rugged man with a crooked nose, the kind that's been broken more than once. With her rosy cheeks and the lazy swagger of her hips, I'd bet she's already tipsy, which begs the question of how she got here in the first place. "Maybe she'll find a ride from someone else tonight," I offer.

The telltale creak of the door sounds—it's become background music to the noise in the Ale House tonight—and Toby's eyebrows arch. "Huh. I think this is a first."

I check over my shoulder to see who stepped in.

And balk at the sight of Roy Donovan standing in the doorway, sizing up the crowd.

"What is he doing here?" I eye the wide-rimmed cowboy hat atop his head, his crisp-collared and clean blue-and-red flannel shirt, blue jeans that look new, cowboy boots that look like they've been polished.

"No idea." Toby glances at the chili table, and his mother, who is too busy gabbing to notice their new guest.

Others have noticed, though. Several heads swivel to the door, curious expressions on their faces.

Roy's sharp gaze meets mine and, slipping his hat off, he strolls toward me.

"Ah, crap," I mutter under my breath, turning back around to face the bar and seek refuge in Toby's kind face. Unfortunately, he's abandoned me to serve someone on the other end of the bar.

"Anyone sittin' here?" Roy asks in that now-familiar Texas accent, his hand on the stool Jonah vacated.

Not only is Roy Donovan here, he's looking to sit next to me.

"Uh ..." I turn to catch Jonah's attention, hoping he'll see my predicament, but he's occupied in an animated conversation with Jack. I admit reluctantly. "No. It's free."

"Don't sound *too* excited on my account." Roy hangs his cowboy hat on a wall peg beside him before settling onto the stool. He hooks the heel of his cowboy boot on the foot rail. "Was wondering if you'd be here."

Really? Why? I take a long swig of my beer, mainly to avoid having to respond.

"You look cleaner than the last time I saw you."

"So do you," I throw back.

Toby returns, saving me from Roy's retort. "What can I get ya?"

"A bottle of beer. Don't care what kind, but make it cheap."

"All right. One Coors comin' right up."

I shoot Toby a panicked "help me" look.

"So, how's your dog doin', Roy?" Toby asks as he fishes a bottle from the fridge.

"Pretty good. He's up and walkin' around again."

"Thanks to Calla."

Roy grunts.

Toby sets the bottle of Coors in front of Roy, and a fresh Corona in front of me, winking. "You look like you're ready for another one."

I'm guessing I'll need twenty more before the night is through, if this conversation goes much longer.

"Here." Roy slaps a twenty-dollar bill onto the counter. His weathered hands are a mess—his cuticles torn, his skin wrinkled, his knuckles cracked. "For mine and hers."

"Uh … Thanks." I steal a quick glance at Toby, who flashes a surprised look before heading to the till. I thought Roy didn't give or do *anything* out of kindness?

Roy stares hard at the bottle in his hand. "How's that old goat doin'?"

Are we attempting small talk? "Still alive."

Roy smirks. "Have you trimmed his hooves yet?"

"We're supposed to do that?" I cringe as I imagine touching those dirty things.

He rolls the bottle in his grip but doesn't take a drink. "You need to keep goats' hooves trimmed, otherwise they could end up infected. Bacteria and all that."

"Oh. *Great.* I'll let Jonah know." I may tolerate Zeke following me around, but I draw the line at goat grooming.

Roy's gaze wanders over all the pictures pinned to the back wall with thumbtacks, seemingly engrossed.

Did he have a wife, as Muriel claims? I can't imagine Roy having another softer side that could lend itself to a loving relationship. Then again, I couldn't fathom what anyone found appealing about Jonah when I first met the angry yeti.

"Had anything sniffin' around your pen lately?" he asks suddenly.

"You mean like your *malamute?*"

His eyes narrow on me, and for a second I wonder if I've expended any goodwill I've earned. "Nah. He's chained up for the time bein' so he can heal. Besides, he won't do nothin' to that old goat." He peers over his shoulders at the people and sneers. "All these campers comin' up here, not storin' their food and trash properly, causin' problems for the rest of us. You two better be keepin' your trash indoors," he warns.

"Jonah grew up in Alaska. He knows what to do." And I grew up in Toronto, with Tim and Sid rooting through our garbage cans at every chance, so I'm not entirely inept when it comes to wildlife. "We keep it in the workshop."

"Calla!" Muriel's husky voice carries over the noise. She waves an apron in the air before her gaze veers to Roy and thins.

"Did my mom happen to mention she was gonna put you to work tonight?" Toby asks with a grin.

"Uh … no. *Seriously?*"

"If there's one thing she doesn't joke about, it's workin'."

I groan as I ease off my chair. Maybe Muriel's doing this to give me an out for having to deal with my neighbor. A "kindness" as she calls it—ending the suffering of wretched creatures. "Thanks for the beer," I offer, because, unlike Roy, I won't be outright rude.

His head bobs slowly, his focus on the bottle within his grasp.

I assume that's all the response I'm getting from him and so I make to turn away.

"I know I can be a real SOB," he says. "But thank you, for what you did for Oscar." His gaze flashes to mine briefly, long enough to show me the sincerity in his words before he turns back to his bottle.

It looks like I got the right side of the coin toss today.

"Hope you like chili," Toby hollers after me, his laughter following me as I cut through the crowd.

CHAPTER TWENTY-FIVE

"What the hell, Jonah? You promised you'd wait!"

In the time it took me to exchange my clothes for my robe, scrub the taste of six different chilies off my tongue—that Muriel badgered me to taste despite my assertions that I'm not a fan—collect two towels, and head back down to the porch, Jonah stripped out of his clothes, climbed into the hot tub, and made himself at home.

"Did I?" His muscular arms stretch out on either side of him along the frame. His head rests back, showing off the sharp jut of his throat. The steam from the hot water mixing with the cool air creates an ethereal mist around him. "Sorry. You took too long."

"I was, like, ten minutes." I set the towels on a small side table and, before leaving my phone there as well, take a stealthy picture of this view—a bare, broad-chested Jonah in the steamy foreground, the sawtooth, snowcapped mountain range in the back.

With a smile of satisfaction—this one will rival the infamous wood-chopping snap, both in sexiness and in the power to irritate him—I move toward the edge of the tub, my hands gripping the lapel of my robe.

Jonah lifts his head to scan me from head to toe, his gaze flashing with mischief. And anticipation.

I've undressed for Jonah countless times. He knows every freckle, dimple, and hint of a scar, and yet every time I'm about to, that same eruption of nerves and excitement stirs in the pit of my stomach, like it did the first time. It's clear why he was so eager to break his promise to me. "Close your eyes, you brat. You don't deserve a show."

The wicked laugh that carries from deep within his chest and echoes over the calm, quiet lake sends shivers down my spine. "I probably don't, but not a chance in hell."

With a quick scan around the property for privacy, which earns a scoff from Jonah, because "look where we live!"—I turn around and make a point of ever-so-slowly sliding the robe off my shoulders, inch by inch down my biceps, uncovering my shoulder blades, my back, that curve above my tailbone, stalling there as the cool night air skates over my naked skin. Stripping outdoors, out in the open like this, with the still lake and the quiet forest and the looming Denali, the last rays of sun touching its westernmost side at ten thirty P.M., certainly adds a certain edge to the moment.

"Get in here already, Calla." Jonah's gruff voice drops an octave.

I let the robe drop to the porch floor next to his pile of clothes and then take a step back to perch on the edge of the tub. I swing my legs over as gracefully as possible and slip into the hot, inviting water. I groan. "This feels so good."

"I'll admit ..." Jonah begins, reaching for me, pulling me across to fit tidily beneath his outstretched arm, my legs pulled over his lap. He curls his body inward, giving him the perfect angle to trace my collarbone with his lips. "This *might* have been worth all that money."

"Wait a minute. Did I hear that right? Did you say that I am the smartest person alive and you are *so* sorry for ever questioning— Ah!" I squeal as Jonah playfully nips at my skin, then licks the spot with his tongue. "Look at them all." I point at the screen and the horde of sizeable, bloodsucking insects perched on the outside, foiled in their attempts to find a way in. There isn't one. The carpenter was meticulous with his work. Not one crack remains, affording us refuge from their nuisance.

"I know. I'm glad I insisted on you hiring that guy to do the screens."

"Hmm ... Yes, that's exactly how I remember it going."

He pulls my body up to perch on the inside of his bent leg. My breasts float just above the waterline. "Yeah, definitely a fucking brilliant idea, getting this hot tub." Jonah's beard tickles my skin as his mouth clamps over a pebbled nipple. Beneath the water, his hand brazenly slides up the inside of my thigh.

There's no question what Jonah's intentions are, and normally I'm more than willing to pander to his physical needs—and my own—but tonight, we need to have an actual conversation first so my focus won't be divided.

I clamp my hand over his, stalling it. "You seemed to have a good time at the Ale House."

As did I, surprisingly. While Jonah was talking to Jack Thomas, Muriel made a point of introducing me to every person who came through the chili line, who in turn asked me about The Yeti, prominently displayed on my chest. I made sure to let them all know how dependable and skilled Jonah is, in case they're ever in need of a pilot. Several people seemed keenly interested.

He groans, finally getting the hint. We shift again, and I shimmy off his leg to immerse myself in the hot water. Jonah leans back against the side of the tub, the hand that was between my thighs settling to a more neutral spot on my knee. "Is this about that woman? Because I didn't encourage that."

"No. I don't care about Jessie Winslow." Though she did nearly end up with Crock-Pot Number Four chili over her head. I wasn't surprised when she took one look at Jonah and eagerly pulled up a chair to their table, touching him at every opportunity. According to Muriel, who must've seen the way my fist curled around the ladle when Jessie pawed Jonah's thigh, the woman has "issues with the drink."

Luckily for her—and for Jonah—he made a point of excusing himself from the table and coming over to sample the food.

And I made a point of sampling his mouth for her to see.

"What'd Roy say to you?"

"That he knows he's an SOB and thanks for saving his dog."

"No shit." Jonah's eyebrows pop with astonishment. "What'd he want with Muriel?"

"I don't know." Roy sat at the bar, staring at his bottle and not speaking to anyone, until Muriel headed over to question him. It was a short conversation and seemed civilized, and then he collected his hat and ducked out of the Ale House without so much as a glance around. According to Toby, his beer was still full.

Muriel offered me nothing more than a tight smile when I asked what Roy had said.

I don't want to talk about lonely, crop-top-wearing alcoholics, or crusty old men, though. I need to talk about something that's been gnawing on my conscience all night.

I drag my fingernail across Jonah's beard, reveling in the scratching sound. "Jack seemed nice." I met the man briefly. He was quiet, soft-spoken. Not at all what I imagined the big game hunter to be.

"He's a good guy," Jonah agrees. "Smart. I've heard he's a helluva hunter."

"Did he mention working for him?"

He hesitates. "Yeah."

"And?"

"And ... nothing. It doesn't work for me." Jonah studies his hand as he skims the surface of the water with his palm.

"What's the job?"

"He wants me for three weeks in September. Seven days a week, doing runs every day and being available on call for game pickups. I'd basically be catering to rich politician assholes from the Lower Forty-Eight."

"And you'd get paid really well doing it."

Jonah nods somberly.

"But you'd have to stay in McGrath."

"Sounds like you already know all about this." He frowns. "Muriel tell you?"

"No. Surprisingly, that is one thing she didn't mention." She told me everything about everyone else, though—births, deaths, marriages, divorces, scandals, bankruptcies, windfalls. "Toby told me."

"Yeah, well ..." Jonah sighs. "Stationing out of McGrath is the only way to do it. It's too far to fly back and forth every day, and he can't risk bad weather through the mountains keeping his pilot from being there. The hunters are paying a ton of money to have one on call."

I take a deep breath and say what I've been preparing to say all night. "If you want to take the job, then you should take it."

His head's already shaking. "I promised you I wouldn't leave you out here alone like that."

"I'll be fine." I hope I sound more confident than I feel. "I'm sure Muriel will be here every day, anyway, whether I want her here or not. And I can always fly home."

"This is your home." He glowers.

"You know what I mean. I can fly back to Toronto for a couple weeks."

He seems to consider this. "What about Bandit and Zeke?"

"I don't know? I'll ask Toby or Muriel to help." I can't believe I have to consider a raccoon and a goat in my plans. I barely even see Bandit, now that the weather's warmer and he's off climbing trees. "We'd make it work."

Jonah slides the elastic from my ponytail. My hair tumbles down over my shoulders, the ends dipping into the water. "If Jack's impressed, he'll want to lock me in every September going forward." Which would lessen some of the pressure to earn money through the long, dark, unpredictable winter months—something I know weighs on Jonah.

"*Of course*, he'll be impressed." I hear what Jonah's really saying, though—that this isn't just for this year. I'll have to be ready to spend *every* September without him.

He chews his bottom lip. "It's not like you'll be stuck here, anyway. You'll be able to drive whenever and wherever you want, to visit people."

I nod and smile; meanwhile I'm wondering, *what people?* I don't know anyone. Agnes and Mabel are all the way on the other side of the state, and I can't get to them by car.

I was right, though. Jonah wants to take this job.

He seizes my chin between his thumb and forefinger, forcing my gaze to his. "Are you sure you're okay with this? Because once I commit, it's a done deal. For this year, at least."

I smooth my hand over his chest. That's twenty-one days and twenty-one nights, unable to touch him like this. Out here alone, possibly. I look out over the vast, quiet space.

This is what Jonah does, though. Off-airport landings are his specialty and he enjoys it. It doesn't feel right, holding him back. I couldn't live with him resenting me for it down the road. "It's only three weeks." Muriel introduced me to a man tonight who's gone for months in winter, up to the North Slope building ice roads for the oil rigs, leaving his wife and kids at home to fend for themselves. When I hear stories like that, it makes me feel silly and weak to fret over three weeks.

Beneath the water, he runs his palm back and forth over my thigh. "Maybe *I* don't wanna be without you for that long. Ever thought of that?"

I smile with the reminder that I'm not the only one who would struggle with this arrangement—Jonah would miss me, too. "You're a big boy. You'll survive. We both will. I mean, come on ... Jessie Winslow's husband leaves her for weeks at a time, and look how well she handles it."

Jonah snorts. "Yeah, I heard *exactly* what she tries to handle. You sayin' I'll come back to you pounding draft beer and hittin' on Toby?"

"If you do, go easy on him. He's probably tried to fend me off."

"Yeah, doubt that," he mutters.

I rest my head on his shoulder. "Jonah, take the job. I know you want it, and I don't want you turning down jobs you want because of me. That doesn't make me happy."

He sighs, and I could be mistaken, but I sense his relief. "I'll call Jack tomorrow. He'd have to accommodate my schedule for those two hunting parties I've already committed to, but he said it shouldn't be a problem."

That guilty prick that's been needling me all night begins to fade, because I know pushing him to accept this offer is the right thing to do. Yet, I don't feel lighter about the decision. But this is what life with Jonah will always be like. I need to learn to take the good with the bad.

I lean in to skate my lips across his neck, ready to pick up where I hindered him earlier.

But his blue eyes are searching the porch's cedar ceiling in deep thought. He swallows hard. "I had an interesting conversation with Sam tonight."

"I noticed." The firefighter pilot is a lot shorter than he looks in his yellow plane. Jonah towered over him. "About what?"

He hesitates. "About flying for him. He's got four Fire Bosses. Alaska Fire Services contracts his company out to help fight forest fires. He wants to know if I'd work for him this summer."

"What do you mean? Like, fighting fires?" I ask warily.

"Yeah. Last year was bad and they're expecting it to be worse this year. It could mean work for me through till August, even until I leave in September. I wouldn't even have to work all winter, if I don't want to, with the kind of money I can make." He peers at me. "I've always wanted to try it."

"Really?" Because he's never mentioned it to me before.

"Yeah." He frowns. "What's that look for?"

"Nothing. I just ... is it safe?"

"As safe as anything I do is ever gonna be."

"Yeah, but flying a plane is one thing. Fighting fires is ... You've never done it before."

"Which is why he'd train me. I've got more than enough experience flying, so that part won't be hard."

That doesn't bring me much comfort, though. What if Jonah has engine problems like we did, while flying over a raging fire? How low will he have to fly? What if the smoke gets too bad and he can't see? But another, more immediate issue stirs in my mind. "But what about The Yeti?"

"The gig with Sam would be contract only, for the summer."

"Yeah, but I'm guessing it's on an as-needed basis?" Forest fires don't follow a schedule. "How am I supposed to book people if you could be called away to fight fires at any given time?"

"I don't know. We'll figure it out." He drags a fingertip over my bare shoulder, down my arm, my exposed skin covered in goose-flesh. But the look on his face is not carnal. It's pensive, as if he's lost in his own thoughts. "I think I'd be good at it."

"You'd be amazing at it." There doesn't seem to be anything Jonah isn't good at, when it comes to planes. "But this is an entire summer." The busiest time for any charter pilot in Alaska. "Don't you think you need to be focusing on building the charter business? At least until you're established? Tying yourself up for an *entire summer* for someone else might not be the best move."

He shrugs. "I'd go out with one of the guys before I commit."

"Right." But he will commit because this sounds right up his alley.

"Are you angry?" he asks.

"No, I'm just ... I don't know what I am." Annoyed, maybe. Here I am, talking the charter company up all night to anyone who would listen, when he might not even be around to fly.

But this also feels like a bit of a reality slap. The Yeti has felt like a joint venture up until now, but have I been fooling myself? Maybe it's always been Jonah's, and I'm lingering in the background, giving myself make-work projects to burn the days away, trying to make it into something it'll never be.

Maybe Agnes was right. Maybe I need to find my own place here, outside of Jonah's world of planes.

But how? Where?

Jonah turns my face to meet his. "You just finished telling me that you don't want me turning down jobs that I want."

I *did* just do that. But that was when I thought it was for The Yeti. This feels like Jonah is casting it aside. "Why this?"

His blue eyes search mine. "Back at Wild, I was doin' things that felt important. I felt like I was helpin' people and, I don't know ... I guess I need to do something that feels important here, too. I can't just be flying tourists around and dropping off coffee grinds to hotels. It's not enough for me. It's felt like somethin's been missing. This opportunity from Sam, though? This is the kind of thing I get a rush from. Plus, the interior gets hit with fires every year. Even around here, sometimes. Imagine having to evacuate and losing all this." He gestures around us. "If I can help stop that from happening, I want to try." He nods slowly, as if convincing himself that this contract with Sam would be the right move.

And it probably is, I must admit. This big, burly pilot of mine thrives off helping people. It's why he gravitated toward Western Alaska to begin with, instead of moving to Anchorage where he spent part of his childhood. He found meaning with aiding the many villagers who populate the roadless tundra.

"Then you should do it. We'll figure everything else out," I offer with a degree of finality in my voice that I don't necessarily feel.

"Wait until January, when we're both cooped up in here because of the weather and on each other's nerves. You'll be begging me to take any job I can get."

"Highly unlikely." This place *almost* feels like home when Jonah is here. "Plus, I may need your help with the outhouse race."

"The *what?*"

"Muriel."

"Say no more." He chuckles. "It was a smart idea to go to the Ale House tonight. Thank you, for pushing me. You are a big part of making all this happen." He traces his fingertip along my jawline before leaning in to press a soft kiss against my lips.

"Glad I could help." And I am, even though the result has me feeling a mixture of relief—that I'm doing the right thing by pushing him—and an unsettled feeling I can't quite put my finger on.

"You know what's an even better idea?"

"No. What?"

He seizes my waist and hoists me up to perch on the edge of the tub.

"It's cold!" I grimace, my sopping-wet skin instantly erupting in gooseflesh. I attempt to slide back into the water, but Jonah holds me in place, smoothly pivoting to part my legs and fit his chest in between.

His icy blue eyes lock on mine as his arms curl beneath my thighs to angle my hips for better access. Despite the shock of the temperature, a thrill erupts inside my belly. I lean back against the porch post and watch with greedy anticipation as he trails soft kisses up the inside of my thigh, all thoughts of the cold temperatures and fighting fires and three weeks without him vanishing the moment his mouth lands on its destination.

CHAPTER TWENTY-SIX

June

"You know you could build your platform solely off naked pictures of Jonah, right? I mean, you'd have a gazillion followers in no time." Dishes rattle in the background as Diana cleans her kitchen, her phone on speaker. She has never been one to sit still while talking on the phone.

I smile, not so much at her words but at the sound of her voice. I haven't heard it since April. "So, you're saying I should sexually exploit my boyfriend for the 'Gram." I crouch to brush off mud that splattered over the carrot marker. Behind it is a tidy row of chartreuse fronds, well-watered by last night's rain. "I don't remember learning that strategy in my marketing classes."

"It's called giving the people what they want, and you're not the only one who does it. The difference is, your guy is universally *hot*. I mean, look how much traction you've gotten on this one!"

"I haven't checked. I've been too busy out here, weeding." A never-ending task, I'm learning. In truth, I didn't post the picture of Jonah in the hot tub for traction, though I knew it'd garner plenty. My Instagram followership has grown exponentially since I started sharing stories about Alaska and the yeti. And ever since I started chronicling our adventure with the log cabin in the woods, people seem to be finding me even faster.

For those on the outside, there's something exotic about my life.

It seems an enviable dream, even when I share the many trials. Of course, I keep the darkest parts to myself. No one would know that, on our second day in our "romantically rustic" log cabin, elbow-deep in Phil's trash, I locked myself in the bathroom and cried. Jonah doesn't even know that secret.

And they'll have no idea, when they fawn over the picture of Jonah in the hot tub, that I feel like I've hardly seen him since the night I took the shot two weeks ago. Sam Reed called him the day after the chili cook-off, enticing him to go out for a day and see how he liked it. It took no convincing and when Jonah arrived home that night, he was buzzing with excitement. I knew, before he confirmed it for me, that he'd already accepted the job, committing to being on call for Sam the entire summer.

Despite what I'd said the previous night, a part of me felt betrayed, that he is abandoning our fledgling charter company, forcing me to block off the booking calendar until October. But I smiled and offered my congratulations, and I convinced myself that Jonah's doing something that makes him happy, which makes me happy.

Which means I'm going to be nothing but encouraging.

The people who gawk at that photo and read my loving, playful caption don't know any of this. They have no idea that there's an inexplicably odd, hollow feeling blossoming in the pit of my stomach as of late; I'm trying my best to be understanding and supportive, but I'm struggling because I like having him around, because I miss him so damn much when he's not here.

They won't know that I posted that picture of Jonah mainly *for* Jonah, because I know I'll get a rise out of him when he sees it, which will earn me a night of playful threats and frisky foreplay. He'll be solely focused on me for a few hours, instead of absorbed by fire-fighting training manuals and textbooks.

So, really, I posted that picture for me.

"Weeding? Did she say weeding?" Diana asks, I assume, Aaron. "Oh my God. It's happened. My best friend has become countryfolk."

"Shut up." I chuckle. "I have to keep myself busy somehow. The days are long around here." There's an official sunrise and sunset but it never truly gets dark. Jonah is up and gone well before I'd ever consider crawling out of bed, stirring my sleep long enough to kiss me goodbye. I've fallen into a predictable routine—check emails over coffee and breakfast, decide what I need to buy for lunch and dinner, followed by a heavy dose of bug repellent to come out here. Sometimes Muriel pops by for a quick check-in on the garden—and on me, I sense. I find I don't mind those visits at all anymore. I've begun to look forward to them, even when she offers her opinions, unwarranted and uninvited.

I passed my road test—with no moose incident—and have gained a degree of freedom I didn't have before. I've joined the gym in Wasilla and now drive in to kill a few hours doing weights and cardio, followed by some shopping. I also visited the car dealership and test-drove a Jeep Wrangler. I'm waiting for a break in Jonah's schedule so he can go in to help me navigate the conversation to buy what I want.

My afternoons are spent entertaining myself with various projects. Last week, I finished the guest bedroom that overlooks the back of the house, garnishing it with new bedding and lighting and chic artwork. As soon as the quilt and dresser I ordered for the other smaller bedroom arrives, I'll be able to finish that, too.

I've booked a contractor to renovate our main floor bathroom and add a shower. He starts next month. I spent a day learning how to style a bookcase, and another two experimenting with surprisingly cute and rustic finds from the Trading Post—antique candle holders, pottery, vintage frames that I filled with pictures from last summer.

I spent a full week organizing the kitchen properly. I've installed additional shelves—by myself, using Jonah's drill. Everything has its own place now, whether it be on a hook or in a labeled jar.

With all this time on my hands, the house is beginning to feel like a home—a well-organized, clean home. I've also discovered that I enjoy trying out new recipes.

But the days are long, my meals are lonely, and I find myself counting down the hours until I hear the familiar hum of an approaching plane.

And counting the months until Jonah's firefighting and his work with Jack Thomas are over, so I can have him to myself again.

"Is Jonah working a lot?" Diana asks.

"Yeah. There's a fire south of here that's been burning for a week." A lightning strike started it, and thanks to the drier-than-normal season, the flames are gobbling up forest like it's kindling doused in gasoline. The fact that it's only mid-June is troublesome, according to the news.

"Oh my God, are you serious? He's fighting fires now, too?" I can hear the thrill in Diana's voice. "Do you know how rugged and sexy your boyfriend is, Calla?"

"I'm sitting *right here!*" Aaron hollers from somewhere in the background, making me smile.

I know how rugged and sexy Jonah is. I'm also learning how frustrating he can be to deal with when it has anything to do with flying his planes. But, I'm not about to get into that with Diana.

"So, how many *years* are you in law school for?" I ask, changing the subject.

She groans. "I can't believe I'm doing this, Calla. I don't even *like* lawyers! Tell me I'm crazy!"

"You're crazy." I smile. "But you're gonna kick serious ass." People often judge Diana as ditzy and shallow based on her flightiness and obsession with drawing the perfect eyebrow, but she's one of the smartest people I know. Her LSAT scores got her into the top law school in Toronto. She's the first paralegal that her boss, a.k.a. Beef Stick, has ever agreed to pay tuition and books for, which tells me how much potential he sees in her.

I'm so happy for her, and yet I'm also sad. It feels like she has found a new life—one that I don't have a place in anymore, especially all the way over here.

"Have *you* decided if you're going back to school yet? Or are you just going to flounder in your newfound wealth?" Diana mocks.

I shake my head. "I don't know. I've looked at the course options but there isn't anything in Anchorage that interests me." Plus, do I really want to commit to an on-campus program? What if we end up deciding to go elsewhere in a year or two? "I've been looking into some online courses. Graphic design, that sort of thing. Something I could maybe do freelance?" Something. I need ... *something*.

"Well ... you've got time to decide, right? It's not like you guys are hurting for money."

"Yeah, I guess." Though Jonah insists on working like we are. "I'm going to a Winter Carnival planning committee tonight." Toby relayed a message from Muriel to be ready for pickup at five forty-five P.M. *sharp*. I keep meaning to ask him if it drives him nuts that his mother, who has a phone capable of texting, uses him as her middleman.

"I guess that makes sense. You *are* a lady of leisure now, so charitable events and party planning need to become part of your daily schedule."

I laugh as I haul myself to my feet and dump a handful of weeds over the fence for Zeke, who trots over to devour them. "Muriel volun-told me so I don't have a choice."

"What does one do at a winter carnival in Alaska?"

"Carnival-y things in the frigid cold. A parade and maybe a race." With outhouses, apparently. I tried searching for information online, so I don't appear completely clueless walking into tonight's meeting, but the event's website lacked for anything beyond sponsorship and vendor opportunities, and a few lackluster pictures from past events of people huddling on the frozen lake. "Maybe I can do some of the marketing?"

"Oh, hey, before I forget, your gift is on back order so it might not come until after your actual birthday."

My birthday. Right. I'm turning twenty-seven in two weeks. I haven't given it as much thought this time around. On the one hand, it's my first one with Jonah, which is exciting. But it'll also be the first one without Mom and Simon hovering over my bed with a slice of cake, singing happy birthday, and the first since I met Diana that we won't be giggling late into the night. "You should fly here and bring it with you, then," I tease, but I'm not really joking.

"Calla—"

"Can't you spare a couple days for me? Come for a long weekend? *Please*? I'll pay for it!" I had no intention of begging Diana or making her feel bad, but the desperate words tumble out before I can stop them.

She makes a strangled sound. "I'm sorry. I'll come next year, I promise. Listen, I've gotta go. Spin class starts soon, and I need to prepare myself mentally for Sergei."

I check my watch, confirming her class doesn't start for another three hours. I know, because we used to take it together. It's not a surprise, though, that Diana would find a way out of our call the moment she begins to feel guilty. She doesn't handle that emotion well. I do my best to keep the disappointment from my voice. "Say hi to him for me." I used to despise Sergei and his militant spin classes. The woman who teaches the spin class at the gym in Wasilla has a docile voice and cranks show tunes.

"Talk to ya later. Keep flaunting that beautiful man."

I laugh, despite my mood. "You have no shame."

"No, what I don't have is a gorgeous naked Viking and a mountainous backdrop to exploit."

"What the hell am I?" Aaron hollers.

"*Not* Norwegian!" she throws back, though with that teasing tone reserved for their verbal jabs. 'Kay, gotta go. Love you!"

"Love you, too. Bye, Aar—"

The phone clicks before I finish getting my words out.

I tuck my phone into my pocket and settle back into weeding, trying to smother my letdown. I knew I couldn't expect my family and friends to fly to Alaska *every* year—no matter how many times they say they want to come. But what will happen, as my parents get older and Diana is immersed in lawyerly things? How many years will stretch between our visits?

I toss the weed over the fence and Zeke bleats. "Maybe I should tell Jonah I want to fly home for my birthday," I say out loud. I know what Jonah's answer will be—he can't leave for a week in the middle of summer, especially after he signed this contract. I *could* go on my own. But the truth is, as much as I begrudge Diana for her unwillingness to leave Aaron on his own, the idea of taking off for my birthday without Jonah doesn't appeal to me much, either.

Zeke bleats again. I've grown familiar enough with the noises he makes to know this one sounds distressed.

I look up in time to see him run along the fence line, away from me, toward his pen. And then he suddenly keels over and lays there, in the grass, his legs stiff in front of him.

"Zeke?" I approach the garden gate, watching with a frown as the goat wriggles his body, struggling to stand. By the time I've exited the garden pen and made it to him, he's on his hooves again. An unexpected wave of relief stirs in my gut. I've gotten used to having the dumb goat as company, trotting behind the ATV every morning, nibbling on grass and devouring weeds. Where Bandit is off in a tree somewhere half the time, Zeke has become my faithful companion, a sounding board when I babble.

He bleats loudly again—that same distressed sound—and darts forward, only to fall over a second time, this time rolling onto his back, his legs held straight in the air.

It clicks. "Oh my God!" I've seen YouTube videos of fainting goats before—compilations of them falling over, temporarily paralyzed, when they're startled. Diana's brother was obsessed with them for a time.

This is the first time Zeke has done it since I've been around, though.

"What is freaking you out so much that—" My question dies in my throat, replaced by a yelp when I spot the wolf standing no more than twenty feet away, watching us.

No, not a wolf, not exactly.

It's Oscar, Roy's dog.

It takes ten seconds for my heart rate to resemble something stable, and then I'm left wondering if I should in fact be worried after all, because in this moment, with his cunning, narrowed eyes and the way his head is bowed forward, Oscar looks every bit the wild animal and not at all domesticated.

But Oscar gives Zeke barely more than a glance as the goat struggles to his hooves again, his keen gaze locked on me. I know for certain now that it's been him all along, lurking within the trees, scaring me half to death.

Does he recognize me from that day?

Why does he keep coming back?

There are pages in that book Jonah got me about what to do when you encounter wild animals. Yell at some, speak calmly to others; don't fight back with this one, arm yourself with sticks and rocks for another. Don't ever run, don't ever turn your back. Those last two seemed universal.

I don't recall any advice about dealing with the grouchy neighbor's wolf dog that repeatedly stalks you on your property.

Oscar hasn't so much as twitched, and when I venture to take a step forward, he takes a quick hobble-step back, heavily favoring his injured hind leg.

Zeke keeps bleating and running and keeling over, clearly aware of the potential danger an animal like Oscar presents. If Oscar wasn't making me so nervous, I would be laughing and recording Zeke's fainting spells on my phone to play for Jonah later. But right now, I need to get the goat back into his pen where he's protected by electric wire, and I'm too afraid to turn my back on Oscar.

He's a dog. He's just a dog, I remind myself. And I did save his life.

"Go home!" I say loudly, attempting authority.

The dog merely blinks.

"Go home!" I yell. I'm sure I don't sound nearly as threatening as Roy does.

After a fifteen-second staring contest, Oscar turns and slowly limps off, disappearing into the trees.

With a sigh of relief, I collect my bag of garden supplies and lead our fainting goat back to his pen, checking over my shoulder frequently.

CHAPTER TWENTY-SEVEN

"Some towns have a main street for events. *This* is the hub for Trapper's Crossing," Muriel explains, charging toward the double doors of the blue-gray community center, a blue folder stuffed with paperwork tucked beneath her arm. "We run pretty much everything out of here. The Carnival in December, which runs over two weekends and includes our annual holiday bazaar and Christmas dinner. We had locals camped out in here during the fires three years ago, when they had to evacuate their homes. People even rent it out for weddings." She waggles her finger at me. "You know ... you and Jonah should think about that when the time comes. With the lake behind, it's quite nice. And, if we can make enough money at this year's carnival, we should have upgraded restroom facilities by next year."

"That's ... something to think about." I school my expression—and my horror at the idea of having my wedding reception in the Trapper's Crossing community center. Meanwhile, I can't ignore the nervous stir in my stomach at the mention of marriage. It reminds me that there is a ring hidden somewhere in our house, meant for me. When I'll see it again, though ... who knows.

"That there is our new covered ice rink." She nods toward a pavilion-like structure on the other side of the enormous dusty gravel parking lot. "Cost us almost half a million dollars and five years of groveling to the Mat-Su Borough to get that put in. Poor kids finally don't have to spend half their hockey practices shoveling snow off the ice. Anyway, it's where we hold our market every Friday afternoon, come end of June through till mid-September, and I'll tell ya, it's been a blessin' on those rainy days."

Inside the center is a long, simple corridor with a few empty folding tables, waiting to be used. To the right is the town's library, a brown-and-beige room with dim lights and only a handful of bookshelf aisles. One lonely woman sits behind a desk, staring at her computer screen. To the left are double doors that, I assume, lead into the community hall. It reminds me of an elementary school—speckled gray flooring, white ceiling tiles, dim fluorescent lighting, and walls lined with team pictures and painted an unflattering lemon-yellow, a color meant to inspire cheeriness but rarely does. It even smells faintly like school—a mix of musty books, white craft glue, and industrial floor cleaner lingering in the air.

The lights flicker overhead. "The money we earn from the carnival each year goes toward upkeep of this building, and we are in desperate need of improvements." A worried frown mars Muriel's face "This is the fiftieth year and, to be honest, attendance hasn't been great lately. We've got to find a way to draw more people out."

"So … who does the marketing?" I ask casually. I don't want to step on any toes.

"Emily. Remember her? You went out runnin' with her that one time."

The super quiet woman with zero personality? Vaguely.

"She's workin' on something special for this year's poster."

"A poster." *Tell me that's not the extent of their marketing campaign?*

"Yes! We put them up all over the Mat-Su Borough. Gets people excited."

Right.

"What if I helped her? I think you could use a new website and a social media campaign and …" My words fade as Muriel waves me off with a doubtful expression.

"Emily's got all that covered. Besides, have you ever been to a winter carnival in Alaska?"

"Well, no. But there's this Christmas market in Toronto—"

"How are you supposed to convince people to come when you've never even been?" She shakes her head but then offers me a reassuring smile. "That social media may have worked where you come from, but none of that stuff works on people around here. Don't worry. We'll keep you busy."

I struggle to smooth the sour look from my face and trail her through another set of doors and into the hall—a dull, sterile, windowless rectangular room. A group of nine women of varying ages and one gray-haired man chatter while rearranging long tables into a horseshoe. One of them—Candace, from the Trading Post—I recognize.

"Lift those legs, ladies!" Muriel croons in a singsong voice, as if to mask that she's giving them an order. "Remember when Sally gouged the floor last year dragging a table? The town council was not happy about that."

"You're on the council, Muriel," Candace says with a chuckle. She's wearing the same pale blue floral-embroidered cardigan and Crocs that she always wears at her store.

"Exactly! And I was *not* happy about wastin' money to fix it." Muriel slaps her folder on the table—in the center of the horseshoe, I note. "Go on and grab yourself a chair, Calla, and come sit next to me."

Several women—including Emily—offer me polite smiles as I pass, heading for a stack of chairs off to the side.

"I found a church pew the other day and I thought of you," Candace says, trailing after me.

I feel my cheeks flush. "Uh, okay?" Because I'm a terrible liar who clearly needs to pray? I've been in the Trading Post a few times and on one trip, she asked me how my mother liked the coffee table. I balked at admitting the truth and instead told her that I hadn't realized how expensive it would be to ship so I've kept it for myself.

She chuckles. "I'm nosy. I asked Toby what you were doin' with all these old things you keep buyin' from me. He said you use 'em around your house. You know, turning them into somethin' else. He said you were really good at that sort of thing." She shrugs. "Anyway, it's a solid piece. Worn to hell and needin' some cleanup, but I thought you might have an idea for somethin' like that."

I've seen church pews repurposed before, as benches, and I have to agree—there's definite potential. "Thank you, for thinking about me." And I genuinely mean it. "Maybe I can come by tomorrow and take a look at it?"

She offers me a toothy grin. Something tells me she enjoys finding treasures for people.

"Okay, everyone!" Muriel shifts her chair over to make room for me and then claps her hands. "Let's get started. We've got *a lot* to cover tonight."

I steal a glance around the table to catch the mixed expressions as everyone takes their seats—everything from eager smiles to a grim stare from the older gentleman. That could be his face, or it could be a reaction to the task ahead.

Or it could be Muriel's abrasive, domineering manner. Toby said his mother feels a certain ownership over Trapper's Crossing, that she has her fingers in every pot when it comes to how the town runs. She's an elected official on the board—and reelected many times over—so people must respect her passion and fortitude.

But I wonder what all the other residents *really* think of her.

Muriel clears her throat. "First things first. Everyone, this is Calla. She's new to the community." Eleven sets of eyes land on me, and my cheeks burn with the attention. I do recognize some of the ladies from the Ale House, I realize. "Let's do a quick round-table intro. Calla, this is John. He manages the overall budget. Gloria runs the volunteer schedule, you've already met Candace ..." She goes around the table, introducing each person.

"Now that that's sorted, how about we start with last month's follow-ups. John, you were going to provide a sponsorship budget update and crunch some numbers so we could figure out how to make the fireworks show bigger ..."

Muriel steers the meeting, rifling through last month's minutes, each member giving their own updates while a small, mousy woman named Ivy takes notes. It reminds me of my corporate days, sitting around a table in a conference room, discussing projects and plans.

I listen quietly for the next sixty minutes as they talk, struggling to quell my simmering annoyance with Muriel for so swiftly dismissing my suggestion to help with the marketing. Sure, this carnival sounds as hokey as I was suspecting it might be—from the pancake breakfast right down to the karaoke competition—but so far, the only marketing that's been discussed is Emily's thrilling, hand-drawn poster and a quarter-page advertisement in the local newspaper a month before the event.

I'm trying to come up with a plan for how to broach the subject with Muriel again later when I feel a jolt in my chair, followed a moment later by a shake that grows more intense by the second. Muriel's voice drifts midsentence, and everyone moves at once, shifting out of their chairs to dive under the tables.

"Come on!" she beckons me, easing her stout body to the floor. I follow her, dumbstruck, and soon, the group of us are huddled beneath the bank of tables, John's wary gaze on the ceiling tiles above us.

The shaking subsides about fifteen seconds later to a chorus of nervous laughter, before people slowly crawl out.

"That one was close," someone says.

"I guess we better go and find out what kind of damage that caused." Muriel wipes her hands over her jeans as if dusting dirt off them. "What do ya think? Five point six?"

"Four point three." John nods to the clock on the wall. "It's barely crooked."

"Wager the first catch of the season?"

His jowls lift with the first smile I've seen from him as he offers his hand, and they shake on it. "Let's hope you catch another thirty-pounder."

They're betting on the magnitude of the earthquake that just shook the ground like we're at a race track on a casual Sunday afternoon.

I stare at them, trying to make sense of their cavalier attitude. There's one explanation I can think of. "Are earthquakes normal around here?" I ask.

Chuckles and sympathetic looks answer me.

—————

I stir as the mattress sinks beneath Jonah's weight. Moments later, his hot, naked body is molding itself against my back. His lips graze my neck, and his hand slips into the front of my panties.

"The ring of fire," I mumble, letting my eyes adjust to the faint glow of the bedside lamp he turned on.

"What?" Humor laces his tone as one talented finger slips inside me to caress my core.

I roll over to face him, checking the clock on his nightstand. It's almost one A.M. "Why didn't you tell me that we live in the *ring of fire?*" That's what the horseshoe-shaped line of volcanos in the Pacific Ocean is called. "And that Alaska has 11 percent of the world's earthquakes and that there are on average 10,000 measured earthquakes each year, and we literally live on a *fault line?*" I spent hours watching the news and then reading articles about Alaska's history with this natural disaster.

Jonah sighs, removes his hand, and flops onto his back, whatever moment he was trying to stir effectively doused. "Is there a way to block you from accessing Wikipedia?"

"It's not funny! I was *hiding* under a table at the community center tonight, Jonah!" But at least I wasn't home alone. I don't know how I would've handled that.

"Five point nine, up in Denali, from what I heard?"

"Yeah. John owes Muriel a fish." Of course her guess would be the most accurate.

He frowns. "Who's John?"

"A guy at the planning committee," I say dismissively. "You should have warned me! Why would I expect earthquakes in Alaska?"

"Most of them are harmless."

"Yeah! Until the day the ground opens up and swallows us whole."

Jonah pinches the bridge of his nose. He's struggling to keep his patience in check. "Honestly, it didn't even cross my mind to warn you. That's how not-a-big-deal it is. It's just something you get used to. You haven't even noticed them until now."

"Great. *Another* thing for me to get used to." As if the long, dark winters, turbulent weather, menacing mosquitos, threatening wildlife, and general isolation aren't enough, now I have to worry about earthquakes—and potential tsunamis. "Why are you home so late, anyway?" And why did he turn on the light?

"I helped get some smoke jumpers back to their base camp. They'd been out there for almost four days."

Right. Those crazy people who jump out of planes to fight fires in remote spots. At least Jonah hasn't told me he wants to try that. Yet.

"We're supposed to get some rain over the next two days."

"Does that mean you'll be home?" My voice, once groggy, is suddenly brimming with hope.

"Depends. Am I gonna have to hear about earthquakes and bear attacks all day?" Jonah rolls onto his side again. "Jim O'Keefe asked me to do a fly-in for him and his sons in the morning, if it's clear enough." He drags the tip of his minty-fresh tongue along my bottom lip before kissing me on the mouth. My breath can't taste nearly as pleasant right now, but he doesn't seem to care. "I missed you."

My chest swells with warmth at his confession, the confirmation that he does still think about me when he's chosen to be out there in the air.

"Anything exciting happen today, besides the earthquake?" he asks, his hand slipping into the back of my panties to fill his palm with my flesh. He squeezes gently.

"Muriel happened today," I grumble, even as my body responds to his touch.

He chuckles. Jonah always finds my stories about that woman amusing. He has an exorbitant amount of patience for her that I don't understand. "What'd she do now?"

"Basically told me that marketing is pointless and that I know nothing." I relay the conversation from earlier.

"Tell her she's wrong. She'd be lucky to have you helping this Emily chick."

"She made such a big deal about how attendance has been down and how important it is that this one succeeds because they need the money for the community center, but she's so stubborn, she's not willing to try. It's not like she'd even be paying me."

"Did you say all this to her?"

"I was going to, but then the earthquake hit, which distracted me, and then, I don't know, I started thinking maybe she's right." I shrug.

"I don't know the first thing about the people around here or marketing a winter carnival in Alaska! What if I completely screw it up? Or make no difference at all?"

"You're not gonna screw it up. Think about it, Calla. You didn't know shit about planes but you designed that whole website for Wild in, like, four days."

"That was just a website. And it didn't mean anything." My father ended up selling the company right after.

"Hey. It meant something. It was the first time I realized you had a big brain in that pretty head of yours. You impressed me." He pauses, as if to let that sink in. "And you basically set up an *entire* charter plane company for us in a few months."

"Agnes helped me."

"She helped a bit, but no, it's because you're smart as hell and you can figure out anything if you put your mind to it. So, if this is something you want to do, then you tell Muriel that you're doing it! End of story."

I chew my bottom lip in thought. His confidence in me is bolstering. "I *do* know a lot about online marketing."

"Probably a hell of a lot more than Emily or Muriel or anyone else in that room, I'm guessing."

"She uses *Twitter* to promote it!" I cornered Emily outside the library after the meeting, while Muriel was occupied, and asked her. "I've already found a ton of problems."

"Yeah? Like what?"

"Like—" My words falter as Jonah tugs my panties down off my hips and coaxes me onto my back. Heat begins to build in my core. "Like, they have no online presence beyond their website, which is junk, and the schedule is confusing. *And* they need food trucks. Throw food trucks into any event and people will come, I swear."

"See? You sound like you know what you're talkin' about."

"Now to convince Muriel."

"You'll figure out a way." He eases my night shirt up, uncovering my stomach and chest. I lift my arms up and over my head to help him slide it off completely. Goose bumps erupt over my body. "Some clever way …"

Material tightens around my wrists and, before I understand

what's happening, my hands have been bound to the headboard using my nightshirt.

"Jonah!" I tug at the binding in vain. "What are you doing?"

It clicks.

The hot tub picture.

Oh shit. With everything that happened today, I completely forgot about it.

But the look on Jonah's face says he knows that I've finally remembered.

This is why he turned on the light. He likes to watch me squirm.

A hysterical laugh escapes my throat before I press my lips together. I fight the urge to wrestle against the ties. "I talked to Diana today."

"Oh yeah?" He throws the covers off my body and settles onto his knees, his powerful thighs coated in soft, ash-blond hair, his erection standing at attention. He's unfazed by his nakedness. "What'd she have to say?"

I manage to peel my attention away to meet his gaze, to find him smirking—he caught me ogling.

"I begged her to come for my birthday, but she said she can't." Admitting that brings a tinge of melancholy to my tone, despite my current predicament.

Jonah studies me for a few beats, the wicked intent in his eyes softening a touch. "I'm taking you away that weekend."

"Really?" My heart stutters, my pending doom pushed aside for a moment. "Where?"

"It's a surprise."

"But what if you get called into work?" Talk of drought is all that seems to be on the state news lately.

"You're more important to me than work, Calla," he says evenly.

My body feels lighter, more relaxed. I didn't know how much I needed to hear Jonah say those words until just now.

He hooks his index finger through the center of my panties and draws them the rest of the way off. "Is there anything else you want to tell me about?" he asks in that overly calm voice. His steely gaze drags over my body.

I struggle to adopt a relaxed pose. "Hmm ... I can't think of anything— Ah!"

Seizing my hips, he flips me onto my stomach with little effort.

I bite my lip to smother my smile—not that he can see it, anyway —and wait with nervous anticipation. What does he have planned this time around? "Oscar came by."

"To thank you?"

I shudder as a single, light fingertip trails down my spine, from the base of my neck all the way down ... down ... down. "I don't know, but Zeke fainted."

His finger stalls a moment. "*Fainted?*"

"Yes. We have a fainting goat. It was funny, actually, once I knew Oscar wasn't going to kill him."

Jonah sighs. "See ... I would have loved seeing a video of Zeke fainting. You know, when I checked my girlfriend's Instagram account during my break today." His fingertip continues past my tailbone. I grit my teeth against the urge to react, which is what he wants. "But instead of seeing a video of that—" The mattress shifts as Jonah moves in to hover over me, his thighs straddling my hips, his hands settling on either side of my pillow, his mouth grazing my shoulder. The slightest nip of teeth catches my skin. "I found out she posted another naked picture of me."

"You weren't naked!" Well, technically he was. "You can't *see* anything!"

"And *tagged* our company's profile in it."

I can't keep my laughter at bay anymore as I turn my head to meet his eyes. "It's *great* marketing."

"Is it really? Because I've got an in-box full of private messages from both women and men who are *not* interested in booking a flight with me."

"But they're definitely looking for a *ride*." I've seen some of those messages. They're equal parts appalling and hilarious.

Jonah's lip twitches. He's struggling to hide his smile. "You know, for someone who was three seconds away from dumping chili on a woman last month for touching my thigh, I'm surprised you find this so funny."

"I trust you." I also block every one of those accounts.

"Good to know." The roguish look that flashes across his face makes my stomach flip. He shifts, and I feel hot breath kissing my spine, followed by the lightest stroke of his tongue.

I swallow my nerves. "What are you about to do?"

His deep chuckle carries through our bedroom as his looming body begins to shift downward, his hands seizing my hips.

"Jonah!"

CHAPTER TWENTY-EIGHT

"Whose dog is that?" I holler into our empty bedroom. The incessant barking woke me ten minutes ago—at first an irritating sound that didn't quite register in the fog of sleep. But it hasn't relented, interspersed with howls that have me kicking my covers off my legs in frustration.

"Jonah?" I call out, a moment before I remember his lips grazing mine an hour ago, and then whispering that Sam had called him in to work.

With that memory comes a hollow feeling. I reach for the pillow next to mine, my fingers crawling over the soft, white cotton. It's dented from where Jonah's head rested but it's cool to the touch. When was the last time I woke to find him asleep in our bed? I can't recall. These days, he's either already in the air by the time I get out of bed or getting ready to fly off.

I find myself yearning for the long winter days again, when we lay tangled in the sheets for hours, planning our future, with no rush to be anywhere.

A woeful howl sounds from outside.

With a huff of annoyance, I throw on clothes and head downstairs.

Oscar is standing at our side door. His tail wags as if we're old friends.

"What are you doing out here?"

He lets out a bark—more high-pitched than anything I've heard from him before. He then takes several limping steps, stopping to turn back and bark at me again, as if beckoning me toward the back of the house where our animal pen and the garden are situated.

An odd sense of foreboding fills me, that something happened to Zeke. Did Jonah forget to secure the clasp? Did Zeke get out?

Am I about to find a bloody goat carcass in my backyard?

I peer down the driveway, hoping in vain that perhaps Jonah hasn't left yet, but Veronica is long gone.

Oscar barks.

"Okay, okay. Hold on!" I say, though the dog can't possibly understand me.

The window in our laundry room overlooks the animal pen. I go to check it and sag against the wall with relief when I spot Zeke pacing the orchard hay Jonah left him this morning, too agitated by Oscar to eat. Bandit's curious triangular face pokes out from the chicken coop window.

It's not our animals that has Oscar riled up, so what is it? Could it be the other dog in trouble? Are there more bear traps on our property, waiting to snag an unsuspecting leg? If so, why wouldn't Oscar go home to get Roy?

Unless he figures Roy will shoot him on the spot.

I shake my head at myself. This is a dog. He doesn't figure *anything*.

What if this is about Roy?

Did he have another heart attack? Is he lying somewhere dead, or close to it?

"Shit." Miserable SOB or not, I can't ignore Oscar and go about my day with that thought in my head. My gut is telling me Oscar is behaving like this for good reason.

And he has come to *me*.

I try calling Jonah to see what he thinks, but there's no answer on either his cell phone or the satellite phone. Toby doesn't answer his phone, either. I even try Muriel, desperate for advice. But her phone is rarely on her person, and she doesn't answer now.

Oscar's frantic barks are not relenting.

I waffle on indecision for another long moment, and then, swallowing my unease, I pull on my rubber boots and a jacket, grab my bug spray, and head out the door to the ATV, where Oscar awaits.

He takes off ahead, running awkwardly on three legs.

I crank the engine and follow, past Zeke, who doesn't trot to the gate as per usual, his creepy horizontal pupils locked on Oscar. Oscar pays no attention, though, slinking past the garden and off to the left, through a narrow clearing in the bramble.

I slow for a moment.

Just long enough to second-guess the intelligence of this. I could use the roads to get to Roy's house, rather than cut through the trees. It's probably safer, given I'm alone.

But what if Roy is not at his house? What if he was out for a walk and he dropped?

Oscar stops and turns to eye me, barking again.

It's not like I'm totally alone here. He *is* a large dog … wolf … whatever.

With a quick text to Toby as a welfare measure—since he's the closest and likely the quickest to respond, I follow Oscar into the woods.

My pulse races with adrenaline.

———

I know how Oscar has been traveling between our houses.

The distance between us and Roy is shorter when you cut through the thicket, rather than use the long driveways and the road. It took some careful navigating around old stumps and fallen trees with the ATV, but Oscar stopped every so often to make sure I was following as he led me all the way here.

I slow to a stop in front of the woodpile and hold my breath, waiting—hoping—for the cantankerous old man to emerge from either the house or the barn. Roy's truck is here, covered in dirt and parked by the pile of firewood. The black dog paces in front of the barn door, not charging me in a barking frenzy as he has the other two times I've rolled in.

A sinking feeling settles into me as the moments pass with no sign of Roy. When Oscar limps toward the barn, it only solidifies my worry.

I cut the engine and hop off, pulling my phone out of my pocket. Thankfully, Toby has responded.

Toby: *Where are you?*

Calla: *Just got to Roy's and I think something bad has happened.*

Toby: *On my way.*

Taking a deep breath, I follow Oscar through the gaping door and into the quiet barn, my heart pounding in my chest.

A pile of lumber of all shapes and sizes lays scattered over the dirt floor. Beneath it, splayed out on his back, eyes closed, a bloody gash on his forehead, is Roy.

"Oh my God." It's not a heart attack but it could prove just as fatal.

With shaky hands, I dial 9-1-1. Meanwhile, Oscar limps over and prods Roy's face with his wet nose, emitting a high-pitched whimper. It's the most doglike I've seen him behave yet.

"Don't need no damn hospital," Roy croaks.

I startle but then sigh with relief that he's alive. I give dispatch directions to send an ambulance as I visually assess the situation. Above us, where I'm guessing Roy stored all this wood, the brackets have snapped, their jagged ends jutting out. It all must have tumbled down on top of him.

Roy is lucky to be alive.

He scowls at Oscar, who is now licking his face. "Go on, get. Don't need that, either."

When I end the call, I'm able to focus on trying to dig him out. "Let me see if I can get these off you." I begin lifting and shifting boards, some of them taking all my strength to maneuver. But there's an enormous beam across Roy's chest, the one that seems to be keeping him pinned. It's propped up on either side by other fallen pieces of wood, saving Roy from its full weight.

"Don't bother," he warns, wincing.

"I've gotta at least try." My shoulder and arm muscles strain as I attempt to lift it. It doesn't so much as budge. "Maybe if you can help lift it from underneath—"

"My arm's broken. Probably a bunch of ribs, too. God knows what else."

"Right. But you don't need a hospital," I say under my breath. *Obstinate fool.* "Toby should be here any minute." I wish Jonah were here, or at least reachable. We might need him, too. I don't know if Toby can lift this on his own. "Does it hurt?"

"Only when I breathe."

"Okay, just ... stay still. We'll get you out of here soon." I settle down onto the floor, leaning in to inspect his forehead, noting, from the corner of my eye, the gun that's propped against the wall.

His aged blue eyes watch me keenly.

"The bleeding seems to have stopped, at least."

He grunts, looking to the broken brackets above. "Must have been that quake yesterday, loosenin' something. Went to pull a board down and it all came tumblin'."

I have no idea if the same quake that made the community center hall's clock crooked would have the power to do that, but clearly, something went terribly wrong. "You're lucky it didn't kill you."

"Who knows. Still might."

Uncomfortable silence hangs as we wait, the minutes dragging too slowly. I survey the vast space, because there's nothing more I can do for Roy, and I'm curious. The barn is huge but crammed—the front half of it a maze of countless tools and saws, of spindles and discarded wood fragments, of boards clamped together on sawhorses. Piles of sawdust have been swept into piles, over into the corners. The smell of damp wood mixes with the stench of the goat pens in the back. I see no finished furniture, though. There's a ladder off to the right that stretches upward to a loft above, where hay four bales high forms a half wall at the edge.

"Why'd you come?" Roy asks, breaking the silence, his gruff voice strained from pain.

"Oscar led me here. He wouldn't stop barking outside my door. I figured something happened. You know, another heart attack, maybe."

"Let me guess, that busybody told you all about that."

I can only assume he means Muriel. I don't bother correcting my source of information. There's no need for Toby to earn Roy's wrath today.

Both dogs have taken sentry positions at the barn's entrance, Oscar easing onto his injured haunches gracelessly, his sharp gaze outward, his ears perked.

"You're lucky Oscar survived that trap." If he hadn't come to get me, how long would it have taken for someone to find Roy out here, buried under a pile of wood? Does he have anyone in his life?

Would anyone miss Roy Donovan?

"What? You want a medal for comin' to my rescue?"

I sigh heavily, loud enough for him to interpret it for what it is —annoyance.

"Joy from the diner woulda' come lookin' for me, eventually," he says after a long moment. "She buys my eggs. I've never missed a week. When I didn't show up on Friday, she would've come lookin'." It almost sounds as if he's trying to convince himself of that.

Maybe he's right, but that means he would've been trapped under this wood for days.

My focus shifts to the shotgun. "Do you always have that thing by your side?"

"I've got twelve goats and a flock of chickens in bear country. What do *you* think?" He winces in pain, reminding me that I probably shouldn't be asking him all these questions. I can't help myself, though—this is the most normal Roy has acted since I've met him.

Plus, I now have a pressing concern. "How often do you get bears here?"

"I lost count years ago."

I think about the distance between here and home, through the woods.

It's too close.

My stomach tightens with anxiety. It's one thing to get used to a roaming fox and a moose. But *bears* in my backyard?

"Don't look so worried, city slicker. You can't raise livestock around these parts without a predator pacing your fence line, trying to find a way in. It's the way things work out here." He pauses. "Muriel didn't tell you, did she?"

"Tell me what?"

"That there's been one hangin' around the past month that could become a problem. A brown bear."

Icy dread slides down my spine. "No. She didn't mention that."

"He gets zapped by the fence every time, but he keeps comin' back. Been comin' during the day, too. The hounds chased him away last week after lunch. Another time, I fired a warning shot to scare him off. But he keeps comin' back."

I look to the wide-open barn door. When will this bear decide to make another attempt? The dogs would sense a bear nearby, wouldn't they? "Are you going to shoot him?"

"Why? You gonna try to stop me?"

"Uh ... *No*, actually."

He smirks. "He hasn't done anythin' that warrants a bullet yet. He's a big boy but young. Probably lost his mama and hasn't figured out how to forage for food. I figure once the salmon are in full swing, he'll move on to the river where he'll be more productive."

This is what Roy was talking about that night at the Ale House when he asked if there'd been anything sniffing around Zeke. He wasn't wondering about Oscar. He was wondering if this bear was coming around our place, too.

Has it been?

I feel Roy's gaze dissecting me. "You know ... you don't belong here, girl."

His words are blunt and yet delivered with a razor-sharp edge, and they stir the twinge of worry deep inside me—that he's right, that there are too many things for me to "get used to" to ever truly feel like Alaska is my home.

But I won't allow Roy to get to me today. I set my jaw stubbornly. "I belong wherever Jonah is."

"Oh. You're one of *those* girls." There's no missing the disparaging tone. The judgment. The disdain.

Even injured—gravely, possibly—Roy is caustic, at best.

"You know, I'm *so happy* Oscar dragged me here today. You're always such delightful company."

He grunts in response, though I note how the corners of his mouth curl, ever so slightly. As if my sarcastic retort amuses him.

The dogs suddenly rush out the door, barking. The sound of squeaking brakes announces a vehicle.

"That should be Toby." *Thank God.* I climb to my feet and head for the barn door, relieved that help is here and I no longer have to bear Roy's acerbic personality alone.

"Go on, get back!" Muriel's commanding voice carries.

I stifle my groan. I'm not sure if having her here will make things better or worse for the man lying on the ground, his body broken.

Toby ignores a barking Gus and slinking Oscar as he strolls toward me, working a dirty rag over his motor-oil-coated hands. "How bad is it?" he asks grimly.

"Not sure yet. An ambulance is on its way."

"Good luck makin' it all the way in." Muriel marches into the barn as if she owns the place. "Well, you gone and buried yourself. How'd you manage that?"

"Dear Lord, end me now," Roy mutters, closing his eyes.

Muriel ignores him, pointing to the boards I already shifted off. "Let's get those pieces farther back to give us some room."

We set to work, dragging the wood away.

Muriel scowls at the beam. "Toby, you help me with this." They grab hold of it together. "Bend with your knees!" she hollers, earning Toby's eye roll. Between the two of them and some grunting, they pivot the beam around and off Roy. His arm, which he must have lifted to brace against the wood as it fell, is bent awkwardly and not moving.

Muriel stands over him with her hands on her hips, assessing the situation with a stern expression. "You put too much wood up there."

"No, I didn't."

"Can you wiggle your toes?"

"If I can't, will you shoot me like you tried to shoot my dog?"

"Your right arm's broken."

"No shit."

"What about your left one?"

Roy answers by raising his middle finger on his left arm and waggling it at her.

I press my lips together to keep from laughing. Apparently being rescued from a dire situation and in pain hasn't softened him at all.

A quick glance over at Toby confirms he's struggling not to laugh, too.

Roy shifts as if attempting to sit up, but manages nothing more than a groan. "Think I'll just stay here for a while, then."

Muriel notes the empty pens. "Toby, go on and check on the goats. Calla, find some blankets inside so we can cover him up."

"I don't need a blanket and she's not goin' into my house!" Roy throws back, whatever civility I caught glimpses of earlier gone with Muriel's presence.

"Yes, you do! Stop bein' such a damn fool!"

"Come on." Toby tugs on my sleeve and leads me out the door.

"Do they always fight like that?" The growing tension in the air is palpable.

"Pretty much. It's like sport for them. You get used to it after a while."

"I don't know how." I eye Roy's little cabin. How often does he allow anyone inside?

"You're probably gonna be the first person to step inside that place ... ever," Toby says, as if reading my mind.

I'm certainly not welcome to. "Do you think he has it booby-trapped?"

"Oh. Definitely." Toby says with a mock-serious face before it splits into a grin. "Holler if you get caught in anything." He walks toward the gate that leads to the clearing behind the barn where several goats graze.

"Hey, wait! Did you hear about that bear that's been coming around?" Is it hiding in the tree line, watching us at this very moment?

"Yeah, Mom said something." He seems unconcerned.

"Shouldn't you bring a gun with you?" How is he so chill about the possibility of a roaming bear, especially after what happened with his brother?

He throws a thumb at the barn where Muriel continues to berate Roy for being stubborn, and he continues to deny his need for any help, despite him lying on the cold ground with God only knows how many broken bones and, possibly, internal bleeding. "You think any animal is crazy enough to come around with that goin' on?"

I shake my head as I climb the steps that lead to Roy's front porch. Oscar slinks behind me, keeping five feet away at all times. With unease, I step inside.

I never put much thought into what the inside of Roy's cabin might look like. It's plainly designed as I would expect of a man who lives alone in the woods—the kitchen on the right, the living room off to the left, two doors at the back, which lead to what I'm guessing are his bedroom and a bathroom. *If* he has a bathroom. There is little in the way of furniture—an old green-and-yellow woven chair that I would bet was rescued from the dump or the side of the road sits next to the woodstove, a small rectangular table for two, but with only one chair, and a gun rack on the wall that holds three guns. I'm sure they're all loaded.

But, what surprises me are the three full walls of floor-to-ceiling, built-in bookcases—all measured and cut and trimmed to perfection. They're the kind of high-end built-ins I've been dreaming about for beneath the stairs at our house. The kind that cost triple what I want to pay.

Roy *must* have made these.

Just as he likely made the countless wooden figurines that fill them. Deer, bears, wolves, fish, pigs, whales ... My amazed eyes graze the shelves, struggling with where to focus. There are people, too. Intricately carved pirates and gnomes, old men with canes, pregnant women cradling their bellies, children running. There's an entire shelf dedicated to a little girl with pigtails—laughing, skipping, sleeping. One has her arms wrapped around the neck of a dog—or maybe a wolf—that's twice her size. There are wooden bowls, wooden spoons with long, narrow decorative handles ...

My mouth hangs open in amazement. There are hundreds of them. Maybe thousands, and the detail in each is astonishing. Some have even been touched by a paintbrush.

That miserable old man out there is an artist.

In fact, *every* detail in this cabin that involves wood seems immaculate. The trim that frames the windows is cut with precision, the wide-plank floorboards are evenly stained, the kitchen shelves that hold dishes for one and several weeks' worth of canned goods look sturdy and secure, mounted to the wall. There are no sloppy, uneven cuts anywhere in here.

"She's not doing anythin' to your damn stuff!" Muriel's scolding voice carries through an open window, reminding me that I have a purpose here and I'm invading Roy's private space against his wishes. I grab the navy wool blanket that sits folded on the armchair, and then head for the door.

A framed picture sitting atop an old trunk beneath the window stops me in my tracks. It's a studio portrait of a man in a cowboy hat with his arm draped over a pretty blonde woman's shoulders. A child sits between them. A doll-like girl of two or three years old, with cherub cheeks and expressive blue eyes. She's been dressed much like a doll, too, in a blue gingham dress, frilly socks, and white Mary Janes, her sable-brown locks secured by a matching blue ribbon. In her chubby grip is a wooden animal like the ones on these shelves.

It's a moment before I realize the man in the picture is Roy.

He's much younger—his face clean-shaven and marred by only a few wrinkles—and a few pounds lighter, but what's the most jarring is the crooked grin he's wearing.

There's no indication of when it was taken, but it has a department store $9.99 sitting fee vibe to it—textured gray background, poor lighting, stiff posing. Roy is in an outfit much like the one he wore to the Ale House—a button-down shirt, jeans, and his broad cowboy hat. He's also wearing a red-white-and-blue tie with a star on it that reminds me of the logo for a restaurant chain back home called the Lone Star. Based on the woman's feathered hair and acid-washed jeans, I'm guessing this was taken some time in the '80s, maybe early '90s.

This must be Roy's wife.

But I don't remember Toby ever mentioning a daughter.

I glance around. It's the only picture in the cabin from what I can see. That he has it on display decades later, and sitting within view of his chair, says these people must be important to him—and that he probably hasn't seen them in a long time.

What happened to them?

"You find the blanket on the chair, Calla?" Muriel's holler pulls me from my snooping.

I rush outside and to the barn to find her still looming over Roy, a stern scowl furrowing her brow. "You don't even know what all needs to be fixed inside you yet. You could be in the hospital for weeks! And how are you gonna milk those goats with one arm, huh? Or fire your gun if you need to?" I wonder if it even fazes her that she's scolding a man as he lies on the ground, injured.

"Carefully," Roy grumbles.

"Yeah, I can see it now." Muriel snorts. "You're liable to shoot yourself in the foot while you're at it."

"It'd be less painful than this conversation."

"You don't want my help? That's fine." She throws her hands up in the air, stepping out of the way to make room for me to stretch the blanket over him. "I wasn't gonna offer, anyway. I don't have time for your chores. Got enough of my own. But don't be an idiot. You got all these chickens and goats and those wild dogs of yours that need carin' for." She pauses a beat. "Calla, here, will come and help you until you're back on your feet."

My head snaps back and I shoot her a wide-eyed "what the hell?" glare.

She smiles encouragingly. "She's a good girl. Smart, and a hard worker."

"I have no idea how to milk a goat," I stammer, broadsided by this sudden turn of events.

"You didn't know how to garden either, did ya? You two will be good for each other. You have stuff in common."

Roy and I have literally *nothing* in common, I want to scream, but I can't seem to find my tongue.

"And we help our neighbors. That's what we do." Muriel nods to herself as if passing her verdict.

Even when our neighbor is an angry, mean old man?

I hold my breath, waiting for Roy to spit on the idea of my aid, so I can bow out gracefully.

But for once, he isn't arguing with Muriel, his shrewd gaze watching me intently.

CHAPTER TWENTY-NINE

Jonah strolls in just after seven P.M. as I'm shoveling the last piece of chicken into my mouth.

"Couldn't wait for me?" He tosses his baseball cap on the hook.

"No. I was hungry." And irritated that he landed forty minutes ago but took this long to make his way home, despite my two texts to tell him dinner was ready.

He leans in to kiss me. "Good day?"

My nose catches a hint of campfire smoke. "*Horrible* day. Possibly the worst day I've had since moving here."

Jonah scrubs his hands in the sink and listens as I give him details.

"How bad is it? Have you heard anything?"

"Muriel called about an hour ago." After all their bickering and posturing, she practically chased the ambulance to the hospital in Palmer. "They're keeping him overnight, but he's doing better than expected. I mean, he has three cracked ribs, a fractured collarbone, his arm is broken in two places, plus he has a mild concussion and bruising all over his body. But it could have been way worse. You wouldn't believe the pile of wood that fell on top of him."

"Barely a scrape, then. When shit like that happens, people die." Jonah settles onto the bar stool beside me. He frowns at the TV where the news broadcasts footage of the wildfire he's been fighting daily down in the Kenai Peninsula. They're already claiming it could become one of the most expensive forest fires in the entire country this year, if they don't contain it.

"So, what's goin' on with his livestock, then? They gonna fend for themselves until he's home?" He picks a piece of chicken off his plate with his fingers and shoves it into his mouth, as if too starved for basic table manners.

"That's the best part! Guess who Muriel tasked with the responsibility of taking care of his twelve goats and flock of chickens, beginning at six P.M. *sharp* tomorrow night? While Roy supervises, of course," I add bitterly. Toby and Teddy are covering until then, at least.

Jonah's face twists with disbelief. "Why didn't you say no?" I catch the accusation in his tone, as if it's somehow my fault I've gotten myself into his predicament.

"How could I? Muriel's all 'help thy neighbor' and the guy was literally lying on the ground, *bleeding.*"

"Why isn't Muriel doin' it, then?"

"Are you kidding?" I snort. "The two of them in the same room is like mixing a vat of bleach and vinegar." The toxic fumes are enough to choke anyone within a mile radius.

Jonah shakes his head. "You still should have said no. That asshole would have said no. He *did*, remember? When we tried to get him to take Zeke."

"Yeah, well, I'd like to think I'm better than Roy."

"You *are* better. Nicer, smarter … A helluva lot prettier." He leans in and plants a quick kiss against my jawline. "Also, a huge sucker."

"I'm not milking his goats," I say with more defiance than I feel.

"You told Muriel that?" Jonah's eyes twinkle with amusement, knowing full well that I haven't.

"He has one good arm. He can do it." Though the instructive YouTube video that I watched earlier suggests otherwise. "Or *you* could do it, if you come with me tomorrow night."

Jonah is already shaking his head before I even finish speaking.

"Come on! I don't want to go there alone!"

"Look at that!" He jabs his fork in the air at the TV screen. "There's no rain anywhere in the forecast and every day gets worse.

I'm lucky I got home when I did tonight. There are hundreds of people on the ground, fighting this. They're there around the clock."

I watch the billow of smoke that pollutes the sky. It's hard to argue with that. It also may be a bad omen for our upcoming plans. I hesitate asking the question, afraid of the answer. "What about this weekend?"

He frowns with confusion.

"For my birthday?" Has he forgotten my birthday?

"Yeah, yeah. Of course we're goin'." His brow furrows. "Look, if I'm home in time tomorrow night, I'll go with you to the asshole's house. But I can't promise anything. There's literally thousands of acres on fire, and what Sam has me and the other guys doin' doesn't seem to be makin' a dent."

Does Sam have all his guys working as hard as Jonah does? Are they putting this many hours in, too? Or is this Jonah, consumed with a task?

I don't ask. I smile and say, "It's okay, I get it." Though I'm beginning to *really* not like it. I'm beginning to pray for heavy rain, for no other reason than to ground Jonah. "Can you also try to be home to go with me to the dealer? I want to buy that Jeep, but I want you there with me. I don't trust that car salesman not to try to swindle me."

"How late is it open till?"

"Eight. We could probably make it tonight."

"Not tonight, Calla. I'm beat. Can we try tomorrow?"

"Sure." I smile, trying to push aside my frustration. "You should see the inside of Roy's place." I describe the impressive built-in cabinetry and the countless figurines. "He may be a jerk but he's crazy talented."

"Maybe after you milk his goats, you can hire him to build us something," Jonah says with a smirk.

"I'm not milking any goats!"

"I heard their udders are soft." Jonah shovels a forkful of salad and chicken into his grinning mouth.

With a heavy eye roll, I collect my dirty dishes, carrying them to the sink.

"Did you talk to Muriel about doin' the marketing for the carnival yet?"

"No. I haven't had the chance."

"Don't be afraid to challenge her, Calla."

"I'm *not* afraid." I tuck my rinsed plate into the dishwasher. "I just haven't figured out exactly how to broach the topic in a way that she can't shoot me down again." And convince me that I have little to offer around here.

"Tell her you're doin' it, end of discussion."

"So I should use your usual charm and brilliant powers of persuasion," I say mockingly.

"I get what I want, don't I?"

"We're living here," I mutter. "Why are you so interested, anyway? It's just a carnival."

He chews slowly, as if deciding how to respond. "Because I'd feel better knowing you're meeting more people around here."

My days certainly wouldn't feel so long if I had places to go, friends to meet for coffee or a meal. Not that I can see myself lunching with John or Candace, or anyone who makes up the carnival planning committee. "The next meeting isn't until the middle of July, so I have time." I wander back over to lean on the island, my thoughts still tangled in the day's events. "I think Roy has a daughter. Or had one. There's this picture of him and a woman and a little girl in his cabin. It was old, from a long time ago. He was smiling." I add, more to myself, "I wonder what happened."

"Divorce or death," Jonah says through a mouthful. "Those are the only two options."

The latter sends a chill of unease down my spine as I think of that little girl's cherub cheeks. "Maybe that's why he moved to Alaska."

"Wouldn't be the first time a person ran here to escape something." Jonah reaches over to click a key on my sleeping laptop. He frowns at the life-sized, motion-activated witch prop that appears. "It's a bit early for Halloween decorating, isn't it?"

"It's not for Halloween." I toggle over to the video and play it so Jonah can watch the witch's eyes glow red and the hair-raising cackle. "I was reading an article today, about how a lady in Eagle

River put one of these by her trash bins and she hasn't had any issues with bears in three years."

"We don't have issues with bears, either. We keep our bins in the workshop."

"It's not for the bins. It's for the animal pen. Roy said there's a persistent brown bear trying to break into his pasture, and we're a lot closer to him than you think, if you cut through the forest. What if it decides to come over here, too?" I ordered three motion-activated cameras but they haven't arrived yet. Not that they'll do anything in the way of protecting us.

"So, you want to put this five-and-a-half-foot, skull-faced, red-eyed *witch* outside our fainting goat's pen, to scare off this bear?" His frown still hasn't wavered, though now it's coupled with amusement.

"No." I set my jaw defiantly, daring him to challenge me. "I want to put one on *each* corner."

Tree branches scrape the paint of our old pickup truck as I coast along Roy's narrow laneway at five after six the next evening, having waited for Jonah as long as possible. I knew not to expect him. I know he's out doing critical, life-saving work, and yet I'm disappointed all the same.

The dogs are barking when I pull up next to Roy's truck and cut the engine. Muriel had Toby text to remind me to be here at six. She drove Roy home from the hospital at noon today—news that had me shaking my head. Those two have the strangest relationship.

I suffer a moment of fear and doubt before I squash it and hop out. Oscar's menacing barks calm and his tail begins to wag. He comes close enough to sniff my thigh before darting back. Progress, I suppose. Even Gus has quieted, as if accepting my presence.

The barn door is already closed. I can hear the goats bleating inside. Even the chicken coop seems to have been tended to—chickens all gathered around what I'm guessing is a feeder, the ground covered in wood shavings. It would seem the evening chores have already been done. Maybe Toby came by?

With no sign of Roy anywhere and not sure what else to do, I climb the porch steps and knock on the door. There's a creak and an unintelligible mutter, and the sound of feet shuffling across the wood floor before the door opens.

A day later and somehow Roy looks worse than he did lying on the barn floor, bloodied and covered in lumber. The gash on his forehead may be cleaned up, but it's camouflaged by a mottle of purple and blue bruising that's extended down to his left eye. His arm is bound with a temporary brace and secured in a sling. Beneath a plain white T-shirt, I can make out the binding that wraps his rib cage.

But probably the most concerning part about his appearance is his ashen complexion.

"Hey ... Muriel told me to be here at six to help you with your evening chores."

He grunts. "Already took care of everything."

My eyebrows arch. "Seriously?" I remember Simon slipping on an icy sidewalk and breaking his collarbone when I was eighteen. He was bedridden and downing Percocet for weeks. My guess is Roy has a much higher pain threshold than my stepfather, but he also has multiple broken bones.

"Let's not play this game where you pretend you wanna be here, Calla." My name sounds odd on his accent. Or maybe it's that he's using it at all, rather than calling me a city slicker or "girl." I wasn't even sure if he remembered it.

"It's not about *wanting* to be here—"

"Yeah, yeah, it's Muriel. I get it. So, let's you and me make a deal— if that old nag asks, you tell her everyone's milked, fed, watered, and in for the night. It'll be our little secret. Everybody wins. So, you can go on home and let me eat my dinner in peace."

I spy the bowl on his table and the opened can of beef stew on the counter, next to a prescription pill bottle. Painkillers, no doubt. The sticker seal on them hasn't been broken yet. "So, tomorrow morning—"

"Like I said, I don't need help. I've managed on my own up until now. I'll figure it out."

His deathly pale complexion is worrisome, but I'm not about to stand on Roy's doorstep and argue with him. "Okay, then ... Have a good night, I guess?" I edge away.

"You like eggs?" he says.

"Uh ... yeah?"

"I hate eggs."

I frown. "Then why do you have all those chickens?"

"Hold up a sec." He turns slowly, and I catch the grimace that flashes across his face. Hobbling over to his fridge, he pulls out two cartons and shuffles back. "Here. Got no use for 'em. They're already washed."

"I thought you sell them to the diner?"

"You want 'em or not?" he snaps.

It clicks—this is supposed to be a gesture. Of kindness, of gratitude.

From a man who gives nothing for free, according to Toby.

I collect the carton from his waiting grasp, noting how his face may have yet turned a shade paler in the slight excursion to the fridge. "Thanks."

"Uh-huh," he adds after a long pause. "Have a good night."

"You, too." I leave Roy's porch, feeling far less relief than I should about escaping a chore list that involves touching udders and shoveling manure.

But all I feel is pity, for an old man who hasn't done a thing to deserve it.

———

I smile at the sound of the metal spoon clanging against porcelain. "What are you going to do when Mom figures out you've been carbing up after she goes to bed?"

"Vehemently deny it, of course," Simon mumbles around a mouthful of instant mashed potatoes. I finally discovered where he'd been hiding his stash of Honest Earth Creamy Mash—in the locked cabinet that holds his patients' files—the only place in the house that is off-limits to my mother.

It's eleven thirty in Toronto, but my stepfather has always been a night owl. I knew, when I arrived home from Roy's and texted him to talk, that he would be awake and available. "So? What are you going to do about this cantankerous neighbor of yours?"

"I don't know. What should I do?"

"What are your options again?"

I sigh. Simon knows my options. As usual, he's making me work through this on my own rather than giving me the answers I seek. He can't help it; it's the psychiatrist in him. "Either I show up there tomorrow morning or I don't."

"Okay. So, if you go there in the morning, what will happen?"

"He'll send me home. And probably yell at me."

"And if you don't go ..."

"Then he'll be doing everything on his own, and what if he falls? Or passes out from the pain? What if that bear shows up and makes a run for him?" I rifle through the list of horrible outcomes to Roy being left to his own stubborn devices. "You should have seen him today, Simon. He looked ready to keel over." Muriel is right. He is a fool, refusing our help.

"So, you feel responsible for his welfare?"

"Responsible? No. But Muriel asked me to help him." More like ordered, because Muriel doesn't know how to *ask*.

"And you don't want to disappoint her?"

"No, that's not it. I just ..." My words falter. What is it, exactly?

"What will happen if you call this Muriel and let her know that he's unwilling to let you help?"

"She'll tell me I must not have tried very hard. And then she'll be there every morning and night, and I know she doesn't have time for that. They're swamped at the resort." I, on the other hand, have *plenty* of time.

"So, you'll feel like you somehow failed her?"

"No, but ... she's helped us out a lot." Whether I've asked for it or not.

"And her opinion matters to you?"

"It doesn't."

"Are you sure?" Simon asks in that gentle prodding way of his.

"I don't know. I guess maybe it does, a little?"

She's a good girl. Smart, and a hard worker.

I can't ignore the blip of pride that stirred in my stomach when

Muriel said that to Roy, shocked as I was by her edict that I'm the person to help him. So, maybe I do care what Muriel thinks of me. "Plus, I know Roy'll be angry if I sic her on him." According to him, we've made a pact to keep Muriel out of this arrangement. *Everyone wins*, he claimed. But it didn't look like he's winning anything except a much slower recovery time.

"And his opinion matters to you?"

I snort. "Are you kidding? He doesn't have a good opinion of *anyone*. But it's sad. I don't think he knows how to let people help him. And I think he's intentionally offensive to keep people at arm's length. Or maybe he's been alone for so long, he doesn't know how to be anything else." And yet he made a rare appearance at the Ale House the night of the chili cook-off to thank me for saving Oscar, and to warn Muriel about this potential problem bear. Whether he did those things because he felt the burden of responsibility or was genuinely compelled, I can't say.

"Maybe both of those things are true."

I sigh. "Maybe."

"You know, it's common for men as they age to become, for lack of a better word, grumpy. It has to do with their decreasing testosterone levels."

I cringe. "I don't want to talk about Roy's testosterone levels, Simon. Besides, according to Muriel and Teddy, he's been this way since he moved here."

"Hmm ... You said he was married once?"

"Yeah. And I think he has a daughter. Or *had* one." My curiosity about Roy's past has taken over my idle thoughts since I saw that portrait yesterday. I'm intrigued about what might have happened, and if it made him into who he is today.

"Well, my dear, it sounds like you don't really have options, then."

Simon's right. Whether it's my guilt or sense of responsibility, or because I know it's the right thing to do, I have to go to Roy's in the morning and offer my help again. Even if he doesn't deserve it. "How do I do it in a way that won't make him reach for his gun?" Not that he could fire it at me at the moment, thank God.

"By beguiling him, of course." I hear the smile in Simon's voice. "If he's isolated himself for this long, perhaps it's best to let him get used to you being around, for starters."

I shake my head, though he can't see it. "I can't believe I'm actually *trying* to find a way to help that asshole milk his stupid goats."

Simon chuckles. "Remember when you used to be terrified of those things?"

"Vaguely. Funny enough, next to bears, they don't seem so scary anymore."

"Yes, perhaps we best not mention that part of this story to your mother, okay? She already worries enough." He pauses. "And how are things otherwise?"

"They're fine." My stock answer these days. "Jonah's been working all the time lately."

"And how does that make you feel?"

I stifle my groan at Simon's favorite question. "Lonely?" I offer casually, but there's nothing casual about that. "Sometimes, it seems like working is more important to Jonah than spending time with me." It's the first time I've ever said that out loud, and it feels like a betrayal.

"Have you talked to him about it?"

"Not in so many words." Not at all, really. "I'm trying to be supportive."

"Are you feeling resentment toward Jonah because of it?"

"No. I mean, how can I? I told him to take the job." Mainly because I felt guilty after overhearing his conversation with Marie. "And what he's doing is important. The wildfires are *really* bad this year." The smoke has gotten so dense, the Chugach Mountains aren't even visible from Anchorage right now.

"It *is* important," Simon agrees. "But so is acknowledging your feelings and deciding how you want to deal with them."

"I'm dealing with them by keeping myself busy and looking forward to things like my birthday." A weekend away is exactly what Jonah and I need. "Besides, it's only for a few more months." And then he's gone for three weeks to fly Jack Thomas's rich hunters around. Quiet days are one thing. My stomach clenches with dread at all those nights alone, listening to every creak the house makes, my overactive imagination conjuring up what might be lurking outside.

I need to start looking at flights to Toronto.

There's a long pause on the other end of the phone, so long that I begin to think the line has cut off.

"Simon?"

"I'm here, I'm here. I thought I heard your mother stirring."

I smile at the thought of my stepfather scrambling to hide his guilty pleasure from her.

And realize how much I miss them both.

———

The front tire of our pickup rolls through a deep pothole in Roy's laneway, jerking my body.

"Crap!" I scowl at the splash of foamed soy milk on my track pants. I was already annoyed about being up this early.

Why am I doing this to myself again?

Roy appears at the opening to the barn with a rake in his one good hand, his face looking as battered and ashen as it did yesterday.

Right, that's why I'm doing this.

Oscar and Gus charge out of the barn, barking. But the moment I hop out of the truck, they calm, coming in close enough to catch a sniff of my leg before darting off again.

"What are you doin' here?" Roy grumbles.

I trudge forward. "Do you like strawberries?"

His gaze drops to the bowl in my grasp, narrowing. "Maybe."

I fight the urge to roll my eyes. "It's a yes or no answer, Roy."

The corner of his mouth twitches. "It's been awhile but, yeah, I like 'em. Who doesn't?"

"*I* don't, actually. And I have Colette's entire patch growing in the garden. These are washed and hulled, ready to eat." I hold out the bowl for him.

He stares at it another moment. Leaning the rake against the wall to free his one hand, he collects the bowl and sets it on a small table. Without so much as a thanks, I note. "You best be on your way, girl.

I've got work to do." With that, he turns and shuffles to the back of the barn, to the empty goat pen.

Arming myself with a deep breath and my conviction, I follow. "So, how often do you milk your goats?"

He glares at me. "Told you already, I don't need your help."

"Oh, I know. But we both know that Muriel is going to show up here one day soon to check on things, and if she finds out you've been sending me away, well ... I guess you'll have her here twice a day for the next month or two."

Roy grunts. "That damn woman."

"It's her or me, but it's going to be one of us, so take your pick." I stared at our wooden ceiling for far too long last night, searching for today's game plan on tackling Roy. The threat of Muriel seemed a guaranteed winner.

His sharp eyes drift over my red rubber boots. "Suit yourself. But don't get in my way."

"Don't worry. I'll just hang back here. And enjoy your charm from afar." I take a long, leisurely sip of my latte, in part to hide any trace of apprehension that may show on my face.

Heavy sarcasm will go one of two ways with Roy—very badly or very well. I'm hoping on the latter, given he admitted to being "a real SOB."

The corners of his mouth twitch before he turns his back to me. "You must be *real* bored over there."

I allow myself a small smile of victory.

————

"Okay, okay ..." I unwind the wire that secures the latch to the animal pen. Zeke was kicking excitedly at the fence post when I rounded the corner, and Bandit had climbed up the chicken coop's enclosure to sit on top of the roof. "Sorry I'm late. I was over at our friendly neighbor's house." Following Roy as he muttered and cursed and refused to let me even fill up a water bucket, all while grimacing in pain.

I prop open the gate with a brick, and Zeke immediately trots over to nip at the bear bell on my shoe. Bandit scurries closely after.

With them free to roam, I hop back onto my ATV and head for the garden, a goat and a raccoon trailing me, bear spray in my holster. I'm hypervigilant of the surrounding forest for movement, now that I know of this brown bear. Perhaps that's why I spot Oscar right away, sitting at the tree line, watching from afar, as if he's been waiting there awhile.

He was at Roy's when I left. He must have headed this way the moment my taillights vanished from sight.

I cut the ATV engine and climb off, but he makes no effort to approach, his sharp gaze flickering once to Zeke before shifting off away, uninterested.

He's like a sentry, on guard for threats unseen.

I can't help but smile. It's ironic that this wolf dog terrorized me for months, slinking through the trees, and yet having him here now makes me feel safer.

I know the moment Zeke has caught wind of our visitor because he begins bleating noisily and then keels over.

———

Roy is dragging a hose from the house to the chicken coop when I pull in next to his truck at five P.M. sharp.

He scowls at his watch. "What're you doin' here so early? I said six."

"And you were lying, so you'd be finished by the time I showed up." Oscar allows me a quick scratch between his ears on my way over. In my other hand, I have a Tupperware container. "I brought you dinner. It's homemade spaghetti." *Real* homemade this time. I even used stewed tomatoes and fresh oregano from the garden.

"I don't need charity from you," he says, but there's no fire in his words.

"It's not charity. I made too much, and I don't like leftovers." Jonah does, but Roy doesn't need to know that.

He opens his mouth and I brace myself for a hostile response, but then he seems to change his mind. He eyes the container. "Well, it's not tasteless beef from a can, but it'll do." The corners of his mouth twitch.

Did Roy crack a joke?

I bite back the urge to make a big deal of the fact that, buried deep beneath his prickly exterior, Roy might have a sense of humor. "I'll drop it off in your kitchen—"

The hint of humor is gone from his face in an instant. "I don't like anyone goin' in my house!"

I was anticipating this. "I've already been inside once, Roy, and I didn't do anything weird. I'll just drop this off in the fridge and then I'll come back outside in, like, *five seconds* to *not* help you, I swear."

He shakes his head. "You're as pushy as Muriel."

"You and I *both* know that isn't true."

He continues toward the coop, grumbling, "Don't know why you keep fightin' to hang around here. I'm rotten company on my best days."

"Self-awareness is the first step to change." At least that's what Simon always says.

He mumbles something incoherent but continues on.

With no further objections, I head up the porch steps and into the cabin.

I wasn't focused on Roy's kitchen the last time I was here, too enthralled by all the wooden figurines. It's basic and functional, but tidy—a small corner of the cabin with a sink, an old white stove, and fridge. A coffeemaker and toaster occupy a four-foot laminate countertop. Two shelves hold a few basic dishes—one of each—and a selection of canned and dried goods. Two pots and one frying pan hang from hooks on the wall. Everything about this kitchen says "one person and one person only."

I note the bottle of painkillers—a prescription to OxyContin for Roy Richard Donovan, the seal still unbroken—sitting on the counter, next to an unopened can of beef stew. His dinner for tonight. And for most nights, based on the grim selection I see. The metal bucket he used to collect milk from the goat this morning and a sieve are drying in the rack beside the sink, along with several glass mason jars. Even in his current state, Roy prepared his goat milk and washed up afterward.

I shake my head as I open the refrigerator.

"Wow." I eyeball all the cartons of eggs and mason jars of milk that fill the shelves. There isn't much of anything else, save for a few condiments, a stick of butter, and the strawberries I delivered this morning. I smile at the nearly empty bowl. There was at least two pints' worth in there. Roy must enjoy them far more than he let on.

Setting the container of spaghetti on top of the bowl, I head back outside, unable to avoid stealing a glance at the trunk beneath the window.

The family portrait is gone.

That only adds fuel to the curiosity fire burning inside me.

Roy is cursing at a kink in the hose when I reach him, unable to nudge it free with his boot.

"So, how often do you fill up their water?" I ask, reaching down to straighten the hose, before grabbing and dragging it the rest of the way to the pen. The door is propped open, but the chickens don't seem in any hurry to escape with Oscar and Gus lingering.

Roy's brow furrows, as if he's trying to figure out a perplexing puzzle. "Every night. Sometimes in the mornin', too."

"In here, right?" The top of the water feeder is open, the conical metal lid already pushed aside.

"Yeah, but I need to rinse out the trough. Dirty little birds like to step in everything."

"Like this?" I aim the nozzle at the bottom where the chickens must drink, and squeeze the trigger, sending several birds scattering away from the spray.

Roy grunts, which I assume is a yes.

Once it's cleared of all shavings and debris, I begin filling the top, my attention rolling over the chicken-wire enclosure and the raised wooden chicken house—that I'm assuming Roy built. "This is a lot nicer than ours." He used real wood as opposed to sheets of discarded plywood. The roof is covered in cedar shingles.

"That's 'cause Phil couldn't nail two pieces of wood together to save his life." Roy shifts on his feet, his good hand twitching at his side, as if fighting the urge to grab the hose from me and take over. It's like he doesn't know what to do with himself if he's not keeping busy. I'm starting to see why he has an army of wooden creatures in his cabin. I'll bet that's what keeps his hands occupied during the long, cold winter nights.

"Yeah, we've noticed. There's a piece of trim in our main floor bathroom that's six inches too short." The gap was conveniently hidden by a magazine rack when we first came through. "And all the shelving units in our cold cellar are crooked. One's so bad, you can't even put breakables on it because they'll slide or roll off. Jonah put a level on it and it was like twenty degrees off." Phil was probably drunk when he put it up.

"You always talk so much?"

I chuckle. "Yeah. According to my father, anyway."

"And what happened to him? You talk him to death?"

I'm guessing Roy's just being Roy and didn't mean anything deliberate by it—how could he? He doesn't know me. And yet I feel the stab of his words, as if they were wielded with intention.

"He died last September. Of cancer." My fingers instinctively reach for my pendant as a ball flares in my throat. For comfort, and perhaps strength, because if Roy says anything else about my father, I'm liable to leave here in tears.

I've caught myself wondering what it'd be like to have Wren Fletcher sitting next to me on our new porch, overlooking the lake and the mountain range, smiling softly as I prattle on about nothing and everything as I always seemed to do, whenever he was around.

I'd do anything to see him fly in for a visit, to talk to him again.

After another long moment of brooding, Roy eases into the coop and to the little chicken house to collect the eggs.

Saying nothing more about anything at all.

I smile through a sip of my morning latte. One of the baby goats—a white one with caramel patches—just leapt off a hay bale and is bouncing around its two siblings as if it has springs on its tiny hooves. "What kind of goats are these?"

"Nigerian Dwarf," Roy says from his spot in the next pen over, his wrinkled fingers working on the goat's udder, a steady-timed squirt of milk shooting into the metal bucket. When I arrived at seven this morning, with another bowl of fresh strawberries, Roy answered the door looking like he'd just rolled out of bed—his shirt rumpled, his salt-and-pepper hair standing on end, his gray beard scruffier than usual, the bags beneath his eyes heavy. I noted, from the front door as he poured himself coffee, that the bottle of OxyContin has still not been cracked.

And his foul mood certainly proves it.

He refused to let me carry the metal bucket out here and snapped at me when I reached for the barn door to unlatch and push it open. I'm learning, though, that if I ignore him and continue with what I'm doing, his resistance fades quickly. I see what Teddy meant about his bark being far worse than his bite.

He didn't argue with me when I left him here to go to the chicken coop to refill the chicken feed and water. I even opened the hatches to the roost and collected five eggs from inside, which was weirdly exciting, seeing what the hens had been up to overnight. It felt a bit like a childhood treasure hunt.

The smallest of the three goats nips at another's side and then bounces away, making me laugh. "I can't believe I'm saying this, but they're cute."

Roy makes a sound. "Those and Nubians are the only milkers I like. The others taste too musky."

"What are you going to do with these three?"

"The two females will be ready to sell next week. I'm keeping the male for breeding." He pauses. "You want one?"

"No. I already have one goat I don't need, thanks."

"Yeah, a useless wether. At least you'd be able to get milk from these."

"I have a dairy allergy."

He snorts. "Your generation and all your sensitive snowflake issues."

I ignore that. "What do you do with all that milk in the fridge?"

"Drink it. Freeze it for the winter. I give a few jars away."

"Can you sell it?"

"Not legally."

Because legalities are a big concern for you. I eye Oscar and Gus—two animals that might have more wolf than dog in them. "So, you drink a lot of goat's milk, then."

"Been drinkin' it all my life. I grew up on a cattle ranch, but they never could get me into the cow's milk."

It's the first shred of anything about Roy's past life he's offered.

"Was that in Texas?" I ask casually.

There's a long pause. "Yeah. In Texas." With a pat against the mother goat's side and an unexpectedly soft "good girl," Roy slowly eases himself to his feet, using the pen's fence post. His grimace of pain says more than words ever could.

"Would you *please* let me carry that bucket of milk to the house?" I can't help the irritation in my voice.

He scowls. "Fine, but don't spill any of it."

"I'll try my best not to." I shoot him a flat look before reaching down to grab the handle.

The sound of an ATV engine approaching along the laneway sends the dogs off in a frenzy.

Roy groans. "Great. Just who I didn't want to deal with right now."

I've reached the porch with the bucket by the time Muriel appears around the corner, her bright orange helmet covering her head of tight gray curls, her gun strapped over her shoulder, the dogs running circles around her.

"Go on and take that inside before the bugs are swimmin' in it," Roy orders, wiping his hand on his jeans as he awaits Muriel, a grim expression on his face.

When I return, to my pleasant surprise, they're not bickering but talking in low, civil tones.

"... probably the same one. Haven't seen or heard him around here the past couple days."

"They said it came way too close to them. The one guy ended up tossin' his catch at it to buy them some time to pack up."

"Dumb ass."

They must be talking about that brown bear.

"My boys are down there tryin' to scare him away before he causes any real trouble." Muriel turns her attention to me and offers me one of those wide, crinkle-eyed smiles. "Just finished up milkin', I see. Told ya you'd get the hang of things around here."

Roy shoots a warning look my way.

If I wanted to punish him, now would be the time to be honest. "Yup. Sure did."

"I got things to tend to inside." Roy shuffles toward his porch as if his conversation with Muriel is over.

"So, I'll pick ya up at eight on Friday?" She hollers after him.

"What for?"

She shakes her head. "So they can put a *cast* on your arm? You know, the one that's broken in two places?"

He grunts. "This brace works fine."

I sigh. *Here we go ...*

"Don't you even think about tellin' me you don't need a cast."

"I'll get myself there!" Roy barks.

"*How?* You can't even carry a bucket of milk inside!"

"The hell I can't! I only let the girl do it so she'd stop buggin' me."

"You *need* a cast." Muriel's hands have settled on her hips. "Unless you don't ever want full use of your arm again. And then what good are you gonna be, livin' out here all alone? You think we're gonna take care of your stubborn ass every day?"

Muriel may be right, but her methods of persuading Roy leave much to be desired. His face has gone from ashen to bright red. It's a wonder he doesn't have a heart attack every time she steps on his property.

I don't have the patience to listen to their bickering, and I have no desire to be calling 9-1-1 again. "*I* will drive Roy to his appointment on Friday. He will get a cast so he can heal as fast as possible, because otherwise he knows he's going to hear about it for the *rest of his life*," I say to Muriel while glaring at Roy.

He grunts in response. "Fine."

"Well ... finally, you're being smart." Muriel's lips twist. "I was just over in your garden, Calla. Looks like the strawberries are ready for pickin'. You'll need to pull all the jars up from the cellar and ..."

Roy hobbles away inside, leaving me to deal with Muriel's grand plans for jam making.

CHAPTER THIRTY

The sun is high in the sky when I hop out of the truck at Roy's on Friday morning. They're calling for temperature in the low eighties, which is only a few degrees less than in Toronto.

Roy steps out of his cabin with his mug of coffee as I'm walking toward his porch, looking slightly less rumpled than he has the last few mornings. Restless goats are bleating in the barn, waiting to be let out, and the chickens cluck. Somewhere in the distance, a chainsaw buzzes as it carves through wood.

Roy inhales deeply.

I'm sure he smells the smoke, too. I caught the faint scent when I stepped out of my house today. At first, I thought it might be a nearby bonfire, but the fire restrictions are so severe right now, no one's burning anything. The radio confirmed that the smoke is coming from the raging fires, more than a hundred miles south of us, carried up on the wind.

Jonah was cursing on his way out this morning. Wind will wreak havoc on their firefighting efforts, fanning the flames that have already laid destruction to almost sixty thousand acres of the Swan Lake area. The only upside to it is that it should help with air quality, which has been deemed "unhealthy."

Roy frowns at my face, my hair, my clothes—a pair of jeans and a pale pink T-shirt I haven't worn in too long. "What are you all gussied up for?"

I assume he's referring to the makeup I put on and the curler I ran through my hair to add some beachy waves. "Your appointment, remember?"

"What, your pilot not good enough anymore? You lookin' to trade in for a doctor already?"

I afford him a flat look. "You know that we're in the twenty-first century, right? Women don't make an effort in their appearance to find a husband. They can also look good because they want to, for themselves."

He makes a sound but says nothing.

I hold out a plate of strawberry muffins. "Here. I baked these last night. I think they actually turned out."

Roy regards the plate a moment before accepting it. "You sound surprised."

"Let's say my track record for baking isn't good. But Jonah seemed to like them." He ate three on his way out.

"I don't eat in the mornin'." Roy's steely eyes dart to mine a moment before shifting back to the plate. "But maybe I'll try one in a bit and let you know if it's awful."

"I knew I could count on you. By the way, do I want to ask how that stir fry I brought last night was?" I've been bringing him dinner every night so far. He stopped complaining about me going into his kitchen to drop it off, and the container from the day before is always washed and waiting for me to collect.

That tiny smirk that hints at amusement touches Roy's mouth. "Not awful."

"Well ... good." At least I seem to be getting the knack for cooking. "So, we have about an hour to get all the morning chores finished before we leave for your appointment." Palmer is fifty minutes away, on the other side of Wasilla. I brace myself, preparing for Roy's stubborn refusal, ready to wave my phone in the air and threaten a call to Muriel.

"There's half a pot of coffee. Help yourself if you want one." With that, he ducks back in the house, leaving me smiling at the simple gesture of hospitality, something I would have assumed Roy incapable of only days ago.

"I don't know what's takin' them so goddamn long," Roy growls. "That idiot technician damn near killed me takin' that X-ray, and now they leave me sittin' out here with my thumb up my ass all damn day long. This was a waste of time."

I shoot an apologetic look to the glowering woman who sits across from us. Thankfully, her son, who can't be more than seven and has his leg in a full cast, doesn't seem to be paying attention to anything besides his iPad screen. "It's been a *half hour*, Roy," I say with forced patience. When Simon broke his collarbone, I sat in the emergency waiting room with him for seven *hours*. Had my father gone through with chemotherapy, the doctor was recommending an eight-hour-a-day, five-days-a-week program. A thirty-minute wait is a blink in time.

I want to tell Roy all these things, but I know it won't make a difference. "Let me go up there and ask them. You stay here." I drop my voice to a whisper, "And maybe stop swearing in front of small children."

I leave Roy scowling as I head to the reception desk. The nurse is busy on the phone, but the doctor who has been tending to Roy's arm—a white man in his fifties with bushy eyebrows and a pinched nose—comes around the corner, a folder tucked under his arm.

"Hi, excuse me, I was wondering if Roy Donovan's X-ray results are ready yet? He's getting a little … *antsy*."

The doctor offers a tight-lipped smile. "He's not too happy to be here, is he? I was just coming to get him, actually. Tell me, has your father been taking it easy?"

"She's not my daughter!" Roy barks directly behind me.

I startle and shoot Roy an exasperated look for sneaking up on me. "I'm his neighbor. But *no*, he hasn't been taking it easy at all. I've had to fight with him every day to let me help around his place." There is something satisfying about tattling on Roy, especially when I watch the deep frown of disapproval that forms on the doctor's brow.

"I had a feeling. There's more swelling than I hoped to see by this point—"

"Well, I ain't comin' back here again, doc, so you better figure it out," Roy snaps.

The doctor shares a knowing look with me. "I was going to say that I think we can set your arm today. Has he been taking the medication I prescribed to manage the pain?"

"Yeah," Roy says at the same time I say, "The seal on the bottle hasn't even been broken."

If looks could kill, the withering gaze Roy spears me with would have them wheeling me to the morgue. "What, are you spying on me?" he growls.

"You sure she's not your daughter?" The doctor chuckles, unfazed by Roy's hostile tone. "All right. We'll get you casted up and on your way."

———

It's midafternoon by the time we pass the sign marking Trapper's Crossing. The ride has been quiet, Roy taking turns scowling at the road and the navy-blue fiberglass cast that stretches from his knuckles all the way to just below his armpit.

"Did the doctor say how long you'd have to wear it?" I dare ask.

"Six to eight weeks, if I don't do anything stupid."

"You mean, like refuse help from everyone around you?" I say lightly but quickly add, "That's nothing. Your arm could have been shattered. If you needed surgery, you would have been in that thing for months. Don't worry, you'll be carving your wooden figurines again in no time."

He doesn't respond, so I assume that's the end of our conversation. I adjust the dial of the radio to find a station with better music.

"And whittling."

"Hmm?"

"Some of them aren't carved, they're whittled. There's a difference."

I wait a moment, and when he doesn't elaborate, I ask, "What's the difference?"

"With carving, you use different tools. Chisels and gouges, and lathes. With whittling, you only use a knife."

"I didn't know that," I say slowly.

"Well ... now you do."

"When did you start doing that?"

"A long time ago." Again, that long pause, where I assume the conversation is done, and then he offers, "I was eight. My daddy was sittin' on the porch after supper, with his pipe and a fresh piece of basswood. He let me give it a try. Stabbed myself here." He holds out his left hand to display the jagged scar on his palm.

"That sounds like a great activity for a small child," I murmur.

"Good way to pass the time." His focus drifts out the window, seemingly lost. "Too many years to ride out, I guess. I'm runnin' outta room." There's something acutely sad about the way he says that.

"You could probably make some decent money off them—"

"They're not for sale," he snaps, his jaw tensing. "Not everything has a price tag on it."

"Relax. It was just an idea."

After a moment, he says, "Who the hell's gonna pay money for a bunch of wooden animals, anyway?"

"People would. Ones as nice as yours, anyway." I feel Roy's narrowed gaze on me as I turn off the main road and onto the one that will lead us home. "Before I forget, I won't be here tomorrow or Sunday to help you with the chores."

"Why? Where are you goin'?"

I can't help but hear an edge of something in his tone. I smother my smile with the idea that Roy might be getting used to me being around, might have begun to prefer it. "It's my birthday tomorrow, so we're flying somewhere in the morning. I have no idea where." I've been needling Jonah for hints, but he hasn't divulged a thing. "Don't worry, though, Toby will be by to help."

"That big, dumb ox," he grumbles.

"Hey! He's a nice guy!" I spare a second to glare at Roy with disapproval. "And a friend. He helped you only days ago, so stop being such a jackass." I've never spoken to anyone besides Jonah like that, and certainly not to any sixty-something-year-old man.

But if there's one sixty-something-year-old man on the planet who deserves it, he's sitting beside me in this old beat-up truck.

"He lets Muriel walk all over him," Roy says, as if that's justification for his harsh words.

"She's his mother! He's being respectful. You should try it sometime." Not that I disagree with Roy's assessment.

Roy glares at his cast as if it's the cause of his discomfort, and not the arm it's protecting.

"Does it hurt?"

"No, it tickles." After a moment, as if catching himself on his sharp response, he admits, "Yeah, it hurts some. They gave me a local anesthetic before they started poking and prodding, but it's wearing off."

"I'll bet one of those painkillers would help, when you get home," I suggest.

He grunts. "I don't do drugs."

I check my side-view mirror as an excuse to roll my eyes at his obstinacy. "It's not crystal meth, Roy. Your doctor prescribed it. Taking a few at night before bed isn't going to kill you. It might even help you sleep." Which, by the heavy bags beneath his eyes, he hasn't been doing much of lately.

"Just a few at night, huh? So easy." His brow furrows. "Me and addictive things don't mix well."

Is that another glimpse into Roy's life? A dark sliver of his past?

It clicks. "Is that why you don't drink, either? I noticed you didn't drink your beer at the Ale House." He held it, he stared at it, but he never took a single sip.

"First a spy, now a detective," Roy grumbles, then purses his lips, as if deciding whether he wants to explain himself. "Haven't had a drink since I came up here, thirty-three years ago."

But he must have had more than one before then, enough to know that he has problems with addiction, enough to not trust himself taking pain meds when he desperately needs them.

"What made you stop drinking?" I dare ask.

"Life."

I hesitate, but only for a second—the opportunity is too tempting to pass up. "You mean, your wife and daughter?"

His jaw tenses.

"I saw the picture," I admit, though he's probably figured that out. *He's hid it since then, for fuck's sake.*

"It's none of your goddamn business." His normally bitter tone is laced with something colder, harder, scarier.

My stomach tightens as regret stirs. I've clearly hit the nerve I knew I would hit if I brought it up. But I've already cracked the proverbial can of worms and, seeing as Roy did open up about his past as, I'm guessing, an alcoholic, I can't help but hope he might tell me more, might tell me something that makes sense. "I know it's none of my business," I offer in as contrite a tone as I can muster. "I was wondering what happened to them."

"They smartened up, is what they did. Got the hell away from me. Is that what you wanna hear?"

So, what Toby said about Roy's wife leaving him was accurate. But has he seen or talked to them since? Does he have any relationship with his daughter? I have so many questions.

Suddenly, Muriel's claim that Roy and I have things in common doesn't sound so farfetched.

I was a daughter estranged from her father.

Is Roy a father estranged from his daughter?

I let a few minutes pass before I ask, "Have you talked to your daughter at all since then?"

He doesn't answer.

We've already passed my driveway, and I know the trip is almost over, so I try a different tactic. "My mom and I left Alaska when I was little and moved back to Toronto. I didn't see my dad again until last summer. I didn't even talk to him for about twelve years—"

"Lemme out here," Roy grumbles. The rustic wooden sign that marks his driveway appears in the bramble ahead.

"*Here*? That's, like, a twenty-minute walk to your house. At least." In good health, and Roy is far from that.

"So what? I like walkin'." He paws at the door handle with his left hand.

"Do you remember the doctor telling you to take it easy?"

"Do you remember me tellin' you to mind your own damn business?" he shoots back.

I sigh, exhausted from a day of dealing with Roy's volatile temperament. "Is this because I brought up your daughter?"

His jaw clenches. "No, it's because you're gonna hit every goddamn pothole from here to my house, and it'll hurt like hell. I can't believe we made it home alive, the way you drive. Whoever gave you your license should be shot."

"There's nothing wrong with my driving!" I snap, my patience finally evaporating. I pull into the laneway—there's nowhere else to go with it being a dead-end road.

He pops open the door the second the wheels slow, forcing me to stop abruptly.

"Are you crazy?"

"Probably." He shifts to move out, but then pulls back, glaring at the laneway ahead. "What're you doin', girl?"

"I'm trying to get you home in one piece!"

"No, I mean, why're you keepin' this up? Comin' around every day, bringin' me dinner and muffins and shit."

"Because you need help?"

"Whatever you're lookin' for here, you ain't gonna find it in me."

I feel my cheeks flush with indignation. "I'm not *looking* for anything—"

"I'm no replacement for your dead daddy, and I don't wanna be."

My jaw drops. "Are you kidding me? Is that *seriously* what you think is going on here?"

His gaze flickers to me before shifting off, as if meeting my eyes is uncomfortable. "I don't know what I think. Been tryin' to figure you out. Maybe ... yeah. Nothin' else makes sense."

"God, you are *such* a—" Just *helping* him doesn't make sense? My hands grip the steering wheel, shaking with rage. "Well, funny, I've been trying to figure *you* out, too, and all I see is a miserable, sad old man waiting to die in the woods, alone."

"Never claimed I was anything else, did I?" With a grimace of pain, he slides out of the passenger side, slamming the door behind him. He hobbles down his laneway.

"You know what, Roy? Screw you!" I holler out the window.

"Maybe you'll listen to me when I tell you to stay away!" he fires back.

"You win! I am done helping you!" My voice is husky with emotion. I add after a beat, "And I don't care if that bear eats you on your way home!"

"Don't worry, it won't. I'm too bitter."

I throw the truck in reverse and jam my foot on the gas, then slam on the brake to keep myself from hitting the tree on the other side. I race home, my tires kicking stones and dust along the way.

CHAPTER THIRTY-ONE

"Hey," I croak.

"Happy birthday to you ... happy birthday to you ..."

Mom's and Simon's singing—Simon's tuneless, my mother's high and rhythmic—fill my ear. I smile despite the pounding headache behind my temple.

"Are you not up already?" my mom asks when they've finished serenading me.

I glance at the clock on the nightstand. It's almost nine. "Jonah let me sleep in." I roll onto my back, squinting at the bright daylight that casts a glow around the edges of the blackout curtains. The other side of the bed is empty. Jonah was supposed to wake me by seven so we could be in the air early, but that plan was made before I opened a bottle of wine last night, waiting for him to get home from work. "Did you know that consuming alcohol while sitting in a hot tub can be lethal? Like, they should put it in the manual." Maybe they did. I only skimmed over the warnings.

"Good time ringing in your twenty-seventh?" Simon asks, amusement in his British lilt.

I groan again, throwing my arm over my eyes. "I think so?" Memories of the night come rushing to me. Jonah, rolling up to the house at ten after finishing his day water-bombing flames. Me, three glasses into a bottle of California Cabernet—my anger with Roy stymied, and my inhibitions dulled—stumbling out of the hot tub to meet him on the driveway, naked and attempting seduction, oblivious to the mosquitos. Things progressed quickly from there.

Or regressed, depending on how you look at it.

Jonah certainly must have had a good night.

I wince at the enormous welt on my arm. I can only imagine how many more I have on my body. I'll be spending my birthday itchy and doped up on Benadryl.

"So, our birthday gift to you is on its way," my mom says, her voice humming with excitement. "We're *so* sorry, we tried to get it to you yesterday. But the courier confirmed it should be there within the hour, so try not to leave before it arrives."

They've piqued my interest. "Is it something I need to sign for?"

"No, but you definitely don't want to leave it on your front porch for the weekend," Simon quips, earning my mother's tittering laughter.

"You two are weird. It's a lemon cake, isn't it?"

"You'll have to wait and see!"

"Whatever it is, I'm sure I'll love it." It has to be lemon cake. They've been "surprising" me with one every year since the local baker mastered a dairy-free buttercream icing for me. But can they even ship that all the way from Toronto?

Of course, my mother would find a way. I applaud her determination.

"We so wish we were there, darling, but you know how June is with all the weddings and graduations and proms. It's like a month of Valentine's Days."

"No worries. I remember." When my mother is home—which isn't often during that month—Simon hides in his office and I tiptoe around her.

"Do you have any guesses for where Jonah's taking you?" Simon asks.

"No, but he promised it doesn't involve an outhouse." Though, at this point, I'd be fine with going somewhere remote, somewhere our phones don't work and there are no TVs to broadcast news of the fires raging on. Somewhere where I have Jonah entirely to myself, where he says the right things and makes romantic gestures and reminds me why I'd chase him to the ends of the earth.

Which, some days lately, it feels like I already have.

I am *desperate* for this weekend away with him, which is absurd given we *live* together.

"Well, I'm sure he's going to spoil you." Again, with my mother's tittering laugh, as if she knows something I don't.

I can't imagine what his gift to me will be this time. Should I be preparing myself for another joke? Matching camo pants to go with the jacket from Christmas?

He'll have a hard time topping the airplane pendant.

Unless he proposes.

My stomach leaps with anticipation. It's been more than a month since we visited the safety cabin, since the pregnancy scare and the potentially disastrous engine failure. I haven't asked and he hasn't hinted.

But that would certainly make this day memorable.

I say my goodbyes to Mom and Simon, and then holler into our quiet house, "Jonah! You promised me coffee in bed today!" He even made me demonstrate how to use the barista machine and write out the steps for making my latte.

A few moments go by with no answer. "Jonah?"

Still nothing.

A vague recollection of his phone ringing early this morning stirs in my memory. I remember the low, gravelly sound of his sleepy voice as he answered, but I remember little else.

I haul myself out of bed and stagger to the bathroom, angling for a long, hot shower to wash the chlorine from my skin and steam the alcohol from my pores.

The Post-it stuck to the middle of the mirror stalls me in my tracks.

Sorry, Sam called. Really needed me. I'll be back in a few hours. Promise. Happy birthday!

I read the note several times over to make sure I haven't somehow misconstrued it, to make sure I'm not still drunk, all while a sinking feeling settles into my stomach. That phone call I heard was Sam. He was calling to ask Jonah to come in to work on his weekend off.

And, instead of saying he can't, instead of saying that it's my birthday and he *promised* me a weekend away, Jonah said yes to Sam and stuck a Post-it Note to the bathroom mirror.

A few hours, my ass. When has he ever been back after a few hours? He could easily be gone all day.

But it's a horrendous fire, I tell myself, trying to settle the gnawing ache in my chest and the lump forming in my throat. A fire that is running rampant, destroying forest, killing animals, chasing people from their homes.

What Jonah's doing is important, I tell myself, even as hot tears trickle down my cheeks, the wave of hurt and disappointment overwhelming.

The most painful thing about this, I realize, is that I'm not surprised.

————

I pull the blanket tighter around my body, as much for comfort as to quash the slight chill lingering in the shade of our porch, despite the climbing temperature outside, and listen to the sound of tires over gravel as our pickup crawls up the driveway. Jonah arrived home half an hour ago, the approaching purr of Veronica's engine bringing both relief—that he has arrived home safe, that it's still early in the day—and a fresh wave of melancholy. I don't know what he's been doing in the hangar since he landed, but he certainly didn't run home to me.

It's left me with far too much time to dwell on my thoughts and insecurities, to dissect fond memories—the weekend he flew across the continent to tell me he can't live without me, the morning he braved the snowy mountains and whisked me off to the cabin for Christmas, all those early nights tangled in sheets, sharing our best intentions.

I'm left wondering if that's all they were—intentions. Has something changed? Have *we* changed in these last few months? Because those memories suddenly feel so far from where we are now—me here, day after day, finding ways to occupy my time until Jonah comes home, telling myself over and over again that what he does is important, that it's only for the summer months, that I knew going in this is how it would be.

I'm tired of telling myself that.

I didn't *really* know this is how it would be. At least, I didn't know how it would *feel*.

I brush my palms against my cheeks, trying to rid any last evidence of tears, and then I shift my focus to the hazy, smoke-filled sky and the small ripples forming over the surface of our quiet lake as I wait to face him.

"You ready to ..." Jonah's words drift when he meets my eyes.

I guess wiping away tears wasn't enough to hide the fact that I've been crying.

"What's going on? Did something happen?" he asks, his voice panicked.

Despite the ache, I almost laugh. He literally has no clue. "Yeah. You told me I was more important to you than work."

A frown slowly forms as realization sets in. "I was only gone a few hours."

"That's not the point!" My voice cracks. Words I hadn't planned on saying out loud fly from my mouth. "I haven't complained *once* about you never being home since you took this job with Sam, have I? But the one day, *the one day* you promised you'd be here, that you'd put *me* first, that *I* would be more important than you flying off somewhere, and you couldn't do that."

A bewildered look flashes across his face. "Calla, you *are* more important to me than work. Or anything," he says slowly. "Where is this coming from?"

"Seriously? I've basically been alone here for the past two months, with a goat and a raccoon for company. I have no job besides being your secretary and your maid and your cook, and I have *one* friend. It feels like you're *never* home anymore. I *hate* it here!"

His eyebrows arch. "You *hate* it here?"

"Yes! No!" I shake my head, the tears rolling again. "I don't know!" It's the first time that thought has taken shape in my mind. It's my emotions talking. Or not? Maybe it's true. Maybe this is as good as it's going to get for me in Alaska. "I want you to be happy, Jonah. But *I'm* not happy. I don't belong here."

"Jesus." He curses under his breath.

A horn tuts several times in rapid succession, cutting into my tirade.

"Oh my God, I don't need this right now." I bury my face in my palms. "Can you please deal with whoever that is? I can't talk to anyone." It must be the courier. I hope it's not Muriel, though she always comes on her ATV and that was the sound of a car door slamming.

"Yeah ... That's gonna be a problem." Jonah sighs heavily. "For the record, I wasn't at work today." He shifts, unblocking the view of the stone path that leads to our porch from the driveway.

And the tall, leggy blonde who's picking along it in a pair of heeled sandals and a brown suede satchel purse swinging at her hip.

"*Diana?*"

"Surprise!" she squeals, throwing her hands in the air.

"I ..." A rush of elation hits me, clashing with the sorrow that had previously taken root and bringing an instant flood of tears. I pull myself out of my wicker chair. "You came?" I manage to choke out, my knees wobbling as I close the distance to the porch door.

She charges in and collides with me in a fierce embrace. "Do you know how hard it was for me to keep this from you? I almost blew it when we were talking on the phone!"

I inhale the familiar floral scent of her perfume. She's been wearing it since we graduated from high school. As far as I'm concerned, they should just change the brand name to Diana. "I had *no* idea."

"Well, you weren't supposed to, *obviously*. God, this is ..." Her big, cornflower-blue eyes are wide and glistening as they drift over the view of the lake and the mountain range beyond. "Indescribable. I get it now."

I look to Jonah who's leaning back against the porch post, arms folded over his chest, a small smile touching his lips. "Did you do this?"

He shakes his head. "It was your mom's idea. They bought the ticket."

"Simon even upgraded me to first class, which was definitely a selling point for this crazy idea." Diana waggles her eyebrows.

"They said my gift was coming by courier and I couldn't leave it on the porch. I thought they meant cake." I laugh, wiping my palms across my cheeks. "When did you get in?"

"My plane landed at 5:10 A.M." She emphasizes the A.M. part with arched eyebrows. "I left right after work last night and I've been flying *all night* to be here." She laughs, and catches a tear from the corner of her eye with her pinky, careful not to smear her eye makeup. "Calla, I'm running on pure adrenaline. I'm apologizing now if I pass out later."

"Oh my God, of course! How long are you here for?"

"Four days. I'm catching the red-eye home on Tuesday night. I already told Beef Stick that I'm going to be useless when I show up there Wednesday."

"I'm so glad you're here. Okay. So ... four days. I don't even know what we're going to do." I look to Jonah. "How long have you known about this?"

"Since she called to bail on you."

That was the beginning of May! I shake my head. "So, there was never any weekend away?"

He shrugs. "Had to make up something to distract you."

"But he promised to take us out today, so let's go before I hit my wall and fall into a coma." Diana takes in my rumpled pajamas that I threw back on after my shower. I'm not even wearing a bra. "You're not dressed. Why aren't you even dressed yet? Is this who you are now?"

"Uh ..." Because I was too busy wallowing in self-pity?

"Of course, I would have been here *hours* ago if not for that debacle in Anchorage."

"What debacle?" I look from her to Jonah and back to her.

She shares a secretive glance with him. "Why don't you two help me unload my things and then I'll tell you *all* about it."

"Really subtle, Di." Jonah shakes his head, but he's chuckling. He leads the way out the door and down the path to the driveway to Diana's rental car.

I stop dead when I spot the pearl-blue Jeep parked beside our old battered pickup truck. It's the exact model I test-drove at the dealership.

Diana takes a break from swatting at the buzzing mosquitos to yell, "I got to drive your birthday present before you did!"

"What?" I spin around to face Jonah, because this could only have come from him. "You bought this for me?"

He bites his bottom lip.

"I can't even ..." My voice drifts, my words failing me.

Diana is grinning ear to ear. "I was supposed to be here by eight this morning, but when I got to the hotel and asked the front desk for the keys, they couldn't find them! So, then I had to wait for that Chris guy to come in and turn over his *entire* office looking for them and when he couldn't find it, he had his wife come in, too, but she couldn't find them, either. I finally called Jonah because I didn't know what else to do!"

Oh my god. It's all making sense now. "So, you flew to Anchorage to find the keys."

"I had the dealership deliver the Jeep to the lodge last night when it was ready because I figured it'd be easy enough for Diana, given the time she was flying in, to cab over there and hop in. Plus, I thought it'd be funny, you know, havin' her roll up in your birthday present. Kind of a double surprise." Jonah's expression sours. "But the dumb ass from the dealer who dropped it off forgot to leave the keys with the front desk. So, we had to wait for the dealership to open and track down the guy, who had both sets in his pocket." Jonah shakes his head. "So much for making things easier."

"And then I somehow got lost on the way here." Diana reaches into the passenger side and pulls out a cooler bag. Inside it is a cardboard cake box from the bakery in Toronto. "Your favorite! We need to get this in a fridge *right away*."

My mind is still on this morning's debacle, and Jonah. "So, that's why you were in the hangar so long? You were waiting until Diana got here."

And then he came home to find me on the porch, hysterical and professing my unhappiness about my life with him in Alaska.

My stomach roils with guilt as I close the distance. "I love it. And you." I stretch to my tiptoes and press my lips against his, lingering longer than I normally would with someone else here.

When I pull back, he's wearing a tiny smirk. "You had to pick the most girlie shade of blue possible, didn't you?"

"It's called Bikini Pearl," I say with a smile. "When did you decide you were getting this for me?"

"I called the dealership after you went to test-drive it," he admits.

"It's *way* too much, Jonah."

"Maybe." His fingertips stroke my cheek as he brushes strands of hair off my face. "But I just want you to be happy here." There's a sadness in his icy blue eyes.

His words are a punch to my gut, given my blowup not even ten minutes ago. "I am." I rope my arms around his neck, pulling him into me. There's no mistaking the tension coursing through his shoulders as I cling to him. Knowing I caused that makes my chest ache. "I didn't mean it," I whisper into his ear.

He makes me feel so slight when he curls his arms around my body, drawing me flush into him. He kisses my temple. "We'll talk about it later, okay? We need to help Diana with her things. I think she's had the roughest morning of all of us."

I climb to my tiptoes to steal one last kiss and then pull away to face my best friend, my heart brimming with pure joy. "Let's get you settled and then we can figure out what we're going to do for the next four—"

A glint catches my eye, drawing my attention to the diamond engagement ring on Diana's left hand.

My mouth drops open as she squeals.

"We have some planning to do!"

CHAPTER THIRTY-TWO

"*He* was in your house when you moved in?" Diana stares pointedly at the moose head that looms over us, the pale pink streamers haphazardly woven through his antlers. Muriel—or likely Toby, by Muriel's instruction—decorated the Ale House in honor of my birthday, a surprise that brought a lump to my throat when we stepped through the doors to the sound of strangers singing. Muriel carried out a strawberry shortcake—made with berries from my garden that she helped herself to while we were out—loaded with candles.

I choked my slice down, not having the heart to tell her the truth about my aversion after she'd gone to all that effort.

"Him. Them." I nod toward the two deer heads that Toby mounted on the other side of the long, narrow room the week after we dropped them off.

"By the way, that lodge that Jonah had me go to get the Jeep?" She flashes a horrified look my way before bringing her martini to her red-painted lips—a special addition to tonight's Ale House menu, for my birthday, and on the house. Teddy said Toby's been practicing his bartending skills all week.

I laugh. "Yeah, I know. I stayed there my first night back, when I was stuck in Anchorage." It feels like *so long ago*. "But it's not bad once you get used to it."

Diana's eyes are glossy and bloodshot. She never managed to get a nap in. Soon after I showed her around, we were in the air, giving her a real look at Alaska—the vast, wild, six-million-acre expanse of the Denali National Park where she saw a grizzly bear feeding off salmon in the stream, the looming, granite-faced gorge of Ruth Glacier, the wreckage of a plane that crashed into a ridge two years ago and can't be recovered, which I was not happy to see—before Jonah landed at an upscale mountain hotel where we had dinner reservations. It's been nonstop since she arrived. How she's awake is beyond me. "We'll finish this drink and go home."

"No, I'm fine!" She waves off my worries, her diamond ring glinting, even in the dim light.

It brings a smile to my face, even as another wave of shock hits me.

Diana is engaged.

Diana is getting married. They won't set a date until she gets a handle on balancing law school and a full-time job, but it's coming and I'm going to be her maid of honor. That was decided years ago, before any potential suitors had even surfaced.

The hard part? I'm now four thousand miles away.

I knew this was the natural next step for her and Aaron, and I'm genuinely happy for her.

But, if I'm being honest, I've also been feeling the weight of envy all day, at how my best friend's life is moving along, with an exciting career and a posh apartment and her family just twenty minutes away from her. At how she didn't have to uproot her life for any of it. She found a man who fits well into her urban, fast-paced life.

Me? I fell in love with a sky cowboy from Alaska.

And ever since those words tumbled from my mouth this morning, despite vehemently denying them, I haven't been able to shake the fear that there is truth to them, that deep down inside, I know this—me here, or Jonah anywhere else—isn't going to work.

Am I happy here?

I'm happy with Jonah. I love him in a way I didn't think existed—wholly and resolutely.

But am I happy *here*, in my life?

Or have I been fooling myself into thinking that one morning I'll wake up and things that feel foreign and temporary will finally feel like home?

I overcompensated for my harsh words by taking every opportunity to touch Jonah today—to hold his hand, to tickle his side, to play with his beard—and prove that they're false. He responded in kind, with smirks and squeezes and back rubs, never withholding an ounce of affection.

But I saw it in his eyes.

The sadness. The worry.

Possibly the worst of all—the same doubt I'm beginning to fear.

And now I'm helpless against that little voice in my mind that purrs terrible, dark thoughts: What if Trapper's Crossing never feels like home? What if I grow bitter with Jonah for what he loves to do? What if he one day decides that I will never fit into Alaska the way he wants me to?

What if I tell Jonah that I want to move, and he refuses to leave?

It's strange how your relationship can feel impenetrable one day and vulnerable the next—with a misunderstanding, a few words, and a mountain of repressed worries that finally swell to the surface.

This roiling in my gut feels like the disastrous trip to the safety cabin all over again. All I want to do is fix whatever I might have broken between us, but what if we can't get back to where we were?

What if I stuck a pin in this bubble of delusion that we've both been floating in?

For the first time since Jonah arrived in Toronto and asked me to move to Alaska, I'm truly afraid that an end date to us is inevitable, no matter how much I love him.

I push those dour thoughts aside before my mask slips and Diana sees through me to the ache buried beneath the joy of having her here. "Relax, Di. You've already earned the ultimate best-friend badge so you can admit that you're dying inside."

"Maybe a little bit." She holds her manicured index finger and thumb up to measure a small space between them, before waving her hand around the Ale House. "But they did all this for you tonight. I'm not going to pull you away yet. I've got another hour or two in my tank. But don't get jealous when your hot Viking has to throw me over his shoulder to get me home, because I'm already drunk." She punctuates that declaration with a hiccup. "Also, I'll probably cop a feel and blame it on the booze. Just so you know."

I shake my head and laugh, imagining Jonah's reaction to that. Not that Diana would *ever* actually do it. "You have no idea how much I've missed you." *I* didn't realize how much until I saw her standing outside our porch.

I steal a glance to the bar where Jonah is nursing a pint while talking to Marie, Toby, and a rosy-cheeked Teddy.

"Do we like her or not?" Diana asks conspiratorially, following my gaze. "Because you've been watching her since we got here."

"That's Jonah's best friend." Marie was sitting at the bar when I walked through the door. He obviously invited her.

"Jonah's best friend is a beautiful blonde?" Diana's eyebrows arch. "You neglected to mention this. Why did you neglect to mention this to *me? Your* best friend?"

Because I know exactly how *my* best friend would react, and I didn't want anyone reinforcing my insecurities, especially not after I left Jonah behind in Alaska. Diana has always been mistrustful when it comes to other females, convinced that their natural instincts are competitive by nature, that a woman who is platonic friends with an attractive man is never that by choice.

In this case, she isn't wrong.

But now is not the time to enlighten Diana about all things Marie, including the boundary-crossing conversation I overheard that morning in the hangar.

"I'm watching her *and Toby*. I'm waiting for them to hit it off."

Diana frowns in thought as she studies them. "Yeah, they could work together. He's cute enough. In that big, burly, teddy-bear kind of way."

"And she's pretty, and nice," I admit begrudgingly.

"Maybe if he stops crushing on you, it'll happen."

"Shut up! He is not!"

Diana's cackle turns a few heads. "Okay, Calla. We're going to play this game, are we? Why do you never see these things?"

"Because I don't want to! *Don't* put things like that in my head! He's, like, my *only* human friend here!" I whine.

She sighs through a sip. "Well, I'm sorry to say this, but I don't think she's interested. Not in Toby, anyway." Her perfectly drawn and filled eyebrows arch as she returns her assessing gaze to the bar, to where Marie is absorbed in Jonah's handsome face.

Teddy says something and they erupt with laughter. Jonah throws his arm around her shoulders to jostle her, as if she was part of the punch line to a joke. She seems to sink closer into him, resting her blonde head in the crook of his neck.

"They're just good friends. They have been for years." I say this even as I sense the uncomfortable prick in my stomach—the one that has been poking me since Jonah steered himself toward the bar as soon as Diana and I settled at this table.

What I would give to go back to this morning, to erase my words, my accusations, my doubt. But I can't, and it is making me especially sensitive to moments like this.

"So, is this *the* place to be in Trapper's Crossing?" Diana asks, taking in the sea of plaid flannel and jean-clad people—about fifty in total, forty of them men by my last count.

"This is *the only* place in town. Well, besides a pizza shop that closes at ten and a community hall. I hear the farmers' market on Fridays is hoppin'." Muriel tried to get me there yesterday, but I was in no mood after the day I had with Roy.

The resort is packed this weekend, as Toby promised it would be come this time of year, and it seems the Ale House is the place they all come at the end of the day, to drink and laugh and share boastful stories about the fish caught, and the fish that got away.

"I'm *so* glad I came, even if it's a short trip." Diana rests her cheek on her palm and smiles wistfully. "I remember that night at the club, when you found out about your dad and you were trying to decide if you should go. Can you imagine if you hadn't?"

"I can't." My chest aches at the thought. Next month will be a year since that phone call from Agnes and my subsequent flight. "That would have been the worst mistake of my life."

"Right? And yet, could you *ever* have imagined yourself *here*, now?"

I fumble with the tiny airplane pendant in my grasp—a gift from two of the most important men in my life—and shake my head.

"Looks like you ladies could use another drink." Toby appears then, replacing our martinis with fresh ones. They even bought proper glasses.

Diana isn't going to be the only one drunk if this keeps up.

"We were just talking about you!" Diana exclaims, her blue eyes twinkling.

Toby's cheeks flush. "All good things, I hope?"

"*Only* good things." She winks, then lets out another hiccup. "For God's sake, this is embarrassing. Excuse me, I need to use the bathroom. Sorry, I mean the 'restroom.' Be back in a minute." Diana stands and strolls for the Ladies' Room sign on the far side, her hips swaying a touch more than normal thanks to the alcohol flowing through her veins, her head held high as usual with confidence, earning plenty of gawking looks. In a room full of jeans, plaid jackets, and baseball caps, she's a leggy, five-foot-ten-inch blonde siren in leather boots.

Jonah sees her passing and steals a glance over my way. He lifts off his stool, looking ready to come over, and my excitement swells. But then Marie stops him with a hand on his forearm and asks him a question that pulls him back into the conversation with two other locals. He eases back onto the stool.

I feel the sour expression take over my face. Am I being a jealous, slightly drunk girlfriend? Or was that an intentional move on her part?

"So? Good birthday?" Toby asks, regarding me curiously.

I force a smile. "*Great* birthday." Despite the rocky start and this lingering sense of doom.

He drags a chair out and settles into it, opposite me. "How surprised were you to see that Jeep roll up?"

I didn't see it roll up, exactly, but no need to get into the details. "More like shocked. Did you know about all this? About Diana coming?"

"Nah ..." A few beats pass and then his grin gives him away. "Yeah, I found out last week."

I give him a playful kick under the table. "You should have told me!"

"You kidding? Jonah would've beat my ass." His gaze drifts over to where Jonah and Marie sit, lingering on her a moment.

"Have you asked her out yet?"

He laughs, his cheeks flushing with embarrassment. "Working up the nerve. By the way, what happened between you and Roy? I went to help him out today, and he asked me if you still wanted him dead."

"Really?" A blip of surprise stirs in my stomach. But what do I care if the curmudgeon's been wondering that? I don't give a shit about Roy Donovan.

"What did he do?" Toby asks in a knowing tone.

I shrug. "Typical Roy, but worse. We had a huge fight on the way home from the hospital yesterday. He said a bunch of mean stuff and told me to stop coming around, and he insisted on walking home from the main road." I don't really want to get into the details of Roy basically claiming I have daddy issues. I know what daddy issues are because I *used* to have them. Now all I have is a desire to keep my father's memory alive.

But there is no way that would *ever* happen in the form of Roy Donovan. Not unless Roy is the evil and monstrous Mr. Hyde version of Wren Fletcher.

Toby chuckles and shakes his head. "I hope you let him walk."

"Not like I had much choice. I think he would have tucked and rolled out the door, broken bones and all."

Toby's face splits into that wide smile that he inherited from his mother.

"So, was he a pain when you went today?" I ask.

Toby frowns. "No, actually. He was decent. Didn't complain much at all. It was weird, now that I think about it."

That *is* weird. Maybe he ended up taking those painkillers after all and they've sedated him to the point of being "nice." If that's even possible for Roy, which I doubt. It sounds like he can swing far in the other direction, though, if what he says about his wife leaving him is true. But how far, exactly, is the question. What made her run, besides his acerbic disposition?

What did he do wrong?

This morbid curiosity with the old man in the woods is getting the better of me once again.

"Well, unless he apologizes to me, I'm done helping him."

"Roy, apologize?" Toby gives me a doubtful look.

"Exactly. So, sorry, but someone else will have to take over. Maybe your mom can find a friendly ax murderer, or someone equally *insane*."

"So, he wasn't wrong about you wanting him dead." Toby grins. "I'll cover until your friend is gone, but be ready. She's gonna try to strong-arm you. That's just what she does."

"She can try all she wants. I'm *not* going unless he apologizes."

Toby's grin falls off suddenly. "Shit. Sorry, I've gotta go hide behind the bar." He scurries away.

When I steal a glance over my shoulder, I understand why. Jessie Winslow has made an appearance tonight, in the same too-tight blue jeans and cropped boots as last time I saw her. She's swapped her leopard-print crop top for a crimson one that clings to her ample curves.

Her large blue eyes scan the heads, quickly spotting Jonah. She indiscreetly fluffs her hair and puffs out her chest and then cuts through the crowd. Another cord of tension weaves its way along my spine. Just what I need. I don't have the emotional capacity to deal with that woman pawing Jonah tonight, on top of all my other issues.

Muriel comes around the bar then and marches straight for our table. "Where's your friend?"

"Bathroom." Probably fixing her makeup. I frown at the soft, camouflage-print gun case in Muriel's hand. "Going somewhere?"

She sets it down on the table, and that's when I notice the pink bow affixed to one end. "Happy birthday, Calla."

Oh my God. "You bought me a gun?"

"Not exactly. This was *my* first gun that my parents gave me. It's a Winchester," she says proudly. "Good for slight females like you. The ownership papers are in the case."

I don't know what to say. Muriel knows I don't like guns and have no intention of ever shooting one. She also knows me well enough to know that I'd never be rude and refuse a birthday present.

But, buried in with all my apprehension is the fact that Muriel is passing along her first gun—a gift from her parents, and probably something she prizes—to me.

Swallowing this confusing swirl of both aversion and appreciation, I settle on, "Thank you." It is the thought that counts, after all, and this is Muriel being thoughtful.

"It's not meant to decorate your wall, Calla," she warns.

I was thinking I'd hide it in the back of my closet, actually.

"You need to be able to protect yourself, especially when Jonah's gone in September, workin' with Jack Thomas."

"Oh, I'm flying home for those weeks."

"What?" That deep crevice forms between her eyes. "But that's garden harvest time! We'll be busy canning!"

"Don't worry, Muriel. She'll be shootin' the stem off apples in no time." Jonah's gruff voice from behind me is an instant balm, saving me from that conversation. Warm, strong hands land on my shoulders.

I reach back to clasp them, and then stretch farther to admire the strength in his wrists and his forearms beneath my fingertips, imagining these hands on the rest of my body later tonight. As much as I love having Diana here, the anticipation of having Jonah to myself— to repair whatever's going on between us—is overwhelming.

A resort guest hollers out to Muriel, distracting her. Jonah settles down in the chair beside me and I waste no time combing my fingernails through his bristly beard and leaning in to capture his mouth with mine in a lengthy, searing kiss that's probably too hot for the Ale House.

When I pull away, he's smirking. "How are you two doin' over here?"

"Fine. How about you? Having fun over at the bar?" I ask as lightly as I can.

"I guess." He nods toward Jesse Winslow whose impressive cleavage is eye level with a rugged-looking fisherman at a nearby table. "Your favorite local just came in."

"Yeah, I noticed. Toby ran away, fast."

Jonah laughs. "Don't blame him. Heard her husband is a bear."

From the corner of my eye, I see Marie watching us. Where I was once sympathetic to her status as the woman with unrequited feelings for Jonah, today I'm finding myself less inclined to care and more determined to make *my* feelings for Jonah—and his for me—clear.

Brash impulse takes over, and I shimmy from my chair to Jonah's lap, wriggling in comfortably, my arm curling around his shoulders. "You've been over there the entire time since we sat down," I say, trying to keep the accusation from my tone.

Jonah frowns. "Yeah, I figured you and Diana would want some time alone."

Leave it to Jonah to be considerate. "What I want is to spend my birthday with my favorite people." I smooth a hand over his broad chest and up over the thick column of his throat, admiring the jagged bump in it. "That means you."

He gives my thigh a squeeze. "Where is Di, anyway? Did she fall asleep in there?"

"Almost," Diana announces, reappearing as if on cue. She flops more than sits in her seat. "I walked into a wall. Both literally and figuratively. I can't tell if I'm really drunk or really jet-lagged, or both, but I'm sorry, I don't have another hour in me. I'm not giving that best-friend badge back, though. I've earned it." Her glossy, tired gaze lands on the camouflage case. "What is *that?*"

"My birthday present from Muriel. It's a *gun,*" I say slowly, giving her a look.

"Wow. A *gun.*" Diana's eyes widen in that "are you fucking kidding me?" way. "You have a *gun.* And it's just right *here,* on the *table* in the *bar,* beside my *martini.*"

Jonah chuckles. "Lemme go lock it up in the Jeep while you two finish your drinks. It's time to go home." He eases me off his lap, his palm smoothing over my backside in the process.

"So, you can do that around here? Just give someone a gun for their birthday? And they can go lock it up in their car and take it home and do ... *whatever* with it?" Diana asks soberly.

"As long as they're not certifiable or a criminal." He smirks. "Is there something we should know about Calla?"

"Oh yeah, she's certifiable all right. Certifiably *in love* with *you,*" Diana draws out her words, earning his snort and my laugh.

Marie appears, her purse slung over her shoulder. "Hey, guys, I'm gonna leave now. I have a sick puppy in the clinic that I should probably check on before I go home."

Relief fills me that I won't have to deal with Marie fawning over Jonah for much longer.

"Perfect timing. I'll walk you out." Jonah collects the gun.

"Happy birthday, Calla." Her smile doesn't quite reach her eyes.

My return smile feels equally forced. "Thanks for coming." I drop into my chair and watch her trail Jonah out the door, full of unease. I don't care what she told Jonah—that woman is only tolerating me because of him.

"A sick puppy in the clinic?" Diana gives me a questioning look.

"She's a veterinarian."

"Huh. So, Jonah's best friend is a beautiful woman who literally saves cute, cuddly baby animals, and you're *totally* okay with this."

"*And* she's in love with him. Don't forget that part," I add bitterly, taking a swig of my drink.

Diana presses her lips together, struggling to hold her opinion to herself.

"No, I'm not okay with it," I finally admit. Not lately, anyway. Not today. "But I trust Jonah." I don't trust her out there with him when I'm questioning the endurance of our relationship in here. "Let's finish these and go."

CHAPTER THIRTY-THREE

Ten minutes later, after guzzling a potent drink that has left my head swimming and thanking Muriel, Toby, and Teddy each in turn for their kindness, we're strolling out the door, arm in arm, a slight stumble to our step. Loud music and voices carry out the open windows into the quiet, clear night.

"This is *so* weird," Diana moans, staring at the sun that clings to the horizon—a hazy orange thanks to the smoke in the sky. We've passed the equinox and the days are already getting shorter, but for now, a near-midnight sun is still a recurring event.

My shiny blue Jeep is parked ahead, where Toby put out a Birthday Guest of Honor sign atop a pylon to reserve our spot for the night. Jonah isn't there. I spot him farther down in the lot, leaning against the side of Marie's pickup, so deep in conversation, he hasn't seemed to notice us yet. I can't see her, hidden by Jonah's broad form and between two trucks, but I can imagine her teal-blue eyes, peeled wide as she gazes up at him longingly.

That's an awfully long goodbye.

My stomach churns with thoughts of what they could be talking about—namely, me. Has he divulged this morning's disaster to her, in the spirit of needing advice again? What would she say? What harsh little truths would she whisper in his ear? They won't necessarily be wrong. He *does* tend to be impatient, and passionate, and move fast.

But who is she *really* trying to help here?

I am *not* the jealous, insecure girlfriend type who doesn't allow her boyfriend to have attractive female friends, who storms in on them and demands to know what's going on, as if there must be something nefarious in the works every time they're alone.

I tell myself this, even as I release my grip of Diana and my feet move of their own accord.

"I'll wait here," Diana's words are followed by a hiss and a slap against her skin. She refused to put on bug spray, claiming it would clash with her perfume. "Get him to unlock the Jeep doors?"

I throw a thumbs-up to her and keep walking. The closer I get, the less the music carries, the more I can hear of their conversation.

And the more I hear, the slower is my approach, the lighter are my steps.

"... fly out in the morning and be back by Monday night," I hear Marie say.

"Yeah, I don't know if that's a good idea anymore."

"Why not? She has her friend here. And I haven't been out to the villages in *months*."

Marie is trying to get Jonah to fly her out west. They used to do that all the time, back when he lived in Bangor. She'd come in on the regional airline that travels between Bangor and Anchorage daily. They'd spend days together, hopping from village to village, Marie the Animal Crusader, saving lives. She could find another pilot to fly her around, of that I'm sure.

But it's becoming more and more clear to me that she doesn't want another pilot.

She wants mine.

He reaches up to work his fingers through his hair, sending it into disarray. The black shirt I bought him clings to his frame, showing off the angles of his muscular shoulders and his trim waist. I can't help but admire him, even as my fists tighten by my sides and I imagine storming in between them to scream my accusations in a fit of rage.

"Yeah, I know, but things aren't great right now," Jonah says, a touch more softly.

I falter. My stomach, already tight, clenches.

Aren't great?

Jonah thinks things *aren't great*? Things between us, he means, obviously.

I mean, I *know*, after this morning, that things couldn't be called perfect, and yet hearing Jonah say it out loud—to *her*—sparks a fresh wave of surprise and hurt and anger.

"Hey, we need to get Diana home. Can you unlock the Jeep?" I call out, not wanting to get caught eavesdropping. I pray they can't hear the strain in my voice.

Jonah turns, sees me approaching, and his eyes soften. "Yeah. Of course. She must be dying." He digs into the pocket of his jeans and hits the key fob. A chirp sounds, followed by Diana's desperate cry of "thank you!" that makes him chuckle.

I could turn back and leave them, but Marie has kept Jonah from me long enough tonight, and so I approach until I'm melding into his chest, roping my arms around his back, and pushing away all emotions but my overwhelming love for this man.

Jonah doesn't hesitate, enveloping me into his warmth. "Ready to go?"

I rest my chin on him, tip my head back, and purr, "Yes." My gaze traces his lips for a moment before giving him an intense look, trying to convey everything I want to do to him tonight in that single glance.

"Got it," he murmurs, his own eyes flaring with heat. To Marie, he says, "I'll give you a call next week."

"Sure. Okay."

I catch a hint of disappointment in her voice, and it brings me a spiteful bubble of satisfaction.

I had no idea what I was going to say on the way over, but it hits me then. "Hey, Marie, I think Toby would love to go out to dinner with you sometime." An innocent-enough suggestion.

"Oh. Really?" She tucks a loose strand of hair behind her ear. A tell, I'm beginning to notice, for when she's uncomfortable or nervous.

"Yeah. You should ask him." I level her with a look while clinging to Jonah. "*He's* single."

Jonah is not.

She opens her mouth to speak but falters, her cheeks flushing as she steals a glance toward Jonah. "I'll keep that in mind. Good night." She ducks her head and climbs into her truck.

Jonah sighs heavily as he leads me out of the way. "What was that about?"

"What do you mean?" I feign innocence.

"Calla ..."

Marie's engine roars to a start. She backs out of her spot and coasts past us, her taillights blinking red.

Jonah throws a hand up to wave goodbye, but his jaw is tight with tension. "Do you want her dating Toby?" he asks in an overly calm voice.

"Sure. He's a nice guy and he's cute. So why not?"

"*Specifically* Toby?" Jonah fixes me with that serious, assessing stare. "Or just anyone besides me?"

"What does it matter?"

He shakes his head. "Because we've been over this before. She knows we're together, Calla."

"But she'd be happy if we weren't."

He curses under his breath. "Come on ..."

"No! You come on! I heard her that day in the hangar. How you're *so passionate* and that's what she *loves most* about you. Don't tell me she meant that in a platonic way. We *both* know she didn't!" His response that day, reminding her how he feels about me, is proof that it didn't come across that way to him, either. I'm tired of pretending otherwise.

He opens his mouth but stalls on whatever he was going to say. "She knows that's not gonna happen, though."

"Are you so sure of that?" A dark thought sparks in my mind, and I don't allow myself the opportunity to weigh it before it tumbles from my mouth. "Do *you* have an issue with Marie dating someone else?"

"Why would I?" he asks, his tone sharpening.

"I don't know." That dark thought is spinning into a convoluted weave with this growing tension between us, and a voice inside screams that it's ludicrous to say it out loud. Yet I can't keep it to myself. "Maybe you want her there as a backup option in case *this* doesn't work out."

He laughs but there's no humor in the sound. "Jesus, Calla. How many drinks did you have?"

"I'm not drunk!" I deny, feeling my indignation flare. Not *that* drunk.

"Are we *really* going there tonight?"

"Never mind!"

"Nah." He shakes his head. "It's too late. What the hell do you mean by that?"

Fine. I push on. "She's perfect for you! She's beautiful and smart and nice. She spends her days saving animals. She belongs in Alaska. She's ready to settle down and have babies like *now*, I'm sure. I don't understand why you wouldn't give her what she wanted."

Jonah's mouth is open but he's struggling with an answer.

Finally, he booms, "Because she's not *you*!"

"Well, things 'aren't great' between us, right? Didn't you just finish telling her that? Why would you tell her something like that?" Tears flow down my cheeks without warning. It feels like a betrayal, to hear him say that to anyone, but especially to Marie, who I know would find some level of delight in that admission. It's what she wants to hear.

It's what *I'd* want to hear if I were in her shoes.

It would give my wounded heart hope.

"Well, it's the truth, isn't it? If you're miserable here, then, no, things aren't great."

"I'm *not* miserable. I just ... you're *never* around!"

He throws his hands in the air. "You're the one who told me I should take this job, remember?"

"Because you wanted it! *I* didn't want you to want it!" I'm amazed we haven't corralled a crowd, the way we're yelling at each other. That seems to be our thing—fighting in parking lots. Thankfully, no one seems to be around to witness this one.

"You're right, I *did* want it. I wasn't gonna take it because I knew it would mean long hours, but then you told me to do what would make me happy, that you *wouldn't* be happy if I didn't. So, I took it.

And what do you want me to say, except that I love it? I'm doin' something important, and I'm good at it."

"And I'm glad that you're doing something you love. I *really* am, Jonah. But where does that leave me?"

He paces in a tight circle, as if to collect his thoughts before coming to a stop in front of me again, his arms folded. "I don't know, because you haven't even given Alaska a chance yet."

My jaw drops. "How can you say that! Look at me, Jonah! I'm riding around on an ATV, and talking to stupid goats and rescuing dogs from bear traps and going to chili cook-offs, and trying to make our house feel like a real home instead of some shack in the woods. I'm growing enough vegetables in our backyard for a family of fifty to survive the entire winter. I've learned how to cook—"

"You're constantly looking for reasons why Alaska is horrible, you keep talking about Toronto like that's still your home and this is only temporary, you're so focused on not fitting in here that you just tried to sell me on dating another woman," he fires back, his tone full of anger and frustration. "You haven't made a single decision about what you might want to do with your life, except to make it clear you don't want a family yet, which is fine with me." He throws his hands up in a sign of surrender. "I'm *not* pressuring you about that. But I thought you were happy! I thought you were making it work! And then this morning, all of a sudden, you're telling me you hate it here, and now I'm beginning to wonder if you *ever* planned on even *liking* it, or if you came here already counting on leaving!"

My jaw drops. "That's not true!"

"Isn't it? 'Cause I don't know anymore." He smooths his hands over his face. "I picked up my life and moved away from what I knew, too. It might not be the same, but it's still a change. Agnes, Mabel … they're like my family, and they're all the way on the other side of the state. I barely talk to them. And, while this might not be the ideal spot for you, you're either in all the way or you're not in it at all. And if you're not even willing to *try* to build a real life for yourself here with me, then …" His words trail.

And my stomach plummets. "Then what?" I manage to get out in a strangled voice.

He swallows and a pained look fills his eyes. "Look, I know I said we'd find somewhere else if Alaska doesn't work, but when I said that, I assumed you'd at least try here first."

"I *am* trying!"

He shakes his head. "No, Calla, I think you came here *wanting* to try, but you're so hung up on not being your mother that you can't seem to figure out a way to be yourself."

Boisterous voices fill the air as a group of five pours out the door from the Ale House.

Jonah sighs, lowering his voice. "As far as Marie goes, you either don't trust me—"

"I do! I swear, I do, Jonah. It's her I don't trust."

"She hasn't done anything wrong, Calla. You're being insecure, and I have no fucking idea why. Haven't I always been crystal clear about my feelings for you?"

"That's not what this is about—"

"You embarrassed her tonight, and you did it intentionally."

A flicker of guilt stirs deep inside, somewhere beneath my jealousy.

"I thought you were better than that." He turns and heads toward my Jeep without waiting for me, his shoulders sagging as if weighed down by a terrible burden.

I trail behind, wiping away tears even as fresh ones trickle, my resentment with Jonah over his claim that I haven't tried to make this work swelling with each step. What will convince him otherwise? What will I have to do?

Learn to fly a plane?

Hunt and cook my own kill?

Have his babies?

No, thank you.

Not a chance in hell.

Not yet.

Or maybe I'll never be able to convince him that I tried. Maybe that'll be his excuse no matter what, when this all falls apart and he refuses to leave Alaska. This is beginning to feel like the fine print in our relationship contract that I somehow missed before I signed on.

We're almost at the Jeep when Jonah stops abruptly. "So, that day when me and Marie were talking in the hangar ... You heard *every-*

thing?" I see it in his eyes—he's playing back the conversation, trying to pick through what all was said. How much does he remember of it?

Me? I remember it, almost word for word.

Not trusting my voice, I meet his gaze and nod.

Yes, I know about the ring—I've even seen it.

Yes, I know you were going to propose that day at the safety cabin.

Yes, I'm aware that it's been six weeks since then and you haven't.

A curse slips from Jonah's lips. "I don't know what to tell you except ..." He peers out at the trees, lost in a moment's thought. "I don't think we're ready for that yet."

"Yeah, I agree." And, after today, I have to wonder if we ever will be.

Wiping my cheeks and pressing my lips together, I ready a fake smile for Diana as we climb into the Jeep.

She's curled up in the backseat, snoring softly.

———

"She's heavier than she looks." Jonah eases down our narrow hallway with an unconscious Diana cradled in his arms, her long blonde tendrils dangling like a thick curtain halfway to the floor. I tried waking her when we pulled up to our house only minutes after leaving the Ale House, but she didn't stir.

"Don't tell her that," I warn, yanking the bed linens down.

He sets her down gently and then backs away. I move in to slip off her boots and socks—she can't sleep with socks on because they make her feet sweaty—before drawing her blanket over her.

Jonah is silent as he watches me unfasten her earrings and slide her bracelet off her limp wrist—jewelry is another irritant for her—and set them in the porcelain dish I bought especially for this purpose. I sense him wanting to say something, but for once, he keeps his thoughts to himself.

I get to her engagement ring and pause on it for a long moment.

Have she and Aaron ever had a fight that left her feeling this bleak?

"You want me to grab her a glass of water?" Jonah asks, his voice grating in the quiet house.

"No, thanks. I'll get it." I'm emotionally and physically exhausted and I want to be alone to try to make sense of my muddled thoughts.

"Calla, I ..." His words drift. "I'll be up soon. Get some sleep, okay? We can talk more in the morning."

Can't wait.

I take my time readying for bed, and when I slip downstairs to fetch water for both Diana and myself, I spy Jonah standing on the porch, his phone pressed to his ear. Who could he be talking to at this hour?

Marie, likely.

My irritation flares. Is he divulging *more* about the weakest points of our relationship, after we literally just finished fighting about him doing this? Is this the way it'll always be? We'll have problems and he'll run off to talk about them with her instead of trying to work them out with me first?

This is beginning to feel like a test.

One we might not pass.

I can't help but think ...

Maybe it's kismet that a pregnancy scare hijacked Jonah's plans for that day, and that our plane almost crashed, forcing his introduction to Sam.

Maybe it's a blessing that I overheard his conversation with Marie about jobs he was turning down.

And maybe it is for the best that I pushed him to accept work he would end up loving.

Because otherwise, where would we be right now? I'd be consumed with planning for a wedding and helping Jonah build The Yeti. Jonah would be faithfully sticking close by and flying, but not loving what he was doing.

And then what?

How long before he grew restless doing supply runs and playing tourist guide, began resenting me for keeping him pinned down by a promise, and confessed his unhappiness? Of course, I'd tell him to do what he loves, and he'd seek out a similar job as the one he has with Sam. The Yeti would fall by the wayside in summer months without its pilot, and I'd be left wondering what to do with myself during the long days. We'd end up exactly back here down the road, only with years and marriage vows between us.

So maybe that all this is happening now is for the best.

On my way back upstairs, I pass the curio cabinet that arrived a few weeks ago. Only one piece sits inside at the moment—Ethel's ivory sculpture. It catches my eye and I stall there a long moment, studying it.

Perhaps Ethel's tale of the raven and his goose wife isn't inaccurate after all.

I manage to keep my composure until I'm tucked beneath our bedcovers, alone. And then I muffle my sobs with my pillow, feeling for the first time since last summer that my relationship with Jonah is surviving on borrowed time.

CHAPTER THIRTY-FOUR

"Calla."

"Hmm?" I crack my eyelids.

Jonah looms over me with a mug in his hand. "Figured you might need this." He sets it on my nightstand. The rattle of a pill bottle sounds as he slips it from his pocket and sets it next to my coffee.

Just enough daylight creeps in from the hallway for me to note the frothy milk. "Did you make me a latte?"

"I owed you one from yesterday, remember? That machine isn't as complicated as I thought it would be." There's no hint of anger or resentment in his voice. If anything, I'd say it's strangely docile.

"Thank you." I check the clock. It's after nine. "Is Diana awake?"

"She's been up since five." Jonah moves to draw the curtains, upsetting the shadows with sunshine. The forecast called for another warm day with no promise of rain anytime soon, in the driest, warmest June on record for this area. "Muriel's here. She took her out to the garden."

"I should get up, then." And rescue her. I groan and heave myself out of bed, wandering to the bathroom to relieve myself and brush my teeth, dismayed by the puffy, sore eyes that stare back at me in the mirror—physical evidence of the disastrous end to my birthday. I'm not sure I can even force a smile at this point.

I climb into the shower, hoping that ten minutes immersed beneath a stream of hot water will help clear my head and my heavy heart. I was *far* drunker than I realized. At least that hopeless despair I carried to sleep has faded with the alcohol. But it's been replaced with an odd emptiness, a melancholy.

Regret.

And lingering confusion.

All the things we said to each other last night ...

I cringe. What would possess me to become *so* wrapped up in jealousy over Marie? In the light of a new day, I feel like an idiot. It wasn't about her at all. Granted, I still don't trust her intentions, but I allowed it to drive a wedge between Jonah and me when we have much bigger, more pressing issues to face.

Jonah thinks I haven't tried here?

Could he have a point? Did you come here seeing Alaska as only temporary?

I hear Simon's British lilt in my mind as readily as if the phone were pressed to my ear. Years with my stepfather have taught me to try to weigh all sides and opinions—even those I don't agree with—but I'm struggling. Maybe because I now have this niggling, gnawing feeling in my gut. Maybe because it would mean I've fallen into the same trap my mother did all those years ago, of not trying with my father when she claimed that she had.

How many times have I told myself—and my mother, and Simon, and Diana, and even Agnes—that I'm willing to try Alaska because Jonah said he was willing to leave?

My stomach clenches with that mental count.

Have I been clinging too tightly to that all these months? From the very beginning?

And is he right? Have I been spending all this time focused too much on everything Trapper's Crossing and this house and my time in Alaska is *not*, instead of everything that it is?

I thought I was embracing it, making the best of my less than ideal situation, but maybe I've been going about it the wrong way. What I do know is that our relationship slid down a steep, muddy slope yesterday. How do we climb back to the top? *Is* there even a way back up for us from this?

Panic begins to swirl. Maybe the docility that greeted me this morning wasn't docility at all, but resignation. Has Jonah recognized something I'm not willing to admit yet?

Has it become not a matter of finding a way back up but a way *out* for him?

What I feel for Jonah, I've never felt a fraction of for anyone ever, and the idea that this could be the beginning of the end—that I might lose Jonah over this—has me slamming my hand on the tap and scrambling to dry off, nausea churning my stomach.

I barrel out of the bathroom with a towel hastily wrapped, intent on dressing quickly and finding Jonah wherever he is downstairs, to fix this mess I've made of us.

But he hasn't left our bedroom. He's perched on the edge of the bed, his focus on his clasped hands in front of him.

I can't get the words out fast enough. "I'm so sorry, Jonah. I'm such an asshole." My voice is unsteady. "Please tell me you're not giving up on me yet."

He offers me a small smile that momentarily distracts me from the dark circles under his eyes. It doesn't appear like he had a good night's sleep, either. "We're both assholes. How about that?" He reaches out, beckoning for me to come.

I rush toward him, but hesitate when I get there—part of me wants to throw myself at him, the other part is terrified that he'll hold me at arm's length, that it's too late, that the slope we fell down yesterday was too steep, the climb up too slippery.

That he's already decided he doesn't want to even attempt it.

But then he clasps my thighs with warm hands and his thumbs stroke my skin, offering me hope. "Using work as my excuse to take off yesterday morning was a dumb move. I just didn't think you'd react like that. But I should have seen it coming." His eyes shine with sincerity. "I'm sorry."

I swallow the growing lump in my throat. "I overreacted—"

"No, you didn't." He steers my body in between his parted legs, pulls me down to sit on one thigh. I use the opportunity to curl my arms around his shoulders and slide in a touch closer. "You *reacted*. To something you've obviously been sitting on and not saying anything about for a while." He presses his forehead against my collarbone. Drops of water linger on my skin.

"I don't want to stop you from doing it, Jonah," I whisper. With tentative fingertips, I stroke his bearded jaw. "I can see how much you love working with Sam. I mean, you've been geeking out with textbooks at night."

He chuckles. "It's been a while since I've learned something totally new. I actually like it."

"I just don't know what I'm doing here, besides being with you. And don't get me wrong, I *love* being with you, and I love it when you come home at night, and there's no one else I'd rather be with, but I feel like …" I struggle to find the right words to articulate this swirl inside me. "I don't know who I am here. At least with The Yeti, we were starting that together—"

"We still have it, Calla."

"I know, but it's different now. You're off, doing your own thing. It's kind of like your backup now. It doesn't feel like *ours* anymore."

Jonah nods slowly. "Fair enough."

"And I don't think I'm made for spending so much time alone. I'm not blaming you for that," I add quickly. "But I'm beginning to think the reason I stayed at home with my mom and Simon all those years had less to do with high rent prices and more about me just liking being around my family." I had the best of both worlds—freedom and privacy, but I never felt alone. I thrive on being on the go and being around people. "I guess I'm more like my mother that way than I care to admit." We both live for schedules packed with appointments to make, social outings to keep, and tasks to complete. "It's a big adjustment for me."

I hesitate. "And, I don't know how to explain it, but I'm beginning to feel like maybe I'm losing a part of who I am?" I remember my mother saying that once—that, isolated in the tiny, mossy-green house in the tundra in the dead of winter, thousands of miles from everything and everyone she knew, she began to wonder, to fear, who she would become in five, ten, twenty years if she stayed.

What choices she would begin to regret.

Is this what she meant?

Jonah studies my features. "Calla, I don't know how to fix that for you. If I could, I would. But you need to stop doin' things because you think *I* want you to, or because Muriel tells you to. I don't give a shit if you know how to cook. Don't get me wrong, I appreciate not living off frozen dinners, but it's not why I fell in love with you. If you burn everything from now until the day I die, I'll still love you."

Warmth fills my chest, hearing those words. "What if I burn down this house?" I ask tentatively, my lips curling into a smile for the first time today.

He gives me a flat look but it softens immediately, as his gentle hand tucks a strand of wet hair behind my ear. "Where's the woman who rolled into Wild, knowing nothin' about charter plane companies or Alaska, and convinced me, the stubborn ass, that Wild was doing it all wrong?"

"It was *just* a website." My dad sold the company before we could ever hope to turn the lagging parts of the business around.

"Where's the woman who got so pissed off at me one night, she shaved my face while I was unconscious?"

I tip my head back and laugh—the sound coming from deep within—and the simple act releases waves of tension that have gripped me since yesterday.

He sighs. "Calla, you're not like anyone else I know around here, and I'm glad. I don't want you to be like Marie. You've got somethin' of your own to add to the mix. You don't have to become someone else. Do what you wanna do. Seriously, if you want to put up motion-activated witches and goblins around our property to scare off bears, do it. If you don't ever want to learn how to fire a gun, fine. If you want to let Zeke in to mow down everything in that garden, go ahead."

"I've actually liked going out there and picking strawberries." Even if I don't eat them. I shrug. "It feels like I've *accomplished* something."

"Then keep doin' it! But do it because *you* want to. Find a way to make Alaska work for you, and soon, you won't even think about the few little things that don't."

"The *few* little things?" I echo. "Man-eating bears, earthquakes, raging forest fires, giant mosquitos, worrying that you'll crash every time you leave—"

"All right, all right ..." He smirks, but then it fades. "*I* can't be the only thing keeping you here. You're too driven to be sitting at home, waiting for me. You need to find something that'll make you want to be all in with this." He presses a gentle kiss against my damp skin.

"Sounds like something Agnes said to me once." I wish I had the answer.

"That's probably 'cause she said it to me last night," he admits.

"That's who you were talking to on the phone?"

He nods. "I needed to know exactly how much of a jackass I was. She's always been good at tellin' me."

"Agnes would never tell you that."

"Trust me, she's got her own special way." He smiles. "Anyway, she helped me see my part in all this."

"I'm sorry for mine." I cup his jaw between my palms. "And I'm sorry about Marie. She didn't deserve that. I'll apologize the next time I see her." My idea of her dating Toby might be good, but my intentions weren't. If the roles were reversed, I'd probably hate me.

His hand slips beneath the hem of my towel to settle on my hip. "Agnes thinks I have a huge blind spot with Marie. I'm startin' to think she might be right."

"What do you mean?"

"Did I ever tell you that she was engaged when I started flying her around to the villages?"

"No." Jonah has never said much about his friendship with Marie.

"Yeah. We hit it off right away. And I'm not gonna lie, I thought she was hot, and super smart, and nice—"

"Okay, I get it." I wonder if I want to hear this.

"If she'd been single, I probably would have made a move. But she was gettin' married, so she was off-limits, right from the start. Anyway, she was only supposed to come out once every two or three months, but she started makin' trips once a month, sometimes more. We'd spend days together. We got to be really good friends. And then about a year in, she told me she'd broken off her engagement. She said they'd grown apart, that she didn't love him anymore. I flew into Anchorage to see how she was doin'. We met up at a bar to have a few drinks, shoot the shit. When we were saying good night, she kissed me."

I knew this. At least, I knew about the kiss—not the how, when, or why. "And?"

"And ..." He hesitates, as if he doesn't want to admit the next part. "For about ten seconds, I was gonna go with it. But then I stopped because it didn't feel right. I hadn't looked at her like that in a long time, and she was too important to me as a friend to screw it up. Plus, I knew she wasn't the kind of girl who was into hookups, that she'd be lookin' for somethin' serious, and I wasn't lookin' for that, with *anyone*. I told her all this, too. She apologized, said she was just drunk and not thinking straight, and that us being friends was too important for her, too. So, we agreed to not talk about it again and left it at that."

"And you believed her?" I can't hide the doubt from my voice. I know the first thing Diana would say if she were hearing this story—Marie didn't love her fiancé anymore because she'd fallen madly in love with a certain bullheaded bush pilot. They were close friends. He was attracted to her. That he denied her that night didn't mean it couldn't happen in the future, once he was ready to settle. I sigh. "Guys can be so dumb."

"What was I supposed to do?" He shrugs. "We went back to things being normal and they seemed fine. She didn't date anyone for a long time. Said she wanted a break after being tied down for five years. She mentioned this guy with a bunch of ferrets who asked her out, and she told him she wasn't interested.

"And then I met that pilot with the coast guard that I told you about."

I nod, and in the back of my mind is that little voice that automatically tosses out curious questions like it does every time there's mention of a woman from Jonah's past: What does she look like? Does she think about him? Does he think about her? If she had been in the picture last summer, would I be here now?

"A few weeks after Teegan came into the picture, Marie started dating the ferret guy. I figured she'd changed her mind, he grew on her, whatever. I didn't think anything of it. She seemed happy. I even met the guy once, and he was decent enough.

"Then Teegan and I ended things, and Marie was single again a week later. Said it wasn't working for her. Again, I didn't think anythin' of it. And she never mentioned dating anyone again. I'd ask sometimes, because I was curious, and she'd say she was too busy with work. Last year, she *finally* admitted that she'd met a guy, but she was waitin' for him to figure his shit out." He frowns. "I'm starting to think she was talkin' about me."

I give him a look—he didn't see *that* coming?—and shake my head.

His gaze drifts along my bare collarbone, over the knot in the front of my towel, and the hint of cleavage peeking out. "And then I met you, and you were like a wrecking ball comin' into my life, Calla." He laughs. "A fucking beautiful, hot-pink wrecking ball. And everything changed for me. All these things I didn't want before, suddenly all I could think about was havin' them all with you." His eyes land on my mouth. "And I haven't stopped thinking about them since."

I capture his lips with mine, coaxing his mouth open with my tongue as a shaky sigh of relief escapes me. It feels like our first kiss all over again—tentative and brimming with raw need. My hand finds his cheek, the coarse hair of his jaw tickling my skin. "Same. You did that to me, too." My entire perspective on life seemed to change, and a big part of that was because of Jonah.

He turns his face in to kiss my palm. "I'm so used to having Marie as my sounding board for everything that at first, I didn't think twice about venting to her after that day up in the safety cabin." He meets my gaze. "But then she said what she did, and I started thinking that maybe I shouldn't be talking to her about us. Not because I think she'd ever try to convince me to leave you. That's not her. But it can't feel good, to listen to me talk about the woman I want to spend the rest of my life with."

His jaw tenses, and when he peers up at me, I see a raw, vulnerable pain that Jonah so rarely makes visible. I can't get close enough to him, twisting and clambering onto his lap, my entire body moulding to his as my thighs wrap around his hips and my arms rope around his head and every other part of me is pressed against him.

I feel a sharp tug on my towel and then it's unraveling, leaving me naked against his dressed body. But there is no playful foreplay this time around. No pauses, no lingering looks or smiles or touches. Our mouths and hands become tangled and rough in a frantic attempt to touch and kiss every part of each other as we maneuver our way fully onto our bed.

Jonah tugs his shirt and track pants off in a hurry, as if he can't wait another second, and then flattens me beneath his weight as we roll into each other. I coil my legs around his hips, opening myself up for him. He pulls back long enough to peer down at me, the agony in his eyes piercing my heart. "I *can't* ever lose you, Calla."

I wasn't the only one panicking about our impending doom—knowledge that brings me great comfort.

"You won't. *Ever*." I grip the back of his neck and pull his mouth to mine. A low moan escapes as he slides into me. His hips move rhythmically, never rushing, never relenting. Over and over again, matching the drumbeat of my heart, as our bodies coil tighter, and our sounds grow hoarse, and our mouths whisper sweet promises of always.

CHAPTER THIRTY-FIVE

"You have everything?"

Diana absently pats the pockets of her denim jacket as she takes inventory of the luggage Jonah unloaded onto the Anchorage airport curb—one suitcase stuffed with twelve outfits for her four-day trip, a backpack, and her oversized purse—and then nods. "I think I'm good. If I forgot anything, it's yours. Okay! This trip was amazing! Oh my God, I'm going to cry!" She throws her arms out.

My eyes are watering as we embrace, and I'm not sure whose grip is tighter. Her flight to Toronto through Vancouver leaves in two hours, and I want to hold on to her until the last possible second. I want to beg her not to leave.

These past few days flew by in a blur of late-night laughter, premature wedding planning, and sight-seeing, visiting some of the same landmarks we did last summer with my father. We made it to Juneau after all, spending all day yesterday marveling at the glaciers, searching for humpback whales and bald eagles, and touring the picturesque and colorful downtown shops. We arrived home late last night, the glow of a hazy orange sun low on the horizon and my soul aching with a mix of emotions.

Diana has to go back to her reality, though—to Aaron and Beef Stick, to lively nights in her pricy Liberty Village condo and getting ready for law school, which I'm guessing is going to take up much of her focus in the coming years.

And I have to go find *my* new reality in this sleepy town in Alaska.

"Thank you for *everything*." She grips Jonah's shoulders in a fierce hug, adding in a whisper that I catch, "Take care of her for us."

"Always," comes his gruff response.

She discreetly brushes a tear from her cheek and then, slinging her backpack over her shoulder and popping the handle on her suitcase, Diana blows us a kiss and strolls through the doors, her furtive gaze already scanning the signs for directions.

We're left standing at the curb with cars waiting to take our spot in the passenger drop-off lane. It's time to go, and yet I can't seem to make my legs move toward the passenger side.

"It's going to be so quiet without her around." A hot tear trickles over my lip.

Too quiet.

"You want me to drive?" Jonah offers.

The prickly lump in my throat flares. "Yes, please."

But instead of moving for the driver's side, Jonah slips an arm around me and pulls me into his side to press a kiss against my forehead. "It's gonna be okay."

I steal a glance at him, in a soft cotton T-shirt and a pair of faded, worn blue jeans—his favorite, I've come to learn. Since our explosive fight on Saturday and epic reconciliation on Sunday morning, things have felt "right" between us again. But now I see worry veiled in his blue eyes. He's afraid it was only temporary. That Diana was a Band-Aid for our ongoing challenges.

And that's exactly what she was, if we allow it.

If *I* allow it.

I hate seeing Jonah like this. He's supposed to be the confident, assured one. *I'm* the one who doesn't have her shit together.

But perhaps that's where things need to change.

I sink into him, reaching up to cup his chin. I offer him a reassuring smile. "Let's go *home*."

My shoes kick loose gravel as I trek behind Jonah, my attention on the mountain range in the distance. Denali looms as it does every day, a silent, imposing expanse of rock, its caps still marked with snow. It has become a constant for me here, an anchor of sorts, and seeing it triggers an odd sense of calm that I can't explain, despite my melancholy over Diana leaving.

"What's all this stuff?" Jonah stoops to pick something up by the front door. "Someone left two dozen eggs here. And our plate?" He holds it in the air.

I spy the red roses bordering the white china dish through the porch screen door. "I left that at Roy's last week. I brought him muffins." That was on Friday, before I took him to the hospital, before our enormous fight.

"You gave *him* muffins?" Jonah glowers. "I was wonderin' where those went."

"Roy must have had Toby drop off these things." Is this supposed to be a peace offering?

Jonah notices something else sitting on the stoop. "What are these?"

I push through the porch door and see the wooden objects in Jonah's grasp. One is a woman in a flowing summer dress, her long hair trailing behind her with a loose braid woven in, her hands clasped behind her back to hold a hat. The other is an animal with large ears, its surface rougher, the details less defined. "Those are Roy's carvings. They're his. He makes them," I mumble, pulling out my phone.

Toby answers on the second ring.

"Hey, did you leave something on my porch from Roy?"

"Uh. No." His voice carries over speakerphone.

"I'm being serious."

"So am I," he says warily.

"What about your mom?"

"My mom? Nah, not unless it was before six. She's been in Palmer since this morning."

This wasn't here when we left for the airport, which means Roy himself must have ventured over.

"Why? What's goin' on? It's not somethin' dead, is it?"

I frown at Jonah. "No. *Why?*"

"Because it's *Roy*."

Jonah snorts. "Yeah. Fair point."

"I passed along your message. You know, about him needin' to apologize before you ever came back again."

Jonah's eyebrows arch. "You expect *that guy* to apologize?"

I shrug. To Toby, I ask, "And? What'd he say?"

"He said something like, 'I am what I am,' and then he got this big grin on his face and he went inside. It was weird. I've never seen that guy smile." There's a pause, and then Toby urges, "What did he leave you?"

"My plate from last week, some eggs, and two wooden figurines that he made. One's a woman and the other is a ..." Jonah holds it up, allowing me to inspect it more closely. "Donkey?"

"A donkey?" Toby echoes, sounding as baffled as I am.

A few beats pass and then Jonah's head falls back, and his booming laughter disturbs the serene calm of the lake. "'I am what I am.'" He shakes his head. "Fucking guy gave you a jackass, Calla."

"What?" I feel the confusion fade as it dawns on me. "That's what I called him on Friday." When he was being disparaging about Toby.

"Yeah, well, this is him admitting it." Jonah sets the wooden figurines in my open palm. "And I'm guessing that's as close to an apology as anyone is ever gonna get from Roy Donovan." He disappears into the house, chuckling to himself.

I study the figurines. He must have plucked them from his collection. There's no way he could have carved these in such a short time, and with a broken arm. The detail on the woman—right down to her delicate face—is astonishing. Ethereal, almost. Is she supposed to be me?

The donkey is far less polished—the surface rough, the chisel marks choppy.

Much like Roy, I guess.

"So, does that mean you're gonna start going back to his place?" Toby asks. "Because I don't mind helpin' out, but I'm kinda swamped at the resort."

"I don't know," I say truthfully. This might be the closest Roy will ever get to saying he's sorry for all that he said, but is it enough?

"He gave you eggs," Toby points out, a hint of surprise in his voice. "He doesn't give anyone *anything*."

I smile as I head into the house to tuck the figurines on their own shelf in the curio cabinet.

CHAPTER THIRTY-SIX

I break from plucking ripe strawberries to brush hair off my forehead with my forearm and look around the garden. The burgundy tops of the beets are breaking the surface of the soil, and two cabbages look ready to cut. Muriel says to leave the carrots in the ground until fall unless we're eating them fresh.

Beside me are three large baskets brimming with fruit. Muriel has another three beside her. I feel like we've barely made a dent. The heat and my excellent watering skills are to be blamed—the crop is better than Muriel's seen in years. "So, the farmers' market ... how hard is it to get a table for a Friday?"

"Not hard at all! Just call the office and pay your fee. You can book one week at a time, if you want. There's always a spot. In fact, I think I remember Laurie sayin' there's still space this week." Muriel pushes her foam knee board over two feet and settles back onto it in front of a new plant. "You're followin' in Colette's footsteps. That's great to hear."

I sigh. It's time for some truth. "Actually, Muriel, I'm looking for a way to get rid of all these, because I don't eat them and there's no way Jonah can get through all this jam in a winter without going into sugar shock." Though I did catch him at the fridge, eating from a jar of last year's batch with a spoon, so maybe I'm wrong.

Muriel settles back on her haunches to frown at me. "This is an awful lot of strawberries to grow for someone who doesn't eat *them*, Calla."

I snort. "No shit."

"You should have said somethin'."

"You should have asked," I say gently, but I say it nonetheless.

I feel her shrewd gaze on me as I search beneath the broad green leaves for any more red berries.

She chuckles. "Colette always said I was part bull."

I can't help but smile. "I think I might have liked Colette."

"Yeah ... she was a good one."

Emboldened, I decide to forge on. "Muriel, we need a proper marketing campaign for this winter carnival if you want it to succeed."

"Emily's workin' on the poster—"

"A *poster*, Muriel? No ..." I shake my head. "That's something to blend into a wall, and flyers end up in the trash. If this is *really* as important as you say it is, then we need something bigger."

She opens her mouth—I assume to argue with me that I don't know what I'm talking about—but hesitates. "What do you have in mind?"

"That fireworks show you were asking John to find more money for? You said it's the biggest winter fireworks show in all of Alaska. Is that true?"

"It is!" she says with indignation, as if I shouldn't even be questioning it.

"Then let's make it bigger and call it the biggest winter show in Alaskan *history*. People around here are so proud of their heritage, we need to give them a reason to celebrate." She opens her mouth, but I cut her off before she can offer a rebuttal or dismissal. "I might not be from around here, but this is what I'm good at, Muriel. *Any one* of you can organize this outhouse race." I set my jaw with determination. "If people haven't been coming around as much over the past few years, then it's time to shake things up. I can do that. *I* can bring fresh ideas, and I can appeal to a younger generation. Plus, hey, if all my efforts don't pay off, you haven't lost anything." I shrug. "It's not like I'm getting paid."

Her brow is furrowed as she seems to mull that over. "I'd have to talk to Emily. She's been handlin' things—"

"*I'll* talk to her." Something tells me I can find a more polite, creative way than Muriel would. "Emily and I can work on it together."

She hums. "Well, what can I say, except ... I'm excited to see what you come up with."

I smile as I shift my focus back to my berry plant. So am I, I think. I have a challenge, a task, and it feels like *me*.

"So, Toby tells me Roy's been givin' you a hard time. You two had a fight last week?"

I stifle my groan. This conversation was inevitable. I only wondered if it would happen before or after she demanded that I bring out my new gun so she could teach me how to shoot.

I steal a glance to confirm that our quiet sentry is there, sitting at the tree line. Since last week, Oscar has ventured over every morning, as if he knows that's when I'm back here, tending to the garden. "Yeah."

"And you haven't been back since?"

"Toby said he would go for me while Diana was here."

"Didn't Diana leave yesterday?" she asks, in a knowing tone.

I shift to a new plant. My knees are beginning to hurt. I recall seeing a foam pad much like Muriel's when I was cleaning the house. I regret tossing it. "Roy and I are working through our issues." With eggs and wooden donkeys.

"Hmm ..."

I keep my head down, plucking and filling my basket, bracing myself for a lecture about helping thy neighbor, even when thy neighbor is an irredeemable asshole.

"Did I ever tell you how Roy came to help us look for my boy Deacon?"

My red-stained fingers stall on a berry. In the months I've known Muriel, the one person she never talks about is her missing son. I look to her now, meeting her steely-gray gaze. "No. You didn't."

She turns back to her plant. "When we got the call that they couldn't find him, Teddy and I jumped in the truck and headed on up there to meet the state troopers right away. But soon enough, others were showin' up. Friends of Deacon's, our regulars at the resort, people from around Trapper's Crossing. Everybody seemed to be rallyin'. It was nice to see. A real sense of community, pullin' together." She smiles sadly. "The official search for Deacon lasted seven days. There was a lot of focus on the river, 'cause that's where the signs led. Toby's bum knee wouldn't let him walk too far, so him and Phil searched as best they could from the sky, while the rest of the volunteers combed the riverbank. But the days passed with no luck."

She presses her lips tightly and then clears her throat. "State troopers called off the search after a week, but we kept goin'. Less and less people came out each day. We understood. People had to go back to their lives. Nights were coolin' off fast. Soon, even Teddy said it was time to pack it in. And that's when Roy showed up." She chuckles and shakes her head. "He came with his gun and his campin' gear, sayin' he was there for some moose huntin' and took off into the bush."

"Alone?"

"The only way Roy does anythin' is alone. But, no." She smirks. "Moose huntin' had ended and even he ain't ballsy enough to go off-season. But he was too stubborn to admit that he knew I'd be too stubborn to call it quits so soon, so he made up this cockamamie story, knowing I'd follow. I did. And Roy and I spent another nine days out there, him in his tent, me in mine, combing the woods for my boy, until the snow made it pointless."

I'm trying to picture Muriel and Roy spending nine days together —alone—in the woods, with guns, but I'm struggling. "You two didn't fight?"

"Oh, we fought." She laughs. "When don't we? It was more to pass the time than anythin'. But he never complained about bein' out there. Never said anything about quittin'. He waited for me to make the call."

"That was ... kind of him." And so unlike everything I know about Roy Donovan so far.

"Yeah. Kind. That's a good word for it. Who knew Roy'd be capable of that?" She snorts. "He's an odd duck, I'll give him that. Not easy to deal with, or even like. But he knows right from wrong, and he chooses right when it counts."

"What made him like that?"

"I don't know if there's any rhyme or reason to the way he is. My guess is he's always been like that, but nobody knows much about Roy Donovan at all. That he ever managed to wrangle a wife in the first place is a mystery to me, if he behaved the way he does with us."

"There's someone for everyone," I echo what I've heard Simon say on more than one occasion. "I think Roy has troubles with addiction. He said a few things ..." My words drift as I hesitate. Am I betraying Roy by talking about this with Muriel? Will she storm over there with her hands on her hips to question him about it? Do I even care?

"Yeah, I've gotten that impression, too." She frowns at the berry in her hand before chucking it over the fence for Zeke. "He told me he got himself into some trouble with the law, back in Texas. Not exactly sure what all happened, but I know it was enough that his wife picked up and left him, told him to stay far away."

So he came to Alaska. I guess that's about as far away as anyone could get while staying within their own country.

"He actually told you that?"

She chuckles. "Nine days is a long time to spend with any one person. We got a pretty good understandin' of each other."

"Did you know he has a daughter, too?"

Her eyes flash to me. "I know about her. How do *you* know about her?"

"I saw a picture in his cabin, the day I went to look for a blanket for him. I asked him."

She makes a sound. "I suppose that's the reason for this *disagreement* between you two."

"Yeah. Part of it."

She nods slowly. "On that last day, when I had to throw in the towel and accept that I'd likely never see Deacon alive again, Roy mentioned how he had a daughter he'd never see again either." Her brow furrows. "I think he was tryin' to relate in his own way. 'Course, I made the mistake of tellin' him it wasn't the same. That was his choice to take off on her, and she was alive and well, as far as he knew. He could see her anytime he wants if he'd get over himself. Me?" She shakes her head. "I can't even visit my boy's grave." There's the slightest quiver in her voice, and it throws me off. Muriel is never anything but loud and strong and certain.

"Well, Roy got madder than I've ever seen him get before, which is sayin' somethin'. We've had an unspoken agreement since then. I don't mention his girl and he doesn't bring up Deacon. It's a good thing, too, 'cause Lord knows he'd say somethin' that would make me pull out my gun and shoot him on the spot." She leans back on her haunches, assessing the rows of plants still prime for picking. "I thought you two spendin' some time together might be good, 'specially after what you told me about you and your own father, how you were estranged and then you weren't. I thought, if you somehow ended up mentioning it to that old badger, maybe it'd give him ideas. Maybe he'd see that it's never too late."

"So there *was* method to your madness," I murmur, more to myself.

"Everyone needs someone to care about. Even that old grump." Her gaze narrows on something in the distance. "You expectin' someone?"

"No?" I follow her sight line to see a small plane descending, angling for our airstrip. I had heard the buzz of the engine but tuned it out, having grown accustomed to the sound.

"This is private property. Pilots can't just land wherever they want. They gotta call it in!" She sounds offended.

"Maybe it's an emergency." And there's no one to call. I'm all the way out here.

When it becomes clear that this plane is in fact landing on our airstrip, I head for my ATV.

———

I feel the blip of excitement the moment Bobbie's blonde head emerges from the plane. George's plane, I realize now, taking in the familiar blue-and-green stripes along the fuselage.

But it's the small figure that pops out from the back passenger seat next that has my heart skipping and my legs propelling me forward in a jog.

"I didn't know you were coming today!" I throw my arms around

Agnes's slight shoulders. I haven't seen her in months. We've tried to plan a visit several times, but between work and school and the weather, it's never panned out.

She returns the embrace with ferocity. "Didn't Jonah mention it?"

"Uh ... *No.*" I greet Bobbie with a hug.

Agnes smiles, the corners of her eyes crinkling. "George and Bobbie are on their way up to their cabin, so we hitched a ride. Thought we'd come hang out here for a while, if that's okay."

"Yeah, of course!" I turn to see a taller Mabel round the other side of the plane, a backpack slung over her shoulder. George lumbers behind her. "Holy cow! You've grown!" It's only been four months but she has changed considerably—her hips rounder in more fitted jean shorts, her legs shapelier, her face thinned out. The biggest change, though, is her hair. She chopped her espresso-colored locks, and they now sit at her jawline in a sleek bob that makes her look years older.

"We tried calling on your birthday but we kept getting your voicemail." Mabel smiles. It's not the wide, toothy grin that I remember, but it's a smile, nonetheless.

I close the distance to give her a tight hug.

"I take it you know these people," Muriel hollers, her approaching footfalls heavy and slow.

"Yes," I laugh and make quick introductions.

"Well, if this isn't perfect timing!" Muriel studies Mabel with keen interest. "We have a *whole* patch of strawberries waitin' to be picked."

———

I step out to the screened-in porch carrying two lattes.

"This is fancy." Agnes accepts her mug with a murmured thanks. "You just missed the fox. He went that way." She points to our left toward a small, covered woodshed used for firewood.

"Yeah, he comes around every night at this time. I think Phil was feeding him." It used to startle me, looking up to see his orange face watching me, but I've grown accustomed to it. I've even snapped a few pictures. The moose haven't been around for months. I'm beginning to think that has less to do with the planes and more to do with Oscar.

Agnes sighs through a sip, her near-black eyes on the lake where Jonah and Mabel float in our aluminum boat, rods propped in their grips. Jonah came home early from work tonight, well before dinner. They've been fishing for an hour, ducking out for some one-on-one time while the sun graces Denali's western side with a late-day glow.

Watching them brings me back to that day on a remote lake with my father—the four of us dangling our lines at opposite corners of a tin boat, Mabel repeatedly mistaking the current for attracted fish, Jonah reprimanding me for my whining, my father chuckling at the lot of us. Nothing bit my line that day, and the hours seemed long and tedious. What I would do to travel back in time to that day, just for a moment.

"You two sure have a good thing here, Calla."

I catch Agnes's gaze flickering to my neck, and I realize I've been toying with my pendant. I smooth my hand over it. "So, when did you decide to come? Was it after Jonah called you on Saturday night?" Is she *that* worried about us, that she'd take time off work and fly here?

She returns her focus to the lake, smiling softly. "This visit was long overdue. For *all* of us."

That's not an answer, but I don't push, because it doesn't matter what Agnes's reason is for being here. She's here, and she brings with her an inexplicable sense of comfort.

"Some days are really hard," I admit in a whisper, leaning against the porch post.

"Some days were *never* going to be easy."

"I know." I watch Jonah adjust his baseball cap. "I guess I was expecting them all in the winter." That's all anyone ever talks about—the long, cold, dark nights that stretch forever. "And now Jonah's fighting fires all day long and I'm trying my best to be supportive. Meanwhile, I feel like I'm constantly worried. About *everything*."

"You'll always worry about him, no matter what. *I'll* always worry about him. That's what you do with the people you love." She sighs. "I think he's still figuring things out for himself." She reaches out to give my forearm a gentle pat. "You'll figure things out for yourself, too. I have faith."

Jonah's deep, bellowing laugh echoes clear across the lake.

I shake my head. "He's *so* loud."

"Jonah's always been loud." Her appraising dark eyes shift over the lake, to the trees beyond and the looming mountains. "But, no, it's just that quiet here. *Peaceful*," she says quickly, as if correcting herself. "Your own slice of heaven."

I think of the way Diana would sink into the wicker chair behind us, donning pajamas, a glass of wine cradled in her hands, and marvel at the vista and the serenity. "I think I like my slice more when I'm sharing it."

"You won't ever catch us complaining." She buries her smile in her mug.

"You know, you two should move here. Come live with us." It's an impulsive invitation, not at all considered, and yet as soon as the words escape, I know I mean them. The idea of having Agnes around warms my heart. She is a piece of my father as I knew him.

"A young couple needs their space, Calla."

Thoughts of last night—of the steady drumbeat of our headboard against the wall, of Jonah climaxing—make me flush. Permanent house guests *would* be hard, especially in our small house. "You could build your own cabin."

"My own cabin." She laughs and shakes her head, as if the idea is farfetched.

I examine the far end of our vast, private lake. "There's an old place on the other side, from, like, the '60s." I point in the general direction, because I'm not entirely sure where it is.

She squints as she searches the trees on the opposite shoreline.

"You can't see it. Everything has grown in, the cabin's old and musty, and *tiny*. Diana thinks I should try to fix it up and rent it out to weekenders." Couples, looking for a romantic escape. I don't know if that's even possible given its state, but I haven't been able to shake that idea since she suggested it. It would be nice to have signs of life within view.

"How'd you ever find it?"

"Muriel. She took me."

"Ah ... Yes." She frowns. "That is one motivated lady."

I snort. "That's one word for it." By the time I'd given Agnes, George, and Bobbie a tour of the house, and led them out to the garden, Mabel's fingers were already stained red with berry juice. George and Bobbie continued on their journey, and we spent the afternoon in the kitchen, filling dozens of sterilized jars with Colette's prized strawberry jam recipe, Muriel instructing through each step. "Anyway, she took me out one day. It's in surprisingly good shape, for as old as it is."

Agnes nods slowly. "Sounds like she's taking good care of you two."

"She gave me a *gun* for my birthday."

"Jonah mentioned." Agnes's eyes twinkle with her laughter. "Have you learned how to shoot it yet?"

"No. But I probably should," I admit reluctantly.

"It would be smart, given where you live," she agrees. "And I think that rental cabin is a good idea, too. I'm sure lots of people would enjoy it year-round."

Mabel lets out a playful shriek, followed by a firm, "No!"

"I haven't heard her like that in a while." Agnes smiles. But I also note how her eyes gloss over as she regards her daughter.

"Mabel is changing, huh?"

Agnes's mouth opens but she hesitates for a long moment. "One of her friends died a few weeks ago. He was from a village nearby."

"How—"

"Suicide."

My stomach clenches. I've never lost anyone close to me that way.

"He was a little older than her. Fifteen."

"Was he a friend? Or ..."

She gives me a knowing look. "I think more, though she wouldn't tell me. She knows I don't want her dating anyone yet. She's too young."

"How is she taking it?"

"She's managing. It happens around us, especially in the villages. It happens *too* much. People are isolated, there aren't a lot of options. They get hold of alcohol as an answer, even though it's not sold anywhere legally." She shakes her head. "This boy had a drinking problem, and I think *maybe* she's been drinking with him sometimes. There have been signs and behavior over the last few months ..." Her words drift.

Mabel? How did the bubbly, innocent twelve-year-old who chased chickens and took me to pick blueberries last summer change so much in a year?

The quiet on the screened-in porch has shifted to something disconcerting. "You should have told us, Agnes," I admonish.

"I didn't want to worry you. You have enough to focus on here. And Jonah, well, I'm not sure telling him is the best idea. He isn't the most graceful with communicating at times."

"Yeah. I get that." He's liable to yell at her, and where will that get him with a rebellious thirteen-year-old girl?

I watch Agnes closely. I had a feeling she was sugarcoating life in Bangor. I've noticed it in our phone calls, when she smoothly diverts the topic away from Aro, away from the new tenant in my father's house, away from her troubles with raising a teenager. Always away from her, and toward us.

I should have pushed, but *I've* been so focused on us, too.

"Are you happy?" I don't think I've ever asked her that outright.

"I'm ..." She frowns. "We're still trying to find our bearings. Without Wren and Jonah, life doesn't feel quite *alive* anymore." She offers a gentle smile. "But I think this little trip was a good idea for *all* of us." She watches the two figures on the lake. "It feels like I have my family back together."

Family.

Yes. That is exactly what this feels like.

CHAPTER THIRTY-SEVEN

When I pull up to Roy's place the next evening, Oscar and Gus charge me with excited barks, giving my pant leg a sniff before darting away to take up their sentry posts. The barn door is open, but the goats bleat noisily inside. Roy must be tending to them in there.

It's been two days since he left his "apology" on our doorstep. I'm not entirely sure why I'm here tonight, except for the simple truth that I spent all afternoon watching the clock and replaying Muriel's words from yesterday while internally debating my choices.

And now I'm here.

Instead of seeking Roy out, though, I head straight for the chicken coop, dragging the hose with me. Someone has shoveled out the chicken poop and replaced the pine shavings. I'd like to think it was Toby, but if there's anyone stubborn enough to attempt that with a collection of broken bones, it would be Roy.

I set to work, cleaning out and refilling the feeders, silently wagering with myself how many eggs I'll find when I check the roosts.

I sense rather than see eyes on me. When I look over, Roy is standing in the entryway of the barn, a rake in his good hand. His face is still bruised but the purple has faded some, now mottled with hints of green and yellow.

"Toby said you got a new truck," he calls out, his voice gruff as per usual.

"I did. A Jeep."

"Why didn't you drive it here?"

"I don't want to scratch up the paint."

He harrumphs but says nothing more about it, disappearing back into the barn.

I finish feeding and watering the flock for the night and then duck into Roy's house to leave the eggs—six!—along with a plate of Agnes's roasted chicken, strawberries that Agnes hulled, and the last slice of my birthday cake.

Roy is lugging a pail of milk when I emerge. The barn door has been pulled shut. It appears chores are done.

I head for my truck. "I have a million berries to sell at the farmers' market tomorrow night, so Toby will be here to help you." I booked my table this morning. Agnes and Mabel have eagerly signed up to help me.

He frowns and works his mouth as if tasting the words he wants to say before letting them out. "Will you be here in the mornin'?"

I pat Oscar on his head. "Yeah. I'll be here." Mabel sleeps until ten and Agnes has no issues entertaining herself. Though, she's been hinting at meeting the infamous Roy Donovan. I pause. "By the way, I have family visiting from Bangor until next week. If one of them is crazy enough to come here with me, you better be on your best behavior," I warn with a stare. "Because if you're a jerk to *them*? No amount of eggs or wooden jackasses on my doorstep will *ever* get me back here again." I climb into the driver's seat.

"Why'd you come back, girl?" he hollers after me, tilting his head with interest.

What *did* make me come back?

My pity for the cantankerous bastard who chases everyone away so they can't get too close?

Or is it my growing curiosity about the man who spent nine days in the woods, keeping Muriel company while she came to terms with the reality that her son was gone?

Or perhaps this has nothing to do with him, and everything to do with me.

Me, sensing that he likes having me around far more than he lets on.

Me, seeing Roy as another monumental challenge in this isolated life, but one that I can overcome.

Me, feeling like, if I can win over the man who keeps reminding me that I'll never fit in, then maybe I *will* belong.

Maybe all three. All I know is, I felt compelled to come.

"I must be really bored." With that, I start the engine and take off, the truck dipping and bumping through the potholes.

I catch a glimpse of Roy watching after me in the rearview mirror.

And I swear I see him smile.

———

"What's this for?" I survey the wooden crate, brimming with Roy's wooden figurines, that sits on the edge of the porch the next morning. Beside it are the dinner dishes I left last night, washed and stacked.

Roy shifts on his feet. The milk pail dangles from his good hand. "You said you're goin' to be at that farmers' market today, right?"

"Right," I say slowly.

"And you think people might wanna buy these things?"

"I do." I'm not sure if a farmers' market is the best place, though.

His weathered face furrows. "I won't be able to build anythin' for another month, at least. I need to make some money."

Roy's asking for my help. And, by the clench of his jaw, he's having a hard time doing it.

"How much should I sell them for?" I ask somberly.

I catch an almost inaudible sigh escape him. "Whatever you think you can get." He turns and trudges toward the barn.

I pull out one figurine, then another, marveling at the detail. "Have you at least signed them?" I ask, turning one over.

"Signed 'em?" He stops, his face twisting. "Why the hell would I do that?"

"Because these are art pieces!"

"They're not art. They're just *wood*," he mutters, as if the very idea is deplorable.

I roll my eyes. "They should be signed."

"Then sign 'em!"

"You want *me* to sign them?"

"I don't care who signs 'em. I ain't signin' shit." He disappears into the barn.

———

"Wait here, okay?"

"Yeah, sure." Mabel's eager eyes wander over Roy's property. "Where's Oscar?"

The wolf dog was at his usual post this morning to greet us when we reached the garden. Once Mabel knew he wasn't there to maul us, she became curious, then enamored. "I don't know. I don't see either of them. Be back in a minute."

I grab the wooden crate from the seat between us and carry it to Roy's front porch. I had planned on leaving it there for him to find in the morning, and yet now that I'm here, I feel compelled to knock.

Moments later, the door creaks open and Roy stands before me in a two-piece pajama set, scowling.

"I'm sorry. I didn't realize it was so … late?" It's only eight. The sun is nowhere near the horizon and won't be for hours. "We just got home from the farmers' market." I can't keep the wide grin from my face as I fish out the envelope of cash and thrust it forward. "We sold *all* but two of them."

Roy's eyebrows arch as he thumbs through the wad of twenties. "Huh … You were right."

"I can sell more next week, if you want. Lord knows I'll have more strawberries to get rid of." And Roy has hundreds of these to offload.

After a moment, he nods, his frown still on the money.

"Okay, well, I'll leave this on your counter for you?" I edge in past him to set the box on the counter, next to the full bottle of painkillers. "Where are the dogs, by the way?"

"Out huntin' for rabbits, probably. They'll be back soon."

"Lovely." I cringe, pushing out the visual of that poor animal's outcome. "I left Mabel in the truck so I should go—" My last word falters on my tongue as I spot the portrait of Roy and his family back in its place, on the trunk beneath the window. That wasn't there last night.

My eyes flash to Roy, to see him watching me, his face hard. Daring me to say something. As if I'd make that mistake again. "So, I'll see you in the morning." I move for the door, noting the rifle propped against the wall next to it. *Good grief, Roy.* I shake my head.

"Her name's Delyla."

I stop. The name spoken in the silence of this house is deafening.

"She's a few years older than you. Thirty-four, I think. Maybe thirty-five." He studies the floor. "I can't even remember anymore. It's been so long."

"That's a pretty name." My pulse pounds in my ears, the urge to ask him what happened overpowering. But I bite my tongue. "Have a good night, Roy." I hold my breath until I duck out the door, and then I let out a long, shaky breath. A smile stretches across my lips.

Mabel's head is bowed, her earbuds in, her attention glued to her phone. As per usual lately, it seems.

I take the stairs down, a slight spring in my step as my gaze drifts over my surroundings—the tidy stack of wood, the chicken coop, the heap of rusted trucks, the collection of water jugs and propane tanks, the brown bear in front of the barn door—

Every muscle in my body locks instantly, except for the one that controls my jaw.

My mouth drops open to scream.

No sound escapes.

Don't scream, I remind myself, clamping my lips together as my heart pounds. I steal a panicked glance toward Mabel, who happens to look up then to see my face. Her brow furrows in question.

"Bear." It's not loud, almost a whisper.

She must read the word on my lips, because her eyes begin frantically searching, spotting it only moments later.

The bear lets out a deep, rattling growl that makes every hair on my body stand on end. It swats at the ground with its paw in warning. It's too close.

I am too close.

"Calla ...?" Mabel calls out with alarm, yanking the cord for her earbuds.

"Close your window and stay in there," I warn, my voice taking on an odd, unfamiliar tone. Walking toward the truck would mean getting closer to it, and so I edge backward slowly, toward Roy's house, hoping it's not too late, that I'm not already too close.

I stumble as I try to climb the steps backward on shaky legs, and the bear takes several charging steps forward.

My breathing stops altogether, and cold calm settles over me as it moves in. This is it.

A horn blasts through the air, once and then a second and third time. Mabel is slamming her palm on the steering wheel in a desperate attempt to distract it. It seems to work, swinging the bear's attention to the pickup truck as it sidesteps to get away from the sudden and menacing sound from another direction.

I use that time to clamber to my feet and rush up the stairs.

Roy's front door flies open. "What the hell is goin'—" He sees my face, must see the terror, because he reaches inside and grabs his gun. "He's back again, is he?" He steps out onto the porch, sounding more annoyed than anything. "Get behind me."

I do as told without question as he searches out and locates the pacing bear. "I've given this thing enough goddamn chances."

A flurry of wild barking erupts from somewhere within the trees then, growing louder by the second as Oscar and Gus charge in, Gus in the lead.

"Heel!" Roy shouts, but the dogs don't listen, each taking a side as they approach the bear. It's more than twice the size of either wolf dog, and yet they herd him back toward the barn door, teeth bared with threatening snarls. The bear roars and swats, its lengthy claws slicing the air as they dive at its haunches before darting out of reach. It's only a matter of time before the bear connects.

Roy must be thinking the same. "He's gonna kill one of 'em. Maybe both," he says with certainly. "Come here."

I step forward without thought.

"Take this." He thrusts the gun into my hands.

I follow on autopilot as he roughly guides my grip, propping the butt of the gun into the ball of my shoulder.

His intentions finally register in my head. "I've never fired a gun, Roy," I admit, my voice hollow.

"It's easy. Point, aim, pull the trigger, watch the kickback. And try not to hit the dogs."

I falter, struggling with the weight and awkwardness of it as I train the muzzle on the massive brown body, silently regretting not taking Muriel's advice to learn how to do this.

"Come on, girl. Before he gets hold of one of them," Roy pushes.

A loud yelp sounds and Gus leaps away. The blood streaming down his side is glossy against his black fur. With him temporarily subdued, the bear turns on Oscar and charges forward. Oscar loses his footing and tumbles to the ground.

"Now, Calla!" Roy roars.

Steeling my shaky hands, I pull the trigger.

"One ... two ... three." Toby, Teddy, and Jonah hoist the body into the back of Toby's truck with a chorus of grunts and groans.

"Damn, this thing must weigh almost three hundred pounds," Jonah says, studying the motionless bear.

I flinch and turn away. The throb in my shoulder radiates from where the base of the gun recoiled upon firing and rammed into my flesh and bone. It all happened so quickly. One second, the bear was lunging for Oscar, and the next, it was on the ground, giving a few last twitches before stilling. Somehow, by sheer luck, and perhaps divine intervention, the bullet landed behind its front leg, to carve through fur and flesh and reach its heart.

An impossible kill shot for a girl who's never even fired a gun, apparently. It had Teddy scratching his head and Muriel nodding her head, impressed.

"You sure you don't want the meat, Roy?" Muriel asks.

He grimaces. "Thing's probably parasitic."

She looks to me and I shake my head. "You want me to call it in for you, or you gonna come by our place to use the phone?"

"I ain't callin' in shit."

Muriel's hands find her ample hips, as if she was waiting for this argument. "Now, Roy, you *know* you need to report this."

"So I can risk havin' someone come sniffin' around here, lookin' to stir up trouble? Hell no!"

I steal a glance toward the barn where Marie works on cleaning and stitching up a sizeable gash on a sedated Gus, Agnes and Mabel acting as observers and helpers. Nearby, Oscar paces on three legs. Thankfully, he earned only minor scratches.

What would the wildlife troopers do to them if they found them here?

"All right." Teddy chuckles, stepping in to settle a hand on Muriel's arm and defuse the shouting match that's about to erupt. "We'll have the hide and skull ready for you in a few days. You do with it whatever you want, okay, Roy?"

Roy grunts, his severe gaze flitting over all the vehicles in the driveway for the umpteenth time. Is he counting them? There are five in total, including my Jeep that Jonah and Agnes hopped into when Mabel called home to tell them what happened. Has he ever had this many people on his property at once? I doubt it. He looks apoplectic.

"Good job tonight, Calla," Muriel calls out and then climbs into Toby's pickup. The truck engine revs to life and then the McGivneys are coasting down the narrow laneway, the lifeless carcass in the back bobbing with each divot.

Jonah checks over his shoulder at Marie who is peeling latex gloves off her hands and collecting her supplies, her stitch work finished. "We should get goin', too."

My legs feel wobbly as I take a step, like they might not be able to carry me all the way home.

Jonah helps Marie carry Gus to the porch on a bedsheet to sleep off his sedative, while Agnes and Mabel load her truck. We thank her for coming—even Roy grants her a nod—and she takes off.

"You have a nice place here, Roy," Agnes offers with her signature soft smile, the one that would make you believe her, even if she doesn't mean it—but she always does. "Minus the bears. Come on, Mabel." They take my Jeep home, leaving Jonah and me with Roy.

"Remember when you said I probably wouldn't see a bear for *years*?" I wince as I test my arm.

Jonah grimaces, pulling me into his side. "Yeah, I'm not gonna hear the end of this, am I?"

I shoot him a glare.

"Put some ice on that shoulder. You'll be fine in a few days," Roy hollers from the porch. He pauses in thought. "Unless you want some painkillers."

"I heard those are addictive."

He snorts, the corner of his mouth twitching.

A curious frown flickers over Jonah's brow as he heads for the truck, not understanding.

Roy and I have an inside joke, I realize.

The porch creaks as Roy's weight shifts, the rifle in his grip. He's still in his pajamas. "Go on home, girl. You look like hell."

"I feel like puking." The nausea has clung to me since my adrenaline slowed. I *killed* something tonight. Worse, I don't know if I feel guilty or not about it. I know I'd feel a lot worse if something had happened to Oscar or Gus, or Mabel.

Or Roy.

"You had no choice. You don't think he could smell that little girl sittin' in the truck? And he *still* came up, lookin' for a meal." He throws a hand toward where the bear fell. Nothing but a small pool of blood remains.

Roy's right. I never noticed how close that bear was to her until now. And she had no clue. That bear could have strolled right past her open window. It could have tried to get in ... A wave of cold dread hits me as my memory replays that deep, grating growl and those vicious claws.

"Can't have bears like that roamin' around. It's only a matter of time before somethin' bad happens. I'll bet you surprised the hell out of him tonight. That could have gone a different way for you." His brow wrinkles, as if he's considering another scenario. When he catches me watching him, he smooths his expression. "Then I'd be dealin' with a pile more people here tonight, and what a pain in my ass that'd be."

I can't help but laugh. "Yeah, that would be a real *inconvenience* for you."

His lips quirk. "That's right. It would be. Go on and get some rest." He turns for his door.

"By the way, I signed your carvings for you!" I call out after him.

He pauses. "You put my name on those things?" I can't tell if he's angry.

"Not exactly. See you in the morning."

After a long moment, he shuffles inside and shuts his door softly.

On instinct, I hang back a few beats, holding my breath as I watch through the tiny window that gives a view of his kitchen. Roy fishes one of the two remaining pieces from the wooden crate, flips it over, and squints at the writing on the base.

His bearded cheeks lift with a smile and a moment later, a low chuckle carries through the quiet night.

I'm disappointed when Jonah starts the truck's engine and drowns out the sound.

CHAPTER THIRTY-EIGHT

August

The shower is running when I arrive home. I head upstairs.

"Hey!" I holler, stepping into our cramped bathroom. I push the toilet lid down and take a seat, eying Jonah's shampoo-laden head rinsing off beneath the stream of water. "You're home early." It's only three and, while Jonah has been working less these last few weeks, this is an unusually short day for him.

"I went north today. There's a fire burnin' up near Mile 91."

"I heard they closed down the highway." It seems like fires are sparking all around us. "How bad is it?" We're only about twenty miles south of there.

"They've got it about 70 percent contained."

I sigh with relief. "Good."

"We're supposed to get rain tonight and into tomorrow."

"Oh! So that means you'll be grounded?"

"Can you try not to sound so excited about that?" His wry tone makes me laugh.

The truth is, mention of rain does get me excited, not just to keep Jonah to myself but also for the garden. We haven't gotten nearly enough. I spend a good hour watering every day. It's therapeutic when I don't have things to do. When I do, it's a pain in the ass.

"How was your day?"

"Good." I examine my fingernails. They're short and naked, but healthier after having months without tips. "I took those pieces of Roy's to that art shop in Anchorage." The more elaborate carvings were too nice to sell at the Trapper's Crossing Farmers' Market, where I have successfully offloaded dozens of pieces for Roy over the last month. I've come to enjoy the surprise in his eyes every time I show up with an envelope of cash, as if he can't believe people would appreciate his woodwork. He's even offered to cover the cost of the table fee, now that I'm out of strawberries to sell. "She's putting them up on consignment. She thinks she can get a good price for each one."

The water shuts off. Jonah yanks the curtain open wide and grabs the towel from the hook.

My mouth goes dry as I watch him wipe down his body.

He steps out, stopping long enough to stoop and kiss my lips, before he tosses the towel back on the bar and strolls into our bedroom. "Does that asshole have any idea how much you're doing for him?"

I trail him, enjoying a sublime glimpse of his backside as he roots around in his dresser drawer for underwear. Things with Roy have become more than tolerable. I go there in the morning and the evening. We work around each other, completing chores. Our conversations are sparse, but that perpetual air of annoyance that used to swirl around him seems to have evaporated. It could be because he's feeling better—the gash and bruising on his face have faded, his ribs and collarbone seem to have mended—but I'd like to think it's something else.

I'd like to think it's because Roy Donovan enjoys my company.

I look up to find Jonah smirking—he caught me with my admiring gaze trained low. "He doesn't need to know."

Jonah chuckles, drawing his boxer briefs up his muscular legs. "Mark Sheppard asked me if I could fly him and his buddy up to their cabin near Murder Lake."

"Fill out an itinerary," I warn him.

He chuckles. "Yeah, yeah. It's not far. Actually, I was gonna see if you wanted to come."

"As much fun as flying to a place called *Murder Lake* sounds and having my ears talked off—" Mark *loves* to talk. I once called his office to arrange billing and it took me forty minutes and five *I should let you go*s before I could break free. "I have to meet Emily in an hour to go over our plans ahead of next week's meeting, and then I'm heading over to Roy's."

I was nervous, approaching Emily about my ideas, given the weak start to our relationship. But she has warmed since then. She's still painfully shy, but she's also collaborative and talented with drawing and photography and willing to help me come up with a fun and creative social media campaign.

"Isn't he all healed up yet?"

"Cast comes off next week."

Jonah tugs on his jeans. "I talked to my mom today. Told her we were staying in Alaska for Christmas."

"How'd she take it?" It's been a few years since Jonah saw his mother.

He sighs heavily. "They want to come here."

"Oh my God, it's actually happening." A week with my boyfriend's mother—whom I've never met—and a stepfather whom Jonah despises. Throw in my psychoanalyzing stepfather and a mother who fusses over minute details, and this could spell disaster.

"Huh?"

I push my worries aside. "That's great! So ... We'll have a full house." We *really* need a dining table.

"Yeah." He snorts. "Both sets of parents *and* Aggie and Mabel? How the hell are we gonna fit everyone in?"

"Are Agnes and Mabel coming, too?"

"Damn right, they're comin'. If I have my way, they'll be living here by then." He shakes his head. "Maybe we can put my mom and Dickhead up in a hotel."

"We *can't* put them up in a hotel on Christmas after they've flown from Oslo."

"Fine. Maybe *we* can stay at a hotel," he mutters, buckling his belt. "I wonder how much one of those places at the McGivneys' would cost to build. We could build a cabin to stick them in for the week. We have enough property."

I watch him pull a T-shirt from another drawer and yank it over his head, hiding his body. But my mind is spinning. This is as good a time as any.

"Hey, can you spare a half hour? I want to show you something."

The hinges creak noisily. "Put that there?" I nod at the small boulder.

Jonah props the door open, and we step inside.

His curious blue eyes roam the four dark corners. "Can't believe Phil never said anything about this place."

"I know, right?" I mentioned the cabin that same day Oscar's foot got caught and intended to bring Jonah out, but time passed and it has sat here, alone.

But not forgotten.

"What do you think about fixing it up?"

"*This* place?" His hand strokes his beard in thought as he does a slow circle, searching the walls. "I don't know. It's small. And it wouldn't be cheap."

"It's not as bad as I thought it would be." I grin sheepishly. "I already had this guy from Anchorage who restores old cabins come up to see it and give me a quote. His name is Steve and he said it was built really well, and it looks like Phil somewhat maintained it through the years."

"So, he did maintain something?" Jonah asks wryly, but he's smiling. "How long have you been thinkin' about this?"

"Since Diana was here, and then Agnes and Mabel." I shrug. "I like having people around. We have an incredible spot here. We could rent it out for weekends. Put it on Airbnb. I'm sure couples would love it."

He ambles outside, peering upward. "Needs a new roof."

"And windows, and some more weatherproofing, and heating, and plumbing, and a laneway in ..." I recite all the expenses I've been tallying. "And I've been looking at ways to make it ecological. I think it'd be neat, you know? To have an efficient cabin here. And see how close it is to the water?" I cut through the trees, adjusting the rifle slung over my shoulder as I push through branches to reach the rocky shoreline, thirty feet away. After the bear incident at Roy's last month, Jonah set up a target in our backyard. I've become adept at loading and firing.

Jonah sidles up beside me to look out on the lake, at our log cabin on the opposite side. "You'd never know this is here."

"We'll have to cut down some of these trees so there's a view."

He looks from our place to the cabin behind us. "We can't get this done by Christmas. There's no way."

I exhale slowly. "Actually? I kind of already hired Steve and started the work. All the permits came through this week. They're coming to cut down trees for a laneway and then they're going to do all the exterior work and plumbing before the snow, so they can focus on the inside in November. This is why I decided to not go to Toronto, so I can be here to make sure the work happens. And I know we agreed to discuss big spending and this is *way* more than a thousand dollars, but I'm really excited about it. I was trying to find the right way to tell you because I was afraid you'd think I was insane." I hold my breath as I offer him a hopeful smile.

Jonah's jaw hangs. He stares at me, his expression unreadable beyond shock.

I want to offload all my fantastical planning before he blows up. "So, the laneway will branch off from our main drive over there." I point to the far end of the lake. "And then we could use all that wood from the trees to build *another* cabin—something bigger—for Agnes and Mabel to live in, because I loved having them here, and I think that if there was a place for them to move in to, Agnes would agree to it—"

"Marry me."

My rambling words die on a croak. "*What?*"

He collects my hands in his and pulls me into him. His earnest eyes roam my features. "Marry me, Calla."

My heartbeat, which was already racing, now pounds in my ears as I search for words. "Because I went behind your back and spent a shit ton of money?"

"No." He leans forward, pressing his forehead against mine, his breath skating across my lips. "Because I want to be here when you renovate this old shack, and build a cabin for Aggie and Mabel, and build *a thousand* more cabins on our property, if that's what you wanna do. I want to be here for it *all*." His throat bobs with his hard swallow. "You're thinking about the future? Well, so am I, and don't want *any* future that doesn't have you in it."

I let out a breathy laugh. The last time Jonah intended to propose, it was a scripted event. Now, we're standing in the thicket, I'm coated in bug spray, a gun slung over my shoulder. I was not expecting this. Not here, not today. "What about not rushing?"

He brushes strands of wayward hair off my forehead. "You think we're rushing?"

"No." I shake my head.

"Me neither."

A bubble rises inside me, of nerves and excitement and emotion, ready to erupt. My eyes burn with tears of happiness. "Are you sure, though? Because you can't ask me something like this and then change your mind later." A sense of déjà vu hits me, of an early morning in the airport last November, surrounded by the bustle of travelers, when I decided to alter the course of my life. Though, truth be told, it had been forever changed the moment I met Jonah.

"I've never been surer of anything in my life," he promises, cupping my face with his hands, brushing his lips against mine. "Is that a yes?"

"My answer will *always* be yes to you, Jonah. *Yes.*"

The kiss he presses against my lips is deep and slow. "I don't even have your ring. I mean, I *have* it, but it's at the house—"

"I know. I've seen it already."

He pulls back, showing me his quirked brow.

"It fell out of your coat pocket. It was totally accidental, I swear! And it's beautiful."

His melodic chuckle carries over the water as he folds me into his arms.

I stare in shock as I set a Tupperware container of dinner—a spicy penne dish with beef and homegrown tomatoes—on the porch. "What the hell happened to your cast?" Roy's appointment to have it removed isn't until next week, and yet here he is, dragging the hose toward the chicken coop, no cast to be seen.

"I didn't need it anymore." He stretches his right arm out in front of him as if to prove it. It seems to be working just fine.

"So you, what? *Cut it off?*"

"Yeah. With a handsaw," he says matter-of-factly, as if that's a reasonable option.

A mental image of a rusted blade cutting through flesh hits me and I cringe. "Jesus, Roy. You could have cut your arm off! What would you do around here? How would you survive?"

He snorts. "No, you don't sound like Muriel *at all*."

I roll my eyes as I reach for the gate to the coop, my gaze landing on my engagement ring. Storm clouds are swiftly moving in, smothering any chance of catching the sun's glitter off the countless facets, but a thrill courses through me, nonetheless. I haven't stopped admiring the intricate snowflake design since Jonah slipped it on my finger.

Jonah and I are engaged.

We're getting married.

He's mine, forever.

Roy does a double take, his focus lingering on my hand a moment, before he moves into the coop to rinse out the chicken feeder. Several birds have darted out the open door, only to turn around and scurry back, clucking as Oscar steps toward them. "So, I guess you can head on home, then. Got no reason to be draggin' yourself over here anymore."

"No, I guess not." An unexpected disappointment stirs in my chest with the reality that my duty here is done, and a week earlier than I anticipated. But Roy has fully mended, almost two months after his accident. He's right, though. There's no need for me to be here, other than for the simple reason that I've grown accustomed to coming. I'm used to the long, bumpy drive up the laneway every day, to completing simple tasks and trading painless barbs with a man who has never once used the words "thank you" for the meals I've drop off or the help I've provided. He's thanked me in other ways, though. With the eggs he tells me to take home and the jars of goat's milk he sends with me for Jonah. I happened to mention Jonah loving moose meat, and the next day Roy thrust a frozen roast into my hands, claiming it was rancid from being in the freezer too long. But I cooked it following Agnes's detailed instructions and Jonah said it was one of the best cuts he'd had in a long time.

No one will ever accuse Roy of being "nice," and yet I've come to believe that if I ever needed him, he would step up. My life here would certainly be less interesting without him in it.

I slip the catalogue page from the back pocket of my jeans. "Hey, so I was wondering if you'd consider building me this." I unfold it before I hand it to him.

He frowns at the picture. "A table?"

"Yeah. Live edge. We have all this family coming in for Christmas, and I don't have a proper table yet." What does Roy do for Christmas? Nothing, I presume.

"Why don't you buy it, then, with all your money."

I shrug. "I'd rather have something locally made, not mass produced."

He grunts. "I don't do custom orders." But he's studying the picture, I note.

Toby did tell me that once, so I was prepared for the pushback. I school my expression. "Well ... what if you just happened to feel compelled to make this table that seats, say, ten people, and then, when it was finished, I just happened to see it and buy it from you?"

His bushy eyebrow arches. "*Compelled*, huh?"

"Yes. Compelled." I pause. "Unless you think it's too hard for you to—"

"I could make that damn thing in my sleep! It's nothin'. Just some lacquered wood and legs."

Jonah said basically the same thing about the overpriced living room tables I want. Something tells me this would be far more complicated.

"Okay, great! So, while you're sleeping, if you happened to make it ..." I back away, moving for the pickup truck, before he can thrust the page back into my hand. I'm excited to get home to see Jonah, anyway. We parted ways soon after he slipped the ring on, both of us having places to be. He'll be back by now. "Oh! Also, I want to hire a carpenter for some built-in shelves beneath our staircase, if you know anyone who'd be interested. Meals and delightful company included, of course." I turn before he can see my smile.

"Hey!" he barks as I'm about to climb in.

I turn, holding my breath.

"Congratulations." He nods once and then turns back to his task.

————

The ramp where Jonah secures Veronica is still empty when I coast up our lengthy driveway, home from Roy's. I frown as I check my watch. Jonah's a half hour late. I know he arrived at Mark's cabin as scheduled because he called to touch base. Which means he's likely standing on his float, waiting for a break from Mark's incessant gabbing to fly home. I look to the north where dark storm clouds hang.

My phone rings and Diana's mocking duck-face profile picture appears on my phone. An excited thrill bubbles in my stomach as I answer. "It took you this long to call me? What kind of best friend are you?" I say in greeting, a wide grin on my face as I continue up the driveway, past our hangar, toward the house. It's been exactly four minutes since I sent her a text with a picture of my ring.

"We're both getting married!" she shrieks.

The truck's cab fills with the sound of our collective screams and laughter.

————

I stand in front of the window, huddled in a sweater, the rain and wind pelting the glass as the storm rages outside. "He should have been home by now, and he's not answering." My heart feels like it's lodged in my throat.

"Mark likes to gab sometimes—"

"No." I'm shaking my head, though she can't see it. "I called Mark. I talked to him." When the minutes began to stretch, I tried his office. Luckily his wife answered and was willing to pass along their satellite phone number. "He said the storm was coming in faster than expected and Jonah didn't hang around at all. He was in a rush to get back home."

Tears stream down my cheeks as the conversation replays in my mind—that the weather looked treacherous, that Mark told Jonah to stay with them for the night. "I have a *really* bad feeling, Agnes." Is this what she felt, that fateful day when Mabel's father didn't arrive at his destination?

There's a moment of silence on the other end, and then Agnes quietly says, "Call it in, Calla."

"You're like a caged bear lookin' for a way out," Muriel chides, handing Teddy another mason jar. He wordlessly dries it with a tea towel, sets it on the counter, and waits for the next.

I ignore her, hugging my chest as I pace back and forth in front of our bay window, my gaze locked on the murky sky, desperately waiting to catch a glimpse of the familiar white-and-black-striped plane.

I *am* looking for a way out, I think to myself.

A way out of this nightmare.

What I've feared most is becoming a reality.

Muriel knocked once and then strolled into the house as I stood in the kitchen, reading off details of Jonah's itinerary to the state troopers, my hands trembling so hard, I struggled to see the words. She listened for a few minutes and then stepped outside, sliding her rarely used phone from her pocket. Shortly after, Teddy and Toby pulled up in Toby's burgundy truck. They've lingered since, Muriel tasking Toby with fetching empty jars from the cellar so she and Teddy can prepare them for canning.

But all *I* can do is pace, my cell and the satellite phones gripped tightly in my fists, and choke down the mounting dread as I wait for news from the Alaska Air National Guard.

It's been almost four hours since Jonah was expected back. The storm has already passed, leaving a cold, steady drizzle. It's darker than usual at this time on account of the weather. Soon, it'll be too dark to see anything on the ground.

My cell phone rings.

My heart stops as I check the screen, only to see that it's my mother calling. I ignore it—I can't deal with anyone right now—and continue pacing.

"Come on. Let's keep our minds busy with—"

"I can't!" I shriek, tears erupting in rivulets as I face off with Muriel. "I can't do *anything* right now! I can barely breathe!"

All three of them pause, sympathy filling their expressions.

"He asked me to marry him today," I continue in a hoarse whisper. The ring on my finger suddenly weighs a hundred pounds. "We're supposed to spend the rest of our lives together. He's my *entire* world. Why can't he just come back?"

Muriel squeezes her eyes shut and nods. She knows what this feels like—this agonizing wait.

How long will it take them to find him?

Hours?

Days?

What if they *never* find him?

My chest feels like it's going to cave in with these foreboding thoughts. "I need air." I rush for the front door.

"Give her some space, Mom," I hear Toby whisper, warning his mother from following.

Out on the quiet front porch, I curl up in a wicker chair, wrapping the blanket around my numb body.

And I wait, for a fate that I fear was inevitable all along.

With my stomach in my throat, I track the small glowing globes of headlights as they crawl up our driveway, just after eleven.

Have the state troopers come to tell me they've found Jonah's body? Have they decided that a phone call is not enough? What is standard protocol for this sort of news?

I breathe a sigh of relief when the floodlight illuminates a plain black truck with scratched-up sides parking next to Marie's truck.

Roy came.

Why is Roy here?

It's a fleeting question that I quickly dismiss. It doesn't matter why, I decide, as I sip on the tea Muriel wordlessly brought out an hour ago—now cold in my grasp. There's nothing else for me to do as I wait for news.

It's been more than five hours.

My vacant stare is searching the dark when the porch door creaks open and Roy slips in, wearing the same outfit he wore that night to the Ale House. Our eyes glance off each other and for a moment, I fear the insensitive comment that will fall from his mouth, that will somehow make this worse.

But then he slips off his cowboy hat and strolls over to settle into the wicker chair beside me, stretching his legs out in front of him, boots crossed, as if to get comfortable.

A loud clatter sounds inside.

"I take it Muriel's inside, rearranging your house?" His Texan drawl is rough and grating as usual.

"Who knows what she's into now?" I don't have that many jars to wash, but I know she'll find something to keep herself busy. She and Marie, who showed up about an hour ago, after Toby called her. By the hushed whispers and the fact that he had her number in the first place, I suspect they've taken my advice and gone on at least one date.

Another long moment passes and then Roy's exhale cuts into the silence. "Any news yet?"

I shake my head.

"Well ... No news is good news."

No news just means they haven't found Jonah's body yet.

It means he could be lying somewhere, alone, suffering.

There are multiple scenarios running through my head, and none of them look *good*.

A fresh wave of tears prick my eyes. "How did you know?"

"Toby came by on his way here."

Why would Toby ... I dismiss the question before it fully forms. That doesn't matter, either. "He wanted me to go with him. I should have gone."

"Then you'd be wherever he is right now."

"It's where I belong." Beside Jonah, in the sky or in the ground.

But always by his side.

I feel Roy studying my profile as I huddle in my blanket.

"You'll survive this. You're tough."

I laugh, the sound hollow. "No, I'm not."

"Yeah, you are. You're tough in your own way, Calla. You'll survive this."

"What if I don't want to survive this?" I'll never complain about Alaska again. I'll live here until I'm old and gray, never thinking of a way out, never wishing I were somewhere else, as long as I can have Jonah. I feel idiotic now. I let such trivial worries consume me for so long.

"It's never up to us, though, is it?"

Heavy footfalls sound from inside a moment before the door creaks open. The low hum of voices on the TV carries out. "Oh, you're here." Muriel nods to Roy as she plucks the cold mug from my hand, still mostly full. "I'm makin' you more tea. Roy, you want tea? I'll make you tea." With that, she turns around and disappears inside.

"I don't like tea," I admit after she's gone.

"Neither do I, but every once in a while, I let that battle-ax get her way."

Despite everything, I feel a small smile curl my lips, imagining the two of them out in the woods for nine days and nights. The conversations those two must have had ... "Muriel told me you helped her look for Deacon, way back when."

He makes a sound but doesn't respond.

I don't care if he's annoyed that I know. Let him yell at me for bringing it up; it'll slide off me like water off a duck's back. Or a goose's back, perhaps. The goose wife who waits to find out if she has lost her raven. "Why'd you do it?"

Roy doesn't answer for a long moment, his eyes roaming the dark, as if trying to make out the tree line from here. "Because I owed her. Because a long time ago, she was the one out there, searchin' for *my* kin."

I frown. "Muriel?"

"I don't remember much, but I do remember bein' hungry and cold and miserable, and listenin' to my parents fight about food." He picks at a button on his shirt. "My father went out to check the snares for rabbits. He couldn't catch his own foot if he stepped in a trap, but the stubborn SOB was determined not to ask for help." He smirks. "In case you were wondering where I get that from. My mother got tired of waitin', so she bundled up and left our house in a blizzard with the last of our money. She was gonna go to the store and see what she could buy, so we wouldn't starve. Told me to stay put. And that's the last time I saw her. Alive, anyway."

An odd sense of recognition tickles me as he tells this story, as if I've heard it before.

"When the locals caught wind, a bunch of 'em spent days combing the forest and the road, lookin' for her. There was this one girl with 'em. She was older than me by a few years and had a gun slung over her shoulder. She seemed tough as nails. I told myself I needed to be tough like her if I had a hope in hell of survivin' up here." His lips quirk. "They finally found my mother. She was frozen solid. They figure she got lost 'cause she was way off course. Probably died that first night."

Cold realization washes over me. "That cabin." I point across the lake. "That was yours." Roy may sound like a Texan, but there was a time that he and his family came to Alaska to try to make a life for themselves here.

And that tough-as-nails girl out there helping search for his mother was Muriel.

"Does Muriel know?" She didn't sound like she did.

He shakes his head.

She doesn't remember, and he's never told her.

I struggle to piece the rest of the story together as I remember her tell it. "So, then ... you and your father went back to Texas. No, wait." I frown. "Muriel said you were from Montana?" The same place her own family was from. That much, she remembered.

"When we left Alaska, my dad didn't want anythin' to do with snow, so we headed south, all the way to a town outside Dallas. That's where I grew up, buildin' houses and barns with my pa. He was always real smart with wood. I learned from him." His fingers trace the brim of his hat. "By the time I found my way back, the land was already sold to someone else. So, I took the closest lot available."

"That cabin was built really well." Steve the contractor was amazed at how well it has withstood the elements. Everything had been done right—the solid foundation, the right wood, the wide overhangs, the drainage slope. The fact that the area has overgrown has helped protect it from the sun. "You can go see it. I mean, if you want."

His lips twist. "I've been by a few times over the years. To clean out the gutters. Phil woulda let it rot."

I think Roy's been doing more than cleaning out gutters. Steve said it looked like someone's been treating the exterior wood—with linseed oil and turpentine, he guessed—and patching the roof.

Roy's been preserving his family's history in Alaska, however tragic it was.

"Why would you ever want to come back after all that?" He lost his mother *and* his brother to this wilderness.

And then he lost his wife and daughter to something else.

Wouldn't be the first time a person ran here to escape somethin'.

That's what Jonah had said, that night after I saw the picture of Roy's family in his house, the day the wood came down on top of him.

Jonah ...

I close my eyes against the terror that floods back to the forefront, dulled by a moment's distraction.

Silence hangs in the cold, damp front porch, until Muriel barrels out with two hot teas, setting them onto the small outdoor side tables I ordered, along with a bowl of sugar and glass of milk. "That's your goat milk, Roy," she says before heading back inside, not waiting for a thank-you. It's shocking that she never put the pieces together to Roy's family history in Trapper's Crossing, being the busybody she is. Then again, she was young, the Donovan family's stint here was brief and secluded, and many decades have passed. Why would *anyone* suspect that the little boy who lost so much to this place would come back years later?

"What are the chances she's put arsenic in mine?" he studies it warily. "Lord knows I'd deserve it."

"Why?" I find myself asking. "What'd you do, Roy?" It's a loaded question—did he do something bad to Muriel? Did he do something

bad to someone else?—and I ask it freely, not caring about reper-
cussions.

The clang of metal against china sounds as Roy fills his tea with
three heaping teaspoons of sugar and stirs. "I wasn't always this
pleasant."

I snort at his twisted attempt at humor.

He brings his tea to his lips, and takes a long, slow sip. "I've had
trouble with vices in the past. Booze … pills … that sort of thing. And
I could get real nasty when somethin' set me off. Truth is, it didn't
take much to set me off. My wife and I went out on the town one
night. Hadn't been out in ages, since Delyla was born. Now, Nicole?
She was a real looker. Turned heads wherever she went. I hated it
and loved it at the same time." He hesitates. "That night we ran into
an old flame of hers. He was the one who got away, and he was back
in town for good. I knew, from the second they laid eyes on each
other, that I was in trouble. At least that's what the whiskey told me.

"One thing led to another and fists started flying. I hit him … I
don't know how many times." He cradles the hot mug in his hand,
staring intently at it. "He wasn't the only one I hit that night."

I try to digest what Roy is admitting to, and I'm suddenly
thankful that I'm already numb.

"So you ran to Alaska?"

"When I sobered up and saw what I'd done to Nicole's face …"
His head shake is almost indecipherable. "It's how I remembered my
mother's face, after one of their fights. Swore I'd never be like him."

"We do that, don't we?" I murmur absently, thinking how many
times I've promised myself the same.

"Nicole was always too good for me. She knew it, I knew it. Her
family damn well knew it. So, I packed my bags and they made sure
she didn't stop me."

No wonder Roy doesn't like talking about his past. Who would
ever want to admit that he hit his own wife?

"Have you talked to Nicole since?"

"Just long enough to tell her where to send the divorce papers.
And she did. My guess is she remarried." He nods slowly. "Good for
her."

I don't know what I'd feel toward Roy right now if I weren't drowning in my own misery.

Anger?

Disgust?

Pity?

Sympathy?

All the above?

Thirty-something years ago, in a drunken rage, Roy laid fists to his wife and then took off to Alaska.

What does he deserve?

Roy has spent three decades in a form of exile, where he couldn't hurt anyone he loved ever again, where he wouldn't let anyone near him ever again, unwilling to take even one painkiller for fear of what he's capable of when he loses control.

What exactly does Roy Donovan deserve?

Maybe on another day, in another headspace, I would have an opinion.

"We were going to restore the cabin so it could be used again," I hear myself say. "They were supposed to start next week."

To that, Roy says nothing.

The steady drizzle intensifies to heavy rain, the drops slapping the water and gravel around us, soaking the ground. Jonah would be glad to see this rain.

Jonah ...

It was supposed to be an easy trip. In and out, back in a few hours, he promised.

The shrill ring of my phone makes me jump. My eyes snap to the screen and the number displayed turns my stomach. I will my shaky hand toward it but find myself frozen—stuck between needing an answer and wanting to cling to this last shred of hope.

Or delusion.

"I can't." The two words are almost inaudible as I struggle to breathe.

Roy hesitates for only a second before collecting my phone. He takes a deep breath and then answers.

I squeeze myself tight.

And I pray.

I pray.

I pray that Jonah will come back to me.

"Uh-huh ... Uh-huh."

Our front door creaks open. Both Muriel and Marie poke their heads out to listen. They must have heard the ring. Marie is clutching her stomach, Muriel is holding her breath.

"Yeah ... Uh-huh ..." Roy's gaze darts to me and he swallows.

That isn't good.

The news can't be good.

I press my lips together in my struggle to control my sobs, as I fight to hold on to hope for the last possible second.

"Yeah ... Okay ... Thank you, sir." Roy ends the call and sets my phone on the table. "They found his plane in a valley north of Palmer," he confirms somberly. "He's alive."

I pray.

CHAPTER THIRTY-NINE

"Two crashes in a year since I've met you. I'm beginning to think you're bad luck, Barbie," Jonah croaks from his hospital bed.

I burst into tears at the sound of his voice as relief overwhelms me.

"Hey, hey, hey ..." He reaches with his good arm out, beckoning me.

"You jerk." I slip my fingers into his and settle on the edge of the bed.

"I'm sorry." He pulls my hand to his mouth. His lips are so dry. "I took a stupid risk. I didn't think the storm would be that bad and if I stayed low in the valley, I'd be fine. I just ... I wanted to get home to you so bad."

"You almost didn't make it back again, ever." The downdraft Jonah got caught in slammed Veronica into the ground. The state trooper I spoke to said it was a good thing he was flying where he was, otherwise those wind gusts would likely have put him into the side of a mountain, and no one walks away from that.

As it is, Jonah has enough broken bones and cuts to keep him grounded and busy with healing.

He tries to adjust his position and winces.

"Stay put," I scold, checking the IV drip attached to him that is administering his pain meds.

"Me and Roy are twins now."

"Yeah. You two would have almost matched." A concussion, a broken collarbone, a shattered left arm that required surgery and pins to put back together, several cracked ribs, a punctured lung, and scrapes and bruises all over his body.

But Jonah's alive, I remind myself, as I've done a thousand times over since that phone call came in. That's all that matters.

His jaw tenses as he stares at the ceiling tile above his bed. "They said Veronica's totalled."

"Yeah. I've already called the insurance company."

"That was Wren's favorite plane."

It *was* his favorite plane. It was the last plane he ever flew, with me in the passenger seat. And I know that wrecking it hurts Jonah more than all his injuries combined.

I smooth a strand of hair off his forehead. "And he'd tell you that it's just a plane and he's happy you're all right. I know because it's what he said *the last time* you crashed his plane."

Jonah snorts, but his face remains serious. "You regretting this yet?" He takes my left hand in his, his thumb smoothing over my ring.

"No. Why would I ever?"

Earnest blue eyes trace my features. "There was a stretch there, when I woke up, and couldn't get out, couldn't move—"

That ball in my throat flares as I'm hit with an image of what that must have looked like from the air. They said they weren't expecting to find a survivor. They said it was a miracle Jonah survived and in the relatively good shape he's in.

"And all I could think about was you, and how I was gonna break my promise about finding my way back. How you were gonna wish you'd never met me."

Fresh tears stream down my face as I shake my head. "I could *never* regret you, Jonah." Not if I'd lost him last night, not if I lose him in five years or fifty.

He swallows. "Are you gonna be able to handle me flyin' again?"

"Jesus. You're insane." I can't help but laugh. "Can we just focus on you healing first?" It hasn't even been twenty-four hours since he nearly died. He won't be flying again for months. His firefighting days are done for the season, and Jack Thomas will have to find himself another pilot for his rich hunters.

"Yeah, fine. Come here," he whispers holding his arm out.

Ever so slowly, I ease in and stretch out against his side, balancing precariously close to the edge of the hospital bed. I gingerly rest my head against the crook of his arm. My tears soak into his blue hospital gown. "I know you're going to fly again, and I would never try to tell you not to. Just please promise me you'll never take a risk like that again. I'd rather spend a hundred nights alone if it means you were going to come back to me safe at the end of it."

"That promise, I know I can keep." He shutters his eyes. The doctor said he'd be groggy.

I bring his hand to my mouth, to kiss his knuckles, and then I ease back to sit, intent on letting him sleep.

"You weren't alone last night while you waited, were you?"

"No, no ... everyone was there." Toby drove me in my Jeep to Anchorage, where they airlifted Jonah.

"Who's everyone?"

"Well, not Agnes, but the McGivneys and Marie, and Roy—"

"Roy?"

"Yeah. I was surprised, too."

Jonah makes a sound, but he says nothing.

"Listen, you need your sleep. I'm going to get Agnes and Mabel before you fall asleep. They're in the waiting room. George flew them in."

"Have you told them about their cabin yet?"

I laugh. "No. You can. Take full advantage of their pity for you and make them agree to it."

He smirks. "Done. Come and give me a kiss first."

I lean in to press a teasing kiss on his forehead.

"Not there."

I peck his nose.

He groans.

With a smile, I savor his lips.

Jonah lets out a contented sigh. "I can't wait to get home so you can wait on me hand and foot."

"Oh, you think so." I laugh. It feels so good to laugh with Jonah.

"Can you get me a cowbell?"

"Sure. I'll also tell you where you can shove it." My gaze trails the gash above his left eyebrow.

"How many stitches?"

I count them. "Six, I think?" I smooth my palm over his beard. It needs a trim. "At least it's smaller than the last one."

He laces his fingers through mine. "Am I still pretty enough for you?"

CHAPTER FORTY

December

The cold bites my cheeks as I sail across the frozen lake on the snow machine, and for a moment, I regret mocking the neoprene face mask Jonah brought home for me ahead of this cold spell. I complained that I would look like a criminal.

But at least I'd look like a criminal without frostbite.

I pull up next to the other snow machine parked at the edge of the shoreline. Oscar and Gus catch up, their tails wagging. "I win!" I tease, giving Oscar a head scratch as I climb off my seat. Lately, the wolf dogs spend more time here than at their home.

I march up the cleared path, marveling at the winter wonderland before me. It snowed for the last four days straight before the drastic temperature drop, blanketing the earth in white. The tree branches sag beneath the weight of their snow coats, sprinkling me with snowflakes as I brush past.

Ahead, the small log cabin sits nestled within the forest, soft light filling the two new windows we cut into the lakeside wall for more light and a view. A steady stream of smoke curls up into the frosty air above it. All around, the trees have been trimmed back to allow for light while also respecting nature.

Behind the cabin, on the narrow laneway we put in last August, sits the scratched-up black truck, with its tires chained and its bed loaded with carpentry tools.

"You two stay here," I order as I kick off the snow from my boots, leaving the hounds on the porch. Warmth envelops me the moment I push through the new red door. "It's *so* damn cold out there." I shudder for emphasis, inhaling the scent of fresh-cut wood as I do every time I come here. While the cabin was in good shape, I wanted a bright, clean feel inside. Everything has been clad with new wood, with a rolling barn-door-type wall to separate the bedroom from the living space and a tiny bathroom in the far right corner, behind the compact kitchen that Roy is putting finishing touches on.

"Too bad you don't have anything to protect your face," Jonah says, shoving another log into the woodstove in the corner.

I smirk at his sarcasm as I haul the basket of lunch onto a small folding table that the guys have been using for meals. "The soup was hot when I packed it, but I don't know how old this thermos is, so don't let it sit too long. There's also roast beef on whole-grain buns—store-bought," I confirm with annoyance, when I see the wary look Jonah and Roy share. I've been testing out recipes with Colette's bread machine and, let's just say I have a ways to go before I'm serving the results to guests. I certainly won't be feeding any of it to Jonah's mom and stepfather when they arrive next week.

Jonah hauls himself to his feet and wanders over to root through the basket, pausing long enough to plant a kiss on my lips.

"Yours is waiting for you at home," I scold, playfully slapping his hand away before I smooth mine over his forearm. It's noticeably thinner, but growing stronger every day. Of all Jonah's injuries, his arm took the longest to heal—almost three months. He was stuck on the ground and grumpy for most of it, and supervising Steve and his crew so intently that they finished ahead of schedule, likely to get away. But he's been cast-free and in the air for the past month, his mood back to normal.

"How long before you have to leave?" I ask. Archie is sitting on his skis at the end of the airstrip, waiting for takeoff. We're down to one plane while Toby overhauls Phil's old plane—it doesn't even have seats anymore—and Jonah decides what he wants to do with the insurance money collected from Veronica.

Jonah checks his watch. "An hour."

"Same here. I promised Muriel I'd be at the Christmas bazaar to make sure everything's running smoothly." We're on the second weekend of the Winter Carnival. Last weekend brought record attendance. I'd like to think it had something to do with the marketing campaign Emily and I launched, targeting radio and news stations between here and Anchorage, tourist companies, schools, markets—basically everyone. We even rallied local celebrities and politicians who were more than happy to attend last weekend's fireworks display and a fun airshow that Sam's Fire Boss planes put on, as a tribute to all the hard work of the firefighters this past summer.

Muriel has already confirmed with glee that the community center is getting its new restrooms in the spring. The library may even get the face-lift it so desperately needs.

She also informed me that the head of the planning committee for Anchorage's Farmers' Market contacted her to find out which brilliant firm they hired to do their marketing because they want to revamp their summer-long program.

"Mabel say how she's doin'?" Jonah reaches for his jacket on the hook by the door.

"Yeah. Sales have been steady." I say this to Jonah but I mean it more for Roy to hear. Mabel and Agnes flew in yesterday to help out. Mabel's been running the table for Roy's carvings at the bazaar. "People keep asking her who The Curmudgeon is."

Roy takes a break from glaring at the level on the countertop to glare at me, before shifting back. "I wish I'd made the bases smaller, so you wouldn't have any room to sign 'em."

"Oh, I'd find a way to make it happen." I wink. "And your website is getting a lot of hits." I launched The Curmudgeon Carvings without asking a month ago, mainly to showcase his work and to take online orders. Since last weekend, three customers have made purchases. "Someone asked for a custom carving—"

"No custom!" He steps back from the counter, level in hand, seemingly satisfied with his work. As with everything wood-related, Roy has been meticulous with each cut and angle of this interior. I knew he would be when I rolled up to his place a week after Jonah's crash to ask if he'd be interested in refinishing the inside of his family's cabin. It was a job I was going to task Steve and his crew with, but my gut told me that given the years of effort and care Roy had secretly put into the place, he might appreciate being the one to help bring it new life.

He seemed surprised to see me that day, and doubtful that I'd actually want to work with him. I assume that's because of the confession he made on what I can only hope will remain the darkest day of my life.

I'm still trying to figure out why Roy divulged those details in the first place.

For distraction?

To warn me away from him?

But I'm not afraid of Roy. And I haven't repeated his sins to anyone, not even Jonah, who likely wouldn't be too keen on this arrangement if he knew.

Roy can't be called a good man, but I also wouldn't necessarily call him a bad one. The question of what he deserves for his past crimes isn't up to me to answer, his punishment not up to me to dole out, especially not when he's spent the last three decades punishing himself.

All *I* know is the man Roy is now, and that man was there for me.

And one day, if and when he decides he'd like to reconnect with his daughter, maybe I can be there for him, too.

"You think we'll be ready to move the furniture in on Monday?" I ask, unpacking the soup thermos for Roy.

"More like Tuesday." His gaze rolls around the space. "Got a few more things I wanna finish, and then it's gonna take at least two days to clean up this mess."

"Cuttin' it close," Jonah says.

"We'll be fine. There isn't a ton to move in." A queen bed, a futon, propane appliances and kitchen supplies, and plenty of blankets and decorative touches to make it cozy.

"Still think we should be the ones stayin' here."

"Your mom is insisting." I've had a dozen conversations with Astrid since they decided they were coming, and she has made it abundantly clear that Jonah and his stepfather would do best with a lake between them. I have to agree.

I'm also learning where Jonah gets his stubbornness from, and I no longer believe it's his father. Part of me is dreading the wedding discussions. Between Jonah's accident, renovating this place, and the planning stages of the cabin we're building for Agnes and Mabel, we haven't had time to make any nuptial decisions. Jonah is all for eloping, and I'm beginning to think it's not a bad idea.

"So, meet you back there?" Jonah gives me a steady look—one that can't be mistaken, his eyes lingering on my mouth—and my heart skips several beats. His recovery time was long for several reasons.

"I'll be out in a minute." I smile softly.

"See ya later, Roy," he calls on his way out the door, not waiting for a response.

Roy grunts, too busy scowling at a corner in the wall to say more. Not that he's ever been one for the "hellos" and "goodbyes," anyway.

"Hey, I was wondering if you'd mind hanging this outside, by the door." Collecting a nervous breath, I slip out the plaque I picked up from Wasilla this morning and hand it to him. "You think they did a good job?"

He pulls out a cheap pair of reading glasses from his pocket and slides them on. His jaw clenches.

"I got the information from town records." It took me several calls and an afternoon of digging through archives to find the original homestead filing from 1965, made by Roy's father—Richard Donovan. It took me another week to track down the names of his late mother and younger brother, because I knew that if I asked, Roy wouldn't give them to me.

The plaque is modest—cast in aluminum and engraved in acrylic, noting the year the cabin was built and the four family members who first lived here.

I hold my breath.

"Where do you want it?" he answers, his voice more gruff than usual.

"Just outside the door. Wherever you think it'd look best. I trust you."

His eyes flash to me, and an emotion I can't read fills them. And then he simply nods.

That's as much as I'll ever get from Roy Donovan.

But it's enough.

I back away, eager to spend time with Jonah before we part ways for the afternoon. "Oh, you wouldn't happen to have a ten-person, live-edge dining table I could buy off you, would you?" My dining chairs arrived three weeks ago, but I know Roy was working on something for me. I've known since the day I showed up at his place to ask him to do the cabin's interior and I found him in the barn, measuring wood while scribbling notes on the catalogue picture.

His gaze cuts to me before shifting back to his work, the corners of his mouth curling upward. "I think I might."

"Can I come get it on Wednesday?"

"It's heavy," he warns.

"That's okay. I've got lots of help." More than I could ever have wished for, and always just a phone call away.

With that, I step outside again, taking a deep breath as the shockingly cold air grips me.

Jonah is waiting on the lake, the old snow machine's engine rumbling. "Race you back?" he hollers.

Instead of hopping onto mine, I scoot onto the back of his. "We can come back for it before you leave." I curl my arms around his torso and press my body against him, reveling in the warmth and strength as my hands wander.

He peers back over his shoulder. "You ready?"

"Probably not." Jonah likes to ride this thing at full throttle. As with everything he does in life, it seems. But that's who he is. He'll always be wild at heart, and there is no way to tame or change him.

Not that I would ever want to.

I smile.

And I hold on tight.

FOREVER WILD

Not ready to leave Calla and Jonah yet?

Forever Wild: A Novella

Visit katuckerbooks.com/foreverwild for more information

ACKNOWLEDGMENTS

These last few months spent with Calla, Jonah, Agnes, Mabel, and the memory of Wren have been utterly enjoyable. I appreciated the opportunity to bring Calla and Jonah's relationship to life in a way I never have before as a writer, as well as to delve into Calla's continued growth. Even though this story is a sequel, it felt fresh, given the new world and new cast of characters to explore, and the chance to incorporate a bear incident. (I spent far too much time researching and watching YouTube videos of bear attacks to *not* include one. My obsession has been sated.)

I'd like to thank the following people for their help pulling this story together (and let me preface this by saying that any mistakes made are my own, either by accident or by creative design):

Trisha Wyrick, for your invaluable help with my questions surrounding the Willow, Alaska, area, the model for my fictional town of Trapper's Crossing.

Suzanna Lynn, for answering my legal questions regarding estates.

Tiffany McNair, for confirming where to tranquilize poor Oscar in his time of need.

Amber Sloan, for confirming my questions around obtaining a driver's license in Alaska (which, after I stopped panicking about having that entire plot thread wrong, allowed me to incorporate the humiliating moose incident).

James "Wild Boy" Huggins, for tolerating my endless questions about how to crash planes. As a pilot, I'm sure you enjoyed the intense focus. I couldn't make that fuel-mistake story work within here, but if I write another book, it's going in.

Hannah Mary McKinnon and Sandra Cortez, for eagerly reading the ugly version littered with murmurs and mutters and a thousand adverbs.

Jenn Sommersby, for your love of syntax, your sharp eye, and your keen wit. Also, for always fitting me into your editing schedule.

Karen Lawson, for providing a second set of critical eyes for those pesky last errors that inevitably slip through the cracks.

Hang Le, for your immense talent and creativity. The cover is everything I wanted it to be.

Nina Grinstead of Social Butterfly PR, for your help and expertise with spreading the word about this book release.

Stacey Donaghy of Donaghy Literary Group, for your endless support and faith in me over the past seven years.

Tami, Sarah, and Amélie, for keeping Tucker's Troop alive and a fun place to be.

My readers, for your excitement behind this sequel. It was palpable, and a bit terrifying, to be honest. I hope you have enjoyed the ride.

My family, for giving me a reason to work so hard.